# ADVANCE PRAISE FOR
# HOW TO SUCCEED AS A TRIAL LAWYER

## ALL THE BASICS, FROM FIRST CLIENT MEETING TO CLOSING ARGUMENT AND BEYOND

"When it comes to litigation, *How to Succeed as a Trial Lawyer* provides the most—and the most useful—advice you will ever find between two covers. It is a must for every trial lawyer's bookshelf."

—Professor Steven Lubet, author of many articles and books on litigation-related topics, including *Modern Advocacy: Analysis and Practice, 4th ed.*

"For any aspiring trial lawyer, *How to Succeed as a Trial Lawyer* includes everything you need to know that you didn't learn in law school. It is fantastically organized, refreshingly straightforward, and includes easy-to-use practice checklists at the end of every chapter. It will be on my bookshelf (or more likely my desk—because I will be looking something up!) for many years to come."

—Nila Bala, Yale Law School Class of 2012

"This is the book I wish I had in my first 10 years as a trial lawyer. It's also the book I wish I could have handed out to trial lawyers while I was on the bench. Edelstein is thorough, concise, shrewd, and wise. The helpful table of contents makes this an efficient handbook, and using it will prevent many a pitfall. Whether the topic is management of emails, drafting settlement agreements, dealing with judicial questions at oral argument, or stipulations at depositions, Edelstein has thought it through and knows what works. His straightforward, approachable style makes *How to Succeed as a Trial Lawyer* a pleasure to read."

—Beverly Hodgson, arbitrator, mediator, former Connecticut Superior Court Judge

"Stewart Edelstein has written a rare comprehensive primer of the trial lawyer's art. I read it when I returned recently to active litigation practice after five years in corporate management, and I found myself learning, or being reminded of, principles, best practices, and "tricks of the trade" on nearly every page. Too much ink has been spilt on how to try cases—how to handle exhibits, examinations, and cross-examinations. Mr. Edelstein touches on those skills too, but he performs a needed service by going much further. These days, most of us who still consider ourselves "trial lawyers" spend our days stating positions in letters and mediation statements more than in complaints, and arguing (if you can call it that) across conference tables rather than from the well of a courtroom. And all the while we need to attract and keep clients, send and collect bills, and, almost as an afterthought, keep ourselves ethical and even sane. *How to Succeed as a Trial Lawyer* covers it all. While law practice is still, I believe, a craft learned by the doing, this encyclopedic overview cannot but give the young trial lawyer a great head start. I sure wish I had it when I began practicing. I cringe to remember the missteps I would have avoided. But I'm glad to have it today, and I expect it will soon become appreciatively thumb-worn."

—Aegis Frumento, partner, Stern Tannenbaum & Bell

"Stewart Edelstein, a veteran civil litigator, trial lawyer, and teacher, has written an interesting and informative text, *How to Succeed as a Trial Lawyer*. Not a traditional text on civil litigation or trial advocacy, *How to Succeed as a Trial Lawyer* contains numerous pearls of wisdom, in checklist format, the do's and don'ts that effective litigators eventually learn "on the job." It shows you how to avoid the mistakes young litigators frequently make, from the first meeting with a new client through presenting a case at trial from the plaintiff's and defendant's perspective. It has what the traditional texts miss: the actual how to do the various tasks of civil litigation and, just as important, the things to avoid doing. This text should be a welcome addition to a young litigator's library, either to read cover to cover, or to use as a reference on a particular litigation task."

—Professor Thomas A. Mauet, author of many articles and books on litigation-related topics, including *Trial Techniques, 8th ed.*, and *Trial Evidence, 5th ed.*

"I wish I had read this book when I started as a civil litigation lawyer 34 years ago. I would also have kept it on my shelf all these years, because *How to Succeed as a Trial Lawyer* can be read by topic, when the need arises, as well as beginning to end. The writing is elegant, to the point, and blissfully free of the legalese and verbosity that afflict other books of this kind. Mr. Edelstein incorporates humor and anecdote when apt, without distracting from his foremost aim, which is to instruct. He has delivered in one efficient and highly readable package a lifetime of learning, some of which I (no doubt like many other lawyers) have had to learn "the hard way" (from mistakes)."

—Martin Domb, partner, Akerman Senterfitt

"Stewart Edelstein's excellent book should be on the desk—not on the bookshelf—of every attorney who is or aspires to be a successful civil litigator and trial lawyer. It should also be read and consulted by students participating in law school clinical programs, and by academic law teachers who wish to bring some of the real world of law practice into their civil procedure and related courses. The book is not only a "how to" manual; it is that and much more. It is filled with information and practical advice about the litigation process, from dealing with clients, to pretrial practice, to mediation and arbitration, to trials and appeals, to dealing with ethical issues, and even to coping with stress and creating a life beyond the practice of law. The book is sprinkled throughout with apt literary and classical references, quotes from prominent jurists, and interesting insights and observations of the author. Each chapter concludes with a helpful "checklist" that summarizes the major points of the chapter. I plan to keep *How to Succeed as a Trial Lawyer* near at hand as I prepare to teach and supervise my clinic students."

—Professor Stephen Wizner, William O. Douglas Clinical Professor Emeritus & Professorial Lecturer at Yale Law School

"This book is to advocacy what *The Elements of Style* is to composition. Not many authors have earned the right to say, "do this; don't do that." When Strunk and White say it about how to write effectively, their authority to give direction proceeds from the force of their prose and the experiential wisdom behind it. The reader has no cause to question either.

The same is true for Stewart Edelstein's instruction in *How to Succeed as a Trial Lawyer*. Edelstein is a teacher and an advocate. He has catalogued in this book a professional lifetime of wisdom about the elements of advocacy as they arise in the daily life of a litigating lawyer. Very little is omitted. Many subjects are covered that are absent from the conventional literature on advocacy skills. Edelstein's edicts are clear, direct, practical. They cover subjects about which the professional reader will necessarily have given great thought—and subjects that such a reader will likely never have considered. Edelstein's gift is the ability to identify and deconstruct all the elements, including the small and unnoticed ones, that make up the craft of the litigating lawyer, and then to speak directly and clearly about the best ways to deploy them. Sometimes the reader will say, "I knew that." Sometimes the reader will say, "I knew that but I never thought about it in quite that way." Sometimes the reader will say, "I never knew that and I never thought about it, but I now see it as a self-evident truth and its recognition will make me better at what I do."

This book should be read cover to cover every so often, so that its messages become woven into the fabric of a professional life. It may also be consulted as a resource on particular practice issues. Mastering its elements will not make the reader a great trial lawyer. But doing so will liberate the ability of each reader to give expression to his or her special and unique talents as an advocate. It is the genius of *The Elements of Style* that its wisdom may be marshaled in the service of every kind of writing, for every kind of purpose, by every kind of writer. So, too, may *How to Succeed as a Trial Lawyer* be marshaled in the service of that personalized and uniquely human brand of advocacy that is the hallmark of every distinguished career.

I hope you enjoy this book. I hope it contributes to your personal fulfillment and success in the honorable and precious role of advocate."

> —Fred Gold, partner, Shipman & Goodwin,
> and Clinical Visiting Lecturer in Law, Yale
> Law School

"*How to Succeed as a Trial Lawyer* may be destined to become the essential handbook for litigators, experienced and novice alike.

Written by Stewart I. Edelstein, this book is an easy and enjoyable read. *How to Succeed as a Trial Lawyer* runs the litigation gamut from intake through trials with detours into alternative dispute [resolution] mechanisms, ethics, marketing, lifestyle, and numerous other topics. Written in deceptively simple prose with great insight, the instructions and tips, complete with checklists, make this a "go to" manual. The text reveals that Mr. Edelstein is an intelligent, seasoned advocate who clearly enjoys plying his trade and sharing his considerable wisdom with his colleagues.

As a litigator with more decades before the bar than I care to admit, I found *How to Succeed As a Trial Lawyer* to be a valuable resource. It is written from a practical perspective, addressing a panoply of topics confronting litigators. Mr. Edelstein leaves little to chance as his explanations and suggestions are rolled out in well-organized fashion. Indeed, the organization and detail present subtle yet helpful devices which are easily overlooked by practitioners but potentially very important.

For example, Mr. Edelstein gives point-by-point tips on how to answer questions from judges. In a more mundane vein, he suggests using note cards at trial to pass between co-counsel to avoid distracting conversation and recommends that each card cover a single point, in order to become a good rebuttal or closing argument outline. Also, Mr. Edelstein reminds us that, when taking a deposition, we should be sure to provide a side chair without arms for the stenographer's use. Such detailed planning avoids wasted time and an unhappy result.

The book's organization extends to the table of contents, which, standing alone, is a useful outline of the various tasks and skills needed to succeed in the courtroom. It also makes finding the sought-after topic a simple task.

I commend Mr. Edelstein for his achievement in laying out his vast knowledge of the litigation art in a practical, enjoyable and extremely useful volume."

—Donald Derfner, partner, Derfner & Gillett, LLP

"*How to Succeed as a Trial Lawyer* is an excellent text for a law school that wants to offer a trial practice course that will produce "practice ready" graduates."

—Fred Ury, President of the National Conference of Bar Presidents, past President of the Connecticut Bar Association

"*How to Succeed as a Trial Lawyer* is a great primer on litigation and life in the law. It is particularly pitched to young litigators—my son Granger, who is just out of law school, read it and got a lot out of it (including advice he would never accept from his Dad). There are tips you might expect with respect to depositions, briefs and the like, and also practical suggestions for dealing with the real thorny problems, like dealing with unfamiliar situations. More seasoned practitioners will benefit from a different perspective on approaches to legal problems and the ever elusive work-life balance. I recommend it highly."

—Daniel Abuhoff, partner, Debevoise & Plimpton, LLP

# HOW TO SUCCEED AS A TRIAL LAWYER

*To Jeremiah
with best regards
Stewart*

# HOW TO SUCCEED AS A TRIAL LAWYER

STEWART EDELSTEIN

# DEDICATION

I dedicate this book to my wife, Lynn,
for her love, for her support,
and for so much more.

# CONTENTS

| | | |
|---|---|---|
| Foreword | | xxv |
| Preface | | xxix |

**CHAPTER ONE**
**DEALING WITH CLIENTS** — 1

1. How to handle the first contact from a prospective client — 2
   *Complete the conflicts check.* — 3
   *When to decline representation, even if you have no ethical conflict.* — 4
   *If there is no ethical conflict, and you can handle the matter, arrange for a first meeting with the client.* — 4
2. How to conduct the first client meeting — 6
   *Establish rapport.* — 6
   *Explain the attorney-client privilege.* — 6
   *Explain the purpose of the meeting.* — 6
   *Get necessary information.* — 6
   *Discuss the document litigation hold requirement.* — 8
   *Get a commitment.* — 9
   *Discuss options.* — 9
   *Don't predict.* — 9
   *Discuss your fee.* — 10
   *Warn your client about preserving the attorney-client privilege.* — 10
   *Ask for more information.* — 10
3. What to do right after the first client meeting — 11
   *If you're not taking the case, put it in writing.* — 11
   *If you decide to take the case, send a confirming letter.* — 11
   *Get help.* — 11

  *Follow through.*    11
  *Determine the case's overall strategy and brainstorm.*   11
 4. How to draft a retainer agreement   12
  *Reduced hourly with performance bonus.*   13
  *Blended rate.*   13
  *Fixed fee.*   14
  *Contingent fee.*   15
  *Retrospective fee based on result.*   15
  *Straight retainer.*   15
  *Volume discount.*   16
 5. How to work collaboratively with your client   16
 6. How to deal with client expectations   17
 7. How to deal with difficult clients   19
 8. How to deliver bad news to your client   21
 9. How to prepare your client to testify in court   22
 10. How to capture and record your time for effective billing and good client relations   23
 11. What to do when you complete your representation   26

## CHAPTER TWO
## DEALING WITH EVERYONE OTHER THAN CLIENTS YOU WILL ENCOUNTER AS A TRIAL LAWYER   29

 1. Your secretary   30
 2. Your paralegals   31
 3. Witnesses   32
 4. Colleagues   36
 5. Co-counsel in other firms   37
 6. Opposing counsel   41
 7. Mediators and arbitrators   45
 8. Judges   45
 9. Jurors   47

## CHAPTER THREE
## MANAGING AND DRAFTING EMAILS AND LETTERS   49

 1. How to manage your emails   49
 2. When not to send an email   50

3. How to draft emails ... 53
4. How to use proper email etiquette ... 55
5. How to avoid inadvertent waiver of the attorney-client privilege when emailing ... 55
6. How to organize and save emails ... 57
7. How to draft letters ... 58

## CHAPTER FOUR
## DRAFTING DOCUMENTS OTHER THAN EMAILS AND LETTERS — 65

1. Principles applicable to all legal writing ... 66
2. How to draft internal memos ... 67
3. How to draft complaints ... 69
4. How to draft motions and memos supporting and opposing motions ... 73
5. How to draft answers and affirmative defenses ... 76
6. How to draft and respond to discovery ... 78
7. How to draft jury instructions ... 87
8. How to draft appellate court briefs ... 88
9. How to draft settlement agreements ... 89
10. Tax consequences of settlement agreements ... 94
11. How to draft cogently ... 95

## CHAPTER FIVE
## PREPARING FOR, TAKING, AND DEFENDING DEPOSITIONS — 99

1. The advantages and disadvantages of taking a deposition ... 100
2. When to take a deposition ... 100
3. How many depositions you can take and how long each deposition can be ... 101
4. How to notice a deposition ... 101
5. Where you can take a deposition ... 102
6. How to prepare to take a deposition ... 103
7. How to prepare your client for his or her deposition ... 103

|     |     |
| --- | --- |
| 8. The procedure at a deposition | 107 |
| 9. How to take a deposition | 108 |
| 10. How to use the funnel method when taking a deposition | 111 |
| *Top of the funnel.* | 112 |
| *Middle of the funnel.* | 113 |
| *Bottom of the funnel.* | 113 |
| *Example of use of the funnel method.* | 114 |
| 11. How to defend the deposition of your client | 117 |
| 12. When to ask questions of your own client at a deposition | 119 |
| 13. How to take and defend depositions of experts | 120 |
| 14. The form of transcript you should order | 121 |
| 15. What you should do after getting the transcript | 122 |
| 16. How to use deposition transcripts before trial | 122 |
| 17. How to use deposition transcripts at trial | 123 |
| 18. What you need to know about video depositions | 125 |
| 19. How to compel attendance at a deposition and compel answers of an appearing deponent | 126 |
| 20. How to get a protective order limiting the conduct of a deposition | 128 |

## CHAPTER SIX
## MEDIATING COMMERCIAL DISPUTES — 131

|     |     |
| --- | --- |
| 1. Whether and when to mediate | 131 |
| 2. How to select a mediator | 133 |
| 3. How to prepare for mediation | 135 |
| 4. Strategies for mediation | 137 |
| 5. How to get past impasse | 138 |
| *Challenge perceived BATNA.* | 139 |
| *Challenge perceived WATNA.* | 139 |
| *Focus on nonmonetary factors.* | 139 |
| *Change the players.* | 140 |
| *Change the venue.* | 140 |
| *Ask: What if?* | 140 |
| *Cut to the chase.* | 140 |

| | |
|---|---|
| *Accept the "double-blind" proposal.* | 141 |
| *Take a break.* | 141 |
| *Resume another day.* | 141 |
| 6. What to do if the mediation is successful | 141 |
| 7. What to do if the mediation is not successful | 142 |
| 8. A few words from Abraham Lincoln | 143 |

## CHAPTER SEVEN
## ARBITRATING COMMERCIAL DISPUTES — 145

| | |
|---|---|
| 1. Advantages and disadvantages of arbitration | 147 |
| 2. How to review an arbitration clause | 148 |
| 3. How to deal with the issue of arbitrability | 149 |
| 4. How to avoid inadvertent waiver of the right to arbitrate | 150 |
| 5. How to select an arbitrator | 151 |
| 6. How to commence an arbitration proceeding | 152 |
| 7. How to deal with statute of limitations issues | 152 |
| 8. How to prepare for the preliminary hearing | 153 |
| 9. How to prepare for the arbitration hearing | 154 |
| 10. How to determine what is admissible at the arbitration hearing | 154 |
| 11. How to make your presentation at the arbitration hearing more persuasive | 155 |
| 12. What to submit to the arbitrator after the hearing | 155 |
| 13. What remedies you can seek in arbitration | 156 |
| 14. How to protect the confidentiality of arbitration | 157 |
| 15. What to do after the arbitrator renders an award | 157 |
| 16. When the Federal Arbitration Act applies | 159 |

## CHAPTER EIGHT
## MAKING ORAL PRESENTATIONS IN COURT — 161

| | |
|---|---|
| 1. How to prepare for argument of pretrial motions | 162 |
| 2. How to answer judge's questions at oral argument of pretrial motions | 165 |
| *Why judges ask questions.* | 165 |
| *How to listen to judges' questions.* | 166 |

|    |    |
|---|---|
| *How to answer judges' questions.* | 166 |
| *How to answer hypothetical questions.* | 167 |
| *What to do if you get an unexpected question, or a question to which you don't know the answer.* | 167 |

3. How to prepare for and make opening statements to the jury — 168
   *What you should do when making an opening statement.* — 169
   *What you should not do when making an opening statement.* — 170
   *How to prepare for your opening statement.* — 171

4. How to prepare for and make closing arguments to the jury — 175
   *Prepare for closing argument.* — 175
   *Determine the sequence of the points you will make in closing argument.* — 176
   *Determine the content of the points you will make in closing argument.* — 176
   *Determine your choice of words.* — 177
   *Use effective body language.* — 177
   *What to avoid.* — 177
   *Miscellaneous tips.* — 178

5. How to prepare for and make appellate court arguments — 178
   *Prepare for oral argument by knowing the record, briefs, authorities cited in briefs, judges' approach to oral argument, and oral argument procedures.* — 179
   *Make your oral argument with the objective of answering questions, not making a speech.* — 180

## CHAPTER NINE
## PRESENTING AN EFFECTIVE PLAINTIFF'S CASE IN THE COURTROOM — 185

1. Choose a compelling theme — 186
2. Draft your complaint so it is consistent with your theme — 186
3. Conduct discovery to get admissions and streamline the trial — 187

|   |   |
|---|---|
| 4. Stipulate to admission of documents as full exhibits | 188 |
| 5. File motions in limine on key evidentiary issues | 188 |
| 6. Prepare a trial notebook | 189 |
| 7. File a pretrial memo, even if not required by the pretrial order | 189 |
| 8. Select as few witnesses as you need and present them in a logical order | 190 |
| 9. Prepare your witnesses to avoid surprises in the courtroom | 190 |
| 10. Ask direct examination questions to get to point B efficiently and effectively | 191 |
| 11. Use exhibits to get to point B efficiently and effectively | 194 |
| 12. If the judge excludes your evidence, consider making an offer of proof | 195 |
| 13. Select an expert who has the required background and experience | 196 |
| 14. Miscellaneous tips | 197 |
| 15. Adjust all this advice for a jury trial | 198 |
| 16. Make the most of your theme | 199 |
| 17. How to deal with settlement shortly before or during trial | 201 |

## CHAPTER TEN
## PRESENTING AN EFFECTIVE DEFENSE IN THE COURTROOM — 205

|   |   |
|---|---|
| 1. Choose a compelling counter-theme | 205 |
| 2. Draft your answer, affirmative defenses, counterclaims, and cross-claims to be consistent with your counter-theme | 206 |
| 3. File a pretrial memo that does more than just refute plaintiff's theme | 207 |
| 4. Take limited notes as plaintiff's witnesses testify | 208 |

5. Keep plaintiff's witnesses' testimony and exhibits
   out of the record to the extent you can     209
   *How to protect the record before trial.*    209
   *How to object to testimony and exhibits during trial.*  210
      Reasons to object to questions.           210
      Objections as to the form of the question.  210
      Objections to the substance of testimony.  211
      Objections to exhibits.                   211
6. Object strategically to questions on direct  213
7. Object strategically to plaintiff's exhibits  214
8. Keep out expert testimony                    216
   *FRE 702 and 703.*                           216
   *Key cases.*                                 216
      Daubert v. Merrell Dow Pharmaceuticals, Inc.,
         509 U.S. 579 (1993).                   216
      General Electric Co. v. Joiner, 522 U.S. 136 (1997).  217
      Kumho Tire Co., Ltd. v. Carmichael,
         526 U.S. 137 (1999).                   217
   *Burden of proof.*                           217
   *Relevance issue.*                           217
   *When expert testimony excluded even if relevant.*  218
   *Reliability issue.*                         218
   *When expert testimony only on general principle.*  220
   *Expert's reliance on hearsay.*              220
   *Appellate review.*                          220
9. Conduct an effective cross-examination       220
10. Impeach on cross-examination effectively    222
11. Use plaintiff's exhibits against plaintiff  224
12. When plaintiff rests, consider filing a motion for
    judgment as a matter of law                 224
13. Adjust your strategy when plaintiff rests   225
14. Limit plaintiff's rebuttal, and consider
    sur-rebuttal                                225
15. Preserve issues for appeal                  226
16. Miscellaneous tips                          228
17. Adjust all this advice for a jury trial     228

# CHAPTER ELEVEN
## DEALING WITH ETHICAL ISSUES     235

   1. Make sure you have the competence before undertaking a representation (Rule 1.1)     237

   2. Get your client's authority, and communicate with your client as required by the ethical rules (Rules 1.2, 1.4, and 1.6)     237

   3. Avoid conflicts of interest with current clients (Rules 1.7, 1.8, and 1.10)     239

   4. Avoid conflicts of interest with former clients (Rules 1.9 and 1.10)     241

   5. Comply with the ethical rules when you represent an organization (Rule 1.13)     242

   6. Comply with the ethical rules when you decline or terminate representation of a client (Rule 1.16)     243

   7. Know your ethical obligations if you discuss a matter with a prospective client (Rule 1.18)     244

   8. Comply with the ethical requirement regarding meritorious claims and contentions (Rule 3.1)     245

   9. Comply with the ethical requirement of candor to the tribunal (Rule 3.3)     245

   10. Comply with the ethical requirement of fairness to the opposing party and counsel (Rule 3.4)     249

   11. Be truthful in your statements to others (Rule 4.1)     250

   12. Comply with the ethical rules when dealing with opposing parties who are represented by counsel, and those not represented by counsel (Rules 4.2 and 4.3)     251

   13. Know and comply with all applicable ethical rules     253

# CHAPTER TWELVE
## MARKETING YOUR LITIGATION PRACTICE     255

   1. How to comply with the ethical rules governing your marketing efforts     256

   2. How to create a niche you can market     258

3. How to create a plan to market your practice — 258
4. How to cultivate relationships with clients and referral sources — 259
5. How to develop in-person networking skills — 261
6. How to make the most of social media to market your practice — 263
7. How to draft and publish articles to market your practice — 266
8. How to cross-sell to benefit yourself and other lawyers in your firm — 267

## CHAPTER THIRTEEN
## COPING WITH STRESS AND CREATING A LIFE BEYOND THE PRACTICE OF LAW — 269

1. Take good care of your body — 271
    *Eat right.* — 271
    *Exercise right.* — 272
    *Sleep right.* — 274
2. Create and nurture your support system — 277
    *Make time for family and friends.* — 277
    *Advise family of trial demands.* — 277
    *Make time for yourself.* — 277
    *Take fulfilling vacations.* — 278
    *Vary your routine.* — 278
    *Expand your horizons.* — 279
    *Create oases.* — 279
3. Work Smarter — 279
    *Keep a current "to do" list.* — 279
    *Plan a realistic work schedule.* — 279
    *Establish realistic expectations.* — 280
    *Don't beat yourself up when you make mistakes, but do learn from them.* — 280
    *Don't internalize your case.* — 281
    *Don't put off the worst until last.* — 281
    *Be organized and focused.* — 282
    *Complete tasks on time.* — 282
    *Be prepared.* — 283

|   |   |
|---|---|
| *Plan ahead.* | 284 |
| *Review all files regularly.* | 284 |
| 4. Take advantage of teamwork | 284 |
| *Get help with work when needed.* | 284 |
| *Keep your client informed.* | 285 |
| *Cultivate staff relationships.* | 285 |
| *Seek feedback.* | 285 |
| 5. Benefit from safety valves | 285 |
| *Expect the unexpected.* | 285 |
| *Discuss your feelings.* | 286 |
| *Listen to your body.* | 286 |
| *Have fun.* | 286 |
| *Evaluate professional satisfaction.* | 286 |
| 6. Navigate up the flow channel to advance your career | 287 |
| 7. Aspire to achieve holistic success | 289 |

## CHAPTER FOURTEEN
## SUCCEEDING AS A TRIAL LAWYER: A PERSONAL ACCOUNT  291

## APPENDIX I COGENCY  307

|   |   |
|---|---|
| 1. Bombast v. Cogent | 307 |
| 2. Cogency: Beyond "Less Is More" | 316 |

## APPENDIX II ETHICS PROBLEMS  325

|   |   |
|---|---|
| 1. Are these conversations forbidden? | 325 |
| 2. How do you deal with what really *did* happen in the car? | 327 |
| 3. How do you solve this joint defense dilemma? | 328 |
| 4. How far does the attorney-client privilege reach? | 330 |
| 5. Is a settlement discussion between parties always ethical? | 331 |
| 6. Is this an ethical negotiation tactic? | 332 |
| 7. How do you deal with a last-minute conflict? | 333 |
| 8. How do you deal with this deposition crisis? | 334 |

9. When can you get out of a case? 335
10. Why contact the passive shareholder? 336
11. Is your e-mail blast ethical? 337
12. Which conversations are ethical? 338
13. How should you handle this blown statute of limitations? 339
14. Is this surreptitious recording ethical and admissible? 340

**APPENDIX III SUGGESTIONS FOR FURTHER READING & FOR VIEWING** 343
**TABLE I FEDERAL RULES OF CIVIL PROCEDURE** 353
**TABLE II FEDERAL RULES OF EVIDENCE** 355
**TABLE III MODEL RULES OF PROFESSIONAL CONDUCT** 356
**TABLE IV AMERICAN ARBITRATION ASSOCIATION COMMERCIAL ARBITRATION RULES** 357
**PRACTICE CHECKLISTS** 359
**INDEX** 381
**PERMISSIONS** 393
**ABOUT THE AUTHOR** 395

# FOREWORD

### BY RICHARD F. ZIEGLER

It is no wonder that Stewart Edelstein's students at Yale Law School have praised the course in Civil Litigation Practice he co-teaches as "the best, most informative class to take at Yale Law School" and "a wonderful experience." The supporting evidence is readily found in this book: Stewart applies his experience, insight, and wit to produce an unusual guide to trial lawyering that is as enjoyable as it is useful.

What does a gryphon—the creature of Greek mythology that combined the body of a lion with the head and wings of an eagle—have to do with civil trial practice? Plenty. The lion and eagle were the top dogs in their respective animal categories, and the gryphon was viewed as the king of the animal kingdom, unexcelled in power and authority. But do not misinterpret the metaphor—it is not intended to embrace those trial lawyers who let their power and authority go to their heads. It is not about those trial lawyers who conduct themselves as if unbridled self-regard is the key to success. This book is not about swagger.

Instead, Stewart explains the gryphon metaphor as reinforcing the key notion that success as a trial lawyer requires mastering multiple different skills. Trial lawyers, like the gryphon, are a hybrid of skill sets. The best trial lawyers are not only persuasive advocates but also creative problem-solvers. Their conduct and demeanor must adjust to the context—one must behave a little differently with a jury than with a mediator, for example—but one must never, ever descend into arrogance. Stewart Edelstein has had an enviable, multi-decade career as a civil trial lawyer by serving his clients effectively and efficiently. According to the *Chambers Guide*, based on independent sources, Stewart is a "truly superb" lawyer. But "swagger" isn't in his vocabulary.

An appropriate vocabulary is important to successful trial lawyering. A trial lawyer must be a master of words, whether written in a brief or spoken in court, at a deposition, or in a marketing pitch to a prospective client. Words are important to Stewart, too. His love of words and skill at deploying them are among the joys of this book. Although Stewart's career has been as a trial advocate and teacher of the litigation process, he is also an accomplished student of etymology. His prior book, *Dubious Doublets*, is solely about words (it discusses unlikely pairs of words that have a common origin, such as "court" and "horticulture.") Both of Stewart's books convey the pleasure he takes from words.

*How to Succeed as a Trial Lawyer* focuses on the intensely practical implications of a trial lawyer's use of words. For example, it provides advice on how to draft an email—and when not to. The book's section on brief-writing, contained in an appendix explaining the importance of "cogency," is a treasure trove of important advice. Some examples: "Write simple, short sentences." "Avoid redundancy." "Use simple English words whenever possible" and "[r]eplace several words with one whenever possible" (so that "subsequent to" becomes "after" and "in the event that" becomes "if"). Although targeted at lawyers who are beginning their careers, all lawyers—no matter how experienced—can benefit from a review of this section of the book (but not only from this section).

Stewart's book is a wonderful compendium of essentially every aspect of the civil litigation process and then some, told with humor and erudition. *How to Succeed as a Trial Lawyer* does not purport to be an academic treatment of the subject. Instead, it provides practical pointers on everything from dealing with clients and adversaries to managing ethical dilemmas to marketing one's practice and learning how to avoid alienating prospective clients at the next fund-raising dinner. The section on effective deposition-taking is a first-rate primer on that subject. Taken as a whole, the book provides a comprehensive checklist and how-to guide for civil litigators. This book is equivalent to having a sophisticated and accomplished trial lawyer in the family who is willing to take the time to share the fruits of his long experience and savvy insight on everything that matters in the civil litigation process.

Two themes permeate this book. First, in the Edelstein view of the litigation process, less is almost always more. As noted, briefs should be edited to the point of gem-like brilliance. Significantly, the cogency that underlies the most effective briefs also informs other key aspects of the litigation process, from determining the necessary scope of discovery to sifting through the claims to present in a complaint or to pursue at trial. Second, every trial lawyer needs to identify the themes that will advance the client's cause and make certain that every litigation judgment is consistent with those themes. Following the precepts of this book will maximize every client's opportunity for success while minimizing the needless costs and expense that have given the contemporary litigation process such a bad reputation.

Litigation is a challenging vocation. It demands not only intellectual ability but attention to detail, perseverance, creative problem-solving, persuasiveness, focus, integrity, and the ability to press the client's position with enthusiasm while maintaining sufficient detachment to provide the objective, independent advice the client requires. *How to Succeed as a Trial Lawyer* is an invaluable guide to each of these requirements and more.

I have attempted in this Foreword to apply some of the principles that this book advocates, including this one: "When you are done, stop." Read it. Enjoy it. You'll get a lot out of it.

—Richard F. Ziegler

*Mr. Ziegler has been a litigator in the federal and state courts for more than 30 years. He was the Senior Vice President, Legal Affairs, and General Counsel of the 3M Company from 2003 to 2007. Earlier in his career he served as an Assistant U.S. Attorney in the U.S. Attorney's Office for the Southern District of New York. A graduate of Yale College and Harvard Law School, he currently is the Managing Partner of the New York office of Jenner & Block, LLP, where he co-heads the firm's International Arbitration Practice and formerly co-chaired its Complex Commercial Litigation Practice.*

# PREFACE

## BUT FOR

We all learned in law school a specialized use of language, including the meaning of "but for" in the tort causation analysis. "But for" applies here as well, to positive effect rather than the cause of harm, beginning with a Yale Law School student's inquiry years ago. He asked Steve Wizner, the Yale professor in charge of clinical programs, if Yale offered an advanced course for students who completed Trial Practice. Yale did not, but Steve told him that if the student could find enough others interested in such a course, he would see what he could do.

The next day, that student delivered to Steve a petition signed by a dozen of his classmates: if Yale offers the course, they will take it. Steve had the confidence in Fred Gold and in me (we had both taught Trial Practice at Yale for many years) to invite us to create that new course. Fred and I had to figure out how to teach what law-school students need to know from the first client meeting through the end of a jury trial in just 13 class sessions. Collaborating closely, we devised a syllabus and, together, we have taught Civil Litigation Practice at Yale ever since.

Knowing how to do something and knowing how to teach it are distinct skills. By teaching Trial Practice and co-teaching Civil Litigation Practice over the years, I have learned—sometimes my students in the role of guinea pigs—what works and what doesn't. *But for* my students, who taught me so much by teaching them, I would not have the insights that made this book possible. As Oscar Hammerstein II put it: "If you become a teacher, by your students you'll be taught." And *but for* Fred Gold's inspirational co-teaching (unless you see him in action, you cannot appreciate his uncanny skill in teaching the art of cross-examination, using nothing more than a yellow highlighter and his wits), this book would not be as comprehensive or instructive.

The *but for* class of people who made this book possible includes many others, of course. My indefatigable and unfailingly cheerful assistant, Ellen Beckwith, endured countless revisions of the text. My firm's trusty librarian, Sandee Molden, who did research for this book on a variety of topics, some arcane, has the rare ability to find whatever I need. Beverly Hodgson, a former judge, now a mediator and arbitrator of renown (and guest mediator for my Yale class who also teaches Trial Practice at Yale), taught me much about mediation and arbitration. My colleagues at Cohen and Wolf, PC have been a constant and unfailingly helpful and encouraging source of advice and inspiration. Our Marketing Director, Kim Brooks, gave me sound advice for the marketing chapter.

George Bakes, a certified personal trainer and certified squash coach (and my nemesis on the squash court), provided useful advice for the chapter on dealing with stress. Merril Adelman, a registered dietician, provided informative and yummy nutrition tips for that chapter. Irwin Sollinger, a psychotherapist, co-wrote an article with me, published in *Trial*, which I adapted for that chapter. Alan Neigher advised me on intellectual property issues, and David Atkins advised me on some ethics issues. Tim Brandhorst, Director of New Product Development at ABA Publishing, provided open-minded and instructive guidance, akin to an always reliable doula, throughout the gestation process. My eagle-eyed proofreader and copyeditor from Lachina Publishing Services caught niggling errors and suggested clarifying stylistic changes, improving the text. Any errors that escaped detection are my sole responsibility. Finally, my gratitude to Richard Ziegler for writing the foreword.

*But for* all these folks, this book would never have come into being. I am ever so grateful to all of them.

## THE GRYPHON

So you want to be a successful trial lawyer! A book could be written about what you must know that you *didn't* learn in law school. This is that book.

This practical guide will show you the way. Whether you are a law student taking a clinical course, or a lawyer learning the ropes, you can read this book at least two different ways. You can read it straight through—from first client meeting through the trial, then explore ethics, marketing, and stress management, with a little philosophy at the end—or you can read chapters as you need guidance on particular issues. The detailed table of contents and index will make it easy for you to pinpoint where in the text you'll find answers to your questions. The practice checklist at the end of each chapter provides you with a cogent summary of what you need to know.

To the extent my advice is based on procedural rules, I apply the Federal Rules of Civil Procedure and the Federal Rules of Evidence. In this book, I refer to each Federal Rule of Civil Procedure as "Rule" and each Federal Rule of Evidence as "FRE." For easy on-line reference to both, with helpful Notes of Advisory Committee as to their intent and purpose, see The Cornell Law School Information Institute website, www.law.cornell.edu/rules. For an excellent and easy-to-navigate primer on the meaning of legal terms, with useful cross-references and case cites, go to www.law.cornell.edu/wex. For a handy table of deadlines in the Federal Rules of Civil Procedure, see the West® version of those rules. For local procedures, you need to check your state court rules.

Studies reveal that at least 10,000 hours of disciplined effort are required to master a skill. *See* K. Anders Ericsson, Ralf Th. Krampe & Clemens Tesch-Römer, "The Role of Deliberate Practice in the Acquisition of Expert Performance," 100 PSYCHOL. REV. 363–406 (1993). Think of tennis great Roger Federer, violinist Isaac Stern, chess grandmaster Garry Kasparov, or opera star Placido Domingo. But the practice of law is never mastered. There is always room for improvement. I learn something about the skills we must master from each meeting I have with a client, each deposition I take, and each case I try.

Over the course of 40 years as a trial lawyer, I have learned some things worth passing on to those with less experience, and have conveyed practical advice, by publishing scores of articles, giving seminars, teaching students at Yale Law School, and mentoring associates at my firm. You will benefit from the lessons my students and associates taught me about instructing them effectively. My writing style for this book, based on my role as teacher and mentor, is direct and utilitarian, just as when I teach one of my students or associates one-on-one.

The skills the successful trial lawyer must seek to master are disparate, a melding of qualities that, together, make up the complete package. Like the gryphon, the ancient Greek mythological beast combining the head of an eagle with the body of a lion (see the cover image), the successful trial lawyer is a hybrid, combining the best qualities of different animals: an eager beaver, busy as a bee, with an eagle eye for key documents during discovery, unearthed with dogged determination, squirreled away for later use; outfoxing opposing counsel; ferreting out the truth by taking effective depositions, while avoiding badgering the witness; preparing for trial with the benefit of an elephantine memory, while not forgetting that sometimes it is vital to horse around to achieve some measure of balance in life.

Just as the gryphon combines the most potent attributes of an eagle and a lion, to formidable effect, the successful trial lawyer is a formidable hybrid, benefitting from the unique skill set this book encompasses. The successful trial lawyer must be adept in such diverse roles as advisor; advocate in mediation, arbitration, and litigation; colleague; adversary; strategist; negotiator; officer of the court; writer; orator; ethicist; and marketer—not to mention all nonprofessional roles in life. This book includes all the fundamentals you need to know as a trial lawyer in all these professional roles, as well as guidance in balancing the personal and professional aspects of your life.

This is not just a formulaic recipe book for success. As you read on, you will encounter obnoxious opposing counsel, perjuring clients, curmudgeonly judges, Batman and Robin, web scammers, insane rabbits, BATNA, WATNA, a man who may have committed suicide, a smoking-gun exhibit, a multiverse of conveyor belts, a death-row inmate about to be executed because of a lawyer's blunder, Lance Armstrong, the Tarpeian Rock from which perjurers were hurled, the Csikszentmihalyi flow channel, the score of Beethoven's Fifth Symphony, a funnel distilling sap into the maple syrup of admissions, psychological concepts such as persistence of belief (also known as confirmation bias), serial position effect, primacy, and recency, a Japanese style of eating known as *hara hachi bu*, Ulysses S. Bombast (of the firm Bombast, Bunkum, Blunderbuss, Billingsgate and Blarney), warm zeal, and a sexually aggressive corporate executive—and you will benefit from words of wisdom of Abraham Lincoln, Will Rogers, Ralph Waldo Emerson, Winston Churchill, Mark Twain, Rabindranath Tagore, Pliny the Younger, Irving Younger (no relation), Shakespeare, Socrates, Montaigne, Oscar Wilde, Pascal, Cicero, Benjamin Franklin, Confucius, Albert Einstein, Eleanor Roosevelt and others.

What will you *not* find in this book? I don't include a discussion of the myriad of issues trial lawyers confront with electronically stored information ("ESI"), because ESI is the subject of hundreds of articles and numerous books. (If you Google "electronically stored information," you will get more than a million hits.) And I don't include what lawyers refer to as "war stories"—personal accounts of adventures as a trial lawyer—except in the last chapter, where you will learn about my first court appearance, which was an unmitigated disaster. You want succinct practical advice, not long stories about my own experience—although my own experience informs everything you'll read in this book.

I don't include a discussion of such specialties as personal injury, divorce, or criminal law, although I do focus on commercial litigation. Even so, this book encompasses all the fundamental skills required of any successful trial lawyer.

Whether or not you are past the ten thousand hour mark, you should find this book worth reading. After all, we can all benefit from advice that gets us closer to the ever-elusive mastery of the skills required of a trial lawyer.

To add an element of humor, I have included New Yorker cartoons that aptly synthesize what I'm trying to convey. Now, taking my own advice about cogency (see the cartoon at the end of chapter 4), I end this introduction. Read on, and learn how to succeed as a trial lawyer.

# CHAPTER ONE
# DEALING WITH CLIENTS

This chapter discusses how to deal with clients, from the first contact from a prospective client through trial. For context, we will start with an instructive etymological exploration.

Unlike the etymology of "lawyer," which is straightforward and uninteresting (from Middle English *lawe*, which derived from Old Norse *lag*, meaning "that which is laid down"—the law), the etymology of "attorney" is revelatory. In Old French, *atorner* meant "turn to," as in "to assign, appoint." The past participle of *atorner* was *atorné* (pronounced ah-torn-AY), which, used as a noun, meant "someone appointed to act as someone else's agent." In the 17th and 18th centuries, "attorney" was also a verb, "to attorney," meaning to act as a proxy for another. The older sense survives in the "attorney-in-fact," in contrast to the "attorney-at-law," which is what trial lawyers are.

What about "client"? Latin *cluere* means "to listen, follow, or obey." The present participle, *cluens*, developed an alternate form *cliens*. Someone who is *cliens* is always listening for another's orders or advice, rather than taking independent action. *Cliens* may be related to Latin *clinare*, which means "to lean or bend," giving *cliens* the related sense of someone who leans on another—you.

Thus, etymologically speaking, an attorney is someone the client appoints to act in his or her stead, on whom the client leans for sound advice. As trial lawyers, we take on tremendous responsibility for our clients. While reading this chapter, keep in mind your role as attorney, and the reliance each of your clients places on you for your expertise, professionalism, and, most of all, advice.

## 1. HOW TO HANDLE THE FIRST CONTACT FROM A PROSPECTIVE CLIENT

Typically, the initial contact from a prospective client is by phone. When you return that call, you must find out the general nature of the case so you can tell whether you are competent to handle it, the urgency of the client's needs, any facts related to applicable statutes of limitations, and the names of all potential parties so you can check for conflicts of interest. If you have handled similar cases, this is your opportunity to tell the prospective client about your experience. On the other hand, if it becomes obvious that you cannot handle the case—because, for example, it is a patent case and you are not a patent lawyer—now is the time to decline representation. Do not give legal advice during this initial contact.

You should explain the ethical requirement that you do a conflicts check, the procedure for it, and how soon you can complete it and call back. Explain that the prospective client must not disclose any confidential information to you until you have done that check.

*Caveat*: If your first contact from a prospective client is by email, beware, and do not open any attachment to it. It may be a scam. Typically, the email is ostensibly from someone seeking help collecting money, supposedly easily recovered if you could just send a demand letter. Warning signs are if the sender, often from a foreign country, is someone you do not know, and making no reference to anyone you do know; the prospective client needs immediate action; and the email may have poor spelling and grammar and generic references, such as "in your jurisdiction."

Here is a typical example, ostensibly from someone in Australia whose email address began with the word "mutilate" (no kidding):

Dear Counsel,

We request your service for business/commercial litigation. You were referred to us from the referral service. Kindly advice [*sic*] if you can be of assistance to the pending issue.

Regards,
C.F.O.

How do these scams typically work? Various ways. Here's one: The attorney undertakes the representation, writes a demand letter, receives a check, and then deposits the check in the firm's trust account. The client presses the attorney for immediate payment. The attorney determines that the deposit was posted to the trust account and presumes that the funds have cleared. The attorney wires the money to the client's bank account. Only when it is too late does the attorney learn that the check bounced, and the money was debited back out of the lawyer's trust account.

Here's what happened to one firm, Milavetz, Gallop & Milavetz, P.A., in Edina, Minnesota. Someone claimed to be a Korean woman hurt in Minnesota who needed help securing a $400,000 legal settlement. The firm received the settlement check for $400,000, obtained assurances that the check had cleared, and forwarded $396,500 to a Hong Kong bank for the client. The check was fraudulent. The law firm sued Wells Fargo in Federal District Court in Minnesota (Docket No. 0:2012 CV 00875, April 6, 2012), claiming that its employees should have known that the check was fraudulent.

According to the complaint in that action, brought in 2012, this type of scam is responsible for $29 million in losses suffered by more than 70 lawyers and law firms. Typically, the scammers contact lawyers through websites, such as lawyers.com. The lesson? Beware of scammers.

## Complete the conflicts check.

The conflicts check must include not only the names of people who and entities that may be parties in the case but also the principals of those entities at all relevant times. For example, if the prospective client is a partnership, you must do a conflicts check on the names of all partners. The most efficient way to do a conflicts check is to use a computerized listing of prior and current clients that includes basic case information. Check that listing for the names of all potential parties in the prospective client's matter. If your check reveals a prior or present representation, you must determine whether that representation creates either an ethical conflict of interest or a practical conflict, as where, for example, one of your colleagues is a good friend of the proposed adverse party. If so, you must call the prospective client immediately so that he or she can seek other representation. See chapter 11, sections 3 and 4, for a discussion of ethical rules governing conflicts of interest.

## When to decline representation, even if you have no ethical conflict.

Know your firm's policies about taking on new matters, independent of your firm's conflicts-check procedures. For example, some firms have policies precluding representation if there is an insufficient amount of money at stake and policies regarding bringing malpractice claims against lawyers and other professionals. Even if you have the competence to undertake a representation, and no ethical prohibition from doing so, you may decide to decline the representation in various circumstances, including the following, all of which raise red flags:

- The prospective client has already discussed the claims with other counsel who have declined the representation.
- The prospective client already has counsel, but seeks new counsel because of attorney-client relationship issues.
- You have a good-faith basis to determine that the prospective claim is not viable.
- You can readily expect that your legal fees will be disproportionate to the likely amount recovered.
- You realize from the outset that you will not be able to work with this prospective client, for any number of reasons, including the client's difficult personality.

If in doubt, discuss with one of your colleagues whether to take on a new matter.

## If there is no ethical conflict, and you can handle the matter, arrange for a first meeting with the client.

*When.* It is preferable to meet as soon as possible after the initial call—certainly long enough in advance of any statute of limitations or other deadline to enable you to do the necessary work before it is too late. Prospective clients call either because they have just been sued or because all less drastic means to resolve a dispute have proved unsuccessful and the matter is hot. Arrange to get together on a day when you will have ample time for the meeting, so you won't need to leave abruptly for your next appointment.

*Where.* It may be best to meet at the client's place of business or at the site of the dispute, especially if the case involves construction or a manufacturing process. Meeting there demonstrates your willingness to go the extra step to get the job done. It is also an efficient way to meet simultaneously with several representatives of your client, while having ready access to your client's files.

In other instances, it may be best to meet at your firm, especially if you are meeting with only one person. Arrange to use a conference room rather than your office. That way, you can work without distraction or interruption and review documents together. This arrangement also avoids having a desk between you and your client, making it easier to establish rapport.

Another advantage of meeting at your firm is the opportunity to introduce your colleagues and impress the client with your well-organized operation.

*With whom.* You want to meet with the principal of the client and, where appropriate, other key employees most knowledgeable about the underlying facts of the case. Be sensitive, though, to a situation where an employee is potentially a hostile witness, as where there is an ongoing dispute about an employee's performance or compensation. In such a situation, it is advisable to have with you at least one other employee of your client who has knowledge of the underlying facts when you meet, both to serve as a witness to the interview and to keep the interviewee honest. Also, consider having the interviewee sign a letter or affidavit that locks him or her into an accurate version of the facts.

*Documents.* Arrange for the client to send you critical documents before the meeting so you can review them to get a rudimentary knowledge of the underlying facts before the first meeting. This gives you the basis to start your factual investigation and helps the client organize his or her thoughts.

*Retainer agreement.* After establishing the terms of your retainer agreement, send it to your client for review before you meet. For more on retainer agreements, see section 4 of this chapter. Your cover letter should confirm the date, time, and place of the meeting. You may want to enclose your firm's brochure.

*Legal research.* If you anticipate encountering any unusual legal issues, complete the appropriate preliminary research even before your first meeting with the client.

## 2. How to conduct the first client meeting

### Establish rapport.

Put your client at ease by engaging in casual conversation before getting down to business. If the meeting is at your office, be welcoming by meeting your client promptly, offering coffee, and otherwise being hospitable. Give your client your contact information (a business card should do). Decide in advance whether to disclose your cell phone number.

### Explain the attorney-client privilege.

Tell your client that this communication is privileged, describing the nature of the attorney-client privilege. Encourage your client to be candid, even about facts he or she is reticent to reveal. Make sure your client understands that the communication remains privileged only if it is not discussed with third parties. If your client is married, discuss the marital privilege that applies in your state.

If you are meeting with an employee or other agent of a corporate client, take care to explain that you represent the corporate entity and not the individual. In these situations, the privilege belongs to the corporation, not its representatives. The corporation may want to waive the privilege even though the individual may not. For more on this, see chapter 11, section 5.

### Explain the purpose of the meeting.

Make sure your client realizes that you need to know both positive and negative information about the case. Explain that your purpose is to gather facts relating to claims *and* to anticipated defenses. Describe the context of the meeting vis-à-vis the bigger litigation picture, and summarize the litigation process as it applies to the case. Make sure your client realizes that litigation is typically no quick fix and may drag on for months, if not years.

### Get necessary information.

Give your client the opportunity to tell the story. Take notes to be sure you have a good record of the facts. Doing so will impress on the client your attentiveness and respect for what the client has to say. Interrupt, but not unduly, whenever you need more detailed information. Most people find it much easier to talk this way than to deliver a lengthy monologue.

In many instances, your new client has made an error in judgment or done something worse, resulting in the litigation. Don't be accusatory or critical. Instead, be supportive and try to get an understanding of just what happened and why. But if something doesn't ring true, call your client on it.

Explain that your client will be cross-examined at a deposition or in trial. Once you have established rapport, question the client closely, preferably changing chairs to dramatize the fact that you are playing the role of opposing counsel. This interrogation will give you a sense of how well your client stands up under cross-examination on that point and will encourage candor.

Ask your client to imagine that the two of you are on the other side of the case. What would the adversary be telling his or her lawyer?

Get a good sense of the bigger picture of your client's business. You can't represent a business properly unless you have a genuine understanding of the context in which the relevant transaction has occurred. Get enough information so you understand the relationship between your client and the opposing party. Find out what business considerations should be factored in when determining your strategy, aggressiveness, and flexibility in pursuing legal remedies. What are your client's business objectives in pursuing or defending the litigation? You cannot give business advice, but knowing your client's business objectives will be useful in giving legal advice.

Learn about the course of dealing and usage of trade in your client's business. This information is important to your understanding of the underlying transaction and is crucial in cases governed by the Uniform Commercial Code. In article 2 alone, one or both of these terms is used in sections 2-202 (parol or extrinsic evidence of an agreement), 2-314 (implied warranty of merchantability), 2-316 (exclusion or modification of warranties), 2-504 (shipment by seller), and 2-723 (proof of market price).

Determine whether your client has insurance that covers the claim. Although insurance policies do not cover claims for intentional torts, some policies provide broad coverage that may apply. If insurance coverage is a possibility, get a copy of all possibly applicable policies.

Establish clear lines of communication with your client. Get the name, title, and address of anyone who should be sent copies of correspondence and pleadings. Find out which representative of your client can give you authority to act.

Get names, titles, addresses, and phone numbers of anyone else who may have relevant information. This may include agents of your client or the opposing party, as well as third parties. Make a list of the documents you require. Find out who the opposing counsel is expected to be.

Find out if any issues can be expected to arise regarding employees of your client who may be key witnesses. Are they likely to be demoted, transferred, or fired? Even if not, are they subject to effective cross-examination as to their credibility, or otherwise?

### *Discuss the document litigation hold requirement.*

A litigation hold, sometimes referred to as a "preservation order" or "hold order," temporarily suspends a company's document destruction/retention procedures for documents that are reasonably anticipated to be potentially discoverable in litigation. The litigation hold is designed to ensure that discoverable documents are preserved, thereby avoiding a claim of spoliation. Courts increasingly impose draconian sanctions on clients and their counsel when a litigation hold is not put in place timely and enforced rigorously.

The litigation hold must be put into effect as soon as litigation is reasonably anticipated, even before an action is brought against your client, whether an individual or entity. You can issue it, or the entity you represent can do so, but you should draft it. Notice of the litigation hold must be sent to any employee who may have documents or electronically stored information that may be discoverable in any action that may be brought. If in doubt about the recipients of this notice, err on the side of caution.

The litigation hold notice should contain the following:

- a brief description of the claim or anticipated claim
- the purpose of the notice
- the scope of what must be preserved, including data in hard copy, on computer systems, laptops, personal computers, PDAs, hand-held wireless devices, mobile telephones, smartphones, and audio devices, such as voicemail
- the actions required by the recipient to preserve data
- the ongoing duty of the recipient to preserve data through the final resolution of the case
- sanctions a court can impose if the recipient does not comply

Keep a list of the names and email addresses of all recipients of your litigation hold letter. Periodically, send reminder notices, to comply with your continuing obligation to avoid spoliation.

### Get a commitment.

Get the client to commit to providing resources to help you prepare for the prosecution (or defense) of the case. Explain that this commitment will save you time and will therefore save the client money, especially if the case involves voluminous documents.

### Discuss options.

Once you have obtained all the preliminary information, generally discuss legal theories that may apply and available remedies. If you represent a defendant, explore possible jurisdiction and venue issues, affirmative defenses, counterclaims, cross-claims, and third-party claims (e.g., for indemnity). Discuss other options, such as removal to federal court (if available) and alternative dispute resolution procedures. To the extent required, make it clear that you will need to do further legal and factual investigation before you can give advice on possible responses to the suit.

If your client wants you to begin a court action, and even if you determine there is a valid cause of action—assuming you can determine this at the first meeting—discuss whether it makes sense to institute suit. Factor in the cost, publicity, disclosure of confidential information, disruption of business, and potential affirmative defenses and counterclaims. In evaluating cost, make sure your client appreciates that expenses involve more than just attorney fees, experts' fees, disbursement, and the like. There will also be indirect costs to the client, including diversion of time, energy, and personnel, as well as emotional cost.

### Don't predict.

Avoid predicting the outcome of the case, except to comment in general terms about the strengths and weaknesses of the claims and defenses. Don't raise unrealistic expectations for your client. If pressed, be conservative in your estimate. See section 6 in this chapter for more about managing client expectations.

### Discuss your fee.

Explain the basis of your fee, billing procedures, whether your client is to pay disbursements such as stenographers' and experts' fees directly, and when invoices are to be paid. Go over the terms of the retainer agreement. If you seek a retainer check, make specific arrangements to get it. Make clear whether you are charging for this first meeting. Remember that once you file a court appearance, it is not easy to withdraw as counsel, so get a reasonable retainer up front.

### Warn your client about preserving the attorney-client privilege.

Caution your client that, from the initial conference, anything your client or a representative of your client says or does that is related to the underlying transaction or dispute may affect the case. Make explicit that all future communications about the underlying transaction and dispute should be between you and your client or his or her representatives only, rather than between the parties, and that your client's representatives should not discuss the underlying transaction, dispute, or case among themselves in the absence of counsel. You don't want to find out at trial that the president of the company sent the head of purchasing a "smoking gun" memo making detrimental admissions or characterizing your client's position in a negative light.

Also caution your client about not forwarding your emails to anyone who is not within the attorney-client privilege and about the use of electronic social media, such as Facebook, Twitter, and LinkedIn. Everything your client has already posted, and everything your client may post in the future, is subject to discovery, if opposing counsel can meet the very low discoverability threshold of Rule 26(b)(1), or your state analog. Opposing counsel need not even conduct formal discovery about such posts, finding them online. Instruct your client to refrain from posting anything even tangentially related to the case, and anything that could be used to challenge your client's credibility.

### Ask for more information.

At the end of the first meeting with your client, suggest that your client or your client's representatives may think of additional facts later, and ask them to advise you of this information as it becomes available. Make a list of documents and information that your client has agreed to provide to you, and set a delivery deadline for them. Send that list to your client.

Tell your client in detail what will happen next. For example, you may draft a demand letter or complaint for the client's review or, if you represent a defendant, you may prepare a particular pleading.

If the meeting is at your office, give your client a brief tour. If you meet at the client's office, ask for such a tour if it would be appropriate.

## 3. WHAT TO DO RIGHT AFTER THE FIRST CLIENT MEETING

### If you're not taking the case, put it in writing.

The letter, preferably sent by both regular and certified mail, with return receipt requested, as well as by email with read receipt, should simply state that even though you appreciate the proposed representation, you are declining to represent the client. If you are aware of any statute-of-limitations concerns or other deadlines, point out that there may be a time bar unless the client acts immediately. In any event, suggest that the prospective client immediately seek the advice of other counsel. Avoid giving legal advice. For a discussion of ethical rules pertinent to declining representation, see chapter 11, sections 1, 6, and 7.

### If you decide to take the case, send a confirming letter.

Your letter should include an itemized list of the documents and information you require. Remind your client of what the next step will be—and follow through.

### Get help.

Arrange for the assistance of other attorneys in your office and for support staff, as needed. After getting authority from your client, retain any experts whose advice or testimony may be required.

### Follow through.

Do whatever you committed yourself to do: conduct the factual and legal investigation, draft the demand letter or pleading, and proceed as you said you would. Keep the client informed of your progress.

### Determine the case's overall strategy and brainstorm.

Develop your themes and causes of action. Plan your further factual and legal investigation. Decide who should be named as parties, your preliminary list of witnesses, and the preferred forum. Evaluate any statute-of-limitations concerns. Consider the strengths and weaknesses of each party's position and defenses to it, at all times keeping in mind your client's business objectives.

If you represent a defendant, consider raising jurisdiction and venue issues, affirmative defenses, counterclaims, setoffs, recoupments, cross-claims, and third-party actions, as appropriate. In any event, put the key deadlines on your calendar.

If you proceed as outlined above, you will accomplish several fundamental objectives simultaneously. You will establish a positive working relationship with a new client. You will obtain, on an expedited basis, the preliminary factual information you need. See Rule 26(a) for mandatory initial disclosures. And you will be well on your way to the successful prosecution or defense of claims for an appreciative client. Horace, the Roman poet and satirist, said it best: *Dimidium facti qui coepit habit*— roughly translated: "Well begun is half done."

## 4. How to draft a retainer agreement

Ethical rules generally require that you have a written retainer agreement for each representation you undertake. Each retainer agreement should, at minimum, clearly identify who the client is, the specific matter you are undertaking, the fee arrangement, reimbursement for expenses, billing and payment procedures, and payment of advances against fees and expenses. When you represent an entity, make sure that the person signing on behalf of your client has authority. For efficiency, provide that the retainer agreement can be signed in counterparts, and by facsimile transmission.

Why not a straight hourly rate in every case? Clients increasingly seek alternate fee arrangements because, with a straight hourly rate fee arrangement, (1) the clients perceive that the lawyer has little incentive to resolve the matter expeditiously; (2) the focus is on input (i.e., the lawyer's work) rather than output (i.e., the result of the lawyer's work); (3) there is uncertainty as to the amount of the fee, making it difficult for a client to budget; and (4) in tough economic times, clients want to reduce expenses, including legal fees. Furthermore, your competitors are offering alternative fee arrangements; you must remain competitive in the crowded legal marketplace.

Here are some alternative fee arrangements to consider, depending on your firm's billing guidelines and your state's ethical rules, especially regarding contingent fees. All these options assume that the client pays disbursements as incurred.

As an underlying concept, to the extent your firm assumes risk contingent on the result, your firm should be compensated accordingly for assuming that risk. In drafting alternative-fee retainer agreements, clarity is all the more important to avoid client misunderstanding; there is no substitute for a careful discussion with your client about the terms of the fee agreement.

All alternative fee arrangements require a careful analysis of the case at the outset, including consideration of the following: What are the client's objectives? What must be done? Who will do it? How long will it take? What is the likelihood of success? What are possible special defenses? What about possible counterclaims? If you obtain a judgment, what is the likelihood of satisfying it?

The following are only some of the alternative fee arrangements available to you. You are limited only by your imagination, common sense, ethical rules, and the client's consent. At the end of the matter, compare the fee with what would have been billed based on hourly billing, to assess whether the option you have chosen is beneficial or detrimental for your firm, thereby learning from experience.

## *Reduced hourly with performance bonus.*

The amount of the bonus is based on a formula related to a predetermined gain or loss in terms of dollars, assets, or savings from the representation. The retainer agreement must be explicit about the bonus terms, which must be fair and reasonable to be ethical.

A performance bonus can be included as part of any fee agreement, subject to the ethical considerations referenced above and client consent. You may decide to agree to a reduced hourly rate as additional consideration for the performance bonus. This type of fee arrangement is not readily applicable where the client seeks equitable or other non-monetary relief.

## *Blended rate.*

One type of blended rate is to charge the same hourly rate no matter which attorney does the work. A variation is to charge one uniform hourly rate for all principals, and a separate uniform hourly rate for all associates.

The blended-rate option raises an issue for the client: Will your firm delegate the matter to the lawyers with the lowest seniority—lawyers who would otherwise charge less per hour than those with more seniority? If so, will the legal representation be compromised, or even adequate?

One way to deal with this issue is to make explicit in the retainer agreement which lawyers are expected to work on the particular matter, after discussing with your client the experience of those lawyers in matters similar to the client's.

An issue for the firm is how to most effectively, but profitably, apply this fee arrangement in delegating work. The best way to accomplish this delicate balance is by doing a comprehensive budget and determining which lawyers are best suited to accomplish the client's objectives.

## *Fixed fee.*

Variations of the fixed-fee arrangement include the following:

- one set fee for all work on a matter
- a set fee for each defined task or stage
- a capped fee, where the amount of the fee is based on the hours worked, but with a cap

The advantages of a fixed fee for your firm is that work can be allocated to lawyers with less seniority—but this same advantage a client will likely perceive as a disadvantage. The advantage to the client is the ability to budget the legal fee going forward with greater predictability.

The types of cases a fixed fee is better suited for include discrete, repetitive cases, where the work to be done and time required for it is more predictable, such as certain bankruptcy and foreclosure matters.

The retainer agreement should clearly spell out what the fee is, how it is to be paid, and if paid based on milestones, what work is included in each phase, and what work will be billed separately as extra work outside the scope of the fixed-fee arrangement.

If the fee is capped, the firm typically charges its standard hourly rates, up to a preset maximum limit, beyond which the client does not pay any further for legal fees. This arrangement requires care in setting the cap and preparation of a carefully analyzed budget.

## Contingent fee.

There are many variations of the contingent fee, including the following:

- no payment of the legal fee until completion of the matter; upon completion, payment of a percent of the amount recovered or saved
- payment at the standard hourly rate up to a specified number of hours or dollar amount of the fee, which is capped, after which the firm gets a percent of the recovery or savings
- a fixed fee for the initial investigation, or through a certain phase of the litigation, and some form of contingency thereafter
- full hourly billing for the initial investigation, or through a certain phase of the litigation, and some form of contingency thereafter

For any of these contingent fee arrangements, you need to address, before entering into any retainer agreement, how to deal with possible counterclaims. Furthermore, if you are only defending a claim, if the issue is money, you can agree on a contingency based on the amount of money saved—but if the relief sought is nonmonetary, a contingency fee arrangement is not as feasible.

## Retrospective fee based on result.

This is one of the more creative (and risky) fee arrangements. The client pays a set amount each month, but the ultimate fee is based on the result. The advantage for the client is being able to budget the legal fee during the course of the representation. The concomitant advantage for your firm is knowing the agreed income stream during the representation.

The issue that arises in a retrospective fee based on the result is the best way to determine the value of the result for the client. This should be spelled out in the retainer agreement, by setting forth in concrete terms the client's clearly defined objectives and what result constitutes meeting those objectives. The retainer agreement should include a minimum for the result-based fee.

## Straight retainer.

The client pays the same amount each month for all work done that month. This is a viable fee arrangement, for example, in representing municipalities in certain types of matters.

## *Volume discount.*

The client agrees to provide your firm with all its work of a particular kind, in exchange for a volume discount. This fee arrangement makes sense only if you can expect ongoing business from this client of sufficient volume to justify giving a discount.

## 5. HOW TO WORK COLLABORATIVELY WITH YOUR CLIENT

Representing a client in litigation is a collaborative process. Your client relies on you for legal advice, and you rely on your client for information, documents, and authority.

Early in your representation, explain the litigation process in detail, both as to substance and procedure. This is all the more important if the client has not already been involved in litigation. Here are some practical tips:

- If you represent a plaintiff, after you have completed a sufficient factual and legal investigation, discuss with your client possible causes of action, the elements of each, and which causes of action you recommend pursuing. If you have eliminated some as weak, explain why you advise not pursuing them, get the client's informed consent, and confirm that consent in writing. Discuss your strategy in prosecuting the case.
- If you represent a defendant, after you have completed a sufficient factual and legal investigation, discuss with your client motions you are considering, possible affirmative defenses, counterclaims, setoffs, and recoupments, whether you have a basis to assert any third-party claims, and your overall strategy in defending the case. If you eliminate any potential courses of action, and your client agrees, confirm your client's consent in writing.
- Early in the representation, explain the need for your client to provide you with all the documents you need for the representation. Discuss all issues related to electronically stored information, and litigation hold requirements. Also explain your continuing duty to disclose information and documents, as provided in Rule 26(e) and your state court analog.
- When you receive interrogatories and document requests, forward them promptly to your client, and explain the procedure for respond-

ing to them. Tell your client that you cannot put in the record at trial any requested document you don't produce, so even if responding to such discovery requests can be arduous and a distraction from your client's business affairs, your client must be thorough and diligent in providing you everything you need to respond. Let your client know that you can seek additional time to respond to discovery requests, if you have a good-faith basis to request an extension. Explain how the attorney-client privilege and work-product doctrine protect from disclosure, and how a privilege log works. See your local rules for the requirements of a privilege log in your jurisdiction.
- Explain to your client why you need information and documents harmful as well as helpful to your claims and defenses, even if opposing counsel has not requested them. An effective way to explain what may be counterintuitive to some clients is that you don't want to get blindsided at trial by opposing counsel putting into evidence something you were not aware of—especially something harmful to your position.
- Explain to your client that the record is not really "closed" until the trial. Even though, as a technical matter, the formal discovery period ends on a date well before trial set by the court, everything your client says or does through and including the time of trial is fair game. So, for example, if your client posts something on Facebook harmful to your case shortly before trial that opposing counsel gets access to, your client may be subjected to surprise, effective cross-examination at trial.

## 6. How to deal with client expectations

To avoid client disappointment, you must manage client expectations as to three things: time, cost, and result. Unless you do so, you may achieve a fine timely result, at a reasonable cost, and still the client will be disappointed. When your client asks questions on these subjects, resist the impulse to respond by saying something only to please the client. Be realistic in advising clients about these sensitive subjects. Clients rely on you for realistic, pragmatic advice, not Pollyannaish prognostication.

*Time.* Business people want results, as soon as possible. In their business world, they are often in a position to impose deadlines, which must be met. In litigation, however, despite such mechanisms as Rule 26(f) conferences and orders, you are not master of the docket, so you must be wary in answering such understandable client questions as: When will we get into court for our injunction hearing? When will depositions be completed? When will our case be tried? How long before the judge rules?

The best way to deal with time-related questions is to provide your most informed response, based on your experience and consultation with your colleagues. Whenever giving an estimate as to time, qualify it by making clear that this is just an estimate, and the actual amount of time can vary—indeed, it may take longer than your estimate, because of the way the system works.

*Cost.* Clients often request estimates of your fees and disbursements. Some corporations require budgets at the inception of a matter, with periodic updated budgets. You must put a lot of thought into preparing budgets. Here's how:

- List each task you expect to perform, from inception through trial.
- Realistically estimate the amount of time required for each.
- For each task, use a range of hours so you have flexibility.
- Include a caveat that this is only an estimate, and that the actual number of hours, and the resulting fee, will depend on certain variables over which you have no control, such as the number of depositions opposing counsel takes and how long they last, the extent to which opposing counsel files pretrial motions, and how the court rules on various motions.

*Result.* It is only natural that clients ask if they have a good case, if you think they will win, or at least the percentage likelihood of success. If you assure a client that you will recover $100,000, but recover only $90,000, the client will be disappointed. If you tell that same client that the likely result will be a judgment in the range of $70,000 to $100,000, that same client will more likely be pleased. Same result, different client reaction to it.

The lesson here is to manage client expectations about the result by realistically assessing the likely outcome, explaining to the client the legal theories and facts in your favor, the legal theories and facts your opponent will rely on, the likelihood of success of counterclaims and other related claims and defenses, and the strengths and weaknesses of both sides' positions. Resist giving a specific percentage likelihood of success, or a specific dollar amount you will recover, but when pressed, provide realistic estimates. If you provide your client with any estimate of time, result, or cost in an email or letter, be realistic, and qualify your estimate to avoid giving your client unrealistic expectations.

## 7. How to deal with difficult clients

Certainly, not all clients are difficult. Even so, you must know how to deal with a variety of difficult clients. Sometimes it seems that our work would be so much easier without the clients. We have a symbiotic relationship with them though, so familiarize yourself with the following cast of characters. As to each, ask yourself what underlying client's concern causes him or her to be so difficult, and attempt to address it.

- *The non-cooperative client.* Even though at your first client meeting you have emphasized the importance of your client working collaboratively with you, including your client's investment of time and effort in the case, and cooperating in providing you with information and documents as needed, some clients are too busy or too preoccupied with other things (like running a business) to enable you to represent your client effectively. In that instance, you need to sit down with your client and explain the importance of working together to achieve your client's objectives. Discuss what is preoccupying your client, and find out if another person at your client's company can take over some of the attorney-client communications.
- *The nonpaying client.* Especially in difficult economic times, some clients do not pay your invoices timely. Even if your retainer agreement provides that invoices must be paid within 30 days of receipt, some clients do not comply. When that happens, you should send a reminder invoice to your client. If that is not successful, call your client to discuss why he or she is slow in paying. If necessary, work out a payment plan. But do not let your client become too delinquent in payment. If you recover, by settlement or judgment, remember that you cannot deduct the balance due your firm without the client's consent, which should be in writing.

- *The micromanaging client.* Some clients, especially business people whose style of managing is hands-on, seek to micromanage your work. They make clear that, before you file anything or make any strategic decision, you must send them a draft for their review and comment and discuss each step to implement your plan of action before they provide written authorization for you to proceed. You should do what is necessary to understand the motivation of such a client (insecurity, wanting to play the role of lawyer, management style, or something else), talk through the issue with your client, come to an understanding, and proceed accordingly. Sometimes input from a micromanaging client can be very helpful, so long as you remember that you are the lawyer, and the business person is the client. You must make that clear to your client, as necessary.
- *The overly aggressive client.* Some high-powered business people are accustomed to getting their way by bullying—or what they would characterize as proactive leadership. Be wary of such clients, especially if they tell you that this is a matter of principle, and that they will fight this to the bitter end, if required. You must explain to such clients what results are realistic, and how you will seek to achieve them. If such a client instructs you to take a position that you cannot take ethically, you may need to terminate the representation.
- *The emotional client.* Especially when the matter you are handling has high-stakes consequences for your client, client emotions can run high. If you have an emotional client, deal directly with the source of your client's emotional state. Is it upset, anxiety, or fear, and if so, about what? Is it about loss of a personal relationship (as can arise in litigation involving the breakup of a partnership or breach of a shareholder agreement)? Sometimes, nonmarital litigation can take on all the emotional baggage of a divorce. Talk through with your client what is causing the turmoil, and do what you can to alleviate the sources of your client's stress, keeping in mind that you are limited in how you can help. You are not your client's therapist.
- *The consistently displeased client.* A cousin of the emotional client is the client who is never satisfied. Find out the source of the problem, which may be unrealistic expectations about timing, procedures, rulings on motions, or ultimate outcome—or more fundamental issues having to do with emotional baggage the cli-

ent brings to the process. Have a frank discussion with your client to get to the root of the problem, within the scope of your professional representation. Address rather than avoid these issues, before they create undue disruption.

If you determine that you just cannot continue working with your client, have a frank discussion with your client about the issues you find unresolvable, and let your client know that you will be discontinuing the representation, as allowed by the procedural and ethical rules in your jurisdiction. Ideally, another lawyer will file an appearance in your place, but if not, you will need court permission to withdraw the representation if you have already brought suit.

If a client owes you money after you discontinue your representation, or after the matter is completed, take steps to recover the balance due you, first by letter, then by phone calls. If necessary, obtain the services of a collection agency. As a last resort, sue the client for the amount due. Keep in mind, though, that a typical client response to such a suit is to file a counterclaim for legal malpractice. Also, know the law in your jurisdiction regarding your right to retain the file until you are paid or until you work out a satisfactory payment arrangement.

## 8. How to deliver bad news to your client

No one likes to deliver, or receive, bad news. However, sometimes you must, as when a judge rules against you in a pretrial motion or you receive a memorandum of decision after trial and the result is not what the client hoped for. What do you do?

Put yourself in the shoes of the client. What would your client want to know, and when? Your client would want to know the result immediately, the significance of the result, a copy of any ruling if in writing, and what can be done next.

You may have a variety of remedies, including a motion to reargue, a motion for reconsideration, a motion for articulation, an appeal, or some other responsive motion. You should realistically explain the significance of the ruling in the context of the case as a whole.

Avoid the natural inclination to delay delivering bad news to a client. If you get an adverse ruling, read it carefully, let yourself feel your disappointment, and then carefully analyze the significance of the ruling and what your options are going forward. Then call the client, deliver the news, explain your strategy going forward, and send your client the ruling. Do the analysis before calling the client.

## 9. How to prepare your client to testify in court

A crucial event in litigation is preparing your client to testify in court. (For advice on preparing your client for deposition, see chapter 5, section 7.) Tailor your preparation to the experience, sophistication, and personality of your client, keeping in mind the following tips:

1. Before meeting with your client, know the facts, and be familiar with all prior client statements relevant to the case.
2. Be sure your client has reviewed his or her prior relevant statements (such as deposition transcripts) and relevant documents.
3. Assure your client that there is nothing improper about your preparing for his or her testimony, and remind your client about the attorney-client privilege as it applies to this meeting. (*Caveat*: When preparing someone other than your client, keep in mind that the attorney-client privilege does not apply.)
4. Discuss your theory of the case, what you must prove, opposing counsel's expected theory of the case, and what opposing counsel must prove.
5. Discuss both positive and negative facts, and how to handle negative facts, including potential impeachment material.
6. Assure your client that there is no script to be memorized.
7. Familiarize your client with the physical layout of the courtroom, the expected demeanor of the judge and of opposing counsel. If appropriate, advise your client about suitable courtroom attire and caution against wearing flashy jewelry.
8. Familiarize your client with all exhibits you plan to use.
9. Familiarize your client with courtroom procedures.
10. Educate your client about effective communication.
    - Eliminate hedging (e.g., "I'm not sure" or "my best guess").
    - Avoid hesitation.
    - Speak openly and frankly.
    - Avoid undue deference to opposing counsel.
    - Avoid agreeing with opposing counsel unless warranted.
    - Avoid arguing with opposing counsel.

- Do not lose your temper.
- Be self-assured.
- Use body language effectively.
11. Educate your client about appropriate attire and demeanor.
12. Remind your client that demeanor is observed at all times in the courthouse, even when you are not "on the record."
13. Conduct the direct examination of your client. See chapter 9, section 10.
14. Advise your client about answering questions on cross-examination.
    - Tell the truth.
    - Understand each question before answering.
    - Seek clarification if necessary before answering.
    - Think before answering.
    - Do not volunteer.
    - Do not guess. If you don't know, say "I don't know"; if you don't remember, say "I don't remember"; and if compelled to estimate, and you can, make explicit that you are estimating; if you cannot estimate, say "I would just be guessing," or words to that effect.
    - Do not exaggerate.
    - If there is an objection, stop talking, but listen carefully to the arguments pertaining to the objection.
15. Conduct the cross-examination of your client. See chapter 10, section 9.

## 10. How to Capture and Record Your Time for Effective Billing and Good Client Relations

Since the practice of law is a business as well as a profession, we must bill our clients appropriately and get paid timely. Many matters you work on are billed by the hour, so you must know how to keep track of the time you spend on each matter. You must do so daily, so your time entries are accurate and timely. Even with contingency billing, your firm cannot assess the cost effectiveness of the contingency arrangement, or monitor your performance, unless you keep accurate track of your time.

You don't want to work hard a full day, only to realize that you have only a half day of recorded time to show for it. Accordingly, you must learn two distinct but related skills: capturing time and recording what you do each day. These skills are essential not only for proper billing but for good client relations.

Capturing your time can be as elusive as capturing a cat for a trip to the vet. Here are some tips:

- Comply with all your firm's timekeeping and recording requirements, in form and substance.
- Comply with all clients' timekeeping and recording requirements. Some clients, such as Fortune 500 companies, have strict requirements. Failure to comply means your firm does not get paid.
- Keep track of your time as you work on each matter.
- As you begin each task, make a note of your start time, on paper or electronically. For this purpose, take advantage of computerized time and billing systems, telephone systems that display elapsed time, and other electronic means.
- Do the same as you *end* each task.
- If you work on more than one task on one matter during the course of a day, keep track of the amount of time you spend on each discrete task so you can itemize it. This enables you to avoid block billing (many entries for one client matter without time itemization), which some clients and some courts do not accept.
- If you engage in a task with another lawyer in your firm, such as a joint meeting or telephone conference with a client, confirm the time spent with the other lawyer for consistency in description and amount of time spent.
- If, while doing research on matter A, you are interrupted by a phone call to discuss matter B, and then a colleague comes to your office to discuss matter C, after which you return to your research on matter A, allocate your time promptly, in fairness to clients A, B, and C.
- If you go to court on a given day for more than one client, as when you argue pretrial motions, allocate your time fairly, based on the amount of time actually spent as to each client.
- Record all your time, relying on the billing partner to write off what is not properly billable. On the other hand, if you engage in a brief ministerial task, such as exchanging emails with a client about scheduling a meeting, don't record that time.

- Do not pad your time. It is unethical, bad for client relations, and you may find yourself out of a job.
- If your firm has minimum annual billable hour requirements, keep track during the year to determine if you are on course. If not, ask for more work.

Here are some tips on recording your billable time:

- Comply with all firm and client requirements.
- Use the present tense.
- Be consistent in describing what you do. For example, a client will wonder what the difference is between "conduct research," "investigate law," and "analyze legal issues."
- Be explicit. If you devote many hours researching a variety of issues for a client, who then receives a bill including your undifferentiated research time, the client may wonder what took you so long, and why the bill is so much. But if you itemize the same amount of time, the client will have a better understanding of the scope of your work. For example, in *Montague v. Capulet*, a defamation case, your time entries could read like this: "research most recent cases for elements of defamation action," "research most recent cases for summary judgment standard," and "research most recent cases for defamation per se."
- If you have a claim to recover attorney fees, discuss with the billing partner how best to record your time. The attorney fees claim may be limited to only certain causes of action, such as where you assert both common law and statutory causes of action, only some of which allow for recovery of attorney fees. If so, you must allocate your time separately for such claims. Be aware that if you include information within the attorney-client privilege in your timekeeping records, it must be redacted before disclosure.
- Put yourself in the position of your client. What information about legal services on your bill would you consider sufficient to be willing to pay it?

Some firms also require that you record non-billable time, such as your meeting with prospective clients, writing articles, attending seminars, engaging in bar associates activities, and the like. You should be just as conscientious in capturing and recording that time as your billable time. Lawyers in the firm who monitor your performance are interested in your development as a lawyer beyond just your billable work. Recording your non-billable time helps them—and you—track that development.

## 11. What to do when you complete your representation

When you complete a matter, send a letter to your client making explicit that you have completed your work in the matter and that you are closing the file. If you fail to do so, your client may expect that you will take some further action—for example, filing a timely appeal.

This is also an opportune time to send your client marketing material about your firm, if you have not done so already. In this electronic world, it is easy to send an email. Even so, it is preferable to send the client a letter, with your firm brochure and other firm information, including your business card, so your client will have something tangible for future reference.

## ❖❖❖❖
## PRACTICE CHECKLIST

- Complete a conflicts check before undertaking any representation.
- Beware of scams in undertaking any representation.
- Decline a prospective representation if red flags are raised.
- If you decline the representation, put it in writing.
- Before doing substantive work, obtain a written retainer agreement.
- Consider alternative fee arrangements:
    - _____ reduced hourly with performance bonus
    - _____ blended rate
    - _____ fixed fee
    - _____ contingent fee
    - _____ retrospective fee based on result
    - _____ straight retainer
    - _____ volume discount
- If you undertake the representation, meet promptly with the client at your client's place of business or your office.
- At the first client meeting
    - _____ establish rapport
    - _____ explain the attorney-client privilege
    - _____ explain the purpose of the meeting
    - _____ get necessary information
    - _____ discuss the document litigation hold requirement
    - _____ get a commitment that the client will devote the resources you need
    - _____ discuss options
    - _____ don't predict outcome
    - _____ discuss your fee
    - _____ warn your client about preserving the attorney-client privilege
    - _____ ask for more information
- Meet with all representatives of your client from whom you need information.
- Early in the representation, obtain the documents you need.
- If you take the case, inform the client what must be done; arrange for the help you will need from support staff, experts, and others; develop an overall strategy; and follow through.
- Work collaboratively with your client.
- Manage client expectations as to time, cost, and result.
- Deal with difficult clients by understanding what concerns cause them to be difficult.
- When you need to deliver bad news to a client, do so promptly, be direct in explaining the significance of what happened, and discuss options in your strategy going forward.

(continued)

- In preparing your client to testify in court, tailor your preparation to the experience, sophistication, and personality of your client, following the tips in the text.
- Be conscientious about capturing and recording your billable and nonbillable time each day.
- After you have completed your representation, send a letter to the client to that effect, and, if you have not done so already, inform the client of other services your firm provides.

CHAPTER TWO

# DEALING WITH EVERYONE OTHER THAN CLIENTS YOU WILL ENCOUNTER AS A TRIAL LAWYER

You play the starring role in the movie that is your career as a trial lawyer, supported by a cast of characters ranging from your secretary to the judges, who decide whether you win or lose motions, and—for that matter—whether you win or lose nonjury cases. In this chapter, we explore how to deal with all of them, except clients, who merit their own chapter. See chapter 1.

This movie analogy is not intended to suggest that you should be play-acting in your role as a trial lawyer. No. You must at all times be yourself, although you can develop different aspects of who you are as you make your way professionally. Other movies are screening at the same time throughout your life—movies of your life as friend, husband or wife, parent, son or daughter, sibling, hobbyist, amateur athlete, and so on. If you abandon all those other roles, you will burn out. See chapter 13 about managing a balanced life.

So who are all these people in supporting roles, other than clients? They are your secretary, paralegals, witnesses (lay and expert), colleagues in your firm (unless you are a sole practitioner), lawyers in other firms you work with, opposing counsel, mediators, arbitrators, jurors, and judges. Your relationship with each has unique benefits and pitfalls for you.

## 1. Your secretary

You and your secretary should be a dynamic duo, like Batman and Robin—but without the costumes—achieving your clients' goals efficiently. Your relationship should be one of mutual respect and cooperation. Even though you are in a position of control vis-à-vis your secretary, you must work as a team to get things done right, and on time. Here are some tips:

- Establish a functional and efficient system for getting work done.
- Encourage your secretary to suggest other ways to improve efficiency, and take your secretary's worthy suggestions seriously.
- If your secretary works for more than one lawyer, establish a mechanism to coordinate work flow. Do not wait for a crisis to deal with this issue.
- If your secretary is ever overwhelmed by too much work that must be done in too little time, have in place a mechanism for overflow work to get done timely.
- Establish a calendar system for a belt-and-suspenders approach, to avoid missing deadlines.
- Establish an electronic form bank, to save time, for such documents as deposition notices, subpoenas, and boilerplate language for settlement agreements.
- Be explicit in all assignments to your secretary to avoid misunderstandings about what must be done, and by when.
- Be explicit about priority of assignments.
- When giving an assignment, explain briefly the purpose and context so your secretary will have a clear understanding of the task and motivation to achieve it.

- Give your secretary positive reinforcement when a task is done well; don't hesitate to express your appreciation for a job well done.
- Whenever you will be out of your office, let your secretary and the receptionist know where you will be and how to reach you.
- Remember that your secretary is not an automaton pumping out work. Express a genuine interest in your secretary as a person.
- If a mistake is made (and mistakes will be made), don't blame your secretary if you can take the blame. So, for example, if a letter is sent out with typographical errors, your secretary is not at fault. Before signing that letter, it was *your* responsibility, not your secretary's, to correct typos.
- If your secretary makes a mistake that you can't take the blame for, discuss what went wrong, why, and how to avoid that kind of mistake in the future.
- If problems with your secretary cause dysfunction over time, do what is required to change secretaries or, when justified, transfer or terminate your secretary's employment. Office managers can play a very effective role in these situations.

## 2. Your paralegals

Paralegals serve the function of doing work that is more advanced than secretarial work but not at the level of legal work, freeing you up to focus on legal work, while saving clients money in legal fees. Their name derives from a Greek root meaning "beside," as in the words parallel and paraphrase. An effective paralegal can work along with you to achieve your client's goals cost-effectively. Tasks paralegals can perform are diverse, including, for example, preparing timelines, Excel spreadsheets, deposition summaries, and digests of documents; assisting you in witness preparation; responding to interrogatories and document requests, searching documents and electronically stored information; and preparing demonstrative exhibits. Some tips:

- Have a written job description for what is expected of a paralegal.
- Whenever possible, avoid giving a paralegal secretarial work.
- As a general matter, do not ask your paralegal to do legal work, such as legal research, appropriate only for lawyers, although paralegals who are properly trained can do rudimentary legal research.

- When giving an assignment, be explicit about the task to be performed, the form of the work (a memo, timeline, computer disc, selection of documents, etc.), and your deadline.
- Follow all the tips above about dealing with your secretary that apply.

## 3. Witnesses

We'll start with lay witnesses, and then discuss expert witnesses, because different rules apply to them.

In all communications with lay witnesses, whether by phone, email, or face-to-face meeting, keep in mind that nothing you say is protected by the attorney-client privilege. So, when that witness is deposed, it's fair game for opposing counsel to ask all about each communication you had with that witness—unless you have a bona fide basis to assert the work-product privilege.

As a practical matter, this means that you should assume that opposing counsel is (hypothetically) copied on each email you exchange with a lay witness and on the phone with you for each conversation with a lay witness, and attends each meeting you have with a lay witness. You have a job to do—find out all the information you need from that witness, and obtain all documents of interest that witness has—but be cautious about any communication with a lay witness that opposing counsel can seize upon. So, for example, don't discuss strategy or strengths and weaknesses of your case with any lay witness.

If your client informs you that someone aligned with your client has information useful for your representation, ask your client to call that person to alert him or her that you will be calling so that, when you do call, that person will not be on guard and will be willing to talk openly. Accommodate lay witnesses by arranging to meet with them at times and places convenient for them. Before you meet, ask them to gather documents that may be of interest to you, for efficiency. If you want the witness to review documents before you meet, send them, knowing that opposing counsel will become aware, through discovery, of everything you are doing vis-à-vis that witness.

Sometimes you need to talk with former employees of an adverse party. Such communications raise ethical issues, discussed in chapter 11, section 12.

Expert witnesses are in a category by themselves, for two reasons. First, you have a choice as to expert witnesses, in a way you don't as to fact witnesses. Second, Rule 26(b) applies to expert witnesses, but not to fact witnesses.

In selecting an expert witness, you must consider many factors:

- What, precisely, is the expertise of this proposed expert? Is it the requisite expertise for your case?
- What is the prior experience of this proposed expert? You need a résumé.
- What is the prior deposition and trial experience of this proposed expert?
- What opinions has this proposed expert expressed in prior depositions and court testimony?
- What has this proposed expert published, and what opinions has the expert expressed in those publications?
- Does this proposed expert use methodologies that withstand *Daubert* scrutiny? See the discussion of *Daubert* in chapter 10, section 8.
- Can this proposed expert explain concepts in simple English, and with the use of apt analogies, so that the trier of fact (whether judge or jury) will understand his or her testimony?
- Can you work with this proposed expert?
- Is the expected fee of this proposed expert reasonable, considering the client's ability to pay and what is at stake in the litigation?

You can get names of prospective expert witnesses by using services that provide testifying experts or, better yet, by finding out from other trial lawyers what experts they have used with success. Whenever possible, you should interview prospective testifying experts to get a good sense of them, how they would approach your particular assignment, and how well they express themselves.

After you select a testifying expert, draft a retainer agreement, keeping in mind that it is discoverable. Avoid anything in the retainer agreement that suggests what the result of your expert's investigation should be, or anything else that could support an argument that your expert is not objective and impartial.

The application of Rule 26(b) to expert witnesses determines the subject matter of your communications with them. In doing this analysis, distinctions must be made among three types of experts: (1) expert non-testifying consultants (we'll call them "Category 1"); (2) testifying experts retained or specially employed to provide expert testimony in the case, or whose duties as your client's employee regularly involve giving testimony ("Category 2"); and (3) testifying experts not in Category 1 or 2, such as employees of your client who do not regularly provide expert testimony ("Category 3").

Opposing counsel cannot, by interrogatories or deposition, discover facts known or opinions held by Category 1 experts, who will not be testifying in your case, except as provided in Rule 35(b) pertaining to physical and mental examinations, or on a showing of exceptional circumstances under which it is impracticable for the party to obtain facts or opinions on the same subject by other means. See Rule 26(b)(4)(D).

Rule 26(b)(4)(B) protects from disclosure drafts of expert reports as to Category 2 experts, and protects drafts from disclosure as to Category 3 experts, regardless of the form in which those drafts are recorded. Rule 26(b)(4)(C) protects communications you have with any Category 2 expert, regardless of the form of the communications, with three exceptions: (1) communications regarding compensation for the expert's study or testimony; (2) the facts or data that you provide *and* that the expert considered in forming the opinions to be expressed (but not communications about the potential relevancy of those facts or data); and (3) the assumptions that you provided *and* that the expert relied on in forming opinions to be expressed—but not assumptions discussed and *not* relied upon, or discussion of hypothetical facts. Note the distinction between disclosure of all facts and data an expert *considered*, on the one hand, and assumptions the expert *relied on*, on the other hand. Communications that remain protected include your theories and mental impressions, and your communications about the potential relevance of facts or data.

Accordingly, make sure that all facts and data you provide your testifying expert, and all other facts and data that your expert relies on, are well-founded, that any assumptions you ask the expert to make are well-founded, and that your expert uses a sound methodology, to avoid a successful *Daubert* challenge. Also, since your expert's invoices are discoverable, the description of your expert's services in invoices should be more generic than specific.

Work-product protection as to communications with testifying experts does not apply to Category 3 experts, except for drafts of the disclosure required by Rule 26(a)(2)(C). So, in dealing with Category 3 experts, assume that what you communicate will be discoverable.

In preparing your expert witness for deposition, discuss which communications are, and which are not, discoverable.

However, if you are working with a Category 3 expert, or are in state court and your state has not adopted the Federal Rules of Civil Procedure or analogous protections, be aware that all of your communications with your testifying experts may be subject to discovery. In that circumstance, limit the record you create by following these tips:

- Explain to your expert that every conversation you have, all writings the expert makes (e.g., the expert's own notes and drafts of reports), all writings the expert exchanges with you (e.g., emails, letters, and draft reports) are subject to discovery, and all will be used against your expert.
- Suggest that your expert limit notes when discussing the case with you.
- Consider retaining your expert initially only as a consulting expert. If your expert's opinions are favorable to your case, then retain him or her as a testifying expert. Even where the Federal Rules of Civil Procedure do not apply, conversations with *non-testifying* experts are generally protected unless opposing counsel can establish exceptional circumstances under which it is impracticable for the party seeking discovery to obtain facts or opinions on the same subject by other means.
- Limit the documents you provide to the testifying expert.
- Do not create a paper trail opposing counsel can use against you. Talk to your expert on the phone rather than exchanging emails or letters.
- Suggest that your expert prepare one draft report on the computer and, as revisions are made, not save prior drafts. If your expert wants to keep drafts, they should be headed "DRAFT ONLY—SUBJECT TO REVISIONS."
- Ask your expert not to send you any draft reports.
- If your expert will interview your client, inform both that the client's conversation with the expert is not privileged.
- To avoid all these issues, seek a written stipulation with opposing counsel that all the protections of Rule 26(b) apply.

## 4. Colleagues

"Colleagues" in this discussion refers to other lawyers in your firm—other associates, your mentor (if the firm has assigned one), and lawyers who assign you work.

Don't hesitate to brainstorm ideas with other associates. One of the main benefits of practicing law with other lawyers is the opportunity to work through tough legal issues, and to develop strategies. When you do brainstorm, feel free to suggest ideas that seem far-fetched, or even outlandish. Sometimes an off-the-wall idea leads to further discussion that is very productive. But don't practice law by consensus—that is, figure things out as much as you can without relying on others. Brainstorm only after you have analyzed an issue as thoroughly as you can.

And don't think Darwinian thoughts—that your future at the firm is a matter of survival of the fittest. After all, you may think, not all of us will make partner, so why should I cooperate with other associates I am competing with for very few slots in the partnership ranks? You might think: it's a dog-eat-dog world. Such an attitude will alienate you from your peers and deny you valuable resources, and could make you a pariah. Think back to law school, and ask yourself: Didn't you learn more from your classmates than from your professors?

You can learn from other associates about firm procedures and culture, practicalities of court procedures, idiosyncrasies of judges, inside information about lawyers in your firm and elsewhere, and information about clients and expert witnesses. And while you're at it, socialize with other associates; let off steam with them. You'll be better off for it. If your firm has a mentor program, make the most of what your mentor can do for you.

When you get an assignment, make sure you know three essentials: (1) what you are being asked to do, (2) the form of the work to be done (find cases, draft a memorandum, prepare a pleading, prepare for a deposition, etc.), and (3) the deadline. If you are already up to your eyeballs in work, don't hesitate to tell the lawyer assigning the work that you can get it done, but not by the proposed deadline, and explain in detail what other work presents the impediment to your meeting it. The lawyer assigning the work will appreciate your candor far more than receiving untimely or inadequate work from you.

If, during your research, you think of related issues worth exploring, ask the attorney who gave you the assignment if you should explore them. Show initiative in other ways as well. For example, if you have completed the research assignment, concluding that the client does have a good basis to pursue a motion to dismiss, offer to draft the motion and supporting memorandum.

If, after working on an assignment, you realize that you may not be able to meet the deadline (for a good reason), inform the lawyer who gave you the assignment before the deadline so an appropriate adjustment can be made. Don't wait until the last minute or turn in inadequate work.

If the lawyer who gave you the assignment does not give you a timely critique, ask for it. When you meet with that lawyer for the critique, be receptive to constructive criticism. The lawyer is investing time and effort in you; you should appreciate advice that will make you a better lawyer.

Throughout this entire process, your attitude should be upbeat, enthusiastic, and energized. If you don't truly feel that way, ask yourself why not, and heed the advice in chapter 13 about dealing with stress.

## 5. Co-counsel in other firms

Co-counsel in other firms fit in two categories: those who represent other defendants in the same case and those who are lead counsel when you are acting as local counsel.

If you are cooperating with co-counsel, obtain your client's consent after consulting with your client about the benefits and potential pitfalls of working with a lawyer who represents other defendants in the same case. Such an arrangement makes sense only when the interests of all defendants are fully aligned, and there is no realistic prospect of any cross-claims between or among defendants.

If such cooperation makes sense for strategic and financial reasons, it is preferable, although not required, to have a written joint defense agreement, which provides that

- The communications between counsel and clients who are parties to the agreement are confidential.
- The confidentiality extends to the maximum extent permissible.
- The parties to the agreement will not disclose those communications to any third parties without first obtaining written consent of the other parties to the agreement.

- Any third parties given access to those communications must sign a document confirming that they are bound by the terms of the joint defense agreement.
- If any party to the agreement receives a demand for documents covered by the joint defense agreement, or a subpoena to testify about communications within the joint defense agreement, counsel must notify other counsel who are parties to the joint defense agreement to provide an opportunity to object.
- The joint defense agreement is binding on any successor counsel.
- The joint defense agreement does not create an attorney-client or other agency or fiduciary relationship between an attorney and anyone other than the attorney's client.
- An attorney's signing the joint defense agreement does not preclude that attorney from representing any interest that may be construed to be adverse to any other party to the agreement or as a basis to disqualify that attorney from representing any other party in any proceeding.
- An attorney's signing the joint defense agreement does not disqualify him or her from cross-examining any witnesses in the case, including clients of the other attorney executing the joint defense agreement, but he or she cannot use documents exchanged pursuant to the joint defense agreement.

Sometimes you are asked to serve as local counsel to a lawyer who serves as lead counsel, both of you representing the same client. In that circumstance, no joint defense agreement is required because you both represent the same client. Different issues arise, however, because you want to make sure you work in concert with lead counsel for the maximum benefit to the client. Keep in mind that you cannot abdicate your responsibilities to your client, and that you are ultimately responsible for what happens in your case, even if acting only as local counsel. Here's a horror story to give you an idea of the potential pitfalls of serving as local counsel:

A communication failure between lawyers came close to allowing the execution of a death row inmate because of a failure to protect the inmate's rights, sending shock waves throughout the bar.

A critical communication slipped through the cracks in a case decided by the U.S. Supreme Court in 2012, *Maples v. Thomas*, 132 S. Ct. 912, highlighting the importance of close coordination between lead counsel and local counsel in both civil and criminal cases.

Cory Maples was found guilty of murder and sentenced to death in Alabama. Two pro bono New York lawyers sought post-conviction relief in Alabama state court, alleging ineffective assistance of counsel. Those two lawyers, as required by Alabama law, engaged an Alabama lawyer, John Butler, as local counsel. Mr. Butler made clear that he would move their admission pro hac vice, but would not undertake any substantive involvement in the case.

While Mr. Maples' post-conviction petition was pending, both New York lawyers left their firm, and their new employment disabled them from representing Mr. Maples. They did not inform him of their departure or inability to serve further as his counsel. In disregard of Alabama law, neither sought the trial court's leave to withdraw as counsel. No other attorney entered an appearance, moved to substitute counsel, or otherwise notified the court of the change in Mr. Maples' representation.

The trial court entered an order denying Mr. Maples' petition. Notices of that order were mailed to the New York firm, which returned them unopened, because the two pro hac lawyers were no longer employed there. Mr. Butler also received a copy of that order, but did not act on it. Mr. Maples was unaware that his appeal period was running. His appeal period ran out.

A month later, an Alabama assistant attorney general sent a letter directly to Mr. Maples, informing him that he missed the deadline to appeal, and that he had four weeks to file a federal habeas petition. The Alabama court denied a motion to reissue its order, which would have restarted the appeal period.

The Alabama Court of Criminal Appeals then denied a writ of mandamus that would have enabled Mr. Maples to file an untimely appeal; the Alabama Supreme Court affirmed. Mr. Maples then sought federal habeas relief. The District Court denied that relief, and a divided panel of the 11th Circuit affirmed, in *Maples v. Allen*, 586 F.3d 879 (2009), because Mr. Maples failed to file a timely appeal.

The U.S. Supreme Court ruled in Mr. Maples' favor, Justice Ruth Bader Ginsburg writing for the majority, with Justices Antonin Scalia and Clarence Thomas dissenting. Justice Ginsburg's rationale was that Mr. Maples could not be charged with the acts or omissions of attorneys who had abandoned him, and could not be faulted for failing to act on his own behalf when he lacked reason to believe his attorneys of record were not, in fact, representing him.

Justice Samuel Anthony Alito aptly described this near catastrophe as "a veritable perfect storm of misfortune." This saga is an extreme example of just some of the things that can go wrong when pro hac counsel and local counsel do not work together effectively. Local counsel must be much more than just a mail drop—and should, instead, provide a hometown advantage.

Here are some tips when you serve as local counsel to lead counsel in a case:

At the inception of the relationship with lead counsel, establish clear lines of responsibility. If counsel in the *Maples* case had done so, Mr. Maples would not have suffered the angst of the prospect of his untimely death, and his counsel would have been spared sleepless nights, to say the least.

Discuss with lead counsel many practical issues, such as: Who will respond to court notices and orders? Who will communicate with the client and draft pleadings? What procedure will be in place for local counsel to review drafts of proposed filings and who will do research on issues as they arise?

When you are retained, reach a clear understanding of the terms of the agreement, including whether the agreement is with the client or with pro hac counsel. One risk is that the client does not establish a relationship with local counsel, and thus minor billing or other issues can take on a greater significance than they deserve.

Maximizing the benefits of your involvement is limited only by creativity. Even though the focus here has been on representation of plaintiffs, the issue is equally important in representation of defendants, albeit on the flip side (e.g., brainstorming affirmative defenses rather than causes of action).

You can assist in pro hac vice applications, assuring compliance with local requirements, not all of which are obvious. You should review the form of lead counsel's draft complaint and other draft pleadings, providing guidance about compliance with the proper format in the local jurisdiction. As well, you should review the substance of the draft complaint to determine whether each count properly sets forth a cause of action in that jurisdiction and is properly pled, based on the law in that jurisdiction and local practice. See chapter 4, section 3, on drafting complaints.

You can suggest to lead counsel other possible causes of action not in the draft complaint and can provide guidance about long-arm jurisdiction, unique to each state; help find the right process server; and provide inside information about judges and their unique chambers practices.

You can also provide lead counsel

- guidance about types of relief that may be available in your jurisdiction, statutory and otherwise, and the likelihood of recovery as to each
- guidance about interlocutory remedies, such as injunctions, beyond what is in the rules, to answer such questions as: What is the likelihood of getting a temporary restraining order? What must be filed with injunction papers? If affidavits are required, how thorough must they be? How long before a temporary injunction hearing? What is the likelihood of going forward when scheduled? How likely is it that the judge will provide temporary relief?
- guidance about implementation of local rules in the jurisdiction
- research unique to the forum state, including benefitting from your brief bank on issues unique to your jurisdiction
- staff for logistical support
- review and comment on drafts of pleadings and memoranda to be filed with the court.

An ancillary benefit, of course, is avoiding legal malpractice. What if Mr. Maples had been executed? No lawyer would want to be a defendant in that malpractice lawsuit. Even if the client's life is not at stake, coordination with local counsel is vital not just to avoid malpractice; it is vital for success.

## 6. Opposing counsel

Two fundamental propositions are crucial: First, opposing counsel is not your enemy; rather, opposing counsel is your adversary. Second, you get what you give. What does this mean? Etymology is informative here.

"Enemy" derives from Latin *inimicus*, a compound of two Latin words, *in-*, meaning "not," and *amicus*, meaning "friend." *In-* begins such words as inefficient, incoherent, incompetent, indiscrete, and insubordinate, none of which you should be. *Amicus* is the root for such words as amicable, and the "amicus brief."

"Adversary," on the other hand, derives from Latin *adversus*, meaning "turned toward," like a faceoff in hockey, or the tipoff in basketball. You and opposing counsel are facing each other, each striving mightily to achieve your respective clients' goals, which are usually—but not always—mutually exclusive.

The point is this: You can and should be amicable with opposing counsel, and not treat him or her as an enemy. If you have an "enemy" mindset, you will only increase the stress you put on yourself and up the ante (now that it is a personal battle of egos, rather than a professional process to resolve disputes), and you will likely end up taking extreme positions that are unwarranted, or act out of emotion, because you have demonized your opponent.

Consider the offer of Tranio (in the guise of Lucentio) to his rivals, all vying for the love of the fair maid Bianca, in Shakespeare's "Taming of the Shrew." He suggests that they "[d]o as adversaries do in the law, strive mightily, but eat and drink as friends." His rivals respond: "O excellent motion! Fellows, let's be gone!" And off they go for a good time together as friends. Be like Tranio, at least in this regard.

Here is what happened to a lawyer who forgot to make the crucial distinction between adversary and enemy. In federal court, trial was scheduled within days of the date a lawyer defending the case, Bryan Erman, was expecting his first child. He filed a motion for continuance. A no-brainer, right? Plaintiff's counsel should have consented—especially since the trial was hundreds of miles from the expectant father's home. Plaintiff's counsel objected on various grounds, including an argument about family planning in the context of a long-scheduled trial, which Judge Eric F. Melgren brushed aside with "For reasons of good taste which should be (though, apparently, are not) too obvious to explain, the Court declines to accept Plaintiffs' invitation to speculate on the time of conception. . . ."

Judge Melgren begins his ruling by noting that "lawyers are trained to handle disputes skillfully but without the emotional rancor," footnoting the quotation from Shakespeare cited above. However, "[r]egrettably, many attorneys lose sight of their role as professionals, and personalize the dispute, converting the parties' disagreement into a lawyers' spat. This is unfortunate, and unprofessional, but sadly not uncommon." He made the personal observation that "this judge is convinced of the importance of federal court, but he has always tried not to confuse what he does with who he is, nor to distort the priorities of his day job with his life's role. Counsel are encouraged to order their priorities similarly." His ruling? "Defendants' Motion is **GRANTED**. The Ermans are **CONGRATULATED. IT IS SO ORDERED**." For a link to the opinion, go to http://graphics8.nytimes.com/packages/pdf/national/14judge/14judge-order.pdf.

In another federal case, a lawyer resorted to cursing and name-calling during a deposition. The judge hit the offending lawyer with a creative sanction. Instead of imposing any monetary sanction, Judge Gene E.K. Pratter ruled that the attorney must take a seminar on "civility and professionalism" and ordered that he sit down for a meal with his opponent. Judge Pratter was inspired by the quote from Shakespeare cited above.

The second fundamental proposition, "you get what you give," simply means that you should expect opposing counsel to mirror the way you interact with him or her. So, for example, if you deny a reasonable request for an extension of time for opposing counsel to respond to your interrogatories and document requests, do not expect opposing counsel to oblige when the tables are turned. If you are not diligent in responding to opposing counsel's emails, you will be hard pressed to complain when opposing counsel likewise is not prompt in responding to yours. Think of the logic behind the legal principal of equitable estoppel, if it helps you understand this fundamental principal of how human beings interact with each other.

"You get what you give" applies across the board in all your dealings with opposing counsel. Now consider the converse: If you are reasonable in your dealings with opposing counsel, it is more likely (but not a certainty) that opposing counsel will be reasonable with you, to the benefit of all parties involved. Consider stipulations that can save all parties time and money, such as

- If you have a discovery dispute, discuss it with opposing counsel before exchanging letters or emails about it. Yes, you must "meet and confer" before filing any motion to compel, see Rule 37(a)(1), but a phone call can be far more efficient than an exchange of letters and emails, at least initially. If you cannot resolve the discovery dispute by a phone call, you can benefit by creating a paper trail.

- Agree to limit the number of depositions each side will take.
- Share the same court reporter and videographer, negotiating a reduced fee.
- Agree that all pleadings will be served by email, as soon as they are filed.
- Work together to draft a mutually acceptable protective order for the court's approval.
- Stipulate to facts that are undisputed.

What should you do if opposing counsel has not been enlightened by the "get what you give" philosophy? Initially, do not react in kind, and see if your refusing to take the bait causes opposing counsel to be more reasonable. In a more extreme case, where opposing counsel rants, screams, and hollers, claiming that you have no right, for example, to object to his or her perfectly proper interrogatories and 127 document requests, instead of responding in kind, keep your temper, and respond something like this, in a calm voice: "I'm happy to discuss with you each interrogatory and document request, as the federal rules require, see Rule 37(a)(1), so let's work through each of my objections you have a problem with, one at a time. The judge can rule on anything we can't work out. What's the first objection you want to discuss?" This approach often defuses the situation, so you can have a productive discussion. Whatever you do, avoid getting into a screaming match with opposing counsel. No exceptions. It's just not worth it.

Early in your career, you will likely encounter some lawyers who try to take advantage of your lack of experience. "Listen, son, that's not how it works. When you've been practicing law as long as I have, you'll understand that you're going to lose on this. Besides, you've never appeared before Judge Hopkins before, and I have, many times, and I know how she will rule on your silly motion." If you are subjected to this, rest assured that your knowledge of the facts of the case, and of the applicable law and procedural rules, will make up for your lack of experience. So, the best way to respond is, "I am prepared and am ready to argue the point, so let's get a hearing date." And then learn what you need to know about Judge Hopkins. Consult with lawyers who have more experience. The same attack on your lack of experience will likely arise in depositions. See chapter 5, section 9, for dealing with obnoxious opposing counsel in depositions.

By following these two precepts—opposing counsel is your adversary not your enemy and you get what you give—you will establish long-lasting professional relationships with other lawyers, relationships of mutual respect. As a result, your practice of law will be more satisfying. Besides, opposing counsel is a source for new work, when he or she has a conflict of interest, and may even become a judge someday.

Whether you win or lose, be gracious in dealing with opposing counsel. What does that mean? If you win, do not boast or gloat. If you lose, extend your congratulations to opposing counsel, unless you have good reason not to.

## 7. Mediators and arbitrators

You and opposing counsel choose mediators for their knowledge, experience, expertise, and demeanor in resolving disputes. Certainly, treat the mediator with respect, and listen to what the mediator says, especially if his or her approach is evaluative rather than facilitative. See chapter 6, section 2, for the significance of this distinction. Even so, be aware that, during mediation, mediators often test the strengths and weaknesses of your position by challenging you. Do not hesitate to stand up to them, and explain why their assumptions about perceived weaknesses in your case are not justified.

Arbitrators serve in the same capacity as judges, but in the context of arbitration rather than litigation. Even though arbitration is more informal than litigation, be respectful of arbitrators, and apply all the tips below that apply to judges. Keep in mind that, unlike your communications with mediators, you cannot have any ex parte communications with arbitrators. Don't be put off or think anything is amiss if the arbitrators before whom you appear seem standoffish. They are required to be impartial and avoid even the appearance of partiality.

## 8. Judges

Judges, sitting up on high, wear the black robe, a symbol of authority, knowledge, and power. Consider this: the only others in our society who wear black robes (except for college graduates) are magicians and members of the clergy. The black robe can work to your advantage or to your detriment, depending primarily on your credibility with judges.

Preserving and promoting your credibility pervades all your dealings with judges. How do you accomplish that? By punctuality, preparation, persuasiveness, and professionalism.

*Punctuality.* Always be on time for all court proceedings and chambers conferences. Being late is disrespectful to the judge, opposing counsel, and clients. Give yourself extra time to get to court. And it is no excuse to say that you were stuck in traffic.

*Preparation.* Know the facts, law, and applicable procedure before you leave for court. Bring to court whatever you will need, whether for a pretrial motion, settlement conference, pretrial conference, hearing, or trial. Consider using a checklist, so you won't forget something crucial. In preparing for an evidentiary hearing, do whatever is required to arrange for your witnesses to be in the courtroom when needed, having served subpoenas as necessary. Bring to court copies of all documents you want the judge to consider, enough for the judge and all other counsel. If, despite all your preparation, you do not know the answer to a judge's question, be direct, admit you cannot answer, and commit to obtaining the answer. Don't assume or guess. See chapter 8, sections 2 and 5, for advice on answering judges' questions.

*Persuasiveness.* In court, be persuasive by incorporating your theme into your presentation of the facts and the law. Give the judge reasons to rule in your favor. See chapters 8, 9, and 10 for more on this.

*Professionalism.* Be organized in everything you say and do in court. Present yourself as a professional in how you dress and act. Demonstrate to the judge that you deal with opposing counsel with the appropriate demeanor—with civility, if not friendliness.

In chambers conferences, adjust your demeanor to the degree of informality the judge demonstrates. Some judges are much more informal in chambers than on the record. If in doubt, don't risk being too informal.

Socrates wrote that a judge should hear courteously, answer wisely, consider soberly, and decide impartially. Alas, not all judges follow Socrates' precepts. Sometimes you will encounter judges who are curmudgeonly, or worse. If you have done your homework, you will know in advance who they are. What should you do? Remain respectful, and make your best argument. Do not interrupt or argue with the judge, no matter how irascible or obnoxious the judge is. Treat all judges with respect, but do not be obsequious.

Assume that judges' clerks will discuss with the judge whatever is of interest about how you deal with them. Always respond promptly to any inquiry from judges' clerks, and treat them with respect. Likewise, treat other court clerks with respect—you need them more than they need you.

## 9. Jurors

You cannot communicate with jurors. During trial, you will encounter them on the elevator, in the hallway, and during lunch. You can say hello, but nothing more. Otherwise, you are risking a mistrial, or worse. And remember that you are always "on the record" within eyesight of jurors, even if not in the courtroom. After the jurors render their verdict and are discharged, you can talk to them, if the judge permits you to do so. Even then, you are constrained by applicable ethical rules. See Model Rule of Professional Conduct 3.5(c), which limits what you can say to a juror or prospective juror after the jury is discharged.

## ❖❖❖❖
## PRACTICE CHECKLIST

- Work in collaboration with your secretary by following the tips in the text.
- Benefit from paralegal assistance by knowing the capabilities of your paralegals and assigning work as appropriate.
- In all communications with witnesses (other than your client), assume that nothing is privileged.
- Know which types of communications with expert witnesses are protected, and which are not, under the Federal Rules of Civil Procedure and the procedural rules in your jurisdiction.
- Limit communications with expert witnesses that are not protected as much as practicable, preferring conversations to writings.
- Brainstorm ideas with colleagues.
- When getting an assignment, know what you are being asked to do, the form of the work, and the deadline.
- As you work on an assignment, if you think of related issues worth exploring, discuss them with the lawyer who gave you the assignment.
- Ask for critiques of your work.
- If you plan to work with a lawyer in another firm representing another party in litigation, obtain your client's informed consent, and draft a joint defense agreement for execution by all affected parties.
- If you act as local counsel only, establish clear lines of responsibility to avoid failure to protect your client's interests.
- Remember that opposing counsel is not your enemy but your adversary, and that you need not be hostile in your dealings. You get what you give in your dealings with opposing counsel.
- Treat mediators and arbitrators with respect, while keeping in mind that mediators often test your position by challenging you.
- Do not communicate ex parte with arbitrators.
- Preserve and promote your credibility with judges by punctuality, preparation, persuasiveness, and professionalism.
- Do not communicate with jurors, while being aware that they observe everything you do, in and out of the courtroom. You can talk to them after they render their verdict, but then only with the judge's permission, within the constraints of Model Rule 3.5(c).

CHAPTER THREE

# MANAGING AND DRAFTING EMAILS AND LETTERS

As a trial lawyer, each day you send and receive scores of emails. This chapter discusses how to manage your emails, when not to send emails, how to draft emails, email etiquette, how to avoid inadvertent waiver of the attorney-client privilege, how to organize and save emails, and how to draft letters.

## 1. How to manage your emails

Unless you focus on each task at hand as you do it, you will allow your attention to be diverted, resulting in slippage caused by each distraction, inefficiency, and waste of time. As a result, you will work longer hours (not all of which can be billed) with less productivity, and your energies will be diluted.

Emails provide an enticing opportunity to lose focus. For example, while working on a brief, your computer flashes a notice, possibly with an enticing "ding," that you just received an email you want to read. Do you break your train of thought, stop drafting mid-sentence, and read that email? Or do you resist that impulse, finish the section of the brief you are working on, and then read that email? Multiply this type of conundrum over a dozen times a day, and you can appreciate the importance of managing your emails.

Knowing that your prompt response to emails is required for you to be diligent in your communications with clients, opposing counsel, judges' law clerks, and colleagues, how do you resolve the tension between being efficient in the work you are doing while being diligent in responding to emails?

The answer is in managing your emails by self-imposed scheduling mechanisms. During the course of each day, restrain the impulse to read each email as you receive it. As emails come in while you are engaged in a task, complete that task first, then read a group of emails together. Whenever possible, do respond to each email the day you receive it, assuming it requires a response.

When you do read your emails, determine which are easily and quickly dealt with. Respond to those first. For emails that require extended time for a reply, respond so the sender knows you are on top of things, even if only to indicate that you received the email and will provide a substantive response by the date you state in your email.

This responsiveness is especially important in dealing with clients. Put yourself in the position of your clients. How would you like it if your lawyer ignored your emails, or even appeared to be doing so? One of the most common client complaints about lawyers is lack of responsiveness. If you are diligent in responding to client emails—even if only to advise when you will provide a substantive response—your client will be more satisfied than if you do not respond at all.

*Caveat*: You have the technological capability to respond to emails 24/7/365, right? Don't. The flip side of being diligent in responding to emails is becoming obsessed with them. Limit the times you read your work-related emails when you are not in the office. Unless you impose such restrictions, you will find yourself on the road to burnout. See chapter 13 on handling stress.

## 2. When not to send an email

Sure, emailing can be efficient and productive, especially if you manage it properly. But emailing is not always the best way to communicate. You have non-electronic options: letters, phone conversations, and face-to-face meetings. There are at least five instances when communication other than by email is preferable.

First, if you are sending a demand letter or other document you may want to use as an exhibit in a pretrial proceeding, or at trial, send a letter by certified or express mail as well as regular mail, if appropriate. Keep in mind that you are making a record in each communication with opposing counsel, whether in formal discovery, emails, letters, or otherwise. If you may want to include a particular communication as an exhibit, write a letter—even if you mail it and email it as well. In pretrial proceedings, it may be necessary to provide to a judge copies of your exchanges to a judge—for example, in pursuing a Rule 37 motion to compel disclosure by opposing counsel. At trial, a certified letter is far more effective than an email, which most people consider more informal and not as "official" as a letter. For tips on drafting letters, see section 7 of this chapter.

Second, a phone call is sometimes more efficient and effective than exchanging a string of emails on a subject. Phone calls present at least two advantages over emails. You benefit from immediate interaction in exchanging ideas in your back-and-forth conversation, rather than an exchange occurring over the course of hours or days. Just as one example, it would be impracticable to accomplish the objections of a Rule 26(f) conference by exchange of emails, even if it were permitted by that rule. Furthermore, a phone conversation gives you the opportunity to establish rapport with opposing counsel in a way not possible with an exchange of emails. And keep in mind that it is easier for opposing counsel to take a tough position by email, with no immediate interaction, than on the phone.

Third, if it is apparent that you need to clear the air with opposing counsel, or with a client, a phone call is far more effective—and far more likely to resolve a misunderstanding—than an email. It is far easier to express negative emotions by email than on the phone. If it appears that the email exchange is becoming inappropriately acrimonious or rancorous, pick up the phone and have a frank, productive conversation to break through all that negative energy. As trial lawyers, we deal daily with plenty of stressors. There is no reason to add yet another unnecessarily.

If you feel the need to draft a blistering email, castigating opposing counsel for being obstreperous or worse, go ahead and draft it, but *do not* push the send button for at least 24 hours. Then, when you are no longer in the throes of emotion, ask yourself if you should send it, soften it, or not send it at all. If in doubt, talk to one of your colleagues before deciding the best course of action.

Here is an example of an email you will never send (and not just because of the typos):

From: Dudley E. Scrivener
To: Julius Throckmorton
Re: Capulet case

Julius,

I just read your brief in connection wtht eh above-captioned case, and I am furious. U know the 1 I mean, the one in which u seek sanctions for what u assert are my failures to comply with discovery orders. Well, u are just plain wrong. Just yesterday, my client confirmed to me that he had provided all me all the documents he could find in his attic, all of which already I produced to u, so u have nothing to complain about. As u well know, I have complied with all discovery orders. Your espersions on my character, and your attacks on my professionalism, are totally out of bounds.

I hereby demand that u withdrw your motion immediately. Your conduct borders on the unethical, and I am considering going to the grievance committee, I'm so mad.

So, withdraw your motion or face the consdequences.
DUdley

Fourth, do not send unnecessary emails. You want to acknowledge receipt of any email to which you need to respond, but do not send any more emails than necessary if you want to be efficient and productive. You will be wasting your time and clogging up the recipient's inbox. And while it is tempting to send personal emails from the office, keep such emails to a minimum, and be mindful that you have no expectation of privacy in any email exchanges when using your firm's computer system.

Fifth, impose rules on yourself about emailing during vacations. You could reduce the stress of confronting hundreds of emails upon your return from vacation by checking your emails constantly while on vacation. But whether a vacation is a break from work is as much in your head as where you happen to be. If you constantly check your emails while on vacation, your head will be at the office, so when you "return" to work *you have already been in the office* during your entire "vacation." It may not be realistic for you to abstain from all work emails when on vacation, but if you cannot, set limits. For example, determine that you will check emails only before breakfast, and have the self-control to put work out of your mind the rest of the day so you can be where you are—on vacation! See chapter 13, section 2, for more about creating meaningful vacations.

Minimize vacation disruption by tying up as many loose ends as possible before leaving, and by arranging for someone else to cover for you. Just before you depart, discuss what might arise during your absence, and suggest how to deal with those eventualities. Make sure that all the lawyers you are working with on active matters know when you are leaving and when you will return. Leave a voicemail message on your phone and an email automatic reply message stating how long you will be away, whether you will be checking your emails, and whom to contact during your absence—and change both promptly upon your return.

When you return from vacation, manage your emails by deleting all junk emails first, respond to emails that you can deal with quickly, and then take the time to respond to emails that require more effort. Get a debriefing from the lawyer who covered for you. Set priorities for the sequence of tasks that you will accomplish. Ease back into work.

Utilize the same procedures when you are involved in a lengthy trial, although you may be able to respond to urgent emails and voice mail messages during the trial, as required.

Sixth, if you get an email that may be from a scammer, do not respond to it, and certainly do not open any attachment to it. For more, see chapter 1, section 1.

## 3. How to draft emails

You have already sent thousands of emails, so what do you need to learn? These tips should improve your emails.

*Recipient.* Send emails only to those who need them. You don't like receiving emails of only tangential interest, so why inflict unwanted emails on others? However, do copy anyone who should be in the loop. For example, know whether the attorney in your firm you are working with wants to be copied on your emails in a particular case, and be diligent about compliance. Whenever you are working with a team of lawyers, agree on what emails all of you will be copied on.

*Subject line.* Be specific! Of course it is easier to type "Montague v. Capulet" in the subject line, but the recipient learns little from it. With little effort, type something that focuses the recipient's attention (and enables you and the recipient to find a particular email more easily), such as "Montague v. Capulet—draft memo supporting summary judgment on defamation claim."

*Content.* Use the fewest words necessary to convey your message. If you have several points to make (for example, key admissions you obtained at a deposition), number them. Avoid long paragraphs. If your message is lengthy, attach a memo rather than drafting a long email. At the end of your email, be explicit about what you will do next or what you expect the recipient to do next. If you are emailing a draft of a document and do not intend to send it out until you receive comments, leave no room for ambiguity.

*Attachments.* Make sure you attach what you intend to attach. If it is a draft brief, for example, confirm that it is the right draft. If it is a signed agreement, confirm that it is the signed agreement, not just a draft. If it is a memo on subject A, make sure you do not inadvertently send a memo on subject B. Read the document that you have attached to confirm that it is the right one before pushing the send button. To avoid forgetting an attachment altogether, as soon as you type the words "I have attached," stop what you are typing, and attach what you intend, if you have not done so already. If you are sending an email with an attachment to opposing counsel, be very cautious about not sending anything you do not intend, or inadvertently waiving the attorney-client privilege, discussed later in section 5 of this chapter.

*Beware of email chains.* Independent of waiver of attorney-client issues, before sending an email, delete whatever appears in an email chain that the recipient should not receive. For example, if your colleague makes a candid observation in an email to you, not appropriate for transmittal to the ultimate recipient, be sure to delete it before sending.

*Read before sending an email.* Think before you click "send." Should you send this email as is, at this time, to this recipient? Check for typos. Spell-check is great, but sometimes "corrects" incorrectly. For example, spell-check will change "tortious" to "tortuous" (Bill Gates does not know the word "tortious"), so when you mean to convey the notion of a civil wrong, whoever reads your email will think of a meandering river. And a spelling mistake can be a real word, so spell-check will not alert you to your mistyping, for example, "our" for "your" or "form" for "from." Check all the components of an email listed above, review the contents carefully, and *only then* click "send." Sure, you are very busy and have little time to read and re-read your emails before sending them, but better to take the little extra time required to avoid the time-consuming distraction of fixing mistakes after the fact—not to mention the blemish on your professionalism.

## 4. How to use proper email etiquette

If sending an email is the most effective way to convey a message, then make the most of it, in a professional manner, by following these etiquette rules. Keep in mind that, in this digital world, the etiquette of your emails can go a long way to establish yourself as a true professional—or as a neophyte fresh out of law school still trying to find your way.

1. Respond promptly.
2. In your salutation, consider mirroring the salutation in the message you received, if appropriate, in addressing the recipient of your email.
3. Use proper spelling, grammar, and punctuation.
4. Use "high priority" and "read receipt" options only when necessary.
5. Do not use all capital letters.
6. Address new contacts with the highest level of courtesy (e.g., "Mr. Montague," "Ms. Capulet") unless informed otherwise.
7. Begin each email with an appropriate businesslike salutation, not too informal.
8. Use normal fonts in normal font size.
9. Copy only those who need to be copied; think twice before hitting "respond to all."
10. Use spell-check and re-read before sending.

## 5. How to avoid inadvertent waiver of the attorney-client privilege when emailing

Using emails can be hazardous to your client's attorney-client privilege, unless you are very conscientious about the email address to which you send your emails and who receives them.

*Caveat about emails to a client's place of employment.* If your client is an entity, and you email an employee of your client, you do not waive the attorney-client privilege, although you should first discuss with that employee who else has access to company emails, and whether a different email address may be more appropriate.

But if your client is an individual, and you send an email to that individual's place of employment, your client has no reasonable expectation of privacy using the employer's operating system. Two possible negative consequences arise. First, your client's employer may read your email exchanges, to your client's detriment. Consider, for example, a case in which your client has a claim against his or her employer. Second, opposing counsel may demand production of all emails you transmit to your client's place of business, contending that, just as if you discussed otherwise privileged matters with your client in a public place or with a third party present, your client has no reasonable expectation of privacy, and therefore the attorney-client privilege does not apply.

*Caveat regarding emails to a client's home email address.* It's not uncommon for a husband and wife to share one email address. If you send emails to that address, you create an avoidable issue about waiver of the attorney-client privilege. Why not avoid the issue altogether by having your client emailing you from home create a separate individual email account for your communications?

*Caveat about copying others on emails to clients and forwarding emails.* If you ever are about to send an email to a client and you copy or blind-copy anyone else, ask yourself if you may be waiving the attorney-client privilege. If you copy another lawyer in your firm, or your paralegal, no problem. But if you copy your expert witness in your case, or counsel in a related case, think twice about clicking "send." Also, check the email chain before you click "send." It may include privileged emails. The same advice applies to forwarding emails. Avoid sending blind copies, because the recipient may respond by pushing "reply all." Rather than using blind copy, forward the email to that recipient.

During your career, you will send tens of thousands of emails. It is just possible that, sooner or later, you will inadvertently send an email to opposing counsel that includes information protected by the attorney-client privilege or work-product doctrine. What should you do? After assuring yourself that the email is within the attorney-client privilege or work-product doctrine, immediately call opposing counsel, say that you inadvertently sent him or her a privileged communication, specifically identify it, and say: Do not read it. Delete it, and then delete it from the deleted emails. Do not print it. Do not forward it to anyone. If already printed, destroy all copies. If already forwarded, instruct the recipient of the forwarded email to follow the same instructions. Confirm that instruction in writing.

Opposing counsel should send you an email confirming that all this has been done. Model Rule 4.4(b) requires that a lawyer who receives a document relating to the representation of the lawyer's client and knows, or reasonably should know, that the document was inadvertently sent, must promptly notify the sender so that the sender can take protective measures. See, more generally, FRE 502(b) and (c), and Rule 26(b)(5)(B), which pertain to inadvertently disclosed information. Opposing counsel should cooperate but, if not, you may need to file an appropriate motion promptly.

Likewise, if you ever receive an email or any other communication opposing counsel sends you that includes such protected information, what should you do? You have the same ethical obligations as opposing counsel has to you. And don't wait for opposing counsel to contact you—initiate the call to discuss the inadvertent waiver issue. Unless you have a good reason to question whether ethical rules in your jurisdiction provide otherwise, you should apply the same procedure as set forth above, in reverse. If in doubt, immediately discuss this issue with a colleague. It may be appropriate to agree to seal the email in question and agree not to read it or do anything with it, subject to a judge's in camera review.

### 6. HOW TO ORGANIZE AND SAVE EMAILS

An efficient way to organize emails is to create subfolders in your inbox of significant emails by case. It takes only an instant to move an email as soon as you receive or send it. You then have ready access to all emails you may need, in each case.

There is no reason to print every email you send or receive, but consider printing those of significance. If you print an email you sent, print the "sent" version so you have a record of sending it. Archive your old emails on your computer. When you close a file, consider putting emails pertinent to that case on a disk, to avoid cluttering a closed file with too much paper.

## 7. How to draft letters

You will draft far fewer letters than emails, but sometimes only a letter will do, as when you may need it as an exhibit for a court hearing or trial, such as a demand letter, or when you are filing a letter brief, which some judges allow.

Here are some practical tips:

- Include a "re" line so it is self-evident at the start what case you are writing about. Be consistent in all your letters in the "re" line you use in a case. If you are writing a judge or judge's clerk, include the docket number, and be sure to copy all counsel of record.
- Be deliberate in deciding how you address the person you write to. Is it "Dear Mr. Hughes," "Dear Charles," or "Dear Chuck?" Decide which form of address is most appropriate.
- Your tone should be businesslike and professional. Some informality is acceptable, though, when appropriate, such as wishing the recipient a happy holiday.
- If this is your first letter to someone, start by making explicit who your client is and the scope of your representation. "I represent Mr. Capulet in the defense of the action you brought on behalf of Mr. Montague claiming defamation."
- If you are drafting a demand letter, include enough detail so that the recipient will take your demand seriously, and so that what you write will be an effective exhibit at trial.
- If you are responding to a letter, simply state at the beginning: "I am responding to your letter dated X."
- Keep in mind that you are making a written record in every letter you write. Have you made an admission of a fact that binds your client? Have you taken a position that a judge may view as unjustified—or worse—when reviewing a chain of correspondence, as with discovery disputes?
- Get right to the point. No one likes to wade through lots of verbiage before finding out why you wrote the letter.
- If you want the recipient to do something as a result of reading your letter, be specific about what must be done and by when.
- Typically, your letters will end with "Very Truly Yours," but if you are writing a judge, you must end with "Respectfully."

- Check the judge's chambers practices (in federal court, available online) before sending a letter, since some judges do not accept letters.
- Think carefully about what names you include in any "cc" line. Be sure to include everyone you should (for example, all counsel of record in a letter to a judge), but no one you should not.
- Be careful not to waive the attorney-client privilege.

How many mistakes can you find in this letter?

> HAND-DELIVERED
> Judge Horatio Prendergast
> Federal District Court
> Southern District of New YOrk
>
> **Re: Montague v. Capulet**
>
> Dear Judge Prendergest,
> I have enclosed my supplimental memorandum in support of the pending motion in the above-captioned case. I filed this supplimental memorandum with the court clerk, and hereby provide you with this chambers's copy, for your review and consideration..
>
> I look forward to receiving your favourable ruling on the pending motion.
>
> Very truly yours,<br>Dudley E. Scrivener

*Non-engagement letters.* Assume a prospective client calls you. As required by the ethical rules, you complete your conflicts check. You have no conflict. You meet with the prospective client. You decide not to undertake the representation. You tell the prospective client you will not be undertaking this representation. Is that sufficient?

No.

You need to create a written record of non-engagement. Otherwise, the prospective client may misunderstand, assume you have taken the case, statutes of limitations may run, and someday you will get a letter from another lawyer putting you on notice of a malpractice claim. Unlikely? Maybe. But why take the chance?

To avoid such a potential disaster, send the prospective client a non-engagement letter. It should state clearly and explicitly that you will not be representing the prospective client in that matter, and recommend that he or she seek advice from another attorney promptly. If you are aware that statutes of limitations are about to run, indicate the need for urgency, while avoiding giving legal advice. Send it in a way that you have a record of receipt.

*Engagement letters.* Engagement letters set forth the terms of your agreement with a client as to the scope of your services, payment of your fees, and other terms. Ethical rules in your jurisdiction may require that you have a written engagement letter for each matter you undertake, except for a client giving your firm ongoing work.

Draft your engagement letter in simple English, and make it as short as possible, while including provisions covering each of the following:

- who the client is
- the scope of services you will render
- the fee arrangement
- the amount of any retainer payment
- who pays for costs
- conditions for termination of representation (e.g., failure to pay fees)
- a procedure to resolve disputes related to the retainer agreement
- a complete integration clause
- a provision that it cannot be amended except in writing, signed by all parties
- a signature line for the firm (not you individually) and each client

The section on fees should disclose the range of hourly rates of all lawyers in your firm and disclose the hourly rates of those who will work on the matter. If you include any contingency element of your fee, make sure it is explicit, avoids any ambiguity, and complies with the ethical rules in your jurisdiction. For alternative fee arrangements, see chapter 1, section 4.

*Completed-engagement letters.* When you have completed your engagement, it is a good idea to send a letter to your client confirming that you have done so and are closing the file. You do not want any ambiguity with your client about whether you will do further work in that matter. This is a good opportunity, if you have not done so already, to inform your client about all the other services your firm provides. If your firm has a brochure, enclose it. Of course, thank your client for the opportunity to be of service, and express your willingness to be of service again, as the need arises.

*Opinion letters.* Some commercial clients ask you for opinion letters, setting forth their legal rights and obligations, something akin to a declaratory judgment, but in the context of seeking your advice. When drafting an opinion letter, state all facts you are assuming in rendering your opinion, what your opinion is, and all qualifications to your opinion. If you need to qualify the absoluteness of your opinion (for example, "it is likely that . . .") then do not hesitate to do so, explaining the reason for your qualification. Avoid categorical statements, unless they are justified. All opinion letters should be signed by the firm, not by you individually, and only a principal of the firm should sign them.

Before sending any opinion letter, make sure a colleague in your firm reviews it. After all, it is the firm, not just you personally, on the hook if you give bad advice.

*Auditor letters.* As part of the normal auditing procedures for many commercial clients, the auditor requests that the client provide information about pending and potential claims and litigation and outstanding fees and cost reimbursements in connection with your firm's legal representation of that client.

Each such letter advises you of the period of time for which the information is requested, and the deadline for you to respond. Your firm should have a system in place for you to determine all pending and potential claims and litigation. Make sure your information is complete before drafting such a letter, which must be signed by a principal of the firm. Do not overstate the likely outcome of pending litigation. Be aware that a letter to an auditor is not protected by the attorney-client privilege. Assume that your opponent may obtain it in discovery.

Qualify your letter with these caveats:

> We have furnished information based on the limitations of our engagement and on the limitations of the American Bar Association Statement of Policy Regarding Lawyers' Responses to Auditors' Requests for Information (December, 1975) ("Policy Statement").

The information included in this letter is current, except as indicated, and we disclaim any undertaking to advise you of changes which may be brought to our attention after the date of this letter.

This response is limited by and prepared in accordance with the Policy Statement. Without limiting the generality of the foregoing, the limitations set forth in the Policy Statement on the scope and use of this response (paragraphs two and seven thereof) are specifically incorporated herein by reference, and any description in this letter of any "loss contingencies" is qualified in its entirety by Paragraph 5 of the Policy Statement and the accompanying commentary (which is an integral part of the Policy Statement).

This letter is solely for your information in connection with your audit of the financial condition of the Company at [LAST DAY OF AUDIT] and is not to be quoted in whole or in part, or otherwise referred to, in any financial statements of the Company or related document. This letter is not to be filed with any governmental agency or any other person without the prior written consent of the undersigned.

## ❖❖❖❖
## PRACTICE CHECKLIST

- Create scheduling mechanisms so you do not get distracted by incoming emails.
- When responding to emails, determine which are easily dealt with; respond to those first and then to those that require more time.
- Be diligent in responding to emails.
- Do not send emails in certain circumstances.
  - _____ when sending a demand letter or other document you may want to use as an exhibit
  - _____ when a phone call is more likely to achieve your purpose
  - _____ when you need to clear the air
  - _____ when it is unnecessary to do so
  - _____ when you are on vacation (with exceptions)
  - _____ when you suspect spam
- Send emails only to those who need them.
- Be specific in your subject line.
- Be cogent.
- Make sure you attach what you intend.
- Beware of email chains.
- Read your draft email carefully before sending it.
- Use proper email etiquette.
- Avoid inadvertent waiver of the attorney-client and work-product protections:
  - _____ Do not send emails to your client's place of employment.
  - _____ Do not send emails to your client's home if not a sole email account.
  - _____ Be wary when copying parties on emails.
  - _____ Do not blind-copy emails.
- If you inadvertently send an email to opposing counsel containing attorney-client privileged or work-product information, take immediate remedial action.
- If opposing counsel ever sends you an email containing attorney-client privileged or work-product information, call opposing counsel immediately so opposing counsel can take remedial action.
- Organize your emails so you can locate them promptly, and archive them appropriately.
- In drafting letters, be cogent, businesslike, and conscientious about each element, from the "re" line to the "cc" line.
- Apply to letters all the advice above about emails, to the extent applicable.
- Send letters when you decide not to take on a matter, when you do take on a matter, and when you complete or terminate a matter.
- Before sending any opinion letter, a colleague in your firm should review it.
- Do a thorough investigation of all relevant matters before responding to an auditor's letter.

CHAPTER FOUR

# DRAFTING DOCUMENTS OTHER THAN EMAILS AND LETTERS

As a trial lawyer, you devote most of your working hours to writing. To succeed, you must know how to write. This chapter discusses general principles for drafting effective legal writing and how to draft internal memos, pleadings, motions, memos supporting motions, jury instructions, appellate court briefs, and settlement agreements. In appendix I, you will learn about the overarching theme of cogency, featuring Molly Cogent in action, taking on Ulysses S. Bombast in a spirited debate, and then mentoring litigation associate Tim Smithers. As in other chapters, this discussion assumes you are in federal court. If your action is in state court, comply with all applicable state court rules.

To learn how to write emails and letters, see chapter 3. To learn about submissions to mediators and arbitrators, see chapters 6 and 7. For guidance in the mechanics of legal writing, read the books on that subject listed in appendix III.

## 1. Principles applicable to all legal writing

While each document you craft has a specialized purpose, certain basic principles apply to everything you write.

*Think before you write.* Sounds simple, right? Of course. But unless you think carefully about what you plan to write, you will not be doing your job. Much of what we write is analogous to playing a chess match—you must think many moves ahead before you make your next move. Ask yourself reporter questions: What am I about to write? Why? What is my objective? For whom am I writing? Why am I writing it now? How am I going to go about it?

*Write for your reader.* Are you writing for a client, colleague, opposing counsel, trial judge, appellate judge, or a jury? Tailor everything you write for your reader.

*Divide the writing process into discrete tasks.* Some legal writing is daunting, because so much is required and so much is at stake. When taking on a substantial writing assignment, divide it up. So, for example, if you need to draft a lengthy, comprehensive memo, divide it into discrete tasks: thinking it through, outlining your memo, doing legal research on each issue, drafting each point, and editing. If a discrete task is very time consuming, periodically take a break and return to the task reinvigorated. An additional benefit of this process is that you get a boost of satisfaction, psychological positive reinforcement, as you complete each task.

*Use simple words.* Even students who can write in plain English when starting law school think, upon graduation, that to write "like a lawyer" they must use sesquipedalian words like sesquipedalian (look it up). The best writing uses simple words. Humorist Will Rogers, in his unique homespun style, drives the point home: "[H]ere's one good thing about language, there is always a short word for it. Course the Greeks have a word for it, the dictionary has a word for it, but I believe in using your own word for it. I love words but I don't like strange ones. You don't understand them, and they don't understand you. Old words are like old friends—you know 'em the minute you see 'em." For examples to emulate, read anything written by Oliver Wendell Holmes, Benjamin Cardozo, or, for a modern example, Chief Justice of the U.S. Supreme Court John G. Roberts. Even if you do not agree with their judicial philosophy, you must admire their ability to convey complex ideas in plain English.

*Edit.* Effective legal writing is hard work. Your first draft may be pretty good, but you can do better. How? By completing your first draft well before your deadline so you have time to improve what you wrote. Then edit, edit, edit. There are no shortcuts. The flip side is that you don't want to be so consumed by the editing process that you are never satisfied with your work, and miss deadlines. Even an artist painting a masterpiece must know when to stop making brushstrokes.

*Eliminate typos.* If I had written *"Elminate typos,"* you would have understood my meaning, but you would question how well I proofread the manuscript of this book, which could cause you to question how carefully I thought through what I wrote. So it is with everything you write. A judge reading your brief full of typos will not be convinced that you did a thorough job in your research, and may very well question the soundness of your underlying thinking, for that matter. Read through whatever you write before sending it out. Spell-check is useful, but it won't catch all your typos. If feasible, ask someone else to proofread your work; a fresh look may very well catch errors you won't. A typo is just as discordant as a wrong note played by a musician in a wide open solo during an orchestral performance. It mars the entire work.

*Write cogently.* Before editing that subheading, I used 10 times as many words to convey the same message. Here is the original draft: "Do not use any more words than you really need in anything you write, to be more effective in your legal writing." That's fine for a first draft, but not good enough. When you edit, eliminate all words that don't do work.

Heed Mark Twain's advice by using "plain, simple language, short words, and brief sentences . . . . don't let fluff and flowers and verbosity creep in."

## 2. How to draft internal memos

*Know your assignment.* In drafting internal memos for your colleagues, you must understand your assignment, think through how you will tackle it, do the necessary factual and legal research, draft using a format that is effective, and respond substantively to what you have been requested to do.

What is your assignment? Make sure you have a clear understanding of what the facts are, what issues you are to address, and the context. When you first get the assignment, ask questions to be sure you have the specific assignment in mind. As you research, if you need more factual information, get it. If you think of related issues you were not asked to research, ask if you should include those in your memo. For each assignment you get, make sure you know the substance, format, and deadline for that assignment. For more on assignments, see chapter 2, section 4.

*Research thoroughly.* Think about avenues of research. Do word searches using computerized research, but only after carefully thinking through what search terms make the most sense, and in what databases. Start with very specific search terms, to capture cases most directly in point. Depending on what you find by specific searches, expand your search by using more general search terms, going up levels of abstraction. For example, if you are researching whether your client can recover legal fees for fraud even if the court awards only nominal damages, and you find no cases in point, you can go up a level of abstraction by researching whether courts award legal fees for *any* common law causes of action in which legal fees are recoverable, even where only nominal damages are awarded.

On the other hand, when your firm is paying a cost per transaction for computerized research, you can reduce such costs by starting with a broad search, and then using narrowing tools provided by the search engine, although the broad search may overwhelm you with many cases of only limited interest.

When you find cases based on search-term research, read each case of interest. Don't just copy and paste sentences that discuss the point you are researching. Unless you know the procedural context, the issues presented, and whether what you are relying on is the holding or merely dictum, you may inadvertently cite as authority cases that do not support the position you are researching. Start with decisions of the highest court in your jurisdiction, and work your way down, proceeding to other states whose decisions judges in your jurisdiction rely upon, if necessary.

Don't stop with computerized research of cases. Research all statutes and regulations that may apply. Browse through the West Key Number System for ideas. Read treatises on the subject. If judges in your jurisdiction rely on the American Law Institute's Restatements of the Law, read applicable sections, and the comments (explaining the rule), illustrations (providing hypothetical fact patterns applying the rule), and reporter's notes (directing you to related authorities) in the text. Find law review articles and *American Law Reports* annotations for in-depth analysis of specific issues. If your firm has a brief bank, take advantage of it. There's no sense in reinventing the wheel, but do bring the research up to date. If your firm does not have a brief bank, create one to share with your colleagues.

For certain assignments, you may benefit from reversing this process by starting with the brief bank, browsing through the West Key Number System and the Restatements of the Law and treatises, before narrowing your search or doing computerized research. By doing so, you will get a better grounding in the more general subject area of your research.

Your purpose is not to persuade, but to inform. Look for cases that go against your position, not only those that support it. You would not want your colleague to get blindsided by opposing counsel's reliance on a recent case holding against your position decided by the highest court in your jurisdiction that goes against you. When you draft, include a discussion based on a devil's advocate position, whenever appropriate.

*Use an effective format.* Your firm may have a set format for you to follow. In general, the best format is as follows:

- Facts. State the salient substantive and procedural facts.
- Issue. State the issue or issues presented.
- Summary conclusion. State your conclusion succinctly.
- Analysis. Discuss each point in your analysis, dividing the text into subparts, as appropriate, with an explicit subheading for each. Include an analysis of the strengths and weaknesses of your position, suggested strategy going forward, and any additional research you suggest.

## 3. How to draft complaints

Complaints control everything in your case—what the issues are, what discovery is permissible, what remedies are available, and what defenses may be alleged. Drafting properly is the sine qua non for achieving your client's objectives. Keep in mind that you assume the burden of proving each fact you allege, each claim you assert, and each affirmative defense you assert.

Before drafting a complaint, you must know your client's objectives, applicable facts, and applicable law, and you must think through possible causes of action and available remedies. Know the elements of each cause of action. After you have done so, ask yourself: *Who* are appropriate plaintiffs and defendants (see Rules 17–22)? *What* common law and statutory relief will you seek? *Where* will you bring suit, keeping in mind *in personam* jurisdictional and *forum non conveniens* issues? If you have a choice of state or federal court, or courts in different jurisdictions, which is preferable, and why? *When* will you bring suit—only after sending a demand letter?—and what about applicable statutes of limitations? *Why* are you bringing suit, rather than seeking some other remedy? Does an arbitration clause apply? *Why* are you asserting these claims against these defendants? And *how* will you make service?

Eliminate weak causes of action, but discuss with your client those you eliminated so you get your client's informed consent. And discuss with your client whether to claim the case to a jury. See Rule 38 for jury claims and chapter 11, section 2 for the applicable ethical rules about informed consent.

These questions are not always easily answered. For example, in deciding who are appropriate defendants, a host of issues can arise: Against which individuals and entities do you have viable causes of action? Do you have a basis to pierce the corporate veil to sue one or more individuals? What about suing individuals who engaged in tortious conduct, even though acting in a representative capacity? If feasible, have you joined all necessary parties (Rule 19)? What about permissive joinder of parties (Rule 20)? If you represent a plaintiff who owns a business interest and your action involves the business affairs of an entity, is it properly a direct or a derivative claim (Rule 23.1)? If you seek declaratory relief (Rule 57), have you included all interested and affected parties as defendants? For entities, do you know the proper legal name, and not just the style in which the entity is doing business (the d/b/a)? Do you have personal jurisdiction over all your proposed defendants, including long-arm jurisdiction over out-of-state defendants? How many lawyers do you want opposing you? You could be battling one lawyer for each defendant you sue.

In federal court, comply with applicable rules. Rule 8(a) provides that a pleading stating a claim must contain (1) a short and plain statement of the grounds for the court's jurisdiction, unless the court already has jurisdiction and the claim needs no new jurisdictional support; (2) a short and plain statement of the claim showing that your client is entitled to relief; and (3) a demand for relief sought, which may include relief in the alternative or different types of relief. Rule 8(d) requires that each allegation must be "simple, concise, and direct"; allows statements of claims in the alternative; and allows for inconsistent claims.

Rule 8 was applied to effect when Lance Armstrong sued the U.S. Anti-Doping Agency and its chief executive, alleging that they had engaged in an obsessive, unlawful, and meritless campaign to strip him of his Tour de France titles and ruin his legacy. Because of a violation of Rule 8, U.S. District Judge Sam Sparks chastised his lawyers. *Sua sponte*, he dismissed Armstrong's complaint within hours of its filing, without prejudice to file an amended complaint.

Armstrong's complaint was neither short nor plain—80 pages containing 261 numbered paragraphs, with multiple subparts. Judge Sparks held that "vast swaths of the complaint could be removed entirely, and most of the remaining paragraphs substantially reduced, without the loss of any legally relevant information." He further admonished: "All parties, and their lawyers, are expected to comply with the rules of this Court, and face potential sanctions if they do not." Judge Sparks advised Armstrong "in the strongest possible terms, and on pain of Rule 11 sanctions, to omit any improper argument, rhetoric, or irrelevant material from his future pleadings." For this ruling (which includes a revealing footnote about complaints not being press releases, Internet blogs, or pieces of investigative journalism), see Judge Sparks' Order in *Armstrong v. Tygart, et al.*, Case No. A-12-CA-606-SS U.S. Dist. (W.D. Tex. Austin Division, July 9, 2012).

Duly chastised, the very next day, Armstrong's lawyers filed an amended complaint of 25 pages, containing 82 numbered paragraphs, with few subparts. Judge Sparks ultimately dismissed the action, because Armstrong had executed a contract requiring that he arbitrate the subject disputes.

Rule 9 provides, among other things, that certain allegations must be pled with particularity. For example, you must plead with particularity fraud, mistake, and items of special damages, but you can plead generally such things as malice, intent, knowledge, and other conditions of mind, and conditions precedent. If you raise a constitutional challenge, comply with Rule 5.1.

Rule 10 requires, among other things, that you state your claims in numbered paragraphs, each limited as far as practicable to a single set of circumstances; it also allows you to incorporate by reference to earlier paragraphs in your complaint. To promote clarity, each claim founded on a separate transaction or occurrence must be stated in a separate count.

Rule 17 defines who can bring a legal action in federal court. Rule 18 allows you to join, as independent or alternative claims, as many claims as you have against a defendant, and allows you to join two claims even though one is contingent on the disposition of the other. For example, you can assert a claim for money, and a claim to set aside a conveyance that is fraudulent as to your client, without first obtaining a judgment for the money. Rule 19 provides for required joinder of parties, and Rule 20 for permissive joinder of parties.

The best way to implement these rules is to divide your complaint into sections. First, identify the parties. Second, state the jurisdictional basis for your action. Third, set forth the facts applicable to all your causes of action. Fourth, set forth each cause of action. Fifth, list your requested relief.

In drafting each numbered paragraph, limit yourself to one fact, or a cluster of closely related facts, designed to make it difficult for defense counsel to deny any more than unavoidable. For brevity, incorporate into later counts allegations in earlier counts, exercising care to be sure you re-allege everything you need, so each count states a cause of action. Be aware, though, that if you re-allege facts from various other counts into an additional count, the result may be confusing.

If the parties have lengthy names, refer to them in a shorthand fashion, but in a way that is intelligible. For example, define Hyperion Widget Manufacturing Corporation as "Hyperion." Avoid such sentences as "ICFA breached Sec. 17.1(d) of the RKO Contract with FLC by failing to give the required notices to FLC or to GLX, GLX Corp., or GLXA Partners." An alphabet soup of acronyms can be nearly indecipherable. And avoid referring to parties in ways that require the reader to do more work than necessary, such as referring to the "Defendant Third Party Plaintiff."

In your complaint, you can demand a jury trial on any issue triable to a jury, as provided in Rule 38. You can also make that demand not later than 14 days after the last pleading directed to that issue is served. Rule 38(b)(1). Otherwise, you waive your right to a jury trial. Rule 38(d).

For complaint forms, see the official Appendix of Forms attached to the Federal Rules of Civil Procedure, which Rule 84 describes as illustrative of the simplicity and brevity that these rules contemplate; complaints drafted by others in your office; and form books. If your firm does not already have a bank of forms, create one, and share it with your colleagues. Whatever form you rely on, be sure to modify it to fit the facts of your case, and make sure it compiles with applicable rules as amended.

Even though your complaint must be a "short and plain" statement of your claim, you should include sufficient facts to tell your story. By the time the judges (or jurors, for that matter) finish reading complaints you draft, they should be convinced of the rightness of your cause, and your entitlement to relief.

Furthermore, you must comply with the requirements of U.S. Supreme Court cases holding that you must state a claim that is *plausible*. This requires more than merely alleging the elements of a cause of action. In a nutshell, a complaint must contain sufficient factual matter, accepted as true, to state a claim to relief that is plausible on its face. While the plausibility standard does not impose a probability requirement, it does demand more than a sheer possibility that a defendant has acted unlawfully. Mere conclusory allegations will not suffice. For more on this subject, read Molly Cogent's advice to Tim Smithers in appendix I.

In drafting the complaint, keep in mind that, by signing it, you are representing to the court that you are not presenting it for any improper purposes; all your claims are warranted by existing law or by a non-frivolous argument for extending, modifying, or reversing existing law or for establishing new law; and your factual contentions have evidentiary support or, if specifically so identified, will likely have evidentiary support after a reasonable opportunity for further investigation or discovery ("on information and belief" allegations). See Rule 11(b). You can amend your complaint, as provided in Rule 15.

### 4. How to draft motions and memos supporting and opposing motions

When you represent a defendant, as soon as you receive a complaint, determine what motions are available to you and comply with applicable deadlines. If you need an extension of time, file a timely motion and comply with all applicable rules. See Rule 12(a). Typically, local rules require that you confer with plaintiff's counsel before filing any motion for extension of time, and so state in your motion. In drafting motions and supporting memos, comply with the Federal Rules of Civil Procedure, local rules, and rules listed in the chambers practices of the judge assigned to your case, available online.

Rule 12(b) lists the following defenses that can be asserted by motion: lack of subject-matter jurisdiction, lack of personal jurisdiction, improper venue, insufficient process, insufficient service of process, failure to state a claim upon which relief can be granted, and failure to join a party under Rule 19. You must file a motion asserting any of these claims before you file your answer. Be aware of the waiver provision in Rule 12(h) to avoid inadvertent waiver of defenses.

Other motions available to you before filing your answer include a motion for a more definite statement if the complaint is so vague or ambiguous that you cannot reasonably prepare a response, Rule 12(e), and a motion to strike a pleading that is immaterial, impertinent, or scandalous, Rule 12(f). These motions are not filed as frequently as motions to dismiss under Rule 12(b), but you should file them in an appropriate case.

In drafting a motion, the title should be explicit. If you represent fewer than all defendants, make clear in the title which defendant is filing the motion. The title should also inform the judge precisely what the motion is.

The body of the motion should be as short as possible, summarizing the basis for the motion, and specifically stating what you want the judge to do. In the motion, refer to your supporting memorandum and any other supporting documents you are filing with your motion, such as declarations or affidavits. Most motions are only a few pages.

The memorandum supporting your motion must convince the judge to rule in your favor. Ask yourself: What does the judge need to know to rule in your favor? Assume that the judge has a pile of motions and supporting memos on his or her desk and gets to yours. What will grab the judge's attention and be most convincing?

Memos involving simple issues do not require many parts and subparts. Simply lay out the pertinent facts, the procedural context, and why your motion should be granted. Motions involving more complex issues justify more detail, although you must comply with any applicable page limits.

The parts of a comprehensive memo supporting a motion are

- *Cover Page.* This informs the judge what this memo is.
- *Table of Contents.* This previews your argument for the judge and enables the judge (and the judge's law clerk) to find specific subparts of your argument, whenever necessary.

- *Table of Authorities.* This enables the judge to find authorities you cite in the text.
- *Preliminary Statement.* Start with a preliminary statement as short as possible, typically no longer than two pages, summarizing your entire argument. By the time the judge finishes reading your preliminary statement, the ruling should be a foregone conclusion.
- *Facts.* Set forth the pertinent facts, and the procedural posture, so the judge is oriented as to the context of the ruling to be made. Deal with relevant facts that undermine as well as support your position, thereby enhancing your credibility, making a pre-emptive strike by putting bad facts in context.
- *Argument.* Divide your argument into subparts, as appropriate, each flowing logically from your previous point, and each headed with a persuasive rather than a neutral heading. Put your strongest point first. Support each argument with appropriate authorities. When citing a case, briefly summarize the holding (a parenthetical summary often suffices), unless you are citing to hornbook law. If a case is of particular interest, discuss it in more detail, but avoid lengthy quotes from any case or from any other source you cite. Do not exaggerate or misrepresent anything, or overstate your argument. If you do, you set yourself up for an effective opposing memo, and impair your credibility with the judge. Use footnotes sparingly.
- *Conclusion.* Explicitly state precisely what you want the judge to do.
- *Supporting documents.* Provide the judge with copies of unreported decisions (those available only online), affidavits, declarations, deposition transcripts, exhibits, and other documents supporting your position. Each should have its own tab. If filing electronically, the "tab" should be a page that says **EXHIBIT 1** or **EXHIBIT A**, etc., and if you are filing a hard copy (including a chambers copy), use real tabs.

The tone of your memos should be professional. Unless absolutely justified, do not contend that opposing counsel's position is "outrageous" or the like. And do not make ad hominem attacks on opposing counsel. Never write anything remotely like this: "It is beyond understanding that opposing counsel asserts such an absurd, disingenuous, and outrageous position, obviously without having bothered to conduct the research even a first-year law student would have realized undermined that position." If you write with such vitriol, the judge will just roll his or her eyes in annoyance or even dismay, and your effort will backfire. A judge subjected to hyperbolic language such as this could well conclude that your argument is weak.

A word about affidavits and declarations supporting memos. The distinction is that an affidavit is notarized, and a declaration is not. See 28 U.S.C. § 1746 for the authority to file declarations. Each must be based on personal knowledge, factually accurate and in numbered paragraphs. Be aware that, if submitted by a fact witness, it will be the basis for deposition questions and cross-examination, so draft accordingly.

In preparing to draft a memo *opposing* a motion, first review the memo you are opposing for any exaggerations or misstatements of fact, analytical flaws, and what of significance is omitted. Then deconstruct it. Read all documents opposing counsel relies on in the fact section. Read all cases and other authorities opposing counsel relies on to support the argument. Case cite each of those cases. Determine if you can distinguish as a group several cases on which opposing counsel relies. Respond to each argument in whatever sequence is most effective, not necessarily the order in the memo you are opposing. Make your most powerful argument first. Give the judge a good reason to deny the motion.

In drafting a reply memo, limit yourself to what is in the opposing memo, analogous to redirect being limited to re-cross in examining a witness at trial. Refer to the specific pages you are rebutting. Make as few points as you need. Take advantage of what opposing counsel failed to address. Make it punchy, memorable. The shorter the better. If the judge allows a sur-reply brief, make it even shorter. Do not repeat arguments you already made.

## 5. How to Draft Answers and Affirmative Defenses

When you first read a complaint served on your client, ask yourself the following questions: Does the court have subject matter jurisdiction? Does the court have personal jurisdiction over your client? Was service made properly? As to each cause of action and each item of relief requested, what defenses are available? Has plaintiff included as defendants all required parties, as provided in Rule 19(a)? Has the statute of limitations run as to any cause of action? Before filing your answer, determine whether you should file any motions addressed to the complaint, discussed in the next section. Also determine whether you have the basis to assert any counterclaims, cross-claims against any other defendants, or any third-party claims, such as for indemnification. See Rules 13, 14.

Review each allegation with your client. Learn what you need to know to be able to admit, deny, partially admit and partially deny, or allege insufficient information (tantamount to a denial) as to each allegation in the complaint. If you admit in part and deny in part, it is preferable to start with "Denied, except . . ." rather than "Admitted, except . . ." to avoid unwittingly admitting something you intend to deny. Anything you don't specifically respond to is deemed admitted. See Rule 8(b)(6).

If the complaint alleges words of a contract accurately in an allegation, you can either admit that allegation or respond by stating that defendant refers the trier of facts to the entire contract for its terms. If the complaint alleges a statement of law in an allegation, respond by stating that this is a statement of a legal claim to which no answer is required.

Comply with applicable Federal Rules of Civil Procedure. Rule 8(b) provides that, in responding to a complaint, you must state in short and plain terms your defenses to each claim. Each denial must fairly respond to the substance of the allegation. Before drafting your answer to each paragraph in the complaint, you must discuss each allegation with your client and perform the required due diligence. Rule 11(b) applies to answers and affirmative defenses, as well as complaints, and specifically provides, in Rule 11(b)(4), that any denials of factual contentions must be warranted on the evidence or, if specifically so identified, are reasonably based on belief or a lack of information.

Rule 8(c) sets forth what defenses must be stated as affirmative defenses, including accord and satisfaction, arbitration and award, assumption of risk, contributory negligence, duress, estoppel, failure of consideration, fraud, illegality, laches, license, payment, release, res judicata, statute of frauds, statute of limitations, and waiver. It even includes "injury by fellow servant." Unless you specifically allege each of these as affirmative defenses when applicable, you will be precluded from relying on them.

Rule 9(a)(2) provides that if you want to raise issues as to a plaintiff's capacity to sue, your client's capacity to be sued, a plaintiff's authority to sue or your client's authority to be sued in a representative capacity, or the legal existence of an organized association of persons that is a plaintiff, you must do so by specific denial, stating any supporting facts within your client's knowledge. The other provisions in Rule 9 applicable to complaints likewise apply to affirmative defenses.

Rule 12(b) provides that every defense to a claim for relief must be asserted in your responsive pleading if one is required, except for enumerated defenses that can be raised by motion.

## 6. How to Draft and Respond to Discovery

You would not try to hammer in a nail with a screwdriver, or tighten a screw with a hammer. Each tool has its own utility. Likewise, each discovery device has its own utility. Just as you need to know which tool to use in building a shed, you need to know which discovery tool to use in building your case or defense.

What is in your toolbox? Informal discovery (such as getting information from nonparties and getting reliable information from the Internet, like the opposing party's website), interrogatories, document requests, requests to admit, and depositions. Depositions are covered in chapter 5.

The scope of your pretrial discovery is broad. Rule 26(b)(1) provides that, unless limited by court order, you may obtain discovery regarding any non-privileged matter relevant to any party's claim or defense. For good cause, the judge may order discovery of any matter relevant to the subject matter involved in the action. Relevant information need not be admissible at trial if the discovery appears reasonably calculated to lead to the discovery of admissible evidence. Thus, it is not a proper objection to a discovery request that what is sought is not admissible at trial. The judge can limit the frequency and extent of discovery, as provided in Rule 26(b)(2). The timing and sequence of discovery is governed by Rule 26(d).

Even though you can use methods of discovery in any sequence, unless the court orders otherwise, typically the most effective sequence is interrogatories, document requests, depositions, and then requests to admit. Interrogatories provide you with certain basic information; document requests provide you with the paper trail you need to examine; depositions provide you with unscripted answers from opposing parties and people with knowledge; and requests to admit lock the opposing party into statements that are conclusory for purposes of the case.

*Interrogatories.* Before drafting interrogatories, review opposing counsel's disclosure as required in Rule 26(a)(1). That rule mandates that, without awaiting any discovery request, a party must disclose

- specific information about each individual likely to have discoverable information, and the subjects of that information, that the disclosing party may use to support claims or defenses, unless the use would be solely for impeachment
- a copy, or a description by category and location, of all documents, electronically stored information (ESI), and tangible things that the disclosing party has in its possession, custody, or control and may use to support its claims or defenses, unless the use would be solely for impeachment
- a computation of each category of damages claimed by the disclosing party, with related document disclosure
- any insurance agreement under which any insurance business may be liable to satisfy all or any part of a possible judgment in the action or to indemnify or reimburse for payments made to satisfy the judgment.

Because these disclosures are mandatory, and are required even before you draft your interrogatories, see Rule 26(a)(1)(c), these mandatory disclosures can provide the basis for you to draft interrogatories to elicit additional useful information. Rule 26(a) disclosures must be supplemented as provided in Rule 26(e).

These mandatory disclosures limit information about witnesses to those the opposing party *may use to support its claims or defenses.* A key witness may be someone opposing counsel will certainly *not* rely on, because that person's testimony would *not* support the opposing party's claims or defenses. Likewise, the mandatory disclosure regarding documents is limited to those the opposing party *may use to support its claims or defenses.* Thus, you can't simply rely on opposing counsel's mandatory disclosure to learn what you need to know about potential witnesses and potential exhibits.

Interrogatories are governed by Rule 33. You are limited to no more than 25, including all discrete subparts, unless otherwise stipulated or the court allows more, as provided in Rules 26(b)(2)(A) and 33(a)(1). The scope is broad, limited only by what is consistent with Rule 26(b)(2). You can include opinion and contention interrogatories that relate to fact, or the application of law to fact, but the judge can order that such an interrogatory not be answered until designated discovery is complete, until a pretrial conference, or some other time.

Here is an example of a contention interrogatory: Assume you represent a plaintiff in an insurance coverage case and there is an issue of late notice to the insurer of your client's claim. If, in your state, the burden is on the insurance company to establish prejudice from such late notice, your contention interrogatory could be: "If Defendant contends that it was prejudiced by the timing of Plaintiff's notice of the claim that is the subject of this case, state all facts supporting any such claimed prejudice."

Each set of interrogatories should include three parts: definitions, instructions, and the interrogatories. Definitions, which must be consistent with your local rules, enable you to define such words as "plaintiff" and "defendant" to include agents, representatives, officers, directors, employees, partners, divisions or other organizational units, corporate parent, subsidiaries, affiliates, or predecessor entities later merged or affiliated with the opposing party (whichever are applicable); "document" to include, among other things, all forms of ESI; "identify," with regard to a person, to include name, address, contact information; to refer to a document or ESI; and to refer to a communication to include the type, subject matter, date and location, author, recipient, or participant, and any document memorializing or concerning that communication.

Instructions, which likewise must comply with your local rules, can encompass such matters as the recipient's continuing disclosure duties, as provided in Rule 26(e), privilege log obligations, and instructions about documents or ESI that have been altered, destroyed, or otherwise disposed of.

Each interrogatory should cover a specific subset of facts. The most useful facts you can elicit from interrogatories are those that pertain to the identities and contact information for people with knowledge of relevant facts, itemization and quantification of damages, and facts related to contention interrogatories, such as the factual basis for a claim or affirmative defense of estoppel. For example, in *Montague v. Capulet*, a defamation action, if you have reason to believe that Capulet made certain references to Montague to third parties, one interrogatory could be: "Identify each person in whose presence Capulet made a reference to Montague using any one or more of the following descriptive terms:

filthy bung; mis-shapen dick; filthy worsted-stocking knave; son and heir of a mongrel bitch; very scurvy fellow; elvish-mark'd abortive rooting hog; canker-blossom; lump of foul deformity; whoreson drudge; knotty-pated fool; crusty batch of nature; swollen parcel of dropsies; bull's pizzle; beetle-headed flap-ear'd knave; and having a brain as dry as the remainder biscuit after a voyage." (Whether these insults are defamatory as statements of fact or only statements of opinion is beyond the scope of this book, and requires consultation with a Shakespearean scholar.)

Keep in mind that, unlike responses to your deposition questions, which are directly from the opposing party and nonparties (and at least somewhat spontaneous), responses to interrogatories are crafted by lawyers, after careful thought.

Some lawyers draft interrogatories such as this: "State all facts that support the allegations in paragraph X of the Complaint." Such an interrogatory will typically be a waste of one of your 25 interrogatories, because it will only produce a response such as this: "Defendant objects to this interrogatory as overly broad and unduly burdensome."

Instead, draft interrogatories that are focused. Form books are available for drafting interrogatories for specific types of cases.

In responding to interrogatories, keep in mind that you have only 30 days to respond or object, as provided in Rule 33(b)(2), unless otherwise stipulated as provided in Rule 29(b) or otherwise ordered by the court. If you miss that deadline, you waive the right to object. If you agree on an extension of time, be sure to reserve your right to object as well as respond to interrogatories. You must make a good-faith effort to obtain all information responsive to interrogatories to which you do not object. If you omit information in responding to an interrogatory, you may be precluded from introducing that information into evidence at trial, so be thorough.

Answers to interrogatories must be made under oath, Rule 33(b)(3), and you must sign any objections. If the answer to an interrogatory may be determined by review of business records, and the burden of deriving or ascertaining the answer will be substantially the same for either party, you can respond by referring to documents, as provided in Rule 33(d).

You must amend your prior response to an interrogatory if you learn that your response is in some material respect incomplete or incorrect, and if the additional or corrective information has not otherwise been made known to the other parties during the discovery process or in writing. Rule 26(e).

Objections to interrogatories you can raise include, among others, those listed in Rule 26(b)(2)(C): overly broad; unduly burdensome; unreasonably cumulative or duplicative; can be obtained from some other source that is more convenient, less burdensome, or less expensive; and the burden or expense of the proposed discovery outweighs its likely benefit.

In responding, you may want to state general objections to all interrogatories, followed by responses and objections to specific interrogatories. If you have a good-faith basis to object to an interrogatory, it is better practice to state your objection, and then answer so much of the interrogatory that is not objectionable.

Typically, the lawyer serving interrogatories will call you to discuss your objections. Pursuant to Rule 37(a)(1), a lawyer cannot file a motion to compel responses to interrogatories (or any other discovery) without providing a certification to the court that the movant has in good faith conferred or attempted to confer to obtain the discovery without court action.

When you get that call, ask yourself: What interrogatory responses is the judge likely to require? Keep in mind that if opposing counsel files a Rule 37 motion and prevails, the court *must*, after giving you an opportunity to be heard, require your client or you or both of you to pay the movant's reasonable expenses incurred in making the motion, including attorney fees, as provided in Rule 37(a)(5)(A). This is a double-edged sword, though, because the same rule works in reverse if you prevail on a Rule 37 motion, as provided in Rule 37(a)(5)(B).

You have the right to move for a protective order, as provided in Rule 26(c)(1), to specify terms for, or even forbid, disclosure or discovery, prescribe a discovery method other than the one selected by the party seeking discovery, forbid inquiry into certain matters, limit the scope of disclosure or discovery, and require that a trade secret or other confidential information not be revealed, or revealed only in a specified way. In business disputes, it is common, for example, for parties to agree on the terms of a protective order regarding confidentiality, for court approval and order.

If a court orders you to respond to interrogatories, and you do not comply, your client can be subjected to the draconian consequences in Rule 37(b)(2), a list of horribles for any trial lawyer. Sanctions include orders that certain facts be taken as established for purposes of the action, prohibiting you from supporting or opposing claims and defenses, striking your pleadings, staying proceedings, dismissing the action in whole or in part, rendering a default judgment against your client, and treating your failure as contempt of court. Additional sanctions apply if you fail to supplement your responses to interrogatories, as provided in Rule 37(c)(1).

What should you do when receiving responses and objections to interrogatories? Review them carefully. Ask yourself: Are all these objections proper? If not, call opposing counsel and attempt to work out discovery issues. If you cannot, and the unresolved issues are sufficiently significant, file your Rule 37 motion.

Use interrogatory responses to formulate questions for depositions, support motions for summary judgment, and prepare for cross-examination of witnesses at trial.

*Document requests.* After reviewing opposing counsel's mandatory disclosure regarding documents, as provided in Rule 26(a)(1)(A)(ii), which may be limited merely to a description by category and location of documents, ESI, and tangible things that the disclosing party has in its possession, custody, or control that it may use, rather than actual production thereof, ask yourself: What categories of documents might opposing counsel seek to put into the record at trial? What categories of documents might I want to get into the record? Then prepare your document requests. Include definitions and instructions, as in drafting interrogatories.

Unlike interrogatories, you are not limited to the number of document requests. Rule 34 governs document requests. You can require the opposing party to produce and permit you to inspect, copy, test, or sample documents and ESI and any tangible things, and to permit you to enter onto designated land or other property possessed or controlled by the responding party, as provided in Rule 34(a). Your document requests must describe with reasonable particularity each item or category of items to be inspected, must specify a reasonable time, place, and manner for inspection, and may specify the form of ESI, as provided in Rule 34(b).

In *Montague v. Capulet*, one document request could be: "Produce each document made known to anyone in which Capulet makes a reference to Montague using any one or more of the following descriptive terms: filthy bung; mis-shapen dick; filthy worsted-stocking knave; son and heir of a mongrel bitch; very scurvy fellow; elvish-mark'd abortive rooting hog; canker-blossom; lump of foul deformity; whoreson drudge; knotty-pated fool; crusty batch of nature; swollen parcel of dropsies; bull's pizzle; beetle-headed flap-ear'd knave; and having a brain as dry as the remainder biscuit after a voyage."

You may want to arrange for opposing counsel to come to your office to inspect documents, and to select among them which to copy. That way, you know which documents opposing counsel is interested in.

You have 30 days to respond or object to document requests, unless a shorter or longer time is stipulated under Rule 29 or ordered by the court. Your response to each document request must either state that you will comply or your objection, including reasons, as provided in Rule 34(b)(2). If you have a good-faith basis to object to a document request, do produce the subset of documents to which you do not object. Keep in mind that you will probably not be able to produce at trial any document you do not produce in response to a document request to which you do not object. Unless otherwise stipulated or ordered by the court, you must produce documents as they are kept in the usual course of business, or organize and label them to correspond to the categories in the request, as provided in Rule 34(b)(2)(E), which also governs ESI production. You must amend your responses the same as for your responses to interrogatories. Rule 26(e).

Before producing documents, give each document a number, a process typically referred to as "Bates stamping" documents. Little-known fact: The Bates of "Bates stamping" is 19th-century inventor Edwin G. Bates who, in 1891, patented a machine. When pressed on a sheet of paper, it printed a number, which a rotating wheel in the machine automatically moved to the next number to stamp the next sheet. Now, it is all done electronically, but is still referred to eponymously for the original inventor.

By Bates stamping documents, you and opposing counsel have a record of what documents you each produced. If opposing counsel ever produces documents to you that are not Bates stamped, stamp them yourself, and send a set of Bates stamped documents to opposing counsel, so you have a good record. You do not want to confront an issue at trial whether opposing counsel produced a particular document.

The procedures for resolving discovery disputes pertaining to document requests are essentially the same as for interrogatories. Use documents produced in discovery as you would interrogatory responses.

*Requests for Admissions.* This sometimes overlooked discovery device is especially potent because facts admitted in response to a request for admission, pursuant to Rule 36, are conclusively established for purposes of the case, unless the court, on motion, permits the admission to be withdrawn or amended. Rule 36(b).

Even if you get useful admissions at the deposition of an opposing party, those are merely evidentiary. The opposing party can testify at trial contrary to his or her deposition testimony and attempt to explain away the deposition testimony as being confused, not remembering correctly, or having memory refreshed after the deposition by review of documents or otherwise. On the other hand, Rule 36 admissions are conclusive in your case.

Consider drafting admissions after reviewing the transcript of the opposing party's deposition, thereby making those evidentiary admissions into conclusive admissions. The scope of admissions is not limited to facts, though. You can seek admissions as to the truth of any matters within the scope of Rule 26(b)(1) relating to facts, the application of law to fact, or opinions about either, and the genuineness of any described documents. Rule 36(a)(1).

Assume that, at his deposition, Montague admitted referring to Capulet in certain specific defamatory terms. You can transform those evidentiary admissions into conclusive admissions by posing the following request to admit: "Capulet referred to Montague in the presence of third parties as a filthy worsted-stocking knave; son and heir of a mongrel bitch; very scurvy fellow; whoreson drudge; knotty-pated fool; swollen parcel of dropsies; and a beetle-headed flap-ear'd knave."

You know that, unlike responses to deposition questions, responses to requests for admissions will be carefully crafted by opposing counsel. So limit each request to one discrete fact. Word it in such a way that opposing counsel will have a difficult time denying it, in whole or in part. You can ask overlapping requests to admit, seeking in one request the broadest admission you can reasonably request on a particular subject, followed by a more limited admission as to that same subject. A request for admissions is also useful to establish conclusively that certain documents are business records, as provided in Federal Rule of Evidence 803(6), and are thus within a hearsay exception at trial. Unlike interrogatories, the number of requests for admission is not limited.

You have 30 days to respond to requests for admission. If you do not respond, the matter is admitted. Rule 36(a)(3). If you do not admit a matter, you must specifically deny it, or state in detail why you cannot truthfully admit or deny it. Any denial must fairly respond to the substance of the matter, and when good faith requires that you qualify an answer or deny only a part of a matter, your answer must specify the part admitted and qualify or deny the rest. You must amend your response as for your responses to interrogatories and document requests. Rule 26(e).

You cannot assert lack of knowledge or information as a reason for failing to admit or deny, unless you state that you have made reasonable inquiry and that the information your client knows or can readily obtain is insufficient to enable you to admit or deny. Rule 36(a)(4). You must state any grounds for your objections, and you cannot object solely on the ground that the request presents a genuine issue for trial. Rule 36(a)(5).

If you served a request for admissions and do not think the responses are sufficient, call opposing counsel to resolve the issue. If unsuccessful, file a motion to determine sufficiency of the responses. The judge must order that an answer be served unless finding the objection justified. The judge may also order the matter admitted, or that an amended answer be served, if finding the answer is not in compliance with this rule. Rule 36(a)(6).

If a party fails to admit pursuant to Rule 36, and you later prove a document to be genuine or a matter true, you can move that the opposing party pay reasonable expenses, including attorney fees, incurred in making that proof. The court must so order, unless the judge held your request objectionable, the admission sought was of no substantial importance, the opposing party failing to admit had a reasonable ground to believe it might prevail on the matter, or there was other good reason for the failure to admit. Rule 37(c)(2).

Consider, for example, a situation where you need to depose an out-of-state witness, because the opposing party denied certain facts, in response to a request for admissions. If the conditions of Rule 37(c)(2) are met, you can seek to recover all expenses and reasonable attorney fees related to that deposition.

A downside of obtaining admissions is that you lose the impact of trial testimony on matters that opposing counsel has admitted if objection is raised at trial based on Federal Rule of Evidence 403. Opposing counsel's position would be: It's already admitted, so no testimony is appropriate as to the matter admitted. This could make a difference in a jury trial. Even so, the benefits of Rule 36 admissions generally outweigh any detriment.

For example, you can use Rule 36 admissions to support a motion for summary judgment and, at trial, you can mark responses to your request for admissions (or some of them) as full exhibits, and read them to the jurors with the court's permission. Remember to take advantage of this valuable discovery tool.

## 7. How to draft jury instructions

Just before deliberating, the jurors hear the judge reading the charge to them—instructions as to the law they have sworn to apply. Assuming no jury nullification issues, the jurors will comply with the judge's instructions. Unless those instructions are easy to understand, the jurors will probably just "go with their gut" in deciding your case.

You have the right to file and serve proposed jury instructions. Rule 51(a). In drafting them, follow these guidelines:

- Use simple English.
- Write in short sentences.
- Include only one concept in each instruction.
- Cite authority for each instruction.
- List instructions in a logical order.
- Include a heading for each instruction or subset of instructions, for ease of reference.

Benefit from form books that provide sample jury instructions, but do not merely copy them verbatim. When you draft, focus more on jury instructions specific to your case than on the boilerplate instructions about such matters as burden of proof and the jurors' role in evaluating credibility of witnesses. Know your rights and obligations regarding specific and general verdicts, as provided in Rule 49.

The judge is obligated to inform you of the proposed instructions, and proposed action on requests to charge, before instructing the jury and before final jury arguments. The judge must also give you an opportunity to object on the record, out of the presence of the jurors, before delivering the instructions. Rule 51(b).

If you object to any proposed instruction, or the judge's failure to give an instruction, you must do so on the record, stating distinctly the matter objected to and the grounds for objection. Rule 51(c). You must object before closing arguments and before the judge charges the jury, unless you are blindsided, as provided in Rule 51(c). On appeal, you are limited in challenging the jury charge unless you object properly and timely. Rule 51(d).

## 8. How to draft appellate court briefs

Review the appellate court pleadings so you know which issues are preserved for appeal. Conduct thorough legal research on all issues presented. Review the entire record. Know the law and the facts in the record. Also know the applicable rules imposing requirements and constraints on what you are about to draft. Follow all the advice above about drafting briefs.

Make a list of the points you may want to make, without caring about which ones you may eventually discard, or the sequence of your presentation in the brief. Then outline your entire brief, discarding weak points. Visualize your entire brief before you begin writing.

Begin your brief by discussing the facts essential to your argument. Exclude all extraneous facts. Your facts should tell a story. Do not misstate or exaggerate any facts. Cite to the record for each fact. Do not ignore bad facts. Deal with them by putting them in perspective.

Frame the issues with care. Your statement of the issues is the lens through which the judge reads your brief. Avoid generic statements of issues. Make them case specific.

Your argument should flow inexorably from the facts. In your argument, make your strongest point first, unless you raise jurisdictional or other procedural issues, such as failure to preserve an issue for appeal. Those take priority. Include only those arguments that you have a legitimate chance of prevailing on. By raising fewer arguments on appeal, you have a greater opportunity to develop each point, and the appellate court judges will be focused on your best arguments.

Explain why the court should rule in your favor. Stress how the law allows the result you seek, and how that result is consistent with the way courts treat the same or similar issues. Ask for no more than you need, but be specific in your request for relief. For example, do you want affirmance, reversal, remand for a specific purpose, or some other ruling on appeal?

In addition to citing cases in your favor, distinguish opposing counsel's cases so the appellate judges will not need to overrule precedent. Focus on why the appellate court should rule in your favor in your case, and why the court's ruling in your case would set a good precedent for similar cases in the future.

Avoid castigating opposing counsel or opposing counsel's appellate court brief. Instead, make your best argument, and rebut opposing counsel's argument, taking the high road.

Finally, proofread! Much of the advice here about appellate brief writing is from an article by former Connecticut Supreme Court Justice Joette Katz. Her final word about appellate court briefs: "Proof read with a passion and get others to do it for you. When you make silly mistakes, at best it tells the court you're sloppy; at worst, it tells the court that you never even bothered to read the brief although you expect it [the court] to."

## 9. How to draft settlement agreements

Because most cases settle, you must know how to draft settlement agreements. Assume that you have worked out the terms of your settlement. How do you memorialize it into a legally enforceable agreement?

In some cases, the matter is resolved by payment of money at the time of settlement and a stipulation of dismissal pursuant to Rule 41(a)(1)(A)(ii). In that event, the only settlement documents to draft and execute are releases. Make sure the parties have no continuing obligations to each other before exchanging *general* releases. They may have ongoing business dealings unrelated to the issues in the case. If so, exchange *limited* releases, tailored to the issues in the case.

Typically, however, settlement of a business dispute is more involved and requires a settlement agreement. In drafting it, avoid any ambiguity so that you will not have problems enforcing it.

Consider including in any settlement agreement provisions covering the following:

- terms of payment, including interest, and recovery of reasonable attorney's fees if breach of the settlement agreement
- mutual releases
- confidentiality provisions
- no admission of liability, fault, or wrongdoing, or any unlawful conduct
- advice of counsel in reaching settlement
- reference to a party includes predecessors, successors, assigns, etc.
- applicability of Rule 408 of the Federal Rules of Evidence regarding inadmissibility of the settlement agreement
- applicable law
- complete integration clause (this is the entire agreement regarding settlement)

- provision for modification only in writing, signed by all parties
- execution in counterparts, which can be conveyed electronically
- effect of invalidity of any provision on other provisions
- authority of agents of parties to sign the settlement agreement
- simultaneous filing of stipulation for dismissal or withdrawal of action
- notice provision

Here is sample language, other than the provision for payment terms:

1. In consideration of the payment specified in paragraph 1 of this Agreement and the other promises and covenants set forth in this Agreement, [Plaintiffs] have remised, released, and forever discharged and by this Agreement do remise, release, and forever discharge [Defendants] of and from all debts, obligations, reckonings, promises, covenants, agreements, contracts, endorsements, bonds, specialties, controversies, suits, actions, causes of actions, trespasses, variances, judgments, extents, executions, damages, claims, or demands of any nature whatsoever, in law or in equity, which [Plaintiffs] ever had, now have, or hereafter can, shall, or may have against them for, upon, or by reason of any matter, cause, or thing whatsoever, whether known or unknown, from the beginning of the world to the day of the date of this Agreement.

2. In consideration of the release specified in paragraph 2 of this Agreement and the other promises and covenants set forth in this Agreement, [Plaintiffs] have remised, released, and forever discharged and by this Agreement do remise, release, and forever discharge [Defendants] of and from all debts, obligations, reckonings, promises, covenants, agreements, contracts, endorsements, bonds, specialties, controversies, suits, actions, causes of actions, trespasses, variances, judgments, extents, executions, damages, claims, or demands of any nature whatsoever, in law or in equity, which [Plaintiffs] ever had, now have, or hereafter can, shall, or may have against [Defendants] for, upon, or by reason of any matter, cause, or thing whatsoever, whether known or unknown, from the beginning of the world to the day of the date of this Agreement.

3. The claims released and discharged by this Agreement include particularly, but are not limited to, any and all claims which were or could have been asserted by [Plaintiffs] against [Defendants], or which were or could have been asserted by [Plaintiffs] against [Defendants], in the action entitled [Caption of Action].
4. All of the parties hereto shall keep the terms, conditions, and existence of this Agreement confidential and shall not disclose the terms, conditions, or existence of this Agreement to any person except (i) as required in response to a valid subpoena or court order, (ii) as required in response to a lawful request of the Internal Revenue Service or other governmental agency, (iii) to a party's spouse or immediate family member who agrees to abide by the terms of this confidentiality provision, (iv) as required in connection with the usual accounting or auditing requirements of any party hereto or as required to obtain legal or tax advice, (v) in connection with any disclosure required to be made to a party's insurance carrier or to a financial institution, or (vi) in any proceeding by a party hereto concerning an alleged breach of this Agreement or in any proceeding in which it is alleged by a party hereto that this Agreement provides a defense. In order to allow the parties hereto to protect their interests of confidentiality, any party hereto served with a subpoena, discovery request, or similar legal instrument that could lead to a court order compelling disclosure of the terms, conditions, or existence of this Agreement shall, within seven days of the receipt thereof, notify the other parties hereto of such subpoena, discovery request, or similar legal instrument, provided, however, that if such seven days' notice would not permit sufficient time to allow the other parties to assert any confidentiality interest concerning the terms or negotiations of this Agreement, the party being requested to make disclosure will give notice to the other parties hereto as soon as practicable, but in any event before actual disclosure.
5. The parties hereto acknowledge that this Agreement represents a settlement of disputed claims, and the parties hereto agree that neither this Agreement nor the furnishing of the consideration provided for by this Agreement shall be deemed or construed at any time for any purpose as an admission by any party of any liability, fault, wrongdoing, or any unlawful conduct of any kind.

6. The parties to this Agreement acknowledge that they have freely negotiated its terms at arm's length, with each party acting under the advice of its or his own counsel. The parties hereto further acknowledge that each party has contributed language to the terms of this Agreement, and hence the terms of this Agreement should not be presumptively construed either in favor of or against any party.

7. Wherever in this Agreement any party shall be designated or referred to by name or general reference, such designation is intended to and shall have the same effect as if the words, "predecessors, successors, assigns, heirs, beneficiaries, attorneys, employees, shareholders, and personal or legal representatives" had been inserted after each and every such designation, and all the terms, covenants, and conditions herein contained shall be for and shall inure to the benefit of and shall bind the respective parties hereto, and their predecessors, successors, assigns, heirs, beneficiaries, attorneys, employees, shareholders, and personal or legal representatives, respectively.

8. In all references herein to any parties, persons, entities, or corporations the use of any particular gender or the plural or singular number is intended to include the appropriate gender or number as the text of the Agreement may require.

9. This Agreement and the negotiations concerning this Agreement shall be deemed to fall within the protections afforded by Rule 408 of the Federal Rules of Evidence, and any similar state or federal statutory, rule or common law protections afforded to compromises, offers to compromise, compromise negotiations, and the like. No portion of this Agreement shall be admissible or may be used as evidence or in any other manner for any purpose, including impeachment, in any legal, equitable, or administrative proceeding.

10. This Agreement and the rights and obligations of the parties hereunder shall in all respects be governed by and construed and enforced in accordance with the laws of the State of [Name of State] (without giving effect to [State's] principles of conflicts of law). The parties to this Agreement consent to the jurisdiction and exclusive venue of the Federal and/or State courts in [Name of State] in any litigation concerning this Agreement.

11. This Agreement sets forth the entire agreement of the parties hereto concerning its subject matter and shall supersede the terms of any other agreement, representation, or understanding (whether oral or written) between the parties hereto concerning the subject matter of this Agreement. This Agreement may be changed or modified only by a writing signed by the parties hereto wherein specific reference is made to this Agreement.
12. This Agreement may be executed in two or more counterparts, each of which shall be deemed an original but all of which together shall constitute one and the same Agreement. Copies of signatures transmitted by facsimile shall have the same force and effect as original signatures.
13. If any provision of this Agreement as presently written shall be construed to be illegal, invalid, or unenforceable by a court of competent jurisdiction, said illegal, invalid, or unenforceable provision shall be deemed to be amended and shall be construed by the court to have the broadest scope permissible under applicable law. If no validating construction is possible, provision shall be severable from the rest of this Agreement and the validity, legality, or enforceability of the remaining provisions of this Agreement shall not in any way be affected or impaired thereby and shall remain in effect.
14. The signatories named below warrant that they are authorized to act on behalf of the respective parties hereto, as indicated, and that by affixing their signatures to the Agreement the parties are bound to the terms of the Agreement.
15. Simultaneously with the execution of this Agreement, counsel for the parties hereto shall execute a Stipulation of Dismissal, as provided in Rule 41(a)(1)(A)(ii), which [Plaintiffs] shall file with the court forthwith.
16. Any statements, communications, or notices to be provided pursuant to this Agreement shall be sent by certified mail, return receipt requested, and also by electronic transmission to the attention of the persons indicated below until such time as notice of any change of the person to be notified or change of address is forwarded in writing to all parties:
    (a) for Plaintiffs, to:
    (b) for Defendants, to:

## 10. Tax consequences of settlement agreements

You must be aware of the tax consequences of any settlement you may be considering. Tax considerations are significant even as you draft your complaint, because the IRS and courts have traditionally given greatest weight to the allegations and claims in the complaint in determining the proper tax treatment for any amounts paid in settlement. Consult a tax attorney when drafting a complaint if you have any question about how best to assert your claims with tax considerations in mind.

The tax consequences are the same whether you settle or proceed to final judgment. Indeed, you can seek to negotiate terms of a settlement agreement that will enhance the likelihood of favorable tax treatment for your client.

In a personal injury or wrongful death case, the recovery is not taxable, even for lost wages arising out of the injury or death, but punitive damages are taxable.

In commercial cases, a number of tax issues may arise, including the following:

- Generally, if there is a business nexus to the payment, it is deductible as a business expense, unless it relates to a capital asset, which may require the payment to be capitalized.
- Whether the amount recovered is properly characterized as ordinary income, return of capital, or capital gain depends on the underlying claim. If the recovery is a substitute for lost profits, then the amount recovered is ordinary income. But if the recovery is on account of loss of good will or harm to other capital assets, then the amount is characterized as capital gain, if the sale or exchange requirement is met, or return of capital.
- A key consideration in determining the tax consequences of a payment in settlement of a claim is the intent of the payor in making it. This factor is even more important when the settlement document is silent on the allocation.
- If different tax treatment applies to different causes of action, allocate specific amounts to specific claims. Even though this allocation is not binding on the IRS or the court, it is evidence of the parties' intent. Any such allocation should be reasonable, to pass muster. Failing to allocate such payments, at a minimum, will raise factual issues as to the reason for the total amount paid.

- Punitive damages are always includible in gross income and are generally deductible by the payor.
- The burden is on the taxpayer to demonstrate what portion of a recovery constitutes a non-taxable or capital item.
- Any fine, or similar penalty paid to a government for violation of any law, is not deductible.
- In employment cases, tax treatment of recoveries is very complex. Consult a tax attorney. As a general matter, most employment-related recoveries are taxable wages subject to withholding, but if the claim is in the nature of a tort, an argument can be made that recovery is not taxable.
- Tax treatment of legal fees generally follows the nature of the underlying claim.

## 11. How to draft cogently

Everything you write should be cogent. You don't want to fill the sky with your words, as in this cartoon of smoke signals.

*"It's from my attorney."*

Read appendix I to learn from Molly Cogent, taking on Ulysses S. Bombast in a debate and mentoring Tim Smithers. You will understand how cogency informs everything we do as trial lawyers.

❖❖❖❖
## PRACTICE CHECKLIST

- Apply the following principles to everything you write:
  - _____ think before you write
  - _____ write for your reader
  - _____ divide the writing process into discrete tasks
  - _____ use simple words
  - _____ edit
  - _____ eliminate typos
  - _____ write cogently
- In drafting internal memos, know your assignment, research thoroughly, and use an effective format by setting forth the facts, issues, summary of your conclusion, and analysis.
- Before drafting a complaint, know your client's objectives, the applicable facts, applicable law, available causes of action, and available remedies.
- In drafting a complaint, do not necessarily include all possible causes of action, after obtaining your client's informed consent.
- In drafting a complaint and other pleadings, comply with all applicable Federal Rules of Civil Procedure and state court analogs.
- Before drafting a pleading responsive to the complaint, ask yourself if the court has personal and subject matter jurisdiction, if service was made properly, and what defenses are available so you can determine whether to file a motion before filing an answer.
- Within the constraints of Rule 11, file motions addressed to the complaint before filing an answer.
- In drafting a memo supporting a motion involving complex issues, include a cover page, table of contents, table of authorities, preliminary statement, facts, argument (divided into subsections), conclusion, and supporting documents.
- In drafting discovery requests, know the practical utility of interrogatories, document requests, and requests for admissions, and use them in a sequence that makes sense in your case.
- In responding to discovery requests, meet deadlines. If you need extra time, comply with rules requiring a conference with opposing counsel before filing a motion for extension of time.
- In responding to discovery requests, conduct a good-faith investigation to respond fully and fairly, while preserving all applicable privileges, and objecting as appropriate, within applicable rules.
- Before producing any documents, Bates stamp them so you have a record of what you produced; opposing counsel should do the same.
- Take advantage of requests for admission to obtain admissions conclusive for purposes of your case.

(continued)

- Draft jury instructions using simple English in short sentences, one concept for each instruction with authority for each, in a logical order with appropriate headings.
- Before drafting an appellate court brief, know the record, standard of review, and applicable law. Discuss facts essential to your argument, frame the issues with care, and make your strongest points first in your argument. Explain why the court should rule in your favor, and distinguish opposing counsel's cases. Be specific in stating what you want the appellate court to do.
- In drafting settlement documents, be explicit and include all provisions discussed in the text, keeping in mind tax considerations.

CHAPTER FIVE

# PREPARING FOR, TAKING, AND DEFENDING DEPOSITIONS

This chapter provides answers to the most common questions that arise pertaining to taking and defending depositions in federal court. It does not cover all questions that may arise, or all procedures. For example, it does not include a discussion of telephonic depositions, because they are infrequent. There is no substitute for reading all rules applicable to depositions.

The outcome of the great majority of cases is determined by resolution of issues of fact rather than issues of law. As eighteenth-century English jurist William Blackstone put it: "Experience will abundantly show that above a hundred of our lawsuits arise from disputed facts, for one where the law is doubted of." Depositions provide the most effective mechanism to ferret out what facts are true during the discovery phase.

## 1. THE ADVANTAGES AND DISADVANTAGES OF TAKING A DEPOSITION

This is your only opportunity to get unfiltered information from opposing parties, and spontaneous answers from them. You can obtain admissions. You can ask follow-up questions. Answers are under oath. You can learn the strengths and weaknesses of your case. You can test potential theories of your case. You can get a sense of how well the opposing party will testify in court. You can obtain information from and preserve testimony of nonparty witnesses.

But depositions are expensive. You must weigh the cost against the benefit. In federal court, each party pays for its own transcript. Your questions can reveal your factual and legal theories of the case. Your deposition gives the opposing party a "sneak preview" of what to expect on cross-examination at trial, and an opportunity to prepare for that cross-examination. If you depose a nonparty witness, opposing counsel learns what you learn from that witness, and has the opportunity to cross-examine that witness at deposition. Your deposition may cause opposing counsel to be better prepared for trial.

## 2. WHEN TO TAKE A DEPOSITION

Complete your research on the legal elements of each cause of action and, where applicable, each affirmative defense, cross-claim, and counterclaim. Unless you know all those elements, you won't know what to ask. Develop a working theme for your case, and give thought to your opponent's likely themes. Obtain all documents you will need for that deposition, by formal discovery and by other means. Do a Google search of the other parties, the deponent, and witnesses. In appropriate cases, before taking a deposition, obtain responses to interrogatories. Complete formal and informal discovery as to the deponent.

Except by court order or agreement of the parties, you cannot take a deposition until after completion of the Rule 26(f) conference. Rule 26(d). Court permission is not required to take a deposition unless you plan to take more than 10 depositions, the person has already been deposed, or you want to take a deposition before the Rule 26(f) conference is completed. You can take a deposition before that conference without court permission, though, if you certify in the notice, with supporting facts, that the deponent is expected to leave the country and be unavailable unless deposed before that time. Rule 30(a)(2).

If you notice the deposition of a party, and you seek that party's production of documents at that deposition, case law supports the conclusion that the party has 30 days from notice to interpose objections to that production. Otherwise, this procedure could circumvent the 30-day period to object in the rules pertaining to document requests. Rule 34(b).

### 3. How many depositions you can take and how long each deposition can be

Unless the parties stipulate or the court orders otherwise, each side cannot take more than 10 depositions. Rule 30(a)(2)(A). This limit applies to all plaintiffs collectively and to all defendants collectively. In the Rule 26(f) conference, discuss the number of depositions required. Unless authorized by the court or stipulated by the parties, a person can only be deposed once, Rule 30(a)(2)(A)(ii), and a deposition is limited to one day of seven hours, not including breaks, Rule 30(d)(1).

### 4. How to notice a deposition

You must provide "reasonable written notice" to every other party. Rule 30(b)(1). This rule, and Rules 30(b)(2) and (3), state what must be included in that notice. You must provide that notice to all other parties. Rule 30(b)(1). If you notice the deposition of a party who has appeared, you must serve that notice on counsel for that party. If you notice the deposition of a nonparty, you must serve a subpoena on that nonparty. Rule 45(a).

If you require the deponent to bring documents to the deposition, include that requirement in the notice of deposition of a party and in a subpoena *duces tecum* on a nonparty witness. Rules 30(b)(2) and 34. If possible, arrange with opposing counsel to receive those documents before the deposition so you can review them and make copies of the documents you want to use at deposition, and to save time at the deposition.

If you depose an entity, comply with Rule 30(b)(6). The recipient of a Rule 30(b)(6) deposition notice is required to designate one or more people who consent to testify on its behalf as to the matters you designate in the deposition notice. Anyone so designated must testify as to the *institutional* knowledge of the entity on which you serve the Rule 30(b)(6) notice, as to all information on the subjects you identify in that notice known or reasonably available *to that entity*. This is in contrast to notices to take depositions of *individuals*, who can testify that they lack knowledge of a particular subject.

The subpoena for the deposition of a nonparty deponent can be served at any place within the district of the court by which it is issued, at any place outside that district that is within 100 miles of the place of the deposition, or at any place within the state where a state statute or rule of court permits service of a subpoena issued by a state court of general jurisdiction sitting in the place of the deposition. Rule 45(b)(2). If the nonparty deponent cannot be served within that territory, you can issue a subpoena from the district where the deponent can be served. See Rule 45(a)(3)(B).

## 5. WHERE YOU CAN TAKE A DEPOSITION

As a general matter, a party noticing a deposition is entitled to choose its location, within the constraints of the Federal Rights of Civil Procedure, and a plaintiff is required to be available for deposition in the district where suit is brought. The rationale is that a plaintiff bears any reasonable burdens of inconvenience that an action presents. However, a plaintiff can file a motion for protective order pursuant to Rule 26(c) if the notice provides for a deposition in a location presenting financial hardship or some other specific burden outweighing any prejudice to the defendant. When presented with such a motion, federal judges consider such factors as cost, convenience, and litigation efficiency.

You can take depositions in the following locations, all subject to successful motions for protective order. *A plaintiff*: in the geographic area where the plaintiff resides, has a place of business, or is employed, or where the action has been brought. *A defendant*: in the geographic area of a defendant's residence, place of business, or employment. *A corporation, through its agents*: at the corporation's principal place of business or the agent's place of employment or residence. *Nonparties*: within 100 miles from the place where the person resides, is employed, or regularly transacts business. See Rule 45(c)(3)(A)(ii). For good cause shown, the court can order that a deposition be taken in a particular location not specified by the federal rules.

## 6. How to prepare to take a deposition

Prepare a list of subjects you want to cover in the deposition. You can list questions you intend to ask, if you are mindful at the deposition to avoid focusing too much on that list—rather than on the deponent. If you must word a particular question to incorporate the words of a statute or regulation, or if the wording must be precise for some other reason, write down the exact words of your question.

Agree with counsel on a date, time, and place for the deposition. Serve the notice of deposition or subpoena. Make sufficient copies of all documents you plan to use at the deposition, enough for each attorney plus one that will be marked as an exhibit. Arrange for a stenographer and reserve a room. To avoid a lengthy lunch break, get menus from a local deli and suggest that sandwiches be brought in.

Put in the deposition room your list of subjects to cover, key pleadings, a working chronology of key events and documents, a legal pad, pens, pencils, a highlighter, stapler, and anything else you may need. Consider giving your client three-by-five-inch index cards at the beginning of the deposition on which to write proposed questions your client thinks of during the deposition, to be handed to you as they are written. Arrange for a chair without arms for the stenographer.

## 7. How to prepare your client for his or her deposition

Meet with your client several days before the deposition to prepare. Let your client know how much time you will need so your preparation is not truncated. In commercial litigation, your client is typically a very busy executive who has many immediate objectives to achieve other than meeting with you to prepare for deposition. You must emphasize the importance of preparing together, highlighting the fact that depositions, if effective, can result in a favorable settlement before trial or victory after trial. Tell your client which documents to review before you meet, including the key pleadings, all of which you will have already provided to your client.

Your objectives are to reduce your client's anxiety about the deposition and to prepare your client for the substance of the deposition testimony. Put yourself in the shoes of your client. The more your client knows about the deposition procedure, and what is likely to be asked, the more comfortable your client will be.

Explain that a deposition is a means by which opposing counsel can learn information useful in trying to defeat your client's claim, so a deposition is a defensive exercise. Your client will be sworn to tell the truth, and opposing counsel will ask a wide range of questions that relate to the case. Explain that, even though it may be counterintuitive to think so, the deposition is *not* the opportunity for your client to tell his story—that is what the trial is for.

Caution your client that opposing counsel may try to disarm him or her by being very friendly, and giving the impression that this is just a casual chat about the case. It is not. The same lawyer can and will use each answer at trial against your client, to the extent it helps defeat your client's claim.

Describe who will be at the deposition and summarize the deposition procedure. Explain that you will be sitting next to your client throughout the deposition, and that you will protect your client's interests as it progresses. Assure your client that during breaks you can discuss anything of concern to your client (unless precluded in your jurisdiction). Explain that the stenographer will prepare a transcript of the deposition testimony, available within a few weeks of the deposition, and that your client will have the opportunity to read the transcript for errors, and make corrections as to typos and substantive mistakes. (At your client's deposition, reserve your client's right to read and sign the deposition transcript to make changes in form and substance, as provided in Rule 30(e)(1)—unless you have a good reason to waive that right.)

Instruct your client about answering questions. Don't just recite a list of "rules" for your client to follow. Instead, provide a concrete example of the application of each rule to your case so your instruction will be useful, not abstract. Here are the rules you must explain:

Tell the truth. This rule has no exceptions.

Listen to each question, and make sure you understand it; take the time to think before answering. If you don't understand a question, say: "I don't understand your question"—and nothing more. Give that answer only if you have a good-faith basis to do so, because the follow-up question may be: "What exactly about my question do you not understand?"

If you understand the question, answer *that* question. Limit yourself to the scope of *that* question. Remember that this is a defensive exercise.

Do not volunteer. Doing so gives opposing counsel an opportunity to ask even more questions. You may feel that you want to get the deposition over with by anticipating opposing counsel's next few questions, and answering them before they are asked. That is a mistake, because opposing counsel may not ask those questions, and the more information you volunteer, the longer your deposition will be. Some lawyers induce deponents to volunteer by looking inquisitive after an answer is given, without saying anything, as if to convey: "And what else can you tell me in response to my question?" Do not fall for this tactic.

If you don't know the answer, or don't remember the answer, say simply: "I don't know" or "I don't remember." (If true, that answer is perfectly acceptable, unless your client is a Rule 30(b)(6) witness, in which event he or she may need to do some homework, or you may need to produce another Rule 30(b)(6) witness.) See section 4 of this chapter regarding such witnesses.

Don't guess or make assumptions in answering questions. If you are asked to estimate, do so only if you have a reasonable basis for doing so.

Avoid being locked in, when you can. For example, if asked what subjects were discussed at a meeting, if you are not sure about all subjects, state: "Those are the only subjects I can think of right now."

If you get a question we haven't talked about, keep in mind the themes of our case, and answer truthfully, consistent with our themes.

Instruct your client about answering questions even after you object, and inform your client when it is permissible for you to tell your client not to answer. Explain that you can object to the *form* of questions, such as ambiguous questions, double questions, questions assuming facts not in evidence, and facts for which there is no foundation in the record.

Explain that, even if you object, opposing counsel is entitled to an answer, because not until the trial will a judge decide whether your objection is well taken, and that you object at the deposition to preserve your right to object at trial if opposing counsel wants to use deposition testimony. If the trial judge sustains your objection, the jury never hears the answer. Unless you explain this seemingly counterintuitive procedure to your client before the deposition, he or she may be flummoxed by being required to answer a question despite your objection.

Explain that, even though you are very limited in what you can say when objecting, your client should listen carefully to each objection you make. Doing so will help your client in answering the question. Keep in mind, though, that your objections must be stated concisely, and in a non-argumentative and non-suggestive manner. Rule 30(c)(2).

Explain that the only circumstances in which you can instruct your client not to answer are to protect a privilege, enforce a court order, or present a motion to the court about the conduct of the deposition. Rules 30(c)(2) and 30(d)(3)(A).

Reassure your client that you can confer during breaks (unless you are in a jurisdiction that prohibits attorney-client conferences during depositions), and that if he or she makes a mistake in answering a question, there are remedies: (a) correct the answer right after giving the wrong answer by saying, "I need to correct an answer I just gave because I made a mistake"; (b) correct the answer later in the deposition, by volunteering the correction (an exception to the do-not-volunteer rule) or by responding to your questions on cross-examination at deposition; or (c) correct the answer on the errata sheet, after reviewing the transcript (the least desirable of these three options, because of impeachment potential).

Explain that your client will have 30 days after receipt of the transcript to review it carefully for mistakes, including substantive mistakes in testimony, and that you will review any corrections with your client before they are made. Rule 30(e).

Conduct a mock deposition of your client, focusing on the more sensitive subjects of testimony. As soon as your client volunteers, or fails to follow any of your other instructions, take a "time out," play back to your client the words he or she just said in response to your question, and suggest specific corrective action. To avoid confusion about which role you are playing (your client's lawyer or opposing counsel), you may want to move to a different seat when you are playing the role of opposing counsel. (Consider also the baseball cap method—donning a baseball cap when you are playing opposing counsel.) When you conduct your mock deposition, remind your client that there is no script; rather, it is a process that enables your client to prepare without memorizing what to say. Unlike the client in the cartoon on the facing page, your client should not sound rehearsed when testifying.

As an ethical matter, you cannot suggest to your client during preparation that his or her answer to a question is wrong if your client believes the answer to be the truth. You can, however, explore the basis for your client's answer, to test its reliability. For more on the ethics of witness preparation, see chapter 11, section 9.

Advise your client about demeanor: businesslike, professional, not hostile. Caution your client not to get emotional, reminding him or her that emotional people sometimes say things they regret. Since every word

*"Why don't we take a break? Your testimony is beginning to sound rehearsed."*

is transcribed, getting emotional is dangerous. If you sense that opposing counsel is getting under your client's skin, ask to take a break, so you can avoid this hazard. During that break, a walk outside is sometimes the best antidote to opposing counsel's tactics. If you ever sense your client beginning to get emotional during his or her testimony, take a break at the earliest reasonable time, to accomplish the same calming objective.

## 8. The Procedure at a Deposition

Ask the stenographer to pre-mark exhibit stickers (but not exhibits). This will save time during the deposition and avoid disruption of your momentum. Don't pre-mark exhibits, because you will determine the sequence of exhibits as you ask questions.

Before going on the record, discuss stipulations. Don't agree to the "usual stipulations," because you can't be certain what the stenographer will insert in the transcript if you do so. Instead, simply agree that Rule 30(c) applies.

Also before going on the record, state whether the deponent reserves the right to read and sign the transcript of the deposition. See Rule 30(e), which provides that *if requested by the deponent during the deposition*, the deponent has 30 days after receipt of the transcript to read it, make corrections, and sign it.

Keep track of the time the deposition starts, and the duration of all breaks, because the deposition for each witness is limited to one day of seven hours (not including breaks), unless that time limit is changed by court order or stipulation of the parties. Rule 30(d)(1). If you are defending and anticipate any problem with the length of the deposition, ask the stenographer to include in the transcript the time the deposition starts and ends, and the duration of all breaks.

Go on the record. State your agreement about stipulations, make explicit that there are no other stipulations regarding the deposition, and state whether the deponent reserves the right to read and sign the transcript. The stenographer swears the witness, and then direct and cross-examination proceed as at trial. Rule 30(c).

If either lawyer seeks to reserve the right to ask further questions after the first day of deposition, the lawyer must make that explicit before stating "no further questions." For example, if a deponent has not brought certain documents requested in the notice of deposition or subpoena, and those documents are available, the lawyer may want to state: "I have no more questions at this time, but I reserve the right to resume the deposition of this witness after I receive the documents the witness did not produce today in response to my notice of deposition." If defending the deposition, limit on the record the scope of what opposing counsel reserves the right to ask at the second day of deposition.

Before completing the deposition, make sure you have all original deposition exhibits, and state on the record who will retain possession of those exhibits. If the deposition is not completed, discuss the next deposition date.

## 9. How to take a deposition

Use the list of subjects you prepared, but do not lock yourself into the sequence you have planned. You may want to cover subjects in a different order, depending on the flow of the deposition.

Typically, lawyers taking depositions start with easy questions about the deponent's background, to get the deponent comfortable and less on guard. However, consider the option of starting with key questions, before the witness has the opportunity to get comfortable or discuss anything with counsel during breaks.

Listen to each answer. You will miss something if you don't, including little asides that reveal much. Deponents sometimes inadvertently disclose information during a deposition. Unless you are really listening, the answer may get by you. If necessary, ask the stenographer to read back the question and answer, or ask that the read-back be done at a break, if you don't want opposing counsel to know that you think a particular answer may be especially significant.

Also be aware of the deponent's body language. Studies show that most of the information conveyed, even in face-to-face communication, is nonverbal. Watch for nonverbal cues to discern when a deponent is holding something back, nervous, lying, or conveying some other message subconsciously. As Montaigne observed: "How often do the involuntary movements of our features reveal what we are secretly thinking and betray us to those about us!" You won't perceive what the deponent is revealing unless you are paying attention.

Use the funnel method to exhaust the deponent's memory on each subject, starting with the general and proceeding to the specific. (See the next section on the funnel method.) To the extent you can, have the witness testify that his or her testimony is complete on each subject, by asking such questions as: "You have told me that the subjects discussed at the meeting were X, Y, and Z. Were any other subjects discussed?" Unless you get an unequivocal "No" in response, the witness has left the door open to testify about other subjects discussed at that meeting at trial. Consider concluding a line of questioning with something like: "Have you now told me everything you can recall about . . . ?"

Do not hesitate to ask questions that will elicit answers that are harmful to your case. You are better off knowing those answers at deposition rather than being blindsided at trial. Besides, in taking depositions, you want to test your legal theories by ascertaining the strengths and weaknesses of possible causes of action. The only exception to asking questions that may elicit negative answers pertains to a witness who is not likely to be available at trial, when you are taking a deposition to perpetuate testimony rather than for discovery purposes.

Ask short, straightforward questions that are not properly objectionable. In framing your questions, keep in mind that you will want to do an electronic word search. For example, be consistent in the way you refer to people's names and dates.

If opposing counsel objects to a question, ask yourself whether the objection is well taken. But avoid engaging opposing counsel as much as possible during the deposition you are taking, even when opposing counsel goads you. No good can come of such engagement, with one exception: if you do not understand the objection, consider asking for clarification. If the objection is well taken, fix the question. Otherwise, you may not be able to use the answer for any purpose.

Keep in mind the words in the transcript. One of your goals is to obtain concrete, unequivocal admissions that you can use in negotiation, in motion practice (such as a motion for summary judgment), and at trial. See the next section for a proven technique to obtain admissions at deposition.

Do not take detailed notes during the deposition, except to the extent necessary to ask follow-up questions, as when the deponent responds with a list of factors or people in answering a question. If you need immediate, comprehensive notes, arrange for a paralegal to take notes on a laptop, or a real-time transcript.

If the deponent does not answer your question, but instead answers a different question, ask yourself whether your question was clear. If so, say: "I may not have made my question clear. You did not answer my question. My question is X." Repeat the question with the same words. If necessary, ask the stenographer to read it to the deponent, and instruct the deponent to answer that question.

If the deponent still does not answer your question, keep asking it, with the same words, until you get the answer. Ask the deponent if there is anything unclear about your question. If your question is sufficiently explicit, the deponent may feel foolish by not answering it. If it becomes apparent that the deponent is being intentionally evasive, be more direct, even confrontational. The deponent will learn that evasive answers don't work. If the deponent is hostile to you, ignore the hostility. Ask your questions and get the answers you require.

If the deponent is trying to play games with you, by evasion, hostility, or otherwise, take a break, and talk to opposing counsel privately. Ask that opposing counsel talk to his or her client about proper conduct, and make clear that the more his or her client tries to play games, the longer the deposition will take.

What do you do if you think the deponent is lying? How can you be alert to perjury? As noted above, most in-person verbal communication is, in fact, nonverbal—conveyed by voice inflection, facial expressions, tilt of the head, body posture, use of hands and arms, and the like. People trained in micro-expressions can even perceive the flicker of instantaneous honest response to a question (such as disdain) before the contrived and dishonest words are uttered. Don't be so mired in your notes and documents that you are blinded to these revealing clues to lying. As you listen carefully to each answer, be aware of internal inconsistencies, "facts" that don't ring true, and any testimony that just doesn't make sense. Then ferret out the truth.

Here are some tips to get adverse parties to tell the truth under oath. Keep in mind, though, the benefits of not playing all your cards at deposition, saving some for trial:

- If the witness testifies to lack of knowledge or of memory, get the witness to admit knowledge of facts related to the facts you want admitted, to make lack of knowledge or of memory implausible.
- Demonstrate, by your pointed questions, the illogic of the testimony.
- Express incredulity by your words and body language.
- Remind the witness of the seriousness of the oath.
- Confront the witness with documents revealing the truth.
- If the witness has memorized a contrived story, ask questions out of chronological order.
- If another witness has already testified under oath to the contrary, confront the witness with this: "Are you telling me that X is a liar? Committed perjury?"

Assume that the deponent will be prepared at trial to testify about all subjects you cover in your deposition, and that the deponent will review the deposition transcript during trial preparation. Consider refraining from using certain documents or asking questions about some subjects, so the deponent will not anticipate all your cross-examination questions at trial. Even though you can obtain valuable information and admissions at deposition, you are also giving the deponent a sneak preview of your cross-examination at trial.

## 10. How to use the funnel method when taking a deposition

The funnel method enables you to gather information on a particular subject, starting with general questions, proceeding to clarifying specific questions, exhausting the deponent's knowledge of that subject, and finishing that subject by obtaining admissions you can use against the opposing party. One funnel applies to each subject you cover in a deposition. For a comprehensive discussion of this method, see *The Effective Deposition: Techniques and Strategies That Work*, listed in appendix III, from which the following discussion is derived. Look at this diagram.

## FUNNEL METHOD

1. DEPONENT'S KNOWLEDGE OF SUBJECT X

2. OPEN-ENDED QUESTIONS

3. REPORTER QUESTIONS

4. FILTER

5. ADMISSION QUESTIONS

6. ADMISSIONS

The beaker (1) once contained the deponent's universe of knowledge on Subject X. It is now empty, because all that knowledge has been poured into the funnel.

### *Top of the funnel.*

The top of the funnel (2) is where you ask broad, open-ended questions about a given subject, which we will refer to as "Subject X." It must be a subject that is relevant to your case; otherwise, you are wasting your limited seven hours per deponent. See Rule 30(d)(1). This phase is designed to encourage the deponent to provide you with extended information without your need, initially, to prompt for details. Typically, such questions begin with "Tell me about . . ." or "Tell me everything you recall about. . . ."

During this open-ended phase, not all testimony you elicit may be of interest, but listen for testimony you may want to learn more about so you know what follow-up questions you should ask in the middle of the funnel.

## *Middle of the funnel.*

The middle of the funnel (3) is where you ask more-specific questions, just as a reporter would: who, what, where, when, why, and how? Get clarification of any non-specific answers. Ask follow-up questions. Exhaust the witness's memory on the subject. Close the door on possible additional trial testimony as to that subject by asking questions that compel the deponent to testify that the information you are getting is complete. Typical of such questions: "What else?" and "Anything else?" as to a subtopic within Subject X. Think of your experience at the deli counter. Complete all your questions about each subtopic before going on to the next subtopic within Subject X. Your objective here is to learn everything the deponent knows about Subject X. You don't want to learn key information for the first time at trial. When you are blindsided that way, you'll be chagrined, or worse, for not exhausting the deponent's knowledge at deposition.

For an entertaining way to learn to ask effective questions in the middle of the funnel, read investigative questioning in detective novels by Robert B. Parker's characters Spenser and Jesse Stone, and Jonthan Kellerman's detective Milo Sturgis.

Prepare for the bottom of the funnel by filtering to determine which deposition answers warrant your seeking admissions. The filter you apply (4) filters out extraneous information, and allows only information to pass through for which you will seek admissions.

## *Bottom of the funnel.*

The bottom of the funnel (5) is where you obtain admissions. Ask only leading questions. "You admit that . . ." "You do not dispute that . . ." "You agree that. . . ." Another effective way to obtain admissions is by making declaratory statements that you want the deponent to agree with. Use the information you obtained higher up in the funnel to obtain admissions (6). Conceptualize it this way: all the information gathering you did higher up in the funnel is the sap you collected, which must be boiled down and distilled to the maple syrup of the admissions you will use to negotiate a favorable settlement, support a motion for summary judgment, and use for cross-examination and impeachment at trial.

You can vary the funnel method by starting in the middle or bottom of the funnel, depending on what sequence most effectively will result in your obtaining the admissions you seek.

There is no magic to starting at the top of the funnel. For example, you can ask admission questions at any time, especially if the deponent is evasive, terse, or adversarial, or if you are approaching your seven-hour limit. You will not know in advance when the opportunity will arise to obtain useful admissions. Seize the moment when it presents itself.

You can also explore a new funnel while you are asking open-ended or reporter questions as you work your way down your original funnel. So, if in answering reporter questions on Subject X, the deponent makes a statement about Subject Y that you consider fruitful to explore, do not hesitate to go right to the Subject Y funnel—as long as you remember to return to Subject X to complete the funnel on that subject. Make the most of the flexibility of the funnel method.

## *Example of use of the funnel method.*

Here is an example of how the funnel method works. Assume you represent Minotaur Microchip Company in the defense of an action brought by Labyrinth Telephonics Inc., a manufacturer of telephone systems. Labyrinth claims that Minotaur sold it defective microchips, known as EPROM (erasable programmable read-only memory) chips, that Labyrinth installed in its Conference Call Express (CCE) telephone systems, causing Labyrinth to suffer millions of dollars of lost profits. Minotaur's primary defense is that the EPROM chips it sold Labyrinth were not defective, and that Labyrinth's problems resulted from defects in other components of the CCE telephone system.

From pre-deposition interrogatory responses and documents produced in response to your document requests, you know that there was a pivotal meeting at Labyrinth during which it was determined that the EPROM chip, not any other component, was the cause of the problems. You are deposing the quality control manager of Labyrinth. Here is how the funnel method works as to that meeting (subject X).

At the top of the funnel, you ask open-ended questions, such as: Tell me about the meeting on X date at which you discussed the causes of the problems in Labyrinth's CCE telephone systems.

In the middle of the funnel, ask reporter-type questions: Who decided to have that meeting? Why? Why that date? What was the purpose? Was that the only purpose? Who was requested to attend? Anyone else? Why them? Who did attend? Anyone else? Where was it? Why there? What was discussed? Was anything else discussed? What documents were reviewed at that meeting? Any other documents? What other possible causes of the problems with the CCE telephone system were considered? Any others? How was it determined that the EPROM chips were the cause? Were any other factors considered? What tests had been done to make that determination? Any other tests? Did those tests comply with Labyrinth's standard procedures? Could other tests have been done? What tests had been done on other components of the CCE telephone system? Did Labyrinth determine that the EPROM chips were the cause of the problems with the CCE telephone system as a result of what was discussed at this meeting? Was that decision based on anything else?

Based on the answers you get, at the bottom of the funnel, ask leading questions in the form of statements to which the deponent must agree. Assuming you obtained information at the middle of the funnel to support each of the following statements, ask the following leading questions in the form of statements. Get a "yes" answer to each:

- You chaired a meeting on X date at which you discussed with others at Labyrinth problems with the CCE telephone system.
- You invited everyone you thought should be there for that meeting.
- You asked Wendell Rogan, who conducted the diagnostic tests on the CCE telephone system, and who concluded they were defective, to attend this meeting.
- It was important to you that Mr. Rogan attend this meeting.
- You invited Mr. Rogan because you knew it was necessary for others at the meeting to discuss with him his methodology and analysis of the results of his diagnostic tests on the EPROM chips.
- You knew before calling this meeting that Mr. Rogan did not test any components of the CCE telephone system other than the

EPROM chips in determining the cause of problems with the CCE telephone system.
- No one else at Labyrinth tested any components of the CCE telephone system other than Mr. Rogan's test of the EPROM chips to determine the cause of the problems.
- Labyrinth could have tested other components of the CCE telephone system to determine the cause of the problems.
- Mr. Rogan did not attend that meeting.
- No one contacted Mr. Rogan during that meeting.
- At that meeting, Corinne Drumheller, assistant quality control manager, proposed that other components of the CCE telephone system be analyzed, because she had reason to believe the cause of the problems may not be the EPROM chips.
- You were under time pressure from the president of Labyrinth to take action on this issue.
- You told Ms. Drumheller at this meeting that you thought Mr. Rogan's test results were conclusive, and that no further testing was necessary.
- You told Ms. Drumheller at this meeting that the diagnostic tests she proposed would take too long, would be too expensive, and would not provide any useful information.
- As of the time of that meeting, you did not have a time or cost estimate for the diagnostic tests Ms. Drumheller proposed.
- As soon as the meeting was over, that same day, you sent a letter to Minotaur, asserting the claim that its EPROM chips were defective, seeking damages.
- You sent that letter with no further discussion with anyone after that meeting.
- Neither you nor anyone else at Labyrinth discussed with Mr. Rogan the methodology, analysis, or results of his testing of the EPROM chips.
- You relied on only Mr. Rogan's testing of the EPROM chips to conclude that, of the 327 components in the CCE telephone systems, the EPROM chips were the only cause of problems with those telephone systems.
- Neither you nor anyone else at Labyrinth ruled out the possibility that any other components of the CCE telephone system were the cause of problems with the CCE telephone system.

## 11. How to Defend the Deposition of Your Client

In *The Curmudgeon's Guide to Practicing Law,* listed in appendix III, Mark Herrmann aptly describes defending the deposition of your client: "Defending depositions is like preventing catastrophes. If you do it well, no one notices. If you do it poorly, there's hell to pay. No lawyer ever won a case through deposition defense, but many lawyers have lost cases that way."

Most of your work in defending a deposition occurs when you prepare your client days before. Tell your client before the deposition starts that you may not say much at the deposition if your client is doing fine, and if opposing counsel is not asking many objectionable questions.

Reserve the right to have your client read and sign the transcript before the completion of the deposition. This right is waived if you do not assert it before then. Rule 30(e).

Object to questions that are objectionable as to form, such as ambiguous questions, double questions, questions for which there is no foundation in the record, questions assuming facts not in evidence, confusing questions, and questions that have already been asked and answered—unless by doing so you are aiding opposing counsel in creating a better record. You must object strategically; do not object to every objectionable question.

Your objections must be concise, non-argumentative, and non-suggestive. Rule 30(c)(2). When appropriate, merely say: "Objection." By doing so, you have preserved your objection for the trial, without giving opposing counsel any guidance about what is wrong with the question. If you need to alert your client to a problem with the question, such as ambiguity, say: "Objection. This question is ambiguous. Which meeting is the subject of your question?" Most lawyers will not have a problem with such an objection.

If opposing counsel shows your client a document at the deposition, make sure your client has sufficient time to review it before answering questions about it.

You cannot talk to your client while a question is pending, but the first time your client completes an answer that includes volunteered information, tell your client: "You just volunteered. You were asked X and you answered X + Y. Keep this in mind as you answer questions—don't volunteer."

During breaks, reassure your client that the deposition is going well if so, and provide guidance as necessary, unless such conferences during deposition are prohibited in your jurisdiction.

If your client makes a mistake in an answer, deal with it: If it is an obvious mistake (e.g., referring to the wrong exhibit number of the document your client is reading), correct the record immediately: "The witness just referred to Exhibit 21. So the record is clear, he was just reading from Exhibit 22." If your client gives testimony inconsistent with what you expected, discuss that testimony with your client during a break. Your client may be testifying truthfully at deposition, or may have misheard the question, or may have merely made a mistake. If your client gave a wrong answer, when you go back on the record, your client should say: "I would like to correct something I said earlier. You asked me X and I answered Y. I meant to respond by saying Z." Prepare your client to answer follow-up questions based on the change in testimony.

If your client forgets something at the deposition, discuss the subject of the forgotten testimony during a break. Your client can fix the problem after the break, but should be prepared for follow-up questions about why he or she now remembers what he didn't remember earlier in the deposition.

Experienced lawyers often save their most important questions for late in the afternoon, when the deponent and defending counsel may be tired, and less alert to the admissions being sought. If you sense that your client is getting tired, at any time during the deposition, take a break, have your client walk around, get some fresh air, drink coffee or soda—anything appropriate to keep your client alert.

Take notes during the deposition only to the extent you will use them during the deposition, as when your client makes a mistake or testifies to something you need to follow up on, any agreement of counsel to produce documents after the deposition, the name and contact information for the court reporter, and the next date for a multiday deposition. You don't want to miss an opportunity to protect the record because you are busy scribbling down everything that is being said. That is the stenographer's job.

If you will need immediate comprehensive notes of a deposition for another deposition that is imminent, arrange for a paralegal to take notes on a laptop. Another advantage of this procedure is that you can review those notes during the deposition, including word searches. This is expensive, though, so your client should be alerted to the cost and be asked to consent. You can also request that the stenographer provide real-time access to the transcript if that cost is justified and approved by your client.

If opposing counsel becomes oppressive, deal with it before things get out of control. For example, if opposing counsel repeatedly asks duplicative questions about the same subject matter, you can say: "You have already asked questions on this subject several times. These questions have already been asked and answered. Go to something else." You cannot instruct your client not to answer, but your admonishment may cause opposing counsel to think twice about revisiting other areas already covered.

In extreme circumstances—and only in extreme circumstances—you can terminate the deposition, if you believe you can convince a judge that the deposition is being conducted in bad faith, or in such a manner as unreasonably to annoy, embarrass, or oppress the deponent or a party. Rule 30(d)(3). Before you resort to such an extreme measure, state on the record that unless counsel ceases doing X (be specific), you will terminate the deposition and seek a court order. It is rare and extraordinary to terminate a deposition on this basis, so be very confident that you are on extremely good grounds before you terminate a deposition.

As a general matter, don't leave your client alone in the deposition room with opposing counsel or his or her client. An exception applies. If you become aware that there is residual goodwill between your client and the opposing party attending the deposition, during a break consider asking your client if he or she wants to meet with the opposing party to discuss a resolution of the entire case before resuming the deposition. If so, discuss such a meeting with opposing counsel. See section 17 of this chapter about use of deposition transcripts at trial.

## 12. When to ask questions of your own client at a deposition

Representing a client in a deposition is a defensive exercise; everything your client testifies about can be used to thwart your position. Thus, in the normal course, you should not ask any questions of your own client at his or her deposition. There are, however, two exceptions.

The first applies if your client gave mistaken testimony when asked questions by other counsel. You can set the record straight by asking questions about subjects that need correcting. Since depositions proceed as at trial, after you complete your limited questioning, opposing counsel cannot ask questions beyond the scope of what you asked.

The second applies if you have reason to believe that your client will not be available for trial, whether due to illness, advanced age, or unavoidable travel plans. Ask yourself: If I ask no questions, and my client cannot testify at trial, will I be disadvantaged at trial by not putting more in the record at deposition? See section 17 of this chapter about use of deposition transcripts at trial.

## 13. How to take and defend depositions of experts

Depositions of experts proceed the same as any other deposition. To prepare for the expert's deposition, read the expert disclosure required by Rule 26(a)(2), review responses to your interrogatories and document requests pertaining to the opponent's expert, do a Google search of the expert, read the expert's report and anything else the expert wrote pertaining to the opinions about which the opponent's expert is expected to testify, discuss this information and these documents with your expert, and then prepare an outline of your deposition questions.

In your deposition, cover the following topics to establish a basis to challenge, or even exclude, the expert's testimony at trial, as discussed in chapter 10, section 8:

- the expert's qualifications and prior experience as an expert
- whether the expert ever rendered any opinions on the subject matter
- each nondocumentary source of information the expert considered (not necessarily relied upon) in doing her or his research and analysis (e.g., discussions with counsel and interviews with anyone)
- each document the expert considered in doing his or her research and analysis
- each treatise the expert considers definitive on the pertinent subject matter
- the substance of each opinion about which the expert is expected to testify at trial
- the basis for each opinion
- all assumptions the expert made as to each opinion
- approaches used by other experts on the same subject matter

- anything the expert has not yet done regarding his or her opinions
- anything the expert did not do in his or her review and analysis that could have been done
- his or her evaluation of your expert's qualifications and report

Note that even though the amendments to the Federal Rules of Civil Procedure effective December 1, 2010, increased the work-product protection of communications between attorneys and testifying experts, it is still fair game to ask about all such communications to the extent they pertain to an expert's compensation, facts or data the attorney provided to the expert that the expert considered in forming opinions to be expressed, and all assumptions provided by the attorney that the expert relied on. Rule 26(b)(4)(C). See chapter 2, section 3, for a discussion of what is discoverable as to expert witnesses.

Consider refraining from asking certain questions at the expert's deposition. For example, if there is a significant mathematical error in the expert's report, and you inquire about it, the expert will fix the error and prepare an amended report before trial. The expert may not have this opportunity if you refrain from inquiring about this error, and will be blindsided at trial.

Review the deposition transcript with your expert to develop your cross-examination for trial.

## 14. THE FORM OF TRANSCRIPT YOU SHOULD ORDER

*Mandatory format.* The stenographer must provide the attorney who took the deposition with a certified transcript in an envelope or package with the title of the action, marked "Deposition of [witness's name]," unless the court orders otherwise. Rule 30(f)(1).

*Alternative types of format.* At the end of the deposition, the court reporter will give you choices of the format of the transcript: paper transcript with full-size pages; condensed transcript with four pages on one; transcript with word index with same as referenced above with index; ASCII disk, disk of transcript in ASCII format; or e-transcript via electronic transcript with no paper transcript. The e-transcript is most efficient and enables you to do word searches.

*Timing of transcript.* The sooner you get it, the more expensive: regular: typically a few weeks; expedited: typically a few days; or overnight.

## 15. What you should do after getting the transcript

Put the sealed transcript in the file so you will have access to it at the trial. If it is the transcript of your client's deposition, and your client has reserved the right to read and sign the transcript, send a copy to your client, with a cover letter explaining that your client should read the transcript carefully and, within no more than three weeks of receipt of the transcript, on a separate page (not on the errata sheet), make a list of every mistake, whether a typographical error or a substantive error, and send it to you.

Calendar the date that is three weeks from your client's receipt of the transcript. Discuss all proposed corrections with your client. Instruct your client about how to complete the errata sheet and sign the jurat, and remind your client to sign it in the presence of a notary. Send the original errata sheet and jurat to the stenographer, and copies to all counsel of record, within 30 days of your client's receipt of the transcript. Rule 30(e)(1).

Prepare a summary of the deposition transcript that includes columns for the page, subject, and the testimony for each statement of interest. If you use uniform terms in your subject column, you can sort effectively by subject. Add to the chronology you prepared before the deposition pertinent information from the deposition transcript, with a citation to each transcript page you reference.

Before trial, discuss your client's deposition testimony with your client, and be prepared to deal with anything that could be fodder for an effective cross-examination.

If it is the transcript of another party or a nonparty, prepare a summary of the deposition transcript, as for a client's deposition; add facts from the deposition to your chronology, as for a client's deposition; and prepare cross-examination of the witness based in part on the transcript.

You can learn from each deposition transcript you read. Whether you have taken or defended a deposition, you will learn from reading those transcripts what works and what doesn't, and whether you successfully followed the advice in this chapter.

## 16. How to use deposition transcripts before trial

Use deposition transcripts to support or oppose motions for summary judgment. The court can consider only *certified copies* of transcripts. Rule

56(e). Use these transcripts in preparation for trial. Discuss deposition testimony with your client in preparing for your direct and anticipating the cross. Also, use deposition transcript admissions in settlement discussions and mediation.

Insert cross-references to pages of opposing parties' deposition transcripts in your cross-examination outline for instant reference when you impeach. If you have taken a video deposition, do the equivalent electronically. Word your trial cross-examination questions the same as your deposition questions of a party so you can conduct an effective impeachment. If there is any disconnect between the two, your impeachment will fall flat. For more on impeachment, see the discussion below in this chapter and in chapter 10, section 10.

## 17. How to use deposition transcripts at trial

*Testimony of an absent witness.* See Rule 32(a)(4) and FRE 804(b)(1). That Federal Rule of Evidence provides, in part, that testimony given in a deposition taken in compliance with law in the course of the same or another proceeding is not excluded by the hearsay rule if two conditions are met: (1) the declarant is unavailable as a witness and (2) the party against whom the testimony is offered, or predecessor in interest, had the opportunity and similar motive to develop the testimony by direct, cross-, or redirect examination.

*An admission of a party opponent.* See Rule 32(a) and FRE 801(d). The party opponent need not be on the stand when you offer such an admission. No witness is required. Mark as an exhibit for identification the pages of the deposition transcript you want in the record (including the title page) and offer it as a full exhibit.

*As a basis for a proffer.* At trial, opposing counsel may object to certain proffered evidence you want to put into the record as lacking a good-faith basis or irrelevant. The judge may ask you for an offer of proof as to the proposed testimony. You can use the deposition transcript to demonstrate to the judge your good-faith basis for inquiring on a particular subject and why that subject is relevant.

*As a means to refresh recollection.* If you must resort to this use of a deposition transcript, here is the procedure: (1) your witness testifies that she has no independent recollection of a fact and that the deposition transcript may refresh her recollection; (2) she silently reads the pertinent passage from the deposition transcript, after you ask permission to approach the witness and identify for opposing counsel what you are showing her; (3) you remove the transcript from her; (4) she testifies that her recollection is now refreshed; and (5) she testifies based on her refreshed recollection. Since the document used to refresh recollection is not put into evidence, there is no evidence rule on this.

*As the testimony of a witness whose testimony cannot be refreshed.* Rule 32(a)(2) allows for the use of a deposition transcript for any purpose allowed by the Federal Rules of Evidence. FRE 804(a)(3) defines a failure of memory as unavailability for purposes of admitting statements that would otherwise be hearsay. A witness's deposition testimony becomes admissible as substantive evidence under FRE 804(b)(1), the provision allowing the use of former testimony, if the witness testifies at trial that he has no memory of a fact and his recollection cannot be refreshed.

*As a means of impeachment.* See Rule 32(a)(2) and FRE 801(d)(1)(A), 801(d)(2). Only impeach on something that matters in the case, and then only if you have solid impeachment material. Make sure that the trial testimony of a witness is contrary to your impeaching material in some material way. In your cross-examination notes, include deposition transcript page and line references for each impeachment point.

Use a three-step process: commit, credit, and contrast. First, *commit* the witness to what the witness testified to at trial, demonstrating that you are skeptical about that testimony by your tone of voice and by your words, such as: "You are telling this jury *today* that. . . ." Beware of appearing to buttress testimony that you are about to impeach on. Second, *credit* the reliability of the impeaching material (whether a deposition transcript or not). In this second step, ask such leading questions as the following, getting a "yes" answer to each: "This is not the first time you testified in this case. You came to my office back in \_\_\_\_, closer to the time of the events that bring us to court, and you took the same oath you took today. You swore to tell the truth. You did tell the truth. Your attorney was sitting right next to you when you answered my questions. You had the opportunity to review the transcript of what you told me. You corrected what needed correcting, in an errata sheet. You signed the errata sheet." Third, *contrast* the witness's sworn deposition testimony with his or her trial testimony. "Let's turn to page 27, lines 3 to 20. Here is a copy of that transcript. I just gave opposing counsel a copy as well. You did not correct anything on that page. Read along with me. I asked you, and I quote: '\_\_\_\_.' And your response, under oath, was '\_\_\_\_.'"

Read from the deposition transcript. Do not rely on the witness to read from it. If you have taken a video deposition, play the tape.

At this point, you will have an urgent desire to ask such questions as: "Are you lying now, or were you lying then? That was the truth, wasn't it, and it's still the truth, right? So, your testimony today is inconsistent with what you told me at your deposition, right?" Do not ask these questions. Why not? Because, by doing so, you open the door for the witness to explain away the inconsistency, blunting the effect of your impeachment.

*As a means to accomplish a phantom impeachment.* After you impeach a witness several times with a deposition transcript, the witness will be conditioned to know that when you are about to make reference to his or her deposition transcript you will nail him or her. A phantom impeachment occurs when you ostensibly prepare to make a reference to the transcript, ask a leading question, and hope that the witness will give you the right answer. This is the least preferred of the ways to use a deposition transcript at trial.

Whenever you use a deposition transcript excerpt at trial for any purpose, keep in mind that opposing counsel has the right to seek to put into the record any other part of that transcript at the same time if, in fairness, it ought to be considered contemporaneously with what you offer. Rule 32(a)(6) and FRE 106.

## 18. WHAT YOU NEED TO KNOW ABOUT VIDEO DEPOSITIONS

In federal court, you have the right to take a video deposition. You must state in the notice of deposition the method for recording testimony. Rule 30(b)(3). The videographer must state the information itemized in Rule 30(b)(5) at the beginning of each unit of recording, and the appearance and demeanor of the deponent and attorneys cannot be distorted through recording techniques. Rule 30(b)(5)(B).

Advantages of taking video depositions include the following: they permit the trier of fact to see the witness's demeanor; they permit the trier of fact to see the witness's physical condition; they are more engaging and easier to follow than reading transcripts at trial; they allow for better presentation of exhibits; they are more effective for impeachment, highlight an opposition witness's evasiveness, fumbling, or hesitating before answering; and they can be edited for use during closing argument and, with the court's permission, during opening statement.

Finally, you are more likely to control the behavior of disruptive opposing counsel than if you have only a stenographic transcription.

However, the disadvantages of video depositions include the following: they are more expensive and require more effort to arrange; they are more likely to have technical or mechanical problems; they are more difficult to use for trial preparation; they may be a waste of money if taken only for discovery purposes, rather than to perpetuate testimony for trial; they require special equipment to use at trial; and they are more cumbersome for impeachment than a stenographic record.

Furthermore, video depositions may preserve testimony harmful to your case more effectively than a stenographic transcript and enable opponent's witnesses to hone their trial performances.

If the video deposition is in lieu of live testimony at trial, prepare as for trial testimony. Present the witness's testimony the same way as if she or he were in the witness box at trial. Avoid interruptions. Enliven the testimony with exhibits, visual aids, use of your voice, and other means, to keep it interesting. Minimize objections by asking proper questions.

Prepare your client for video deposition by discussing dress and demeanor, explaining the procedure at a video deposition, and cautioning your client about appearing honest and straightforward in answering questions, while avoiding unnecessary or distracting movements and gestures. Your client should come across as self-assured and confident.

See Rule 32(c) regarding how to present video depositions at trial.

## 19. How to Compel Attendance at a Deposition and Compel Answers of an Appearing Deponent

The court may impose an appropriate sanction, including the reasonable expenses and attorney's fees incurred by any party, on anyone who impedes, delays, or frustrates the fair examination of the deponent. Rule 30(d)(2).

If you have issued a subpoena on the deponent, you can seek an order that the deponent be held in contempt for failing to comply with it. Rule 45(e).

If a party fails to appear at a deposition, or appears and fails to answer questions, you can seek relief pursuant to Rule 37. Be sure to comply with all its requirements.

If a deponent fails to answer a question within Rule 30 or 31, you can move for an order compelling any such answer. Rule 37(a)(3)(B)(i). Some judges make themselves available for phone calls during depositions to resolve such disputes. Even so, refrain from making that call, except as a last resort.

If an entity fails to make a designation under Rule 30(b)(6) or 31(a)(4), you can move for an order compelling such designation. Rule 37(a)(3)(B)(ii).

When taking a deposition, you may complete or adjourn the examination before moving for an order. Rule 37(a)(3)(C). As a general matter, you are better off completing as much of the deposition as you can before adjourning it, to get responses to questions that are not the subject of the court order you may seek. Besides, it is far better to resolve deposition-related disputes during a break on the day of the deposition than to engage in avoidable motion practice.

For purposes of Rule 37(a), an evasive or incomplete disclosure, answer, or response is the same as a failure to disclose, answer, or respond. Rule 37(a)(4).

The prerequisites for any motion under Rule 37(a), as provided in Rule 37(a)(1), are a good-faith conference, or attempt to confer with the party failing to comply with deposition requirements; certification regarding that good-faith conference or attempt to confer; and notice of that motion to all parties and all affected persons, including that certification.

As provided in Rule 37(a)(5), if the motion is granted *or* if you obtain compliance after you file the motion, the court *must*, after giving the parties an opportunity to be heard, require the party or deponent whose conduct necessitated the motion, the party or attorney advising that conduct, or both to pay your reasonable expenses in making the motion, including attorney's fees, unless you filed the motion before attempting in good faith to obtain the disclosure without court action *or* the opposing party's nondisclosure, response, or objection was substantially justified *or* other circumstances make an award of expenses unjust.

If you file a motion pursuant to Rule 37(a) and lose, the court *must*, after giving the parties an opportunity to be heard, require the movant, you personally, or both to pay the party or deponent who opposed the motion its reasonable expenses in opposing the motion, including attorney's fees, unless the motion was substantially justified or other circumstances make such an award unjust. Rule 37(a)(5)(B).

If the court grants a Rule 37(a) motion in part and denies it in part, see Rule 37(a)(5)(C). If the deponent fails to comply with a court order, you can move for contempt and sanctions, as provided in Rule 37(b). If a party fails to appear for a properly noticed deposition, you can seek sanctions as provided in Rule 37(d).

## 20. How to get a protective order limiting the conduct of a deposition

The court can order limits on the number of depositions and their length. Rule 26(b)(2)(A).

As provided in Rule 26(b)(2)(C), on its own or on motion, the court *must* limit the frequency or extent of discovery otherwise allowed if discovery sought is unreasonably cumulative or duplicative, or can be obtained from some other source that is more convenient, less burdensome, or less expensive; *or* the party seeking discovery has had ample opportunity to obtain the information by discovery in the action; *or* the burden or expense of the proposed discovery outweighs its likely benefit.

At any time during a deposition, the deponent or a party may move to terminate or limit it on the ground that it is being conducted in bad faith or in a manner that unreasonably annoys, embarrasses, or oppresses the deponent or a party. If the objecting deponent or party so demands, the deposition *must* be suspended for the time necessary to obtain an order. Rule 30(d)(3)(A). This is a difficult burden to sustain, so do not file such a motion except in extreme circumstances.

The court may order that the deposition be terminated or limit its scope and manner as provided in Rule 26(c), and may award expenses as provided in Rule 37(a)(5), in connection with a motion pursuant to Rule 30(d)(3). You can move to quash or modify a subpoena. Rule 45(c)(3).

## ❖❖❖❖
## PRACTICE CHECKLIST

- Take a deposition only after you have completed necessary factual and legal research and developed a working theme for your case.
- Obtain all necessary documents and review them before taking a deposition.
- If an opposing party is an entity, serve a notice to take the deposition of the entity, not just individuals, listing topics to be covered, as provided in Rule 30(b)(6).
- In preparing your client for a deposition, explain the deposition procedure in detail; discuss the themes, claims, and defenses of the case; discuss how to answer questions; and put your client through a practice deposition, playing the role of opposing counsel. Explain how you will protect your client's interests at the deposition, and explain how your client can correct any mistakes in his or her deposition testimony.
- In taking a deposition, use the list of subjects or questions you prepared, listen to the answers and observe the deponent's body language, ask follow-up questions, exhaust the deponent's memory, and use the funnel method to obtain admissions you can use.
- In defending a deposition, caution your client the first time he or she volunteers; limit your objections to the word "objection" unless you have justification to say more; during breaks, provide guidance to your client as needed unless prohibited in your jurisdiction; take notes only as you need at the deposition; and know when it is permissible to instruct your client not to answer.
- Ask questions of your own client at a deposition only to correct mistakes or to create a more complete record if your client may not be available at trial.
- In deposing an expert, prepare by learning everything you can about the expert and the expert's writings, cover all subjects that may be useful in cross-examining the expert at trial and for a *Daubert* challenge; and consider refraining from asking certain questions to blindside the expert at trial.
- Unless, for strategic reasons, you have not preserved your client's right to read and sign the transcript of the deposition, preserve that right during the deposition, and make sure that you submit the errata sheet within 30 days of your client's receipt of the transcript.
- After receiving the transcript, prepare a summary of it and include significant facts from it in your working chronology.
- Use deposition transcripts to support motions for summary judgment, in settlement negotiations, and at trial. You can use deposition transcripts at trial as follows:
    - _____ testimony of an absent witness
    - _____ admission of a party opponent

(continued)

- _____ basis for a proffer
- _____ means to refresh recollection
- _____ testimony of a witness whose testimony cannot be refreshed
- _____ means of impeachment
- _____ means for phantom impeachment

- In an appropriate case, consider taking a video deposition, keeping in mind the advantages and disadvantages of doing so.
- Take advantage of applicable Federal Rules of Civil Procedure to compel attendance at deposition and to compel answers to deposition questions.
- Take advantage of applicable Federal Rules of Civil Procedure to obtain a protective order limiting the conduct of a deposition.

CHAPTER SIX

# MEDIATING COMMERCIAL DISPUTES

You must be prepared to try each case—yet the reality is that the vast majority of cases settle before trial, many by mediation. Unlike arbitration, mediation is not binding. But it can be an effective mechanism to resolve cases long before you ever get to trial.

## 1. WHETHER AND WHEN TO MEDIATE

The threshold question is whether a particular case is a good candidate for mediation. In some circumstances, the parties are obligated by contract to mediate before arbitrating or litigating, so find out if your client has signed such a contract. Also, if you have a corporate client, determine whether it is one of more than 4,000 companies that signed the CPR Corporate Policy Statement on Alternatives to Litigation, a commitment to seriously explore mediation and other alternative dispute-resolution methods before pursuing full-scale litigation. See www.cpradr.org for more on this.

Factors you should consider in determining whether to recommend mediation include the need for confidentiality; desire for resolution without protracted litigation; avoidance of the expense, uncertainty, and disruption of litigation; need to preserve an ongoing business relationship; concern about establishing an adverse precedent; and collateral issues that cannot be addressed in litigation but are within the ambit of mediation. Factors militating against mediation include the need to establish a legal precedent, likelihood of succeeding in a motion to dismiss or for summary judgment, need for immediate equitable relief, the additional expense of mediation, and your client's unwillingness to mediate.

You should consider mediation only after you have a solid grasp of the facts supporting all claims and defenses, and a thorough knowledge of the applicable law. For example, you may want to complete key depositions or certain document discovery before you mediate. On the other hand, you don't want to wait too long before mediating. It is preferable to propose mediation well before trial, by which time the parties will have invested so much time, effort, and money and positions will have likely so hardened that clients may perceive that it is too late in the process.

Clients sometimes perceive your mere suggestion of mediation as a sign of weakness. This is especially so if you have a high-powered, master-of-the-universe client.

"You tell them we're not ready to make nice until they're ready to make nice."

It is important to explain the speed, cost savings, time savings, and privacy benefits of mediation, emphasizing that merely proposing mediation is no sign of weakness at all. Rather, such a proposal, made by one trial lawyer to another, is commonplace and signals nothing other than a willingness to resolve the dispute without putting both parties through litigation to the last appeal. Emphasize that mediation is not binding; instead, it is guided negotiation. You can also advise your client—if true—that the merits of your claims are so strong that a mediator is likely to validate your position, encouraging the opposing party to resolve the dispute favorably for your client.

Assure your client that, when you propose mediation to opposing counsel, you will emphasize that a successful mediation will benefit both parties, and is therefore worth pursuing. After all, your client and the opposing party are in the same boat—neither wants to incur the expense, disruption, aggravation, and uncertainty of litigation. They each have a business to run, and better ways to utilize their financial and other resources than to spend it on litigation. Discuss these benefits of mediation with your client.

If the parties agree to mediate and do not have a preexisting mediation agreement, work out a written agreement for the terms of the mediation, including the identity of the mediator, location of mediation, terms for paying for the mediator and for mediation facilities, and a provision about confidentiality. FRE 408 and state analogs make privileged certain statements made during the course of settlement negotiations, but those rules do not protect statements of fact. Nor do they protect against the use of mediation-related statements and documents in depositions, arbitrations, the press, or public. Accordingly, agree in writing before the mediation that all statements made in connection with the mediation are privileged and cannot be disclosed to anyone. On the other hand, the mere fact that someone uses a document in connection with a mediation does not make that document privileged. Furthermore, information you disclose at a mediation is known to the other side, and may be the subject of discovery, deposition, and trial questions.

## 2. How to select a mediator

Selecting the right mediator can make all the difference. Some mediators take a facilitative approach, identifying and exploring parties' interests, concerns, motivations, goals, common ground, and possible resolutions. Such a mediator—who need not be a lawyer—will typically be unable, though, to evaluate the case, assess legal positions, or predict potential litigation outcomes. Instead, a facilitative mediator is primarily interested in discussing terms of the settlement, in an effort to have the parties come to a meeting of the minds for resolution. Typically, a facilitative mediator's focus is on offers and counteroffers in attempting to settle a case, rather than on an analysis of the strengths and weaknesses of each party's position.

Other mediators take an evaluative approach, offering opinions on the strengths and weaknesses of each party's position, challenging the parties' predictions on the litigation outcome, and initiating settlement proposals. Of course, many mediators combine both approaches.

You want a mediator who is impartial, with no conflict of interest or close bond with either counsel or party (after all, the word "mediator" is from Latin *medius*, meaning "middle"); has a strong track record for effective problem-solving and excellent negotiating skills; is a person of patience, trustworthiness, and a keen business sense; and has a good sense of humor. In certain types of cases, you may need a mediator who has expertise in a particular area, such as in construction, securities, employment, and patent disputes. Find out from colleagues and other lawyers whose opinions you trust which mediators are the best around. Also consult organizations that recommend mediators, such as JAMS (www.jamsadr.com), CPR Institute for Dispute Resolution (www.cpradr.com), the American Arbitration Association (www.adr.org), and the valuable reference book, *The Best Lawyers in America*, which has a separate listing for each state under the topic "Alternative Dispute Resolution." Go to www.bestlawyers.com for more imformation about this book and related publications. Call mediators you are considering and ask them about their approach, availability, fees, and whether they have experience mediating cases like yours.

Discuss with opposing counsel which mediators you are considering, and get assurance that opposing counsel and the opposing party agree on the selection. Unless all counsel and all parties have confidence in the mediator, when it comes crunch time during the mediation, the necessary mindset to really listen to what the mediator has to say will be absent, as will a resolution. Keep in mind that any recommendation by a mediator who is viewed as likely to favor one side or the other will be considered suspect and will be discounted.

## 3. How to prepare for mediation

Of the three worst mistakes lawyers make in connection with mediations, one is lack of preparation. Before mediating, you must know the key helpful and harmful facts in your case, and you must know the applicable law. Know your initial demand or offer, but make sure your client is open-minded about terms of an ultimate settlement.

In deciding on your initial demand or offer, discuss with your client the outcome you seek in this mediation. In doing so, consider the best and worst alternatives to a negotiated agreement (BATNA and WATNA, respectively), as discussed in *Getting to Yes: Negotiating Agreement Without Giving In*, referenced in appendix III. BATNA is your best-case scenario, and WATNA is your worst. By doing this analysis, you can evaluate in advance of mediation whether a settlement proposal makes sense. This requires a cold, hard look at the strengths and weaknesses of each party's position, the likely result of litigation, and the likely expense of litigating through the last appeal. After all, as a businessperson, your client views the financial aspects of the case globally—what the ultimate result will be in dollars. For example, if a client is defending a monetary claim, the question is: How many dollars must your client pay before this dispute is resolved, whether paid to the claimant or to you?

Make sure you get clear authority from your client as to the initial demand or offer, as you must for each settlement proposal during the course of mediation. See chapter 11, section 2, regarding your ethical obligations to obtain such authorization. Keep in mind that sometimes mediations succeed because parties propose nonmonetary resolutions, even in cases that apparently present only monetary claims. For example, in an employment case, consider a work reassignment, early retirement, training, a letter of reference, or an apology; in a business case, consider an agreement to continue doing business together or to do new business together on mutually acceptable terms; in an intellectual property case, consider a license and royalty agreement, or an agreement not to challenge the validity of intellectual property in the future. Discuss such creative resolutions with your client before mediation. You are limited only by your imagination, your client's authority, and the ethical rules.

Consider a principle both parties can agree on, around which to build a settlement. For example, in a contract dispute, such an operating principle could be: "We agree that Jones is entitled to all amounts properly due him under the contract." As you evaluate the application of this principle, focus on the motivations of *both* parties in seeking a resolution. As a useful exercise, when meeting with your client to prepare for the mediation, play the roles of opposing counsel and client as they prepare. Verbalize the devil's advocate position; then analyze it.

Keep in mind that most commercial disputes result from the breakdown of a relationship. Ascertain the source of that breakdown, evaluate the relationship issues, and strategize accordingly. To the extent you can, separate the personal from the substantive issues. It may be appropriate, at some point in the mediation, for the two principals to meet by themselves to smooth things over—but consider this option only if you have confidence in your client's good sense and ability to handle such a potentially explosive situation.

The mediator will likely request a pre-mediation statement from each party. This gives rise to the second of the worst mistakes lawyers make in connection with mediations: failing to submit a proper pre-mediation statement. Find out from your mediator what is expected in that statement and any page limit.

Typically, mediators request that pre-mediation statements include a brief summary of the facts, the claims, and the prior negotiations between the parties, imposing a limit of about 10 pages, allowing exhibits, as appropriate. Make the most of this opportunity by giving it as much thought and careful drafting as when you draft a pretrial memo, even though in the mediation context. Mediators will assess your skill as an advocate based in part in the quality of your pre-mediation statement—and your skill level affects the value of your claim or defense.

Consider whether it is advantageous to your client to exchange position papers with opposing counsel, or whether it makes more sense to submit confidential position statements only to the mediator. As an alternative, consider submitting one that is exchanged and one that is not.

Also consider preparing demonstrative exhibits for the mediation and including smaller versions of them in your position statement. For example, a time line or an organization chart may graphically convey what is difficult to put in words alone. In addition to demonstrative exhibits, bring to the mediation all key pleadings, documents, admissions, deposition excerpts, photos, and videos, as appropriate. Also bring the right people.

Bringing the wrong team to the mediation is a third common mistake lawyers make. Unless you have the decision-maker at the mediation, you're looking for trouble. Do not rely on the person with authority being available by telephone, because that person does not have the benefit of experiencing the mediation process firsthand, which is a significant detriment to resolution. And don't bring anyone you don't need, because they can interfere with the mediation process.

Discuss with your client proper demeanor at the mediation, which is more cooperative than adversarial, including the appropriate way to greet the adversary—businesslike, not hostile. Make sure your client realizes that, while you will present your position persuasively, this is not a time for emotionally charged language or theatrics. The atmosphere is more like negotiation of a business deal than making a closing argument to a jury. Your client should be aware that opposing counsel and the mediator are sizing up you and your client based on what you say, how you say it, and your body language.

## 4. Strategies for mediation

You already know the final result you seek. How do you get there? Often, mediators give each counsel the opportunity to make an opening statement in a joint session. Decide in advance whether your client will say anything during that joint session, based on the likelihood that your client will be persuasive without resorting to vitriol. If your client is sophisticated and well prepared for the mediation, he or she can speak in the opening joint session, ideally appearing reasonable, convincing, and sympathetic. This is probably your only opportunity in this mediation to convey directly to the opposing party that you are a formidable adversary prepared to litigate this case to conclusion, if necessary—but that you nevertheless realistically recognize the benefits to both parties of resolving the case on a sensible basis through this mediation process. It is also your only opportunity in mediation to demonstrate that your client will be a formidable witness at trial, if that is so. When you make your opening statement, focus your remarks and attention on the opposing party rather than on the opposing lawyer or mediator.

As the mediator engages in shuttle diplomacy, meeting with each side separately, expect that the mediator will play devil's advocate, emphasizing all the weaknesses in your position, as well as in your opponent's position, in turn. Acknowledge such weaknesses when they exist, and explain why some perceived weaknesses in fact *do not* exist. Make proposals to generate movement, aware that if you consistently change your position parallel to your opponent's, you will likely end up halfway between your opening positions. To signal that you are getting close to the limit of your authority, reduce the increments in your position. Track each change in position of each side so you can monitor the progress of the negotiations, and be aware of where you are heading if you stay on this course. Be patient. Typically, in a one-day mediation, not until late afternoon does the negotiation either reach resolution or fail. While the mediator is meeting with the other side, remind your client that this process takes time, and evaluate where you are in the negotiation process to consider your next move. Even though you have predetermined your desired result, remain flexible because, as the mediation progresses, you may need to alter your analysis of the strengths and weaknesses of each party's position.

Keep your mind open to creative resolutions during the entire process of the mediation, and ask the mediator to recommend substantive proposals, as appropriate. Listen very carefully to the words that opposing counsel uses in making a proposal, as conveyed by the mediator. It is one thing to say: "My client will not settle for a penny less than $750,000," but quite another to say "My client is looking to settle in the range of $750,000" or "My client may consider $750,000 if you offer it." Likewise, be aware of the words you use in discussions with the mediator to convey your authority.

Be very clear with the mediator what information (not just your settlement proposal) and documents you authorize the mediator to share with the other side. For example, to support your position, you may rely on a key document that is not yet the subject of any discovery, and you may benefit if you disclose it for the first time at the deposition of the opposing party, or at trial. Should you authorize the mediator to show it to the other side? The answer depends on whether doing so will resolve the case then and there.

## 5. How to get past impasse

It is not unusual for the parties to reach an impasse late in the afternoon of a one-day mediation. How do you break the impasse? If you have chosen an effective mediator, he or she will deploy strategies to get to a resolution—and you can utilize impasse-breaking strategies yourself. This is the time to be creative, recognizing that a good settlement is one that neither party is delighted with, but that both parties can accept, even if begrudgingly. Keep in mind that the value of a case depends on many factors, beyond the merits of claims and defenses, such as expense and disruption of litigating all the way, insurance coverage, personal exposure of a party's representative, settlement of comparable cases, and the experience and track record of counsel. And keep in mind that many commercial cases settle for reasons unrelated to the technical merits of claims and defenses. Here are some impasse breakers:

### *Challenge perceived BATNA.*

The mediator may challenge your perceived BATNA. If your BATNA is unrealistic, your position may be more extreme than it should be. Well before the mediation, analyze your BATNA and discuss it with your client. Play devil's advocate to focus on weaknesses in your position.

When the mediator challenges your BATNA, you may want to challenge the other party's perceived BATNA because, if that is unrealistic, the other party should be more flexible.

### *Challenge perceived WATNA.*

The mediator may challenge your WATNA on such matters as likelihood of success as to each cause of action, the amount of damages that may be awarded and recovered, the amount of future legal fees, and the likelihood of success on any counterclaims. As with BATNA, analyze your WATNA well before the mediation. Also be prepared to challenge the opposing party's apparent perceived WATNA.

### *Focus on nonmonetary factors.*

Expect that the mediator will encourage the parties to bridge that final gap by emphasizing the nonmonetary as well as monetary benefits of settlement. Do the parties have an interest in preserving their business relationship for their mutual advantage? If so, a handshake and signed settlement agreement are far preferable to months of potentially acrimonious litigation. Do the parties have an interest in preserving the confidentiality of the subject matter of their dispute? If so, that confidentiality is lost in litigation.

Do the principals want to suffer the disruption, inconvenience, and anxiety of litigation, with its uncertain result, over many months, at great expense? Or would they rather enjoy the benefits of immediate finality so they can devote their energies to running their businesses?

### Change the players.

The negotiators may have become so entrenched in their respective positions that they are unwilling or just too stubborn to be open-minded about settlement alternatives. One way to break through impasse is to change the players. Variations include principals meeting without lawyers; lawyers meeting without principals; experts meeting with each other; and one person meeting with the opposing team. Remember, though, that even though a mediation is confidential, the information disclosed and admissions made, other than settlement positions, can be used in legal proceedings unless the parties otherwise stipulate.

### Change the venue.

Typically, the mediator engages in shuttle diplomacy between conference rooms in a formal setting. In that venue, it can be easier to take "hard" positions than in a more relaxed setting. Consider suggesting that the decision-makers meet elsewhere, possibly over a meal or drinks, to enhance the likelihood of greater flexibility in positions. Of course, you can change the players *and* the venue simultaneously.

### Ask: What if?

Be prepared for the mediator to ask both parties: "If I can get the opposing party to alter its settlement position by $X, how much are you willing to alter your position?" By this process, a mediator attempts to narrow the gap to the point that any remaining dispute is negligible. Be sure to obtain your client's consent before answering this and any other settlement position questions. This may be an opportune moment to highlight for your client all the risks and costs of litigating to the bitter end—your WATNA—as well as the nonmonetary factors that militate toward settlement.

### Cut to the chase.

Be prepared for the mediator to ask: "How far are you willing to go to settle this case?" Make sure you have your client's authority to answer this question, which you should have discussed before the mediation, although the answer may change during the course of the mediation.

The mediator will ask the same question to the opposing party to determine whether the parties are close enough to make it worthwhile to attempt to bridge the final gap.

## Accept the "double-blind" proposal.

If both parties agree, the mediator presents to each party a "double-blind" proposal, by which the mediator confidentially presents the same final number to each side to accept or reject. Be prepared to give your final offer or demand.

## Take a break.

If the mediation has developed momentum toward resolution, a break can slow down that momentum. However, once you reach impasse, a break can provide a welcome respite for everyone involved, during which everyone can re-evaluate their positions. Refreshed after the break, the parties or the mediator may come up with a new approach, some creative way to break through impasse.

## Resume another day.

This is the last resort, when all else has failed. It is possible that one party needs more information before completing the mediation process, or that one party wants to consult with someone as a result of the mediation process thus far. Or it is possible that the parties need a "cooling off" period before resuming.

Renewed mediation can be by telephone, another meeting, or by any other exchange of information. Whatever process the mediator and parties adopt, imposing a deadline at some point is advisable, to bring things—finally—to a head, to either settle or try the case. Of course, if mediation fails, arbitration is an option that should be considered, especially if the parties require confidentiality.

These impasse-breakers are not mutually exclusive, nor are they the only ways to break through impasse. Use whatever combination of strategies that may be effective in breaking through impasse.

## 6. WHAT TO DO IF THE MEDIATION IS SUCCESSFUL

If you are successful in the mediation, get the settlement terms in writing before the mediation session is over, keeping in mind the tax consequences of a settlement, as discussed in chapter 4, section 10. Unless representatives of each party with binding authority sign on the dotted line before everyone leaves for the day, each party has the opportunity to reconsider the terms of an agreement so painstakingly worked out. Finality is key here. Consider having a computer accessible to draft the terms of the final settlement agreement so it can be printed and signed on the spot. You may even want to draft the boilerplate provisions of a settlement agreement and have it on your computer before you begin the mediation session. Unless you follow this advice, you risk misunderstandings about the settlement terms and "buyer's remorse."

If the settlement agreement is complex and the best you can do before leaving the mediation is to draft a term sheet, include a provision that the mediator's ruling on the settlement terms is final, and make sure both principals, and their attorneys, sign it. Your goal is finality.

### 7. What to do if the mediation is not successful

If you are not successful in breaking the impasse, do not despair. Use the mediation as a basis for later negotiations. It may take time for the matters discussed in the mediation to sink in. Consider transforming the process to baseball arbitration, by which each party submits to an arbitrator (without disclosing it to the other side) a number that is acceptable. The arbitrator then picks one of those two numbers—conclusive and binding on the parties. This process forces each party to be reasonable in submitting a final number to the arbitrator. Consider also "bounded" or "high-low" arbitration. The parties agree that the defendant will pay, within an agreed range, an amount to be determined by the arbitrator. The person who served as the mediator can serve as the arbitrator for these types of resolutions or for straight arbitration, or you can select someone else to arbitrate, depending on whether, during the course of mediation, you or your client revealed to the mediator something detrimental to your client's position that may not come out in an arbitration. Make sure your client understands that, unlike mediation, arbitration is final and binding, subject to very limited exceptions. See chapter 7 for more about arbitration.

## 8. A FEW WORDS FROM ABRAHAM LINCOLN

If you apply these strategies, you will enhance the likelihood that your mediation will be successful and your client satisfied (although not delighted—in a successful mediation, no party is delighted) so that you will then be able to turn your attention to all the other cases you should consider mediating. And remember—the more cases you mediate, the better you will be at it, having learned from experience.

Whether or not you are successful in the mediation of a particular case, heed the advice of Abraham Lincoln: "Discourage litigation. Persuade your neighbors to compromise whenever you can. Point out to them how the nominal winner is often a real loser: in fees, expenses and waste of time. As a peacemaker, the lawyer has a superior opportunity. . . . There will still be business enough."

❖❖❖❖
### PRACTICE CHECKLIST

- Determine whether your client has a contractual obligation to mediate before commencing litigation.
- Weigh the advantages and disadvantages of mediation before advising a client whether to mediate; discuss them with your client.
- Explain to your client that offering to mediate is not a sign of weakness.
- Mediate only after you know the facts and law of your case, but before the parties have spent so much on legal fees and their positions are so entrenched that they conclude it would be a waste of time and money to mediate.
- Unless the parties have a preexisting mediation contract, draft one.
- In deciding on a mediator, determine whether you want a facilitative or evaluative mediator, or a mediator who combines both approaches.
- Select a mediator in whom all parties have confidence.
- Prepare for mediation:
  - _____ Know your BATNA and your WATNA.
  - _____ Decide on your opening demand or offer.
  - _____ Get authority from your client regarding your settlement position.
  - _____ Discuss with your client nonmonetary as well as monetary resolution components.
  - _____ Consider principles all parties can agree upon.

(continued)

_____ Determine whether the dispute results from a breakdown in a relationship; if so, determine the best way to deal with it.
_____ Prepare demonstrative exhibits for the mediation, as appropriate.
_____ Bring to the mediation all documents you may need.
_____ Bring to the mediation someone with authority to settle, but no one you do not need.
_____ Prepare your opening statement.
- Use effective strategies during the mediation.
  _____ Deliver an effective opening statement.
  _____ Be prepared for the mediator's shuttle diplomacy, including the mediator's taking a devil's advocate position with you.
  _____ As you make each demand or offer during the mediation process, get your client's prior authority, be aware of how the opposing party will interpret it, and be very careful in the words you use in transmitting each demand or offer.
  _____ As you approach the limit of your authority, decrease each increment in the amount of your offer.
  _____ Keep in mind creative resolutions.
  _____ Be very clear with the mediator what information you authorize the mediator to share with your opponent.
- Use strategies to break through impasse.
  _____ Challenge perceived BATNA.
  _____ Challenge perceived WATNA.
  _____ Focus on nonmonetary factors.
  _____ Change the players.
  _____ Change the venue.
  _____ Ask: What if?
  _____ Cut to the chase.
  _____ Accept the "double-blind" proposal.
  _____ Take a break.
  _____ Resume another day.
- If your mediation is successful, before leaving the mediation session, get a signed agreement.
- If the mediation is not successful, consider other dispute resolution mechanisms.
- Learn from each mediation so you will be more adept in your next mediation.

# CHAPTER SEVEN
# ARBITRATING COMMERCIAL DISPUTES

Commercial disputes often arise out of claims of breach of a written agreement that includes an arbitration clause. By such a clause, the parties agree in advance that if a dispute arises regarding performance of that agreement, they will arbitrate rather than litigate it. Accordingly, when taking on a new matter, determine whether the parties have agreed to arbitration, and proceed accordingly.

Not all arbitration clauses are alike, and the exact wording is crucial in determining the scope of and procedures for arbitration. This chapter discusses the advantages and disadvantages of arbitration, how to review an arbitration clause, the issue of arbitrability, waiver of the right to arbitrate, how to select an arbitrator, strategies for the arbitration process, and post-arbitration award procedures.

This discussion assumes that the Commercial Arbitration Rules of the American Arbitration Association (AAA) apply (referred to as R-___), because most commercial contracts with arbitration clauses so provide. The rules in effect when filing the demand for arbitration govern. R-1(a). Go to adr.org for the most recent version. Note that these rules provide that, by written agreement, the parties can vary them. R-1(a). The

AAA has separate rules for disputes involving claims of at least $500,000, employment claims, construction claims, securities claims, consumer claims, and patent claims. In reviewing the arbitration clause in connection with any dispute, be sure to take note of which arbitration rules apply.

Be aware that parties can agree in writing to arbitrate a dispute *even after* a dispute arises, without any pre-existing arbitration contract clause. So don't rule out the possibility of arbitration in that circumstance. If you can reach agreement with opposing counsel, sometimes it *is* possible to change venue to an entirely different legal system.

If you draft an arbitration agreement, ask yourself these questions:

1. Unrestricted submission (arbitrator renders an award on all disputes) or limited submission of disputes to arbitration?
2. Any conditions precedent to arbitration, such as non-binding negotiation or mediation?
3. Panel of one or three arbitrators?
4. Any specific qualifications of the arbitrators required?
5. What rules govern the arbitration process, AAA rules or otherwise?

*"We would like to request a change of venue to an entirely different legal system."*

6. If AAA rules apply, which ones—commercial, construction, employment, securities, consumer, or patent?
7. Where will the arbitration take place?
8. What law controls the arbitrator's award?
9. What preliminary relief can the arbitrator award?
10. What limits are imposed on pre-arbitration discovery?
11. What limits are imposed on what the arbitrator can award?
12. Do you want a provision for recovery of attorney's fees?
13. What will be the form of the arbitrator's award?
14. What is the agreement about confidentiality of the arbitration process?
15. What other ways can you customize the arbitration clause to fit your client's needs?

For sample provisions dealing with all these issues, read the AAA publication, *Drafting Dispute Resolution Clauses: A Practical Guide*, available at no charge at adr.org.

## 1. Advantages and disadvantages of arbitration

The principal advantages of arbitration over litigation, when conducted properly, is that arbitration is less expensive, more efficient, and therefore a more cost-effective mechanism for resolving commercial disputes; it is private, unlike the public forum of litigation (but see the discussion of confidentiality issues in section 14 of this chapter); the arbitration procedures and hearings are less formal than in litigation; and you have the opportunity to choose the arbitrator, unlike the chance appointment of a judge in litigation. Final and binding arbitration awards are enforceable in court.

You can take advantage of the flexibility available in arbitration, unconstrained by state and federal court rules. Your creativity is limited only by the authority of the arbitrator, applicable arbitration rules, and ethics rules.

Be aware, though, that unless the arbitrator controls the pre-hearing procedures (for example, by limiting pre-hearing discovery) and reins in the attorneys for both parties, the cost effectiveness and efficiency of arbitration are diminished. The risk is that, without such controls, arbitration will look and feel too much like litigation. Thus, selection of the right arbitrator is crucial for the success of the arbitration process, as discussed in section 5 of this chapter.

Arbitration also has disadvantages. Discovery is limited in arbitration, compared with litigation. The rules of evidence do not apply, and thus the scope of what you can get into evidence at the arbitration hearing depends on the broad discretion of the arbitrator. The award of the arbitrator is very difficult to vacate, as discussed in section 15 of this chapter. Unless you have strong grounds to vacate an arbitrator's award, you have no effective appeal, unlike your right to appeal from a trial judge's decision. You cannot establish a precedent by the arbitrator's award, as you can in litigation.

As a practical matter, if the parties have a pre-dispute arbitration clause, you have no choice about arbitrating a dispute that is arbitrable, unless both parties waive that right. However, if the parties discuss the possibility of a post-dispute arbitration agreement, consider all the advantages and disadvantages of arbitration vis-à-vis litigation before deciding which is better for your client.

## 2. How to review an arbitration clause

You confront several issues when dealing with arbitration clauses. Unless you deal with them up front, you will create needless issues.

*Conditions precedent to arbitration.* Some arbitration clauses provide that, before arbitrating any dispute, the parties must mediate it, on terms and conditions set forth in their written agreement. Be sure to comply with those conditions precedent before initiating arbitration proceedings. Pre-arbitration mediation may resolve the dispute and, even if it does not, you will avoid a successful motion to vacate your arbitration award by complying with such contractual requirements.

*Scope of the arbitrator's authority.* The authority of the arbitrator is limited to what the parties provide in their arbitration clause, and the specific disputes submitted to the arbitrator for resolution. The precise wording of an arbitration clause can make quite a difference. An unrestricted submission provides that all future disputes are resolved by arbitration. Here is a typical unrestricted submission:

> Any controversy or claim arising out of or relating to this contract, or the breach thereof, shall be settled by arbitration administered by the American Arbitration Association in accordance with its Com-

mercial Arbitration Rules, and judgment on the award rendered by the arbitrator(s) may be entered in any court having jurisdiction thereof.

On the other hand, a restricted submission limits the authority of the arbitrator to only certain issues. Here is an example of a restricted submission:

> Any controversy between the parties to this Agreement involving the construction or application of any of the terms, covenants, or conditions of this Agreement shall be settled by arbitration administered by the American Arbitration Association in accordance with its Commercial Arbitration Rules. The arbitrator's sole authority shall be to interpret or apply the provisions of this Agreement.

This restricted submission does not, for example, empower the arbitrator to rule on the issue of arbitrability.

*Unique arbitration clause*: Since the parties, by contract, can vary AAA rules, they may insert unique clauses regarding the method of selecting the arbitrators, required qualifications for the arbitrators, location of the arbitration, the law governing the arbitration, the preliminary relief a party may seek in arbitration (e.g., injunctive relief, or mandatory placement of funds in escrow), pre-arbitration hearing discovery procedures, time limits, remedies available to the arbitrators, and award of attorney's fees. Be sure to comply with the specific provisions of the arbitration clause applicable in the dispute you are handling.

A final word about arbitration clauses: Certainly, the parties to an agreement containing an arbitration clause are bound by its terms. But who else may be bound? Depending on the circumstances, non-signatories may be bound, including corporate parents, corporate subsidiaries, third-party beneficiaries, assignees, and successors.

## 3. How to deal with the issue of arbitrability

Arbitrability pertains to the authority of the arbitrator to act. Since parties are required to arbitrate only those issues they have agreed in writing to arbitrate, an issue sometimes arises whether a particular dispute is subject to arbitration. This is an issue of contract construction, based on the language in the arbitration clause.

A challenging question arises in connection with this analysis: Does the court or the arbitrator determine the issue of arbitrability? You must research case law in your jurisdiction for the answer. Keep in mind that there is no publication of arbitration awards, so you must rely on case law in dealing with this issue, typically in decisions ruling on motions to confirm and vacate arbitration awards, and appeals therefrom.

Rule 7(a) provides: "The arbitrator shall have the power to rule on his or her own jurisdiction, including any objections with respect to the existence, scope or validity of the arbitration agreement." Some judges rely on this AAA rule in holding that the arbitrator, not the court, determines arbitrability issues.

Keep in mind that the authority of the arbitrator to act is a function of two things: (1) the scope of the arbitration clause, which vests authority in the arbitrator, and (2) the scope of the submission to the arbitrator of the issues for resolution by arbitration. If an arbitrator makes an award beyond the scope of either, that award is subject to a successful motion to vacate it.

## 4. How to avoid inadvertent waiver of the right to arbitrate

The right to arbitrate, as with other contract rights, is waivable. Even if the parties have agreed to a pre-dispute arbitration clause, they can intentionally waive that right by one party commencing litigation and the other party intentionally not invoking the right to arbitrate.

More often, the issue of waiver of the right to arbitrate arises in the context of inadvertent waiver. Such waiver occurs in the following circumstances:

- A party acts in a way inconsistent with the right to arbitrate.
- Litigation has proceeded substantially before a party asserts the right to arbitrate. Some judges hold that a party's merely commencing litigation, knowing of an applicable arbitration clause, gives rise to a rebuttable presumption of waiver of the right to arbitrate.
- A defendant asserts a counterclaim without moving for a stay of litigation to proceed with arbitration.
- A party takes advantage of discovery available in litigation, of a nature not available in arbitration.
- The delay in seeking arbitration has negatively impacted, misled, or otherwise prejudiced the opposing party.

If your client has signed an agreement with an arbitration clause, and the opposing party commences a court action, ask whether you are better off in court or in arbitration. You can intentionally waive the right to arbitrate, or you can file a motion to stay the legal proceedings and seek to compel arbitration. Make sure your arbitration clause covers the dispute in question before seeking to compel arbitration.

## 5. How to select an arbitrator

The selection of the right arbitrator is crucial. The AAA will send you a list of proposed arbitrators, with their résumés. You can choose among them or you can agree with opposing counsel that the arbitrator will be someone not on that list—even someone who is not certified by the AAA. R-11(a) and R-12. The AAA sends each party the same list of 10 potential arbitrators. If all parties agree on an arbitrator from that list, you have your arbitrator, if he or she takes on the assignment. If you do not agree, each party crosses off the name of any arbitrator who is not acceptable, and ranks the others. The AAA case manager then makes the best match. If none, the AAA case manager appoints an arbitrator not on either list, without any input from the parties.

Some arbitration clauses provide for a three-arbitrator panel, rather than just one arbitrator. Be aware that, on average, the cost of a three-arbitrator panel is more than *five times* the cost of one arbitrator, and the time to an award is, on average, *six months longer* than with one arbitrator. So, even if the arbitration clause provides for three arbitrators, consider agreeing on one.

Before selecting an arbitrator, make sure you learn everything you need to know about each candidate. You can do a web search, and ask colleagues what they know about each candidate—and you can do more. Consider submitting written questions to potential arbitrators, or calling them to learn about their arbitration practices, within two constraints: First, you cannot have any ex parte communications with potential arbitrators. Arbitrators cannot have ex parte communications with counsel, without the consent of all counsel. See R-18, which includes an exception for a candidate for direct appointment. Second, you cannot ask any questions about the specific dispute to be arbitrated. You must, however, disclose to the proposed arbitrator the names of everyone and every entity involved in the arbitration, including all principals of entities and all witnesses, to avoid disqualification of the arbitrator. See R-16 and R-17.

## 6. How to Commence an Arbitration Proceeding

The AAA has a self-explanatory one-page form you can file electronically, with a copy of the arbitration agreement. The amount of the administrative fee payable to the AAA is based on the amount of your claim. To institute proceedings, you must send a copy of that AAA form with your claim, and file in an AAA office two copies thereof with two copies of the arbitration provisions of the subject contract. R-4(a). No formal service of process is required.

It is advisable, but not required, to submit to the AAA and send to the opposing party a detailed statement of your claim when you initiate the arbitration proceedings. Your statement of claim can look much like a complaint, except without any jurisdictional allegations, but greater informality is acceptable. See chapter 4, section 3, on drafting complaints.

*Caveat*: Even if the agreement between the parties that includes an arbitration clause does not provide for the recovery of legal fees, if all parties to the arbitration seek recovery of legal fees in their submissions to the AAA, then the arbitrator is authorized to award legal fees. See R-43(d).

The parties to an arbitration are referred to as claimant and respondent, rather than plaintiff and defendant. The respondent has 15 days from receipt of the arbitration claim to file an answer. See R-4(b). If respondent does not file an answer, the claimant's allegations are deemed denied. Rule R-4(c). The same procedure applies to counterclaims. R-4(b).

## 7. How to Deal with Statute of Limitations Issues

If the statute of limitations is about to run on your claims, which are within the ambit of an arbitration agreement, whether you need to concern yourself with statutes of limitations raises complex issues. In some jurisdictions, initiation of arbitration proceedings is not "commencement of an action" within applicable statutes of limitations, and thus arbitration claims are not time-barred by such statutes. If so, you may not have any statute of limitations issues, although you may have laches issues.

To determine the best course of action, you must analyze case law, rules of practice, and statutes in your jurisdiction. You don't want to be hit with a motion to dismiss well into the arbitration process, based on your opponent's contention that your claims are all now time-barred by operation of the statute of limitations, because you did not file a timely court action.

If, in your jurisdiction, the statute of limitations may apply even though the parties agreed to arbitrate their disputes, consider filing a court action timely, then moving to stay it to proceed with arbitration, unless doing so constitutes an arbitration waiver.

## 8. How to prepare for the preliminary hearing

The preliminary hearing, typically by telephone, is procedural. It is the opportunity for the arbitrator to deal with prehearing procedures, scope of discovery, deadlines, hearing dates, and the form of the award. Before the preliminary hearing, discuss with opposing counsel all the issues you can expect will be raised at the preliminary hearing, which is a case management conference, analogous to a Rule 26(f) conference in federal court. For the scope of the preliminary hearing, see R-20.

Be prepared to answer these questions: Have counsel informed the arbitrator of all names necessary for a conflicts check? What agreement, if any, have the parties reached about pre-hearing discovery, including depositions? See R-21. What have the parties agreed to about e-discovery? Do the parties anticipate a bifurcated hearing and, if so, on what basis? See R-30(b). Does the respondent expect to file a motion to dismiss? Does either party expect to seek an interim award? See R-34. In a complex matter, what are the issues the parties need the arbitrator to decide? What about scheduling? Will the parties file pre-hearing briefs? Does either party want a stenographer at the hearing? See R-26.

Do not be surprised if the arbitrator limits pre-hearing discovery, including restricting the number of depositions each side can take, despite counsel's agreement to the contrary. In doing so, arbitrators seek to avoid arbitration discovery that looks just like pretrial discovery in litigation, while achieving an efficient and cost-effective resolution of your client's dispute. See R-21.

It is advisable to agree at this preliminary hearing on the dates for the arbitration hearing. Once you lock those days in as immutable, you can discuss other deadlines, such as the dates for the respondent to file the answering statement, R-4(b), termination of discovery, filing of pre-arbitration motions, pre-arbitration briefs, stipulations of fact, witness lists, and proposed exhibits.

Finally, at this conference, confirm the form of the award: bare (one sentence stating who wins and what relief is granted, if any); reasoned (like a judge's memorandum of decision); and reasoned with findings of fact and conclusions of law. A bare award is more difficult to vacate, because it does not include the arbitrator's reasoning, but it is less satisfying for the clients.

## 9. How to Prepare for the Arbitration Hearing

Once you have completed your pre-arbitration discovery, including the required pre-hearing exchange of all exhibits, see R-21(b), and you have prepared your witnesses for the hearing, what else should you do before the hearing starts?

Agree, to the extent possible, on which facts are not disputed, so you can file a stipulation of facts, and which exhibits can be entered into the record by stipulation. At least five days before the hearing, you must exchange with opposing counsel copies of all exhibits you intend to submit at the hearing. See R-21(b). Prepare a chronology to give the arbitrator. Arrange for the experts to exchange reports, and consider implementing procedures to expedite the hearing, discussed below. See R-30 for the flexibility the arbitrator has in the conduct of the hearing.

Assuming you and opposing counsel agree to file pre-hearing briefs, draft yours to include the key facts, referencing proposed exhibits, a statement of issues presented, and an argument supporting your position. It should be focused and cogent. See chapter 4, section 1, for drafting tips.

## 10. How to Determine What Is Admissible at the Arbitration Hearing

Since no court rules of evidence apply, the arbitrator has broad discretion in deciding what is admissible at the hearing. R-31. Because state statutes typically provide that an arbitration award can be vacated for an arbitrator's refusing to hear evidence pertinent and material to the controversy or for taking any other action by which the rights of any party have been prejudiced, and because the parties have agreed, by arbitrating rather than litigating, that the constraints of court evidentiary rules do not apply, arbitrators are generally very liberal in what is admissible at the hearing. Assume that everything will come into the record, unless it is clearly not pertinent or material, or obviously cumulative. Prepare yourself—and your witnesses—accordingly. If possible, learn in advance your arbitrator's preferences in this regard.

Despite this liberality in admissibility, arbitrators typically do look to the rules of evidence for guidance, so be prepared to make an evidentiary argument based on those rules, especially when complex evidentiary issues may arise.

## 11. How to make your presentation at the arbitration hearing more persuasive

Have all your witnesses available when needed; be prepared for direct and cross of witnesses in this setting, in which the rules of evidence do not apply, R-31(a); know your exhibits and opposing counsel's exhibits; prepare an exhibit book for the arbitrator with stipulated exhibits; and know the basis to get each contested exhibit into the record, even though technically unconstrained by the rules of evidence.

Consider less traditional ways to make the arbitrator's job easier. Give the arbitrator a list of the dramatis personae, including a brief description of the role each person plays in the story that will unfold during the arbitration hearing. Prepare a bullet-point sheet to give to the arbitrator as you put on each witness, to give the arbitrator a road map of where you are going with each witness, and give the arbitrator a chronology of key events. If you have many witnesses, consider providing the arbitrator with a photo of each, to make the recall of your witnesses' testimony more vivid.

Consider agreeing with opposing counsel that the direct examination of witnesses will be by affidavit, in which event witnesses answer questions only on cross (a time-saver, but a possible strategic disadvantage). You might also reach an agreement that opposing experts testify consecutively, each being given the opportunity to ask questions of the other, and that the sequence of testimony be by subject so that all witnesses testifying on a particular subject do so the same day, even if some of those witnesses also testify another day.

In general, follow all the advice in chapter 9 and 10, to the extent applicable to arbitrations.

## 12. What to submit to the arbitrator after the hearing

You should file a post-hearing brief, unless the arbitrator makes explicit that he or she will not accept one. In addition, consider submitting copies of all cases, statutes, and other authorities on which you rely; arbitration hearing transcripts, highlighting key testimony (if you have arranged for a stenographer, as provided in R-26); an index of hearing exhibits; highlighted key exhibits; a list of all claims and the relief you seek as to each; and even a proposed award. Consider providing all this to the arbitrator in a thumb drive or by other electronic means. In an electronic brief, you can hyperlink exhibits and copies of cases, highlighting key passages.

Put yourself in the shoes of the arbitrator, and ask yourself: What would make it easier for the arbitrator to review the record, and your contentions, to be persuaded in your client's favor? Keep in mind that, unlike in mediation, you must submit to opposing counsel everything you submit to the arbitrator.

## 13. WHAT REMEDIES YOU CAN SEEK IN ARBITRATION

Depending on the authority vested in the arbitrator in the arbitration agreement, and the claims submitted to the arbitrator for resolution, you can seek any remedy a judge is empowered to order, and additional remedies, R-34 and R-43, although an arbitrator cannot hold a party in contempt. As noted above, an arbitrator can award legal fees if all parties request such an award, even if not explicitly provided for in their arbitration agreement. R-43(d). In contrast, a judge cannot award legal fees on the merits (as opposed to legal fees as a sanction) unless authorized by statute, contract, or in connection with recovery for an intentional tort, such as fraud.

Arbitrators can award more than just monetary damages, and can award equitable and other forms of relief, including specific performance, injunctive relief, imposition of a constructive trust, and award of consequential damages, liquidated damages, and punitive damages, as well as attorney's fees, if within their authority. You have an opportunity to be creative in your requested relief. See R-43.

You can also seek interim relief in arbitration, before the arbitration hearing takes place, as provided in R-34, which is broadly worded to include whatever interim measures the arbitrator deems necessary, including injunctive relief and measures for the protection or conservation of property and disposition of perishable goods. Check statutes in your jurisdiction to determine what court relief is available in aid of the arbitration process, including, for example, motions to compel a party to participate in arbitration, and securing respondent's assets before an arbitration award is made, so you can recover if you are successful in the arbitration.

## 14. HOW TO PROTECT THE CONFIDENTIALITY OF ARBITRATION

One advantage of arbitration is that it is confidential—right? Even though the ethical rules governing arbitrators require that *arbitrators* keep confidential all matters relating to the arbitration proceedings and decisions, R-23 and THE CODE OF ETHICS FOR ARBITRATORS IN COMMERCIAL DISPUTES Canon VI(B), no rule of the AAA requires that the *parties* maintain such confidentiality. If you want to preserve confidentiality, enter into a confidentiality agreement at the outset, unless already provided for in the arbitration agreement.

## 15. WHAT TO DO AFTER THE ARBITRATOR RENDERS AN AWARD

The arbitrator has 30 days from the close of the hearing to render an award, unless otherwise agreed by the parties or specified by law. R-41. The arbitrator may decide not to close the hearing even after the close of evidence, especially if the parties submit post-evidence briefs and make oral arguments after filing them. If the parties have waived the hearing, the 30-day period runs from the date of the AAA's transmittal of the final statements and proofs to the arbitrator.

As soon as you receive the award, read it carefully. Determine whether the arbitrator ruled on all the issues presented, and whether the form of the award is as agreed (bare, reasoned, or reasoned with findings of fact and conclusions of law). If the award is unacceptable for any of those reasons, call the case manager and deal with it promptly. If the arbitrator has made a clerical, typographical, or computational error in the award that makes a difference, you have 20 days after transmittal of the award to request the arbitrator, through the AAA and with notice to the other party, to make the necessary corrections. R-46. Also check applicable state statutes to determine your deadline to move in court to modify or correct an award, based on such defects as an evident material miscalculation of figures or some other evident mistake; an award on a matter not submitted to the arbitrator; or an award imperfect in matter of form not affecting the merits of the controversy.

Discuss the award with your client. If you are satisfied with the award, promptly file a motion in court to confirm it. If you have a basis to vacate the award, promptly file a motion in court to vacate it. Be aware of state statutory deadlines to file motions to confirm and vacate arbitration awards, and comply with them. Typical statutory bases to vacate an arbitration award are

- if the award has been procured by corruption, fraud, or undue means
- if there has been evident partiality or corruption on the part of any arbitrator
- if the arbitrator has been guilty of misconduct in refusing to postpone the hearing upon sufficient cause shown or in refusing to hear evidence pertinent and material to the controversy or of any other action by which the rights of any party have been prejudiced
- if the arbitrators have exceeded their powers or so imperfectly executed them that a mutual, final, and definite award upon the subject matter submitted was not made

In addition, you should research the case law in your jurisdiction for common law in addition to statutory bases to vacate an arbitration award. Courts have vacated arbitration awards on common law grounds if the award

- is arbitrary and capricious, where the award cannot be inferred from the facts of the case
- fails to draw its essence from the underlying contract
- is contrary to an explicit, well-defined, and dominant public policy
- is in manifest disregard of applicable law, upon a showing that the arbitrator was aware of a controlling and well-defined legal principle but did not follow it when rendering the award

If an arbitration award is confirmed, and confirmance is upheld on appeal, the award, as confirmed, has the same force and effect in all respects as a judgment or decree in a civil action and may be enforced as such. If the award is vacated, and vacatur is upheld on appeal, the award is a nullity.

## 16. When the Federal Arbitration Act applies

Generally, the Federal Arbitration Act (FAA), codified as 9 U.S.C. §§ 1–16 applies where the transaction subject to an arbitration clause involves interstate commerce, based on the Commerce Clause of the U.S. Constitution, Article 1, Section 8, Clause 3. The FAA is quite short.

The FAA's most salient provisions pertain to the validity, irrevocability, and enforcement of arbitration agreements; stay of court proceedings where the parties have agreed in writing to arbitrate the subject dispute; authority of federal courts to compel arbitration when warranted; procedure for appointment of arbitrators if the parties have not agreed on a method for doing so; authority of arbitrators to summon witnesses to appear before them, with or without documents; confirmation, vacatur, modification, and correction of arbitration awards; and appealability of court orders pertaining to arbitrations.

### ❖❖❖❖ PRACTICE CHECKLIST

- At the inception of a new matter involving a written agreement, determine whether your client has agreed to arbitrate disputes.
- Be aware that, even after a dispute arises and the parties have no pre-dispute arbitration agreement, they can agree to arbitrate their dispute.
- Know the advantages and disadvantages of arbitration, and advise your client accordingly.
- Review the arbitration clause, focusing on what arbitration rules apply, conditions precedent to arbitration, scope of the arbitrator's authority, and unique provisions regarding what is arbitrable and agreed arbitration procedures.
- Know the law in your jurisdiction on the issue of arbitrability.
- Unless your client authorizes you to waive the right to arbitrate, do not inadvertently waive that right by proceeding in a way inconsistent with arbitration, as by prosecuting or defending claims in litigation.
- Know the procedure under the applicable arbitration rules for selecting arbitrators.
- Learn as much as you can about potential arbitrators before making your selection.

(continued)

- When you commence an arbitration proceeding, include a detailed statement of facts in your statement of claim.
- If the statute of limitations may run soon after you take on a new matter where the parties have a pre-dispute arbitration agreement, bring a legal action, and then move to stay that action to arbitrate the same claim if required in your jurisdiction to avoid the running of the statute of limitations.
- Prepare for the preliminary hearing by discussing with opposing counsel all the issues you should expect will be raised at that hearing, which is analogous to a Rule 26(f) conference in federal court.
- Prepare for the arbitration hearing by completing your factual and legal investigation, stipulating to facts and exhibits, preparing a chronology, and discussing with opposing counsel creative ways to expedite the arbitration hearing.
- Even though the evidentiary rules do not apply in arbitration, be prepared to argue the evidentiary basis for getting testimony and documents in the record.
- Prepare for the arbitration hearing as you would for trial, but keep in mind your greater flexibility in arbitration, enabling you to provide the arbitrator (copying opposing counsel) with such persuasive aids as bullet-point sheets regarding the testimony of each witness, a chronology, and demonstrative exhibits.
- In your post-hearing brief, consider including, in an appendix, copies of the authorities on which you rely, transcript excerpts, an index of exhibits, and anything else that may make the arbitrator more likely to rule in your client's favor.
- Be aware of the nonmonetary as well as monetary relief available in arbitration, and seek all relief appropriate in your matter.
- Protect the confidentiality of arbitration by entering into a confidentiality agreement.
- When appropriate, file a motion in court to modify or correct an award within the time allowed by statute.
- If the arbitrator rules in your favor, file a motion in court to confirm the award within the time allowed by statute so that the award becomes a court order.
- If the arbitrator rules against you, determine whether you have a good-faith basis to file a motion in court to vacate the award; if so, file it within the time allowed by statute.
- Be aware that the FAA applies in certain matters, and comply with its provisions when it does apply.

CHAPTER EIGHT

# MAKING ORAL PRESENTATIONS IN COURT

This chapter discusses your oral presentations to the court in arguing pretrial motions and making opening statements, closing arguments, and appellate court arguments. If you prepare properly, these oral presentations can provide tremendous professional satisfaction—your only opportunity on the record to engage in a back-and-forth colloquy with a judge, and your only opportunity to address the jurors directly.

Any oral argument you prepare must be cogent. Paring your argument down to its essence is hard work. As Mark Twain observed: "If you want me to give you a two-hour presentation, I am ready today. If you want only a five-minute speech, it will take me two weeks to prepare."

You must also deal with the stress of making oral presentations. Jerry Seinfeld quipped: "According to most studies, people's number one fear is public speaking. Number two is death. Death is number two. Does that seem right? That means to the average person, if you have to go to a funeral, you're better off in the casket than doing the eulogy."

## 1. How to prepare for argument of pretrial motions

Trial court judges' approaches to oral argument vary widely. At one end of the spectrum is a judge who asks very few questions; at the other end of the spectrum is a judge who peppers you with probing questions as soon as you start your presentation, referred to as a "hot bench." Discuss with colleagues what you need to know about your judge's approach to oral argument of pretrial motions, and find out applicable chambers practices regarding oral argument in federal court, available online. Call the judge's law clerk to find out how much time you will have for oral argument, if you don't know from the notice.

By the time you prepare for oral argument, the motion has been fully briefed. Assemble all the briefs on the issue, applicable pleadings, exhibits, key cases, statutes and other authorities, and anything else related to the motion. Find a time and place where you will not be disturbed and focus on how to present the most effective oral argument. You know that you do not want merely to read or paraphrase your memorandum, which the judge has presumably already read—although some judges are more diligent than others. But what *should* you do?

Ask yourself: What is the procedural posture of this case? What standard applies to the ruling on this motion? (For example, the standard for ruling on a Rule 12 motion to dismiss is different from the standard for ruling on a Rule 56 motion for summary judgment.) What makes a difference in this judge's ruling on this motion? List the key points that you consider most persuasive to support your position. Then, play devil's advocate, and list the key points most persuasive to support your opponent's position. Determine what facts and legal authorities provide the most persuasive authority to support each position. Know the facts, analysis, rationale, and holdings of each case that is of particular significance, especially cases you rely on as a close precedent to your case.

Based on the psychological theory of primacy (what you present first has greater impact than what you present in the middle), you want to argue your strongest points first. What are your strongest points? How can you present them in a way that each follows inexorably to the conclusion you want the judge to reach? What is the first thing you should say, after introducing yourself to the court? If you can encapsulate your message into one initial sentence, do so.

If you are arguing in favor of your own motion (rather than opposing other counsel's motion), in structuring your oral argument, first make the key points—with supporting authority—that support your position. Second, rebut opposing counsel's position. Third, explain why, considering all the factors, you win.

If you are opposing a motion, start by exposing the biggest weaknesses in opposing counsel's argument. Then launch into your argument, distinguish the authorities opposing counsel relies on, and finish by summarizing why the judge should deny the motion.

What should you plan to bring to the podium? At a minimum, have ready access to the memoranda filed by both sides, copies of key cases and other applicable authorities, and other documents, such as transcript excerpts, as appropriate. You don't want to be in the middle of oral argument without immediate access to the documents you may need. Tab them as necessary to locate the key pages.

What about notes for oral argument? By the process described above, you will distill your argument down to its essence. At oral argument, have notes to remind you of the main points you want to make, but do not write down every word you plan to say. A sentence or phrase outline should be sufficient. You want to make eye contact with the judge as much as possible, to convey your message convincingly and to watch the judge's reaction to what you are saying. If the judge appears to be nodding in approval, emphasize the point; if the judge is scowling, figure out a way to get the judge to come around to your point of view. If the judge is reading while you are arguing, ask, respectfully, if the judge wants you to wait.

How do you achieve the ability to argue with very few notes in front of you? Write out your entire oral argument, if you find it useful to do so. Distill it down to a sentence outline, or even a phrase outline, preferably on one page. Stand in front of a mirror. Make your argument. Be aware of how much you look in the mirror and how much you look down. Keep practicing until you look down very little. While you're at it, listen to your voice. Is it strong and convincing? Are you talking too fast? Are you too meek or too strident?

If the motion is sufficiently significant, ask your colleagues to be a hot bench for a dry run of your argument. They should know the file, and should pepper you with questions. You can then workshop how you can improve your answers.

Consider bringing to court extra copies of key documents so that, if the judge does not have them accessible, you can, with the court's permission, hand them up, at the same time giving copies to all other counsel.

When your case is called, and you are walking up to the podium, you will probably be nervous. Yes, you have prepared, and you are eager to get started, but your anxiety level may be understandably high: What if I forget something? What will the judge ask? What if I don't know the answer? What if I make a mistake? So much is riding on this motion, what will I tell my client if I lose? What effect might this have on my career?

Calm yourself, secure in the knowledge that you have prepared well and that you'll do just fine. Slow your breathing. Before you begin speaking, inhale deeply several times. Increasing oxygen intake helps reduce stress, to calming effect. Professional basketball players do the same thing as they prepare to make a crucial free throw shot. Be confident. Think of it this way: This is your golden opportunity to have a one-on-one exchange with the judge, an opportunity to convince the judge of the persuasiveness of your position. Seize the moment, and make the most of it.

Keep in mind that oral argument is more like jazz than classical music. That is, when performing classical music, if a musician plays any note other than the one on the score, that note is a mistake. In performing jazz, on the other hand, you are free to improvise. In oral argument, you do not read from a script. Instead, you have a more free-flowing back-and-forth with the judge, giving you the opportunity to express yourself persuasively as you make your argument and respond to questions, at liberty to say what you need. Even so, you may want to memorize the first and last things you plan to say.

Do not expect to make your presentation just as you planned. Do expect to be interrupted within the first minute of your presentation. If you have prepared properly, you will be able to answer questions, no matter what the sequence.

How about your physical presentation? You want to appear prepared and confident. Whatever you bring to the podium should be neat and tidy. As you argue, stand still at the podium. Use your hands to gesture as is comfortable for you. Avoid having anything in your hands, such as a pen, because you're likely to fidget with it. Keep your hands away from your face. Avoid doing anything that will distract or annoy the judge. The focus should be on the argument.

Don't speak too fast. Because you may feel an adrenaline rush as you approach the podium and argue, you may have a tendency to do so. Be aware of the pace of your speech. To slow yourself down while arguing, take a breath. And watch the judge's hand. A judge can't take good notes if you talk faster than the judge can write. If speaking too fast is an ongoing problem for you, write in large block letters at the top of each page of your notes **SLOW DOWN!**

## 2. How to answer judges' questions at oral argument of pretrial motions

### Why judges ask questions.

Judges ask questions at oral argument for several reasons. You must understand the distinct function of each, and know how to answer based on the judge's reason for asking each question.

- To obtain information. If asked a question about the record, or authorities on which you rely, answer succinctly. Since the judge expressed an interest in that information, weave it into your argument.
- To test the efficacy of your argument. Is it logical? Is it supported by the authorities you cite? What about contrary authority? If the judge rules in your favor on this motion, what kind of precedent might it set for similar cases? You can give more expansive answers to these questions, staying focused on what concerns the judge.
- To obtain concessions. Be wary of making any concessions about the facts or legal principles, but do make concessions when you need to. If, in good faith, you must make a concession, ask yourself: Why is the judge focused on this as a matter for me to concede? How can I weave that concession into my argument, either by demonstrating that it is of little significance in a proper analysis of the issues, or by explaining that, despite the concession, other factors militate in favor of your position? Concede no more than you need to, but do concede what you must. Otherwise, you risk losing credibility and antagonizing the judge.

## *How to listen to judges' questions.*

As you hear each question, ask yourself: Do I understand what the judge is asking? If in doubt, ask for clarification. Don't guess at what the judge wants to know. You will only confound the judge and create confusion. As you hear each question, ask what motivates the judge to focus on the subject of inquiry. Consider how you can incorporate your answer into your theme.

## *How to answer judges' questions.*

- Think before you answer, even if you need to pause before answering.
- Answer the question asked, not the question you wish the judge asked. If it calls for a yes or no answer, say "yes" or "no," followed by an explanation that supports your theme.
- Do not evade, say "I'll get to that later," or defer answering in any other way.
- Whenever possible, weave your themes into your answers.
- When answering, make sure you state the facts and legal propositions correctly. Any misstatement of fact or law erodes your credibility as to everything you say in oral argument, and everything in your memoranda to the court.
- Answer each question in a way that is clear and responsive. You don't want the transcript to look like this (from oral argument in April 2012 before the U.S. Supreme Court on the constitutionality of Arizona's 2010 immigration law, Justice Sonia Sotomayor to Solicitor General Donald B. Verrilli): "I'm terribly confused by your answer. O.K.? And I don't know that you're focusing on what I believe my colleagues are trying to get to."
- If you make an erroneous statement during oral argument, and realize it, correct your mistake at the earliest opportunity during oral argument.
- Do not argue with the judge. Judges sometimes build a premise into a question you may disagree with. If so, with respect, state that you disagree with the premise, but even if the premise were so, you win, and explain why. Sometimes judges ask questions that you perceive to be hostile. Remain professional and respond with your best answer. Stick to your guns. Don't allow yourself to be

bullied into retracting a position you know is valid or conceding something you should not concede.
- Never suggest that a judge's question is off the mark or of no consequence. Answer the question, and then explain how your answer ties into your theme.
- Never interrupt a judge. No exceptions.
- If it appears that you are losing ground in an argument, consider offering an alternative argument that the judge may find more persuasive. This requires careful thought well before the day of oral argument.
- Be respectful in giving answers, but not obsequious.
- Engage in a dialogue, more like a conversation than a debate. Be spontaneous, engaging, and forthright.
- Learn from oral arguments you observe, but be yourself when you argue. Do not attempt to adopt a persona that is not you. It won't work.

### *How to answer hypothetical questions.*

One way judges test the persuasiveness of contentions is by posing hypothetical questions. Judges ask such questions to identify which facts make a difference in the analysis, isolate legal issues, seek concessions, and understand the possible precedential effect of a ruling in your favor.

When answering a hypothetical question, make sure you understand it. Seek clarification if you do not. Determine what in the hypothetical distinguishes it from your case. Answer the question based on the hypothetical, and then distinguish it from your case, as appropriate.

### *What to do if you get an unexpected question, or a question to which you don't know the answer.*

Even if you have prepared thoroughly, and you know the record, the case law, and other authorities in play for a particular oral argument of a pretrial motion, you will get questions you did not expect. What do you do? You could ask the judge to ignore the facts (or the law, for that matter), but that's not a winning strategy.

Stay calm. You know your case better than anyone. You are prepared. Ask yourself: How can I tie my answer into the themes of my case? Give the best answer you can and move on.

"Can we, just for a moment, Your Honor, ignore the facts?"

If you think you know the answer, but are not sure, say so. If you simply don't know the answer, be straightforward about it. Say the words no trial lawyer likes to say: "I don't know." But follow those dreaded words with: "But, with the court's permission, I will promptly provide that information to the court through the law clerk, with a copy to opposing counsel."

### 3. How to prepare for and make opening statements to the jury

Even if you do not try as many jury cases as a personal injury lawyer, you must not shy away from claiming appropriate cases to a jury, and you must know how to try a case to a jury. The opening statement is your first opportunity to address the jurors directly, person to person. An effective opening statement is vital. Studies show that about 80 percent of jurors make up their minds on the issue of liability—irrevocably—immediately after hearing oral arguments, before hearing any testimony whatsoever!

Why is that so? One factor is the psychological principle of primacy, referred to above, by which information presented initially is remembered better than what is presented in the middle, possibly because initial items are more effectively stored in long-term memory as a result of the greater amount of mental processing devoted to them. So the jurors will remember better what you say in your opening statement—and what you say at the beginning of your opening statement—than what they hear in the middle of the trial. See the discussion of confirmation bias in chapter 10, section 1.

Of course, you must know your theme before you can begin preparing your opening statement. Even though you are limited in your opening statement to the facts you will prove, all those facts must be woven together to support the theme of your case.

Put yourself in the position of your jurors. What do they want to know from your opening statement? What is this case about? Who are the players? What went wrong? What do I need to decide? What should I pay attention to? Will it be interesting? Will I be able to understand it?

## *What you should do when making an opening statement.*

- Reintroduce yourself to the jury—who you are and whom you represent.
- Start with a statement that will capture the jurors' attention and evoke feelings favorable to your client and your theme. "This is a case about _____." Make the jurors want to learn more.
- Provide the jurors with a basis to identify with your client.
- Tailor your opening statement to your jurors. You know something about each of them from the jury selection process.
- Create images that bring the jurors close to the action.
- Consider using the present tense in describing what happened, to vivid effect.
- Describe what you will prove in a way that captivates the jurors. Humanize the story. You may choose to start in the middle of the story with the most fateful event, and then tell the rest of the story from there.
- Use simple language.
- Include only facts that matter, that is, facts that make a difference in the outcome of your case. Keep it simple. Each fact should support your theme.
- Inject a sense of morality, when you can.
- Weave in key phrases jurors will hear from witnesses.
- Weave in key phrases jurors will hear in the jury charge.
- If there is a genuine fact dispute, so indicate to preserve your credibility, but demonstrate that your facts are more compelling on that issue.

- Inform the jurors who will testify about what.
- If you represent a plaintiff, discuss damages.
- If you represent a defendant, take advantage of what plaintiff's counsel said in the opening statement in making your opening statement, as appropriate.
- In the middle of your opening statement, exploit weaknesses in the opposing party's case, and deal with weaknesses in your own case. Tread lightly to avoid overemphasizing those weaknesses, while innoculating the jurors from the impact of opposing counsel's opening statement.
- Use stipulated exhibits and demonstrative exhibits if the judge allows you to do so.
- End with something powerful, and let the jurors know that you will have the opportunity to address them again after all the evidence is in.
- Follow all the advice elsewhere in this chapter regarding your physical presentation. Use no notes at all if you can. If you want a safety net, leave your succinct outline on a nearby podium, and refer to it if you need to. Make eye contact with the jurors as much as possible.

## *What you should not do when making an opening statement.*

- Don't make a closing argument. That is, you are limited to a statement of the *facts* you will prove at trial. Save your persuasive argument for your closing. If you present the facts effectively, they alone will be persuasive.
- Don't refer to anything that you may not be able to get into the record. If you do, opposing counsel, in closing argument, can take advantage of what you promised to prove but did not.
- Don't overstate or exaggerate anything.
- Don't be theatrical or go for dramatic effect. Movies and television series about trials make for great entertainment, but they are not realistic. (However, see appendix III for movies of interest.) Just be yourself and you'll do fine. Sincerity is far more effective than theatrics.
- Don't refer to the "golden rule." You cannot say, in effect: "How would you like to be in the shoes of my client?"

- Do not state your personal opinion. "I know the defendant perpetrated a fraud on my client. How do I know? Well, let me tell you!" No.

## How to prepare for your opening statement.

After you have distilled your facts to those you should present to the jury, focus on those that best support your theme, and those that undercut your theme for which you must make a preemptive strike in your opening statement. After you have decided the most persuasive way to begin your opening statement and you have outlined your entire opening statement, write down what you plan to say. Read it aloud. Change anything that is out of place, unnecessary, sounds pedantic, or does not flow. Read it again. Edit. Keep polishing.

Then reduce what you have revised to a sentence outline. Give your opening statement referring only to the sentence outline. Reduce that sentence outline to the fewest words necessary to remember what you plan to say. Make your opening statement in front of a mirror. Be aware of how much you are looking down. You want to look down less and less, so you will have full eye contact with the jurors.

Present your opening statement to people who are totally unfamiliar with your case—people who are not lawyers, and who will give you honest feedback. Then ask what they think the case is about, what they may be confused about, what they are looking forward to learning more about during the trial, who should win and why. Revise your opening statement accordingly.

The best way to demonstrate an effective opening statement is by example. What follows is an opening statement in a National Institute for Trial Advocacy case file, *Dixon v. Providential Life Insurance Co.* Judge Dixon was found dead in his home office. If he died by accident while cleaning his hunting rifle, Providential must pay his widow twice the amount of the policy, but if he committed suicide, as Providential contends, it must reimburse her only the premiums paid on the life insurance policy. So, the issue is: accident or suicide?

As you know from the introductions at the beginning of this case, I represent Mary Dixon, the widow of Judge Dixon. [**REMINDER TO JURORS WHOM YOU REPRESENT**] Providential made a promise. Providential made that promise in writing—in a life insurance policy—a contract. That promise was that if Mary Dixon's husband, Judge Dixon, died as a result of an accident, she would receive $500,000.

The evidence will show that even though Judge Dixon paid his premiums in full, on time, and they were up to date; even though this contract was in full force and effect the day Judge Dixon died; and even though Mrs. Dixon filed her application for benefits to which she was entitled on time and in the right way, Providential refused to pay her the amount due her—$500,000. Providential broke its promise, a promise it made in writing—in a contract. [**STATEMENT OF THE THEME**]

Instead, Providential offered to pay her less than $2,000 as the full amount it was willing to pay. That's why we are here today.

Judge Dixon was in his fifties when he tragically died of an accident two years ago. A devoted husband, who took care of his wife and his family's finances, he was a longstanding justice of the peace right here in Nita City, a successful lawyer who often met with clients in his home office, a member of the bar association's committee on ethics, a member of the school board, and an active church member—and a man who enjoyed hunting. [**CHARACTER OF JUDGE DIXON**]

Several witnesses will testify that Judge Dixon was a very experienced hunter. He had a favorite shotgun, but sometimes it discharged accidently, as it did two months and one month before the accident with the same gun that killed him.

Who will tell you about these accidental shotgun blasts? [**STATEMENT OF KEY FACTS**] Sheriff Fred Webb, the longstanding sheriff of Darrow County, who hunted with Judge Dixon four or five times each hunting season; Mrs. Dixon, who will testify about what her husband told her about problems with this shotgun; and Mrs. Dixon's sister, Anna Martin, who was living with the Dixons for a short period, who hunted with Judge Dixon just a couple of months before he was killed, when she had trouble with the same gun.

Let's turn to the night before Judge Dixon was killed. The evidence will show that Judge Dixon has dinner at home with his wife and sister-in-law, Anna Martin. [**SHIFT TO PRESENT TENSE FOR GREATER IMPACT**] At dinner, he is laughing, joking, in good spirits, cheerful. He tells his wife that some people would be coming over to meet with him after dinner—people who have some difficult problems. He has that meeting that night, during which Mrs. Dixon hears some loud voices.

Judge Dixon comes to bed around 11:30 that night. He jokes with her about her falling asleep with the TV on, and lets her know that he will be hunting with Sheriff Webb the next day. He sleeps soundly that night.

The next morning, about 6:30, Judge Dixon has breakfast with Anna Martin. As Anna will testify, he is fine that morning. After breakfast, he works in his home office. Around 8:30, Mrs. Dixon goes to the supermarket. At 9:15, Judge Dixon calls Sheriff Webb to confirm their hunting plans that day. He is already wearing his hunting clothes when he makes that call. Judge Dixon tells Webb he is looking forward to hunting that day, especially because he has been working on that troublesome shotgun, and thinks he has figured out how to fix it. He says that when he is done with that repair he will give it a good cleaning.

When Mrs. Dixon returns home, she finds a horrible scene. Judge Dixon is in his home office—dead—a shotgun blast through his left eye, through his brain and through his skull. Next to him is the very same gun that had accidently discharged several times during two months before this tragic accident.

Sheriff Webb arrives on the scene that morning. Sheriff Webb is a friend of Judge Dixon, but he is also a professional. He has a professional responsibility to investigate the circumstances of Judge Dixon's death. As sheriff of Darrow County, he oversaw the work of twenty deputies. He was trained at the State Police Academy, even taught courses in crime scene investigation at that academy. Sheriff Webb will describe for you what he did to investigate just what happened. He will also inform you that he concluded that Judge Dixon died when that same shotgun that had caused problems before accidently discharged.

Sheriff Webb is not the only one who concluded that Judge Dixon's death was accidental. You will hear the testimony of Edward Sharpe, the coroner of Darrow County for more than ten years, a person trained in forensic medical investigation, and who has investigated more than a hundred violent deaths. He had seen Judge Dixon for a few minutes the day before this tragic accident—they were friends, and Dr. Sharpe was Judge Dixon's physician. Dr. Sharpe will testify that he noted nothing out of the ordinary about Judge Dixon that day.

What will you hear from Providential's lawyers about all this? [**PRE-EMPTIVE STRIKE ATTACKING PROVIDENTIAL'S POSITION**] Despite this extensive record that Judge Dixon died as a result of a tragic accident, Providential has asserted the defense that Judge

Dixon committed suicide. The insurance policy Providential issued provides that if Judge Dixon killed himself, it only had to return the amount of the premiums paid.

I expect that Providential will put on witnesses to testify that Judge Dixon had some financial difficulties, including amounts he owed the state for probate court fees he received, and that Judge Dixon had made a stock investment in an oil company that went bad. I expect that Providential's lawyers will also point out some check marks on the insurance policy relating to the suicide provisions. But those check marks were made during a ten-day period when several people other than Judge Dixon—including employees of Providential—could have made them on that policy.

Coroner Sharpe will testify that he concluded that Judge Dixon's death was accidental for several reasons. [**REINFORCEMENT OF DIXON'S POSITION**] You will hear him testify about the fact that Judge Dixon had no history of depression or ever talked about suicide; the scene was consistent with an accident; he left no suicide note; and the fact that Judge Dixon was shot through the eye is not a way people commit suicide. And, he concluded, Judge Dixon would not have killed himself the way he died, for his wife to find his body in such a horrible scene.

Sheriff Webb and Coroner Sharpe were not the only ones to conclude that Judge Dixon's death was accidental. There was a formal proceeding called an inquest to determine whether Judge Dixon's death was by accident or some other cause. After the testimony of witnesses, the jurors in that inquest rendered a verdict that Judge Dixon's death was accidental.

So, you will hear the testimony of two professionals, Sheriff Webb, and Coroner Sharpe, that Judge Dixon's death was accidental, and you will have the verdict of the jury at the inquest, that Judge Dixon's death was accidental. Providential's insurance policy assured Mrs. Dixon that if Judge Dixon died an accidental death, she would receive $500,000. Providential has failed to make good on that promise. Providential broke its promise, a promise it made in its contract, so Mrs. Dixon would be provided for upon Judge Dixon's death. [**RESTATEMENT OF THEME**] That is why we are here today.

I thank you in advance for your time and close attention to the testimony and evidence in this case. [**STATEMENT OF GRATITUDE**] I look forward to talking with you again, in closing argument, after all the evidence is in.

## 4. How to prepare for and make closing arguments to the jury

Closing argument is your second and final opportunity to address the jurors directly. You must persuade the jurors to render a verdict in your client's favor by making an argument that sets the jurors at ease, makes them sympathetic to your position, and motivates them to do the right thing. You must be straightforward, logical, and sincere.

Your closing argument is a singular opportunity to persuade jurors, because of what psychologists refer to as the recency effect. Barring other factors, people tend to remember better what they learn most recently before recall, perhaps because that information is still present in working memory when recall is required. Besides, that information is fresher in memory than information presented days or weeks earlier. Immediately after your closing argument, the judge will instruct the jurors. Then they deliberate, with the words of your closing argument ringing in their ears.

Make the most of this golden opportunity by following these tips.

### *Prepare for closing argument.*

- Know how much time you are allowed for your closing argument.
- Prepare a draft of your closing argument before trial, but make changes based on what happens during the trial.
- Determine what trial testimony and exhibits are most persuasive to support your position.
- Determine what trial testimony and exhibits are most persuasive to support opposing counsel's position.
- Determine whether you want to use any demonstrative aids during closing argument. If so, get court permission before using them.
- Think of apt analogies, metaphors, illusions, aphorisms, and images, and find quotations from literature and references to popular culture that will resonate with the jurors. You have wide latitude in making closing arguments.
- Determine the best way to minimize the impact of opposing counsel's position.
- Ask yourself: If I were a juror in this case, what would I want addressed in closing argument? What would be persuasive?
- Review your notes from jury selection so you can tailor your closing argument to what you learned about individual jurors' backgrounds,

experience, and beliefs, without being too obvious that you are doing so in your closing argument.
- Know what the judge will charge, so you can incorporate into your closing argument references to the charge, and words of the charge, as the court permits.
- Consider psychological factors of closing argument: Jurors tend to remember better what has meaning to them, what is familiar to them, what is associated with what they know, what is vivid, what evidence fits your theme, and what is repeated (but not too often). Jurors tend to remember less well what is difficult to follow, what is too complex, and what is presented too fast.

### Determine the sequence of the points you will make in closing argument.

- Start by thanking the jurors with sincerity, not in a patronizing way.
- State your theme succinctly.
- Provide the framework for a verdict in your favor.
- Start your review of the record with your strongest evidence.
- Topics should follow with continuity, in a logical sequence.
- Systematically, support each element of your claims.
- Make a preemptive strike as to major defenses you expect opposing counsel to raise in closing argument.
- End strong, reiterating your theme.

### Determine the content of the points you will make in closing argument.

- Include references to testimony and exhibits in the record that make a difference in the outcome of the case.
- Humanize your client, even if you represent an entity, by focusing on the people involved in your case. You do not represent a nameless, faceless entity.
- Remind the jurors of any commitments they made to you during voir dire—for example, that they will keep an open mind until completion of evidence, and that they will follow the judge's instructions.
- Discuss burden of proof.
- Encourage jurors to use common sense.
- Discuss credibility of witnesses.

## Determine your choice of words.

- Choose words carefully. You have many synonyms to choose from. Pick the best one. Find synonyms in a thesaurus or on the Internet. For example, go to www.synonyms.net and merriam-webster.com/dictionary/synonym.
- Use simple, powerful words.
- Use the active rather than the passive voice.
- Consider using the present tense in describing what the evidence shows.
- Use quotations from crucial testimony and exhibits.
- Use rhetorical flourishes, but nothing too fancy.
- Use analogies, metaphors, allusions, and aphorisms, but beware of doing so in a way that opposing counsel can make them backfire on you.
- Use apt quotations from literature, poetry, and elsewhere, and make references to popular culture, as appropriate.
- Use images.
- Use words that engage as many of our five senses as appropriate.
- Incorporate words from the request to charge.

## Use effective body language.

- Be aware of your posture, movements, facial expression, and tone of voice.
- Appear confident, relaxed, and forthright.
- Do not hold anything.
- Do not bring your hands to your face.
- Move naturally, but do not pace.
- Do not use the podium, except as a place to put your outline.
- Stand close enough to the jurors so you have their attention, but not so close that you invade their space.
- Make eye contact with all jurors as you argue.
- Use your voice like an instrument. Your voice should be strong, yet nuanced, using pauses, changes in how loudly you speak, and in the pitch of your voice.

## What to avoid.

- Do not ask the jurors to put themselves in the shoes of one of the parties.

- Do not state your personal beliefs.
- Do not state your personal view of any witness's credibility, although you can challenge credibility of witnesses by demonstrating inconsistencies in testimony, bias, prejudice, and other means.
- Do not state: "What I am about to say is not evidence."
- Do not misquote or exaggerate any testimony or evidence.
- Do not yell, be theatrical, or try to be someone you are not.
- Do not talk too fast.
- Do not assume any burden of proof you do not have.
- Do not be too slick.
- Do not use notes, but have an outline handy if you need it as a safety net.
- Do not make your presentation so complex or so long that you will lose the jurors.
- Do not merely recap all the evidence.
- Do not attack opposing counsel.
- Do not be dogmatic. Jurors should arrive at their own verdict after you have led them almost all the way down the path to success. Jurors should own their verdict, rather than feel that you have dictated what they must do. No one likes to be told what to do.

## *Miscellaneous tips.*

- If opposing counsel says something improper in closing argument, raise an objection at trial to preserve your argument on appeal. Do not interrupt opposing counsel's closing argument except in extreme circumstances, such as if opposing counsel makes a "golden rule" argument.
- If you represent a defendant, tailor your closing argument to what plaintiff's counsel stated in closing argument, using what opposing counsel said to your advantage.
- If you represent a plaintiff, save time for rebuttal. Make only the most important points, and then sit down before your time is up.

## 5. How to prepare for and make appellate court arguments

Context is key here: The case has already been tried, and you are now limited to the record. All counsel have already identified the issues for appeal, completed thorough research, and submitted extensive appellate court briefs. How do you prepare for oral argument? Do you just rehash what is in your brief? What about preparing to answer questions from a hot bench? And once you're standing there in front of the appellate court judges, what do you do?

You can assume that all the judges on your panel have read the briefs and the record, and are prepared to pepper you with questions. You can also assume that they have at least a predisposition about how they will rule before hearing oral argument. Even so, your mindset should be that you can convince them of the rightness of your position by answering their questions knowledgeably and persuasively.

## Prepare for oral argument by knowing the record, briefs, authorities cited in briefs, judges' approach to oral argument, and oral argument procedures.

- Know the record cold so that, when asked about it at oral argument, you will be prepared. Tab key pages of the record, so you will have ready reference to them at oral argument.
- If you were not trial counsel, do not tell an appellate judge that you cannot answer a question because you were not the lawyer who tried the case.
- Highlight key passages in all appellate court briefs and tab key pages.
- Outline the argument of each side, determining which issues are most significant for argument. Determine your strongest arguments and your opponent's strongest and weakest arguments.
- Determine which cases and other authorities are the most significant in the analysis of issues on appeal. Mark them up. Know them cold.
- A few days before oral argument, do a moot of your argument, with two or three of your colleagues who know the record and briefs in the appeal acting as a hot bench. The moot helps you identify difficult and likely questions, and enables you to practice articulating the answers in the stress of something approximating being at the podium. Your colleagues should critique your performance so you can improve it—especially your answers to tough questions.
- Find out which judges will be on your panel. Know their approaches to oral argument, such as whether each judge on your panel is known for a barrage of questions, drawing lawyers out on

tangents, asking many hypothetical questions, and the like. If possible, observe those judges at oral argument before it's your turn.
- Know your opponent. If, for example, your opponent has a reputation for arguing facts beyond the record, or overstating holdings of cases, you will be on your guard.
- Know the rules for oral argument in your jurisdiction. How many minutes are allocated to each side? Are time limits strictly enforced? What is the system of warning lights? What is the procedure to reserve time for rebuttal? What forms must you fill out the day of oral argument? Generally, what is the protocol?
- Put yourself in the shoes of the appellate court judges. What are they likely to ask about? What are the logical extensions of the positions you take? Appellate court judges set precedent binding on trial courts. Is the precedent you espouse one that should bind the trial court judges—not just in your case—but also in similar cases? What are the consequences for the future if the appellate court rules in your favor, not just as to your client?
- Bring with you to the appellate court all the appellate court briefs, copies of key cases and authorities (all tabbed for quick reference to what matters), trial transcripts you may need, and, whenever possible, a colleague who can assist you at oral argument.
- Prepare notes for your oral argument, but the fewer the notes the better—preferably not more than two pages. Do not write sentences. Instead, write only key words, to trigger your memory as to the most important points you want to make. If you write sentences, you will read them—a big mistake.

## *Make your oral argument with the objective of answering questions, not making a speech.*

You may think that the purpose of oral argument is to summarize the key points in your brief, reinforcing all the reasons you should prevail on appeal, so that at the end of your speech all the appellate judges on your panel will be convinced to rule in your favor. No.

The purpose of oral argument on appeal is to find out what the appellate court judges consider the key issues, what they are in doubt about, and what they may be confused about. You are there to answer questions, not make a speech.

How do you ferret out what the judges want to know? There are various ways to encourage colloquy with the panel, and to answer questions persuasively.

- Tell the judges what you think is the most important issue. Refer the judges to something in the record or a brief, and focus on it. Explain what matters: a flaw in the trial judge's reasoning, a holding of a key case, a significant exaggeration or misstatement in opposing counsel's appellate brief.
- Draw the judges' attention to the most important language in the most important case regarding your most important issue.
- Inform the judges what issues you do not intend to discuss. If a judge on the panel has questions on one of those issues, you'll find out.
- Sometimes appellate court briefs give the judges the impression that each side is talking about a different case below, causing confusion as to the precise issues on appeal, what is and is not supported by the record, or the scope of review. If so, set the record straight.
- Make eye contact with all judges on your panel.
- Adjust your presentation to what occurs during oral argument. For example, incorporate prior questions and answers during oral argument into your answers to later questions.
- Know which cases in point members of your panel ruled on, and incorporate those cases into your responses to questions. But don't pander.
- Do not be afraid to make concessions, particularly on points that are not crucial. You will gain credibility with the court. But be wary of making any unnecessary concessions or implicitly accepting a fact or point of law with a concession built into a question. Think about the predicates of the question and qualify your answer accordingly.
- Be prepared to make an uninterrupted argument. It does not often happen that the judges ask no questions, but if they are convinced of your position, or if they have already decided against you, they may ask very little or nothing at all.
- If noteworthy opinions have been published since briefs were filed, refer to them, but only after notifying the court and opposing counsel before oral argument, in accordance with applicable appellate court procedures.

- If you represent the appellee, adjust your presentation to what the appellant's counsel just stated in oral argument. Having paid attention to what appears to be troubling the appellate judges about appellant's position, make the most of it. If it appears that appellant's counsel scored some points in oral argument, explain why appellant's position lacks merit. Make your strongest arguments and pounce on the weaknesses of appellant's argument.
- If you represent the appellant, reserve time for rebuttal. If you need it, use it. Even if you don't need it, you'll keep appellant's counsel honest.
- Whether you represent the appellant or the appellee, when you have completed what you need to say, stop, even if you have not used all your allotted time. Do not exceed your allotted time, unless the chief judge hearing your argument gives you permission to complete your answer or otherwise exceed it.
- Apply all the advice in sections 1 and 2 of this chapter on oral argument of pretrial motions.

One final bit of advice, from Justice Robert H. Jackson, who described his appellate experience as follows: "As Solicitor General, I made three arguments in every case. First came the one that I planned—as I thought, logical, coherent, complete. Second was the one actually presented—interrupted, incoherent, disjointed, disappointing. The third was the utterly devastating argument that I thought of after going to bed that night."

So, prepare, expect the back-and-forth of oral argument, do your best, and wait as patiently as you can for the appellate court's ruling. Learn from each appellate court argument you make, and each one you observe.

## ❖❖❖❖
## PRACTICE CHECKLIST

- In preparing for oral argument of pretrial motions, learn what you need to know about the judge before whom you will argue, find out how much time you will have for the argument, read all briefs and other documents related to the issues presented, and decide what points are most persuasive.
- In preparing for oral argument of pretrial motions, take a devil's advocate position, and determine how you can undercut that position in your presentation, while focusing primarily on arguing your position.
- Bring to court all briefs and other documents related to the issues presented and an outline of the key points you plan to make.
- Expect to be interrupted during your argument.
- As you argue, appear prepared and confident, don't fidget, and don't talk too fast.
- Listen carefully to the judge's questions during oral argument. Think before you answer. If you do not understand a question, seek clarification.
- Answer each question directly, weaving your themes into your answers.
- In answering questions, do not evade, put off until later, misstate anything in the record or any point of law, or answer a question other than the one asked.
- Do not argue with the judge or suggest that the judge's question is off the mark or of no consequence.
- Never interrupt a judge.
- Be respectful, but not obsequious.
- Make concessions, but only as necessary.
- Be wary of hypothetical questions, because they may contain hidden concessions.
- In your opening statement to the jury, introduce yourself, start with a persuasive statement of your theme, provide the jurors with a basis to identify with your client, describe what you will prove in a way that captivates the jurors, use simple language, focus only on facts that matter, inject a sense of morality, make a preemptive strike on your opponent's theme, and end with something powerful related to your themes.
- In your opening statement to the jury, do not make an argument, do not refer to anything unlikely to get into the trial record, do not overstate or exaggerate anything, do not be theatrical, do not refer to the "golden rule," and do not state your personal opinion.
- In your closing argument to the jury, address what you think the jurors will find most persuasive, weave in your theme throughout your argument, and start and end strong. Use simple, powerful words, analogies, metaphors, allusions, aphorisms, apt quotations, images, and words the jurors will hear in the charge to the jurors.

(continued)

- In your opening statement and closing argument to the jury, use as few notes as possible.
- In preparing for an appellate court argument, know the record cold, the issues on appeal, the standard of review, and the key cases. Prepare an argument based on the amount of time the court allows, planning to make your strongest point first. Find out which judges are on your panel and learn what you need to know about them.
- During your appellate court argument, expect to be interrupted constantly and follow the advice as for argument of pretrial motions.
- If you represent an appellant, reserve time for rebuttal.

CHAPTER NINE

# PRESENTING AN EFFECTIVE PLAINTIFF'S CASE IN THE COURTROOM

Unlike cases involving medical malpractice, personal injury, divorce, and alleged criminal acts, commercial cases typically lack drama and can be, well, boring. This chapter discusses ways to make the plaintiff's presentation in a commercial case not just engaging, but compelling.

Picture yourself as the intrepid leader of an expedition. Your goal is to get from point A (the start of the trial) to point B (a plaintiff's judgment). You want to arrive there by the most direct route, avoiding swamps, boulder fields, treacherous stream crossings, and the like. Your opponent's goal is to divert you from that path and, worse yet, to lead the judge (this chapter assumes a bench trial, except in the last section) from point A to point C (a defendant's judgment)—somewhere you definitely do not want to go. So, how do you get to point B most efficiently and effectively? You must begin preparing for this expedition well before trial. Here are some useful tips.

## 1. Choose a compelling theme

From your first client meeting, you should be thinking about the theme that will guide the judge along the path to point B. As you learn additional facts and conduct legal research, ask yourself: What theme fits the facts and the law best, and will make the judge want to rule in your favor? Think beyond just establishing the elements of each cause of action you assert. Your theme should be based on common sense—it must ring true—and it should be so succinct that it would fit on a billboard or bumper sticker.

For example, consider these themes, all of which put the dispute in human terms: people should live up to their promises (breach of contract); cheaters should pay the price for their deception (fraud); people should think before they speak, and a victim of someone who doesn't should recover his due (negligent misrepresentation); no one should take unfair advantage of another (unjust enrichment); someone who betrays another's trust and confidence should suffer the consequences (breach of fiduciary duty); and everyone must play by the rules or be punished (violation of an unfair trade practices act).

## 2. Draft your complaint so it is consistent with your theme

In drafting your complaint, you could just mechanically recite the bare-bones facts of your case, without telling the story that promotes your theme. Even though Rule 8(a)(2) provides that a complaint must be "a short and plain statement of the claim showing that the pleader is entitled to relief," you have some leeway in drafting your complaint. The judge will read it before the trial starts. Within the bounds of proper pleading practice, draft a complaint that tells your client's story in such a way that, by the time the judge finishes reading it, the conclusion is just about inexorable that your client is entitled to all the relief you seek. As you draft, ask yourself: How does each paragraph promote my theme? In early drafts, include all causes of action that you may consider viable; then discard the weaker counts, because they detract from the stronger ones. Write short sentences in simple English, in short numbered paragraphs with subheadings, as appropriate. See chapter 4, section 3, for more about drafting complaints.

*Presenting an Effective Plaintiff's Case in the Courtroom* | 187

## 3. Conduct discovery to get admissions and streamline the trial

Conduct all pretrial discovery with an eye toward gathering information and documents useful in the courtroom to promote your theme. You can establish facts for elements of your causes of action or corroboration about them by getting admissions of the opposing party. You can also streamline the trial, without the risk of getting answers at trial that divert you from your path, by putting the opposing party's admissions into the record at trial. Here are some techniques.

Use the deposition of the opposing party not just to gather facts but to get admissions. Make sure, as you take that deposition, that you have obtained the admissions you need so that you can put them in the record at trial. See chapter 5, section 10, for techniques to obtain admissions in depositions. Putting such admissions into the record at trial goes well beyond their use as impeachment. Pursuant to FRE 801(d)(2), such statements are not hearsay, and you can introduce such admissions as the admissions of a party. If the opposing party is an entity, take a Rule 30(b)(6) deposition, in which you can obtain an entity's admissions. See chapter 5, section 4, and Rule 32(a)(2), which authorizes use of deposition transcripts of an opposing party—whether an individual or an entity—for any purpose allowed by the Federal Rules of Evidence. A real-time transcript is useful, if the client can pay the expense, so that during the course of the deposition you can be sure you have the admissions you need. If you take a video deposition, the judge at trial can observe your opponent making such admissions—more compelling than mere words on a page.

Take advantage of requests for admissions, as provided in Rule 36. See chapter 4, section 6. Such admissions are conclusive for purposes of your case, unless the judge permits their withdrawal or amendment. Rule 36(b). In drafting requests for admissions, remember that they are not limited to facts, but can include admissions pertaining to "the application of law to fact, or opinions about either," as well as "the genuineness of any described documents." Rule 36(a)(1). You can include similar but not identical requests for admissions so that even if the opposing party can figure out a way to deny all or part of one request, you can get an admission on a similar request. You can also use requests for admissions to establish certain documents as business records so that at trial you do not need to go through the cumbersome and sometimes time-consuming process of establishing that certain documents are within FRE 803(6), the business record exception to the hearsay rule.

Obtain documents from third parties and from the public record. Do Web searches, but keep in mind that not everything you find on the Internet is reliable. If your case involves public records, obtain certified copies so that you can put them into evidence without the need to call any public official as a witness, as provided in FRE 803(8).

When appropriate, seek judicial notice of adjudicative facts, as provided in FRE 201. A court must take judicial notice of such facts if requested by a party and supplied with the necessary information. FRE 201(d). Such a fact must be one that is not subject to reasonable dispute in that it is either generally known within the jurisdiction or capable of accurate and ready determination by resort to sources whose accuracy cannot reasonably be questioned. FRE 201(d). Such facts include, for example, prevailing interest rates; contents of court records; Securities and Exchange Commission (SEC) filing requirements; federal regulations; scientific, technological, and mechanical principles; facts involving history, geography, locations of buildings, distances between places, and topological characteristics.

## 4. Stipulate to admission of documents as full exhibits

In most commercial cases, a subset of documents will be admissible at trial, without any bona fide objection. Seek agreement of opposing counsel for the admission of as many of these documents as you can, to streamline the trial. Of course, you must expect that defense counsel will likewise seek your stipulation to documents he or she wants in the record, but that is a small price to pay for the benefits to your client of such a stipulation. Pretrial orders often include the requirement that parties so stipulate to the extent they can. Read all pretrial orders carefully to be sure that you comply with this and all other pretrial requirements.

## 5. File motions in limine on key evidentiary issues

A motion in limine is a procedural device by which a party seeks a ruling on admissibility of testimony or evidence before trial starts. It is pure Latin, meaning "at the threshold," from the same root as for "preliminary," "eliminate," and "subliminal." Even though no rule explicitly provides for filing such a motion, the court's power to rule on it derives from FRE 103(c) in jury cases and FRE 104(a) in any case.

It is a useful device serving several functions. First, it alerts the judge that, during trial, an evidentiary issue will likely arise requiring more careful deliberation (possibly including research by the judge's clerk) than run-of-the-mill evidentiary issues. Second, it gives you an opportunity for the judge to see an evidentiary issue your way, with the benefit of your analysis of applicable evidentiary rules and precedents. Third, you avoid having the presentation of your case bog down just as you are building up a head of steam, while the judge hears extensive oral argument on a predictable evidentiary issue. Fourth, your successful motion in limine may result in a pre-trial settlement favorable to your client. One typical use of this motion is to challenge expert testimony, as discussed in chapter 10, section 8.

The downside of filing a motion in limine is that it highlights the evidentiary issue for your opponent, and gives your opponent the opportunity to review and analyze your view of that issue and the authorities you rely on, and to file an opposing memo on that issue. But the benefits of filing a motion in limine on key evidentiary issues typically outweigh this downside.

Even though judges sometimes postpone ruling on motions in limine until the trial is in progress, the first three advantages referenced above still apply.

## 6. Prepare a trial notebook

This three-ring notebook will be your bible for the trial. Make separate subsections for key pleadings; chronology; list of plaintiff's exhibits; list of defendant's exhibits; each witness (inserting direct and cross-examination notes and deposition summaries); key exhibits (if not voluminous); and trial notes. Begin preparing your trial notebook at the inception of your representation, amending and revising it as the case progresses.

## 7. File a pretrial memo, even if not required by the pretrial order

Keep in mind your role as the intrepid leader of this expedition from point A to point B. The pretrial memo is your map for the judge, showing how to get there. Distill your case down to its essence. Write as few pages as possible. Every sentence should promote your theme. By the time the judge finishes reading your pretrial memo, he or she should want to rule in your favor, needing only the trial record to justify getting to point B.

## 8. SELECT AS FEW WITNESSES AS YOU NEED AND PRESENT THEM IN A LOGICAL ORDER

Put on only as many witnesses as you need to establish all the elements of each cause of action. With few exceptions (such as strategically important corroboration of key testimony), duplicative testimony may not only violate the rules, see FRE 403; it can result in inconsistent testimony. Confusion only aids the defendant, whether by inconsistent testimony or otherwise. Even if duplicative testimony is not inconsistent, consider whether the additional testimony will bog down the trial.

In deciding the sequence of witnesses, consider what psychiatrists refer to as the serial position effect, which refers to the fact that, barring other factors, people tend to remember information as a function of the sequence in which it is presented, primarily based on primacy and recency. Under the theory of primacy (what we hear first we tend to remember better), your first witness should be very strong. Generally, you should present your witnesses so they can relate the facts in chronological order, although this is not always possible. Under the theory of recency (what we hear last we tend to remember better), end with a strong witness. Put in the middle those witnesses whose testimony is required, but who either are weaker or whose testimony is less important or unavoidably tedious. These same psychological principles likewise apply to your deciding the sequence of questions of each witness. Start and end strong with each witness.

## 9. PREPARE YOUR WITNESSES TO AVOID SURPRISES IN THE COURTROOM

If your witnesses have a good idea what to expect in the courtroom, they will be less ill at ease when they testify. When preparing your client, ask the same questions you plan to ask in the courtroom, while assuring your client that there is no script, so this is not a memory contest. In this respect, the trial of a case is more like performing jazz than classical music—jazz musicians can improvise, whereas classical musicians are limited to the notes on the sheet music. If you plan to use exhibits or demonstrative exhibits during your client's testimony, make sure your client is thoroughly familiar with them, and comfortable with their use. Anticipate the cross of your client, and put your client through cross-examination before trial. Depending on your client's prior courtroom experience and sophistication, it may be appropriate to take your client to the courtroom where the case will be tried, to get the feel of the place and a sense of the judge.

Discuss with your client the theme of your case and the legal theories supporting it, as well as defendant's theme to get to point C, so that when your client answers questions on the stand, he or she understands the context. This is especially useful when your client answers questions on cross-examination. Your client will be less likely to be surprised by cross-examination questions that even you didn't think of if your client has an understanding of the strategy underlying those questions. Your client will then be more likely to answer cross-examination questions consistent with your theme, keeping you on the path from point A to point B, avoiding detours and staying off the path to point C, a place you want to stay far away from.

When preparing witnesses other than your client, you don't have the benefit of the attorney-client privilege. So, assume in any conversation you have with a non-client witness that opposing counsel is sitting next to you.

## 10. ASK DIRECT EXAMINATION QUESTIONS TO GET TO POINT B EFFICIENTLY AND EFFECTIVELY

Keep your questions short. Shorter questions are easier to understand, for the witness and the judge, than long, convoluted questions.

Ask questions using plain English words.

Ask questions using a pace that moves things along nicely, but not so fast that the judge will be unable to follow the testimony, or take notes. If the judge is taking notes during the testimony, as most judges do, keep an eye on the judge's writing hand. If you are going too fast for the judge to write, slow down.

Ask only questions that further your theme.

Vary the types of your questions to avoid a dull back-and-forth with your witness. Include leading questions for preliminary matters. See FRE 611(c).

Use headnotes, such as, "Let's turn to the day you signed the agreement with Jones." Such headnotes are signposts along the trail, guiding the witness and judge to let them know just where you are, and where you are headed. They serve a useful function analogous to subheadings in a brief.

Use loop-backs, by which you incorporate into a question the answers from the prior question or two. Loop-backs reinforce the testimony your witness just gave, provide context for the question you are now asking, and strengthen the flow and logic of your presentation. Use them sparingly, to emphasize the most important testimony.

To achieve all these objectives, what notes should you use? Whether on paper or an iPad or other electronic device, have handy a numbered list of points you need to cover with each witness, as specific as necessary but using the fewest words possible, to avoid reading it. But don't be locked into that sequence. Vary your questions as appropriate, depending on the courtroom testimony.

In direct examination, the focus should be on the witness, not you. Do not move around the courtroom. Stand at the podium or, unless the judge prohibits your doing so, stand closer to the witness.

Once you have the answers you need, do not try to "gild the lily" by asking the one question too many that too often results in a bad answer.

Avoid objectionable questions. Each time you do so, your opponent is presented with an opportunity to place obstacles in your path, transforming a nice, easy trial into one full of rocks, roots, and ruts. If you inadvertently ask an objectionable question, and realize that it is truly objectionable, withdraw it (don't say "stricken," which only a judge can do), and ask a proper question. You don't want to be derailed by asking objectionable questions, like the lawyer in the cartoon below.

If opposing counsel objects to a question as irrelevant, use the opportunity in response to reinforce your theme, explaining how the answer to your question is relevant to get to point B.

Don't allow opposing counsel to take the judge on a detour off your trail in the guise of voir dire on a document as to its admissibility, on competency of a lay or expert witness, or otherwise. When a judge does allow voir dire, object to the first question beyond the scope of proper voir dire.

*"Objection sustained."*

Use your voice like an instrument. Avoid the monotone Q and A that puts everyone to sleep.

When eliciting key testimony, build up to it. Through the witness, bring out the significance of the event, creating anticipation, so that the judge is eager to hear that testimony.

Make a preemptive strike by asking your own witnesses questions revealing weaknesses in their testimony. This may seem counterintuitive, but far better that you introduce this testimony first, so long as you don't let it overshadow the helpful testimony. You can insert such testimony in the middle of your witness's testimony, presenting it in the most favorable light that is reasonable, even though it is negative. You will not be able to explain it away, but you can put opposing counsel to a disadvantage, because by the time the judge hears the cross on this vulnerability, it is old news, with comparatively little impact.

Before you end your direct examination of each witness, ask for a moment to review your notes. Once you say "no further questions," it is awkward—and sometimes futile—to ask the court's permission to ask further questions of that witness. Likewise, review your notes before resting your case, to satisfy yourself that you have put into the record at least a prima facie case. This is a turning point in the trial, enabling defense counsel to file a motion for judgment as a matter of law (see chapter 10, section 12). Consider your list of facts and exhibits you needed to get into the record to be your malpractice checklist.

## 11. Use exhibits to get to point B efficiently and effectively

Put into evidence only exhibits that advance your theme. Cull from all the documents you have obtained from your client and from discovery only those documents that make a difference in your case. By this distillation process, you will choose to put into the record at trial only what will advance your theme.

There are three types of evidence: documentary, real, and demonstrative. For example, in a construction case, you could seek to put into the record the construction plans (documentary), the part that failed (real), and a three-dimensional model of the construction site (demonstrative).

Know the evidentiary basis for the admission of each proposed exhibit. Be prepared with evidence rules, precedent, and other authorities to support the admission of each. Keep in mind that the mere fact that the opposing party produced a document in response to your pretrial discovery, or a document was made an exhibit at a deposition, does *not* make it automatically admissible at trial.

Unless the exhibit is pre-marked for identification or stipulated as a full exhibit, ask the court clerk to mark each proposed exhibit for identification before inquiring about it. After you ask questions to establish the requisite evidentiary foundation, state: "I offer Exhibit X for ID as a full exhibit" or "I offer Exhibit X for ID into evidence."

Build up key exhibits to highlight their significance before introducing them, just as you do with key testimony. Do so by eliciting testimony as to the reliability of the exhibit, and why it matters to the outcome of your case, in context.

Introduce into the record the admissions in the transcript of the deposition of the opposing party (see Rule 32(a)(2)) and the admissions in response to your requests for admissions (see Rule 36(b) and FRE 801(d)(2)). Keep in mind, though, that pursuant to FRE 106, opposing counsel can put in the record any other portions of the transcript of the deposition of the opposing party, or other responses to requests for admissions, which "ought in fairness to be considered contemporaneously with it."

Introduce into the record the deposition testimony of anyone (not necessarily a party) within the scope of Rule 32(a)(4), which includes, among others, any witness who is more than 100 miles from the place of trial, any witness unable to attend the trial because of age or infirmity, or anyone whose attendance cannot be procured by subpoena. Be aware that FRE 106, the rule of completeness, applies to this transcript as well as to party admissions.

To save time, and increase persuasiveness, introduce summaries of documents into evidence, as appropriate, taking advantage of FRE 1006. Remember that you cannot introduce summaries unless you make originals, or duplicates, of all the documents you summarize available for examination or copying, or both, at a reasonable time and place. So, consider the utility of summaries well before trial and comply with FRE 1006.

Make an extra set of exhibits for opposing counsel, the judge, and the judge's law clerk.

Use demonstrative exhibits, as appropriate, to clarify complex testimony or documents. Examples include timelines, organization charts, and flow charts. Limit the amount of information in each demonstrative exhibit, so it is easy to understand. If sufficiently accurate and probative, a demonstrative exhibit is admissible in evidence. Use such exhibits in a way to avoid being faced with a challenge pursuant to FRE 403 and 611(a), which give the judge discretion to keep out cumulative evidence and evidence that needlessly consumes time. Well before trial, play devil's advocate by asking yourself how opposing counsel might use your proposed demonstrative exhibits against you, and make any necessary revisions.

Consider using electronic demonstrative exhibits, as well as projection of exhibits electronically. If you do so, make sure you have the proper power sources and equipment in the courtroom, permission to use them as required, and the ability to use them under pressure. For advice on cutting-edge use of electronics in the courtroom, see *Law on Display, The Digital Transformation of Legal Persuasion and Judgment*, listed in appendix III.

At trial, keep a list of all documents that are made full exhibits, so you know what you and opposing counsel put into the record, and all exhibits marked only for identification.

## 12. IF THE JUDGE EXCLUDES YOUR EVIDENCE, CONSIDER MAKING AN OFFER OF PROOF

If a judge sustains opposing counsel's objection to testimony or to a document you want in the record, you have the right to make an offer of proof. FRE 103 provides, in part, that if a judge excludes evidence that affects a substantial right of a party, error is preserved by informing the court of its substance by an offer of proof, unless the substance was apparent from the context. By an offer of proof, you inform the judge what would be put in the record but for the judge's exclusionary ruling, giving the judge the opportunity to reconsider. Once the court rules definitively on the record—either before or at trial—you need not renew an objection or offer of proof to preserve a claim of error for appeal. Only make an offer of proof as to evidence that makes a difference in the outcome of your case.

The court may make any statement about the character or form of the evidence, the objection made, and the ruling, and may direct that an offer of proof be made in question-and-answer form. To the extent practicable, the court must conduct a jury trial so that inadmissible evidence is not suggested to the jury by any means, so offers of proof are made outside the presence of the jury.

### 13. Select an expert who has the required background and experience

Select an expert who can speak plain English and knows how to use effective analogies.

In establishing your expert's credentials, intersperse leading questions, see FRE 611(c), to move the testimony along.

Anticipate any *Daubert* issues and make sure they are resolved before trial. See chapter 10, section 8, for more on *Daubert* challenges.

In federal court, it is not necessary to ask the judge to find that your expert witness is an expert on the subject for which you offer his or her opinion testimony. Accordingly, there is no reason to put this obstacle in your path to point B. On the other hand, if it is self-evident that a judge would rule favorably on your tender of a witness as an expert of a particular subject, jurors will likely give that witness's testimony extra weight by making that succesful tender.

Do ask your expert his or her opinion on the ultimate issue the judge must decide, as allowed by FRE 704(a).

Use the expert's report to guide the judge through the expert's testimony. Even though the expert's report is hearsay, judges typically allow it as a full exhibit. Your expert is the teacher, the judge is the student, and you are the moderator.

## 14. Miscellaneous tips

Here are some more ways to get from point A to point B.

If you expect the judge to follow your lead, you must be trustworthy. In your pretrial memo, make sure that each fact will be supported in the record, and that each legal authority you cite supports the proposition for which you cite it. During trial, be yourself, and don't seek to have any witnesses exaggerate anything about themselves or distort the truth in any way. In your post-trial memo, deal with the entire record, not just a skewed selection from only part of the record while ignoring anything inconsistent with or adverse to your position. One misrepresentation taints everything you do. If you lose credibility, you risk losing your case.

When you get a bad answer from your own witness, don't panic. Ask yourself if you have asked the question in a way that confused the witness. If so, rephrase the question. If the witness is hopelessly confused at that point, go to a different subject. If the witness is your client, discuss the troublesome testimony during the next break, unless the judge precludes such discussions. If your client was confused, but your discussion clarifies what you were seeking, deal with what will be apparently inconsistent testimony head-on. Make clear on the record, after the break, that your client understood by your earlier question as "X," whereas, reworded, he or she now understands the import of the question is "Y." This detour off your path is usually avoidable by careful preparation.

When the judge is activist, asking your witnesses many questions, the witness should not be surprised by this turn of events, and should be advised before trial to look the judge square in the eye and answer the judge's questions directly. You should listen carefully to the judge's questions, and make the most of any follow-up questions you may want to ask on a subject that obviously has the judge's attention.

Stay organized. Your space at counsel table should be neat and tidy. You should have on it only what you need, and nothing more.

If you are trying the case with co-counsel, have a stack of note cards with you at counsel table. They are handy for communication between you and co-counsel without any conversation that could interfere with your undivided attention on the witness, judge, and opposing counsel. Each card should have only one point on it. You can then discard cards (in a recycling bin) as you cover each point.

Keep in mind your role as leader of this expedition. Even when you are diverted from your planned route to point B, keep your composure and remember that there is more than one way of getting from point A to point B.

When defense counsel rests, consider putting in rebuttal evidence, which must be limited to the scope of the defense evidence. For more on this, see chapter 10, section 14.

Don't burn out during trial. Make the time each day to do something relaxing. Even an intrepid expedition leader needs time to unwind during an arduous trek.

## 15. Adjust all this advice for a jury trial

All the advice in this article is as useful in a jury trial as in a bench trial, with some modifications. To avoid waiving your right to a jury trial, file a timely jury demand, as provided in Rule 38. Such a demand is typically included in the complaint, although any party can demand a trial by jury no later than 14 days after the last pleading directed to anyone triable to a jury is served.

Well before trial, get advice from a non-lawyer. Describe the facts of your case, without disclosing whom you represent. Start with the most basic facts, and ask what additional facts would be required to decide who should win. Provide that additional information. Find out what facts make a difference, and why. Then present your theme to determine if it is effective. Brainstorm other themes. More formally, you can do this with a focus group or mock jury.

As in a bench trial, be trustworthy. In your opening statement, throughout the trial, and in your closing argument, do not promise what you cannot deliver, and do not misrepresent or distort anything.

Even though you should reinforce your theme throughout the trial, don't bludgeon the jury with it. Generally, people do not like to be told what to think and prefer to arrive at their own conclusions. As an analogy, consider Georges Seurat's pointillist masterpiece *Sunday Afternoon on the Island of La Grande Jatte*, the pixilated paintings of Chuck Close, or the connect-the-dots puzzles you did as a kid. Each is nothing more than dots; but, together, the dots form an image. Each dot is a fact, and it is for the jurors to connect those facts to come up with their own image—which is, of course, what they find at point B.

Unlike in a bench trial, you risk confusion or worse, using legal terms that a juror will not understand. The judge is a seasoned trekker, who generally knows the territory, although the judge has not been down this particular path. The jurors are novices, just learning the ropes, and need more guidance on the path to point B. And in both bench and jury trials, make sure your witnesses explain any terms that are not in common parlance—especially in expert testimony.

Consider using more demonstrative exhibits in a jury trial, to keep the expedition more engaging to laypeople.

Make sure you include the jury as each document is made a full exhibit. Think of effective and creative ways to publish each exhibit to the jury, such as blowups, copies for each juror, and displays on computer monitors in electronically enhanced courtrooms. When asking questions in a jury trial, stand at the back of the jury box, if the judge allows you to do so. That way, your witnesses are looking at the jurors while answering your questions, and jurors will likely be more engaged.

Unlike in a bench trial, in a jury trial you make an opening statement and closing argument (both of which you should practice in front of a mirror), and you have input on the charge to the jury (see chapter 4, section 7). Each should be no longer than necessary, be in simple English, and promote your theme. Your opening statement is your opportunity to show the jurors the map of the trail along which you will lead them. Your closing argument is a recap of the route you took together, weaving in your theme to explain why the destination you brought them to is where they ought to be. The charge to the jury, ideally, is the judge's explanation of how it is that they can arrive at your destination.

## 16. MAKE THE MOST OF YOUR THEME

As noted at the beginning of this chapter, your theme dictates all that you do in preparing for and trying a case. Consider a musical analogy. The theme of your case is analogous to the theme of a symphony. Take, for example, the theme of Beethoven's Fifth Symphony. Here it is:

Even if you don't know how to read music, you can see how simple this theme is. Four notes. The same note repeated quickly three times, followed by a lower note held longer. If you ever heard this symphony (undoubtedly you have), you know how stirring this music is. You feel it in your bones. How does Beethoven manage to evoke such passion from two notes, one of them repeated three times? Orchestration, to be sure, but he does what you should do in presenting your case. Beethoven works this simple yet compelling theme into his symphony as a leitmotif that pervades his entire work. If he merely repeated the same notes over and over, it would be boring. Visually, the music score would look like this:

Even if you can't read music, this will put you to sleep. Now let's take a look at the actual score:

Observe how Beethoven masterfully repeats his theme, but with variants—employing different rhythms, different intervals between notes, and different notes, but all based on the very same theme of "da-da-da-DUM!"

And so it is when you present your case. In your closing argument, for example, you would not state to the jurors: "The insurance company broke its promise—a promise it made in a written contract! The insurance company broke its promise—a promise it made in a written contract! The insurance company broke its promise—a promise it made in a written contract! The insurance company broke its promise—a promise it made in a written contract! The insurance company broke its promise—a promise it made in a written contract! The insurance company broke its promise—a promise it made in a written contract!"

You would, though, weave that theme into everything you say to the jurors in your closing argument, analogous to the music score as Beethoven wrote it.

As you see, just as Beethoven did not merely repeat his theme "verbatim" interminably, instead weaving it into his score so artfully, you can weave your theme into each question you ask on voir dire, what you say in your opening statement, each question you ask on direct, your choice of each document you put into the record, each objection you raise at trial, each question you ask on cross, as well as your proposed jury charge, and, in a courtside trial, in your post-trial brief. By the time the jurors enter the deliberation room, they should all be singing "da-da-da-DUM!" in unison. In a courtside trial, the judge should be humming "da-da-da-DUM!" even before reading your post-trial brief!

By implementing all these tips, you enhance the likelihood that you and the judge or jury will arrive at point B, having made the trek at a steady pace, on your well-planned route, charted with your theme in mind each step of the way.

## 17. How to deal with settlement shortly before or during trial

About 98% of federal civil actions settle before trial is completed, many on the eve of trial. If you work hard to prepare for trial and it settles, you will feel mixed emotions. Sure, you will feel satisfaction in resolving the dispute without the uncertainty of a bad result, achieving finality for your client, and ending legal and expert fees and related expenses for your client. But you will likely also feel some frustration and disappointment that you are denied the opportunity to put on your case after so much time and effort during the pleading, discovery, and pretrial preparation phases, and you are denied the experience of the trial.

Your mindset should be that you achieved something of great value in settling your client's claim as favorably as you did, and that it settled on that basis only because you were prepared to put on an effective presentation in court—and opposing counsel knew it. If a case settles shortly before or during trial, you have already carved out days for the full trial. Reward yourself by taking off a day or two, if you can, and then apply yourself to the next case. Move on.

❖❖❖❖
## PRACTICE CHECKLIST

- Choose a compelling, succinct, common-sense theme.
- Draft your complaint so it is consistent with your theme.
- Conduct discovery to get admissions and streamline the trial:
  - _____ Get deposition admissions and judicial admissions in response to requests for admissions to promote your theme.
  - _____ Obtain certified copies of public records.
  - _____ Get judicial notice of adjudicative facts.
- Stipulate to admission of documents as full exhibits.
- File motions in limine on key evidentiary issues.
- Prepare a trial notebook.
- File a pretrial memo.
- Select as few witnesses as you need and present them in a logical order.
- Prepare your witnesses to avoid surprises in the courtroom.
- Ask direct examination questions efficiently and effectively:
  - _____ Ask short questions in plain English at a comfortable pace.
  - _____ Ask only questions that promote your theme.
  - _____ Vary the types of your questions.
  - _____ Use headnotes and loop-backs.
  - _____ Don't ask the one question too many.
  - _____ Avoid objectionable questions.
  - _____ Counter defense counsel's objections in a way to reinforce your themes.
  - _____ Cut off voir dire that derails your case.
  - _____ Use your voice like an instrument.
  - _____ Build up significant testimony.
  - _____ Make a preemptive strike on weaknesses in your witnesses' testimony.
  - _____ Review your checklist before ending your questions of each witness, and before resting your case.
- Use exhibits efficiently and effectively:
  - _____ Put into evidence only exhibits promoting your theme, and know the evidentiary basis for each.
  - _____ Build up significant documents.
  - _____ Put into evidence deposition testimony and responses to requests for admissions.
  - _____ Put into evidence summaries of voluminous documents.
  - _____ Use demonstrative exhibits.
  - _____ Make sufficient copies of documents.
  - _____ Keep track of which documents are in evidence and which are for identification only.

(continued)

- Select an expert who will support your theme efficiently and effectively:
    - _____ Select an expert with the requisite background and experience who speaks in plain English and who is not subject to a *Daubert* challenge.
    - _____ Have your expert testify on the ultimate issue.
    - _____ Introduce your expert's report into evidence.
- Miscellaneous tips:
    - _____ Do not misrepresent or distort anything.
    - _____ Be prepared for a bad answer from your own witness.
    - _____ Prepare your witnesses for questioning by the judge.
    - _____ Stay organized during trial.
    - _____ Use note cards to communicate with co-counsel during trial.
    - _____ Be flexible during trial.
    - _____ Avoid burnout during trial.
- Adjust all this advice for a jury trial:
    - _____ Workshop your case with a non-lawyer, focus group, or mock jury.
    - _____ Don't promise more than you can deliver in your opening statement and don't mischaracterize the record in your closing argument.
    - _____ Don't bludgeon the jurors with your theme.
    - _____ Try your case at the level of the jurors.
    - _____ Use more demonstrative exhibits than at a bench trial.
    - _____ Publish each exhibit to the jurors in a meaningful way.
    - _____ Promote your theme in opening statement, in closing argument, and in the charge to the jury.
- Listen to Beethoven's Fifth Symphony, focusing on his use of the theme.
- When you settle a case shortly before or during a trial, keep in mind that your case settled so favorably only because you were prepared to try it.

CHAPTER TEN

# PRESENTING AN EFFECTIVE DEFENSE IN THE COURTROOM

This chapter complements the prior chapter on presenting an effective plaintiff's case in the courtroom. For example, the discussion in this chapter about cross-examination of plaintiff's witnesses applies equally to crossing defendant's witnesses. As with that chapter, the tips offered here focus on what happens in the courtroom during a bench trial (except for section 16, which provides tips for a jury trial), although the discussion necessarily encompasses pretrial preparation as well.

The goal of plaintiff's counsel is to get from point A (start of the trial) to point B (a plaintiff's judgment). Your goal in defending is to get from point A to point C (a defendant's judgment).

## 1. CHOOSE A COMPELLING COUNTER-THEME

Persistence of belief (also known as confirmation bias) is a psychological concept explaining a common way people deal with indecision. Assume you are planning to buy a new car. Until you decide which car you will buy, you are in a state of some discomfort, eager for a resolution of the dissonance your indecision has created. You find relief by finally making your decision, after which you will likely focus on information supporting your decision, minimizing the information challenging it, such as in magazine and television car ads. For more on confirmation bias, see the work of Dan Kahan, Professor of Law and Psychology at Yale Law School, and Jeffrey Rachlinski, Professor at Cornell University Law School.

And so it is with trial themes. Plaintiff's counsel has the advantage of presenting the first theme. If the judge or jury is so beguiled by that theme as to be swayed (while trying to keep an open mind, of course), you must present a counter-theme at least as compelling as plaintiff's in order to overcome the "persistence of belief" created by plaintiff's theme.

Ideally, your theme should be more than "Plaintiff is wrong," although you certainly want to undermine the plaintiff's theme. You should present your own independent theme that takes the legs out from under the plaintiff's theme. For example, if plaintiff is suing for breach of contract for the sale of goods and plaintiff's theme is that "people should live up to their promises," your counter-theme (assuming you have the facts) may be that "people should not be required to pay for shoddy goods." You may also be able to co-opt the plaintiff's theme and turn it against the plaintiff (again, assuming you have the facts) by a counter-theme like "people should live up to their promises by delivering what they promise." Of course, such counter-themes are possible only if you have pled effectively, as discussed in the next section.

## 2. Draft your answer, affirmative defenses, counterclaims, and cross-claims to be consistent with your counter-theme

From your first meeting with a client when defending a commercial case, you must learn everything of potential interest about the underlying transaction and about your client's business. It is often beneficial to meet at your client's place of business, where you can tour the facility to learn the ins and the outs of the operation in a way that is not possible by merely talking with your client and reviewing documents. Such a meeting also gives you the opportunity to meet with other client employees in their work setting, giving you insights otherwise not available.

Early in your representation, glean enough information to enable you to determine what allegations in the complaint you must admit, and whether you have any viable affirmative defenses, counterclaims, or cross-claims. It is always preferable to put a plaintiff at risk—not just of losing but of having to pay your client money or provide your client other relief.

Brainstorm with your colleagues possible affirmative defenses, counterclaims, and cross-claims. Doing so often sparks new ideas about such pleadings. Be familiar with Rule 12 regarding what affirmative defenses must be pleaded, and Rule 13 regarding compulsory counterclaims.

Before filing your answer, affirmative defenses, counterclaims, and cross-claims, discuss them thoroughly with your client to assure that you have your facts straight and your client is comfortable with what you allege. Otherwise, you risk a meltdown of your case in the courtroom if your witnesses can't support key allegations in your pleadings.

Be cautious about pleading defenses in the alternative. To borrow from the memorable hypothetical of law school professor and jurist Irving Younger, assume the claim is that Farmer Jones' goat ate Farmer Smith's vegetables, causing damage to his crop. You would lose credibility if you allege that the goat did not belong to Jones; if it *was* Jones' goat, it did not trespass on Smith's property; if it *did*, the trespass was unintentional; if it *did* intentionally trespass, it did not eat Smith's vegetables; and if it *did* eat Smith's vegetables, it was insane.

Keep in mind that you assume the burden of proving each fact that you allege in an affirmative defense, counterclaim, and cross-claim. The burden of proof can sometimes tip the balance between winning and losing, so draft carefully. For more on drafting pleadings, see chapter 4, sections 3 and 5.

## 3. File a pretrial memo that does more than just refute plaintiff's theme

Consistent with creating a "persistence of belief" for the judge to arrive at point C rather than point B, you should guide the judge in the right direction and give the judge a very good reason to get to point C, in a cogent, compelling pretrial memo—even when such a memo is not mandated.

Put yourself in the judge's shoes and ask: "What counter-theme is most compelling, and how can I present it most effectively?" Include facts you are confident you can establish at trial, weaving them into your counter-theme. When the judge hears the testimony and admits into evidence a key document to get to point C, the judge will be primed to understand the significance of what you are putting into the record, and how it fits into your counter-theme. Otherwise, you risk presenting a smattering of data without context.

## 4. Take limited notes as plaintiff's witnesses testify

Some trial lawyers make the mistake of taking copious notes during the direct examination of the plaintiff's witnesses. If you have conducted proper discovery, you know before trial what each witness for the plaintiff is likely to testify to on direct. No significant purpose is served by your scribbling down as much of that testimony as possible. Besides, it is difficult to object timely or effectively when you are preoccupied in this way. You must be prepared to object to each question (although you will pick your shots, as discussed in the next section) in the instant between the end of that question and the beginning of the witness's answer—a matter of one or two seconds.

So what notes should you take when a witness for the plaintiff testifies on direct? You should only take notes useful to you in cross-examining that witness and other witnesses, and in putting on your own witnesses. Listen carefully. Sometimes a witness will use a certain word or make an unexpected admission that you can seize upon. Make a note of anything the witness says on direct that you can use on cross. Your trial notebook already includes an outline for your cross of each witness. Consider writing your trial notes from direct examination right on your cross outline so those notes are readily accessible as you stand up to begin your cross.

Of course, it can be helpful as the trial unfolds to have someone else take detailed notes summarizing what each of the plaintiff's witnesses says on direct. Various strategies include having a paralegal in the courtroom taking notes on a laptop (thereby giving you the opportunity to search for key terms instantaneously), having a second-chair attorney take notes, and ordering daily transcripts. Each of these options adds to the cost of the defense, so you must weigh the benefits against the cost and advise your client accordingly.

## 5. Keep plaintiff's witnesses' testimony and exhibits out of the record to the extent you can

You have many weapons in your arsenal to object to testimony and documents at trial. You must be poised to object before the witness has answered each question. Object strategically, which means that you will object only when the proffered testimony or document will be detrimental to your case and you have a good-faith basis to object, keeping in mind the judge's prior rulings on evidence during the course of the trial. Know the evidentiary basis for each objection so you can articulate it instantaneously. Unless you object *before* the witness responds to a question, you are relegated to making a motion to strike, which is not nearly as effective.

Here is a list of the most common objections to seek to exclude testimony and documents your opponent attempts to put into the record. This list is not intended to be all-inclusive.

### *How to protect the record before trial.*

- During the discovery phase when defending depositions, strategically object to questions that are objectionable, to preserve your objections for trial, and, if the deponent is your client, instruct the deponent not to answer when appropriate. See chapter 5, section 11, for more on defending depositions.
- During the discovery phase, be vigilant about not disclosing documents within the attorney-client and other privileges and those protected by the work-product doctrine. For the scope of the work-product privilege, see Rule 26(b)(3). If you make an inadvertent disclosure, be aware of the procedure in FRE 502 and Model Rule 4.4 for ethics issues that arise. See the discussion in chapter 3, section 5, regarding such inadvertent disclosure, which applies to responses to discovery requests as well as to emails mistakenly sent to opposing counsel.
- Anticipate the testimony of each witness opposing counsel is likely to call at trial; determine what objections you can properly raise. Some pretrial orders require disclosure of all such witnesses, and procedural rules require disclosure of all testifying expert witnesses. See Rule 26(a)(2).
- Anticipate all documents opposing counsel will likely seek to put into the record at trial and determine what objections you can

properly raise. Some pretrial orders require disclosure of all documents each side intends to put into the record, giving you advance notice of those documents, except for rebuttal or sur-rebuttal.
- File motions in limine when appropriate so you alert the judge before trial of key evidentiary issues, provide the judge with authorities on those issues, and seek a ruling on those issues before trial. Be aware that some judges reserve decision on motions in limine until trial. It is appropriate to file a motion in limine when you seek to keep something out of the record, or get something into the record, and the evidentiary issue is sufficiently complex that a pretrial motion and supporting memo would aid the court. Be mindful that filing a motion in limine also gives your opponent advance notice of the evidentiary issue and of the authorities you rely on regarding that issue. See chapter 9, section 5, for more on motions in limine.
- If opposing counsel intends to put deposition transcripts into evidence in lieu of live testimony (as when an out-of-state witness has been deposed and will not be appearing at trial, a witness who has been deposed cannot attend the trial, or opposing counsel seeks to put in an admission of a party from a deposition transcript), carefully review the transcript to determine what excerpts from that transcript are objectionable, for which you have preserved your right to object. Rules 29, 30(c)(2), and 32. In addition, get into the record other excerpts that help your case. FRE 106 and Rule 32(a)(6).

## *How to object to testimony and exhibits during trial.*
### Reasons to object to questions.
- exclude prejudicial evidence that is properly excludable
- make a record for appeal
- prevent unfair treatment of a witness
- break up the testimony of an opposing witness, if you have a proper basis to object
- reinforce your theme when objecting, unless the court does not allow speaking objections

### Objections as to the form of the question.
- leading question during direct examination, unless preliminary question or necessary to develop the witness's testimony, FRE 104(a) and 611(c)

- compound
- ambiguous or unintelligible
- already asked and answered
- argumentative
- too general or calls for a narrative answer
- misquotes the witness or misstates prior evidence
- assumes facts not in evidence

**Objections to the substance of testimony.**
- irrelevant, FRE 401, 402
- immaterial
- hearsay, FRE 801–807
- lack of personal knowledge, FRE 602
- no foundation
- speculation
- waste of time or cumulative, FRE 403
- prejudice outweighs probative value, FRE 403
- confusing or misleading, FRE 403
- inadmissible opinion of lay witness, FRE 701
- privileged, FRE 501 and 502
- voir dire question beyond the scope of proper voir dire
- cross beyond scope of direct, FRE 611(b)
- redirect beyond the scope of cross, FRE 611(b)
- improper impeachment, FRE 613
- prior consistent statement, FRE 801(d)(1)(B)
- testimony admissible only for a limited purpose, FRE 105
- answer beyond scope of question (motion to strike)

**Objections to exhibits.**
- irrelevant, FRE 401 and 402
- immaterial
- waste of time or cumulative, FRE 403
- no foundation
- hearsay, FRE 801–807
- prejudice outweighs probative value, FRE 403
- confusing or misleading, FRE 403
- inadmissible opinion of lay witness, FRE 701
- privileged

- not authenticated, FRE 901 and 902
- improper copy, FRE 1003
- public record not certified or insufficient supporting testimony, FRE 902(1) to (5) and 1005
- summary if underlying documents not made available as required, FRE 1006
- not disclosed as required by mandatory disclosure, Rule 26(a)
- not disclosed as required by a document request to which opposing counsel did not object in the discovery phase, Rule 34(b)
- not disclosed as required by a pretrial order
- document admissible only for a limited purpose, FRE 105

The hearsay objection deserves further discussion, because it arises so often. Hearsay is an out-of-court statement offered in evidence to prove the truth of the matter asserted. FRE 801(c). Thus, the *purpose* of the offer is crucial. If something is not offered for the *truth* of the matter asserted, but instead, for example, to elicit testimony or evidence about state of mind or notice, it is not hearsay. Also, verbal acts, such as the statement of an offer or acceptance in a contract action, are not hearsay.

FRE 801(d) enumerates the kinds of statements that are not hearsay, including, among other things, certain prior inconsistent statements of a witness, and admissions by a party opponent (which include admissions by others than the named party opponent), when offered *against* that party. Prior *consistent* statements of a witness are admissible only in very limited, unusual circumstances. See FRE 801(d)(1)(B).

Hearsay is not admissible, subject to numerous exceptions as provided in FRE 803, 804, and 807. Opposing counsel cannot take advantage of the residual exception in FRE 807 without providing you advance notice, as required by that rule.

One challenge is being sufficiently alert to a question that does not obviously call for hearsay testimony. Red flags go up, of course, when opposing counsel asks: "What did Henry Horton tell you about who attended the meeting?" But what if the question is: "Who attended the meeting?" If opposing counsel has not laid a proper foundation for *how* the witness knows who attended the meeting, the source of the witness's knowledge may be hearsay. So, object based on lack of foundation. If the foundation is that Henry Horton told the witness, then object on the ground of hearsay.

Also be on the lookout for hearsay within hearsay. For example, even if a document is within the business record exception to the hearsay rule (FRE 803(6)), it is still subject to a hearsay objection if the *contents* of that document include hearsay. See FRE 805.

## 6. OBJECT STRATEGICALLY TO QUESTIONS ON DIRECT

Listen carefully to each question posed by the plaintiff's counsel. That's one reason not to take copious notes of the witness's answers. As each question is asked, consider: Is the question improperly leading? Does it call for hearsay *or* irrelevant or immaterial testimony, assume facts not in evidence, or seek an answer for which there is no foundation? Is it otherwise objectionable? Be poised to stand and object before the witness can answer.

Make objections timely. Don't interrupt the question posed by the plaintiff's counsel, but don't wait until the answer is in the record before objecting. If you wait until the answer is given, you are relegated to making a motion to strike. As discussed in section 17 of this chapter, the untimeliness of your objection is especially a problem in jury cases. Stand up when you are about to object. By standing, you signal that you have an objection to a question. Address your objection to the judge, not to opposing counsel.

You have an arsenal of objections to keep out testimony and exhibits. At trial, you could object to each potentially objectionable question, and you may even keep some things out of the record by doing so. It is far more effective, though, to object strategically.

Objecting strategically means asking yourself, before you stand up to object, whether you can accomplish something meaningful by objecting. If a question is readily fixable and you have good reason to believe that opposing counsel will fix it, don't bother to object. For example, if opposing counsel has not established all the elements for the business record exception to the hearsay rule, FRE 803(6), but can easily do so by asking a follow-up question—and will get the right answer—then what do you accomplish by objecting? On the other hand, if you doubt opposing counsel can satisfy the requirements of FRE 803(6), certainly object.

When you object, you may decide not to telegraph more than necessary, especially when opposing counsel is struggling in attempting to get something into the record. If the judge does not require more from you and knows the rules of evidence, simply say, "Objection." If the judge sustains your objection, without explanation, plaintiff's counsel will have the burden of figuring out what the problem is. Be prepared, though, to state the basis for each objection. And when given the opportunity, weave your counter-theme into your objection so you can frame the evidentiary issue to your client's benefit. If you have more than one basis to object to a question, inform the court of that fact and present your best objection first.

How do you know what to object to? In preparing for trial, ask yourself what testimony and exhibits plaintiff's counsel will want to get into the record and whether you have a proper basis to keep out any of it. Strategically, object to testimony and evidence that both hurts your case and is objectionable. By picking your shots, you will find that the judge is more likely to pay close attention to the objections you *do* raise, and you will have greater success in limiting plaintiff's evidence. Also consider filing a motion in limine. Even if you don't file that motion, be prepared at trial to state the basis for each objection and have appropriate authorities at your fingertips, including the applicable section of the rules of evidence.

Listen carefully to the judge's words when ruling on your objections, and adjust your later objections based on what you learn. For example, if a judge's interpretation of what is a leading question is far more limited than yours (allowing answers to questions you consider leading but the judge does not), you accomplish little and risk antagonizing the judge by repeatedly objecting to such questions.

This does not mean that you should refrain from protecting the record. On evidentiary issues that truly make a difference in a case, you must object and create a record at trial sufficient for a successful appeal if you get an adverse ruling. Keep in mind, though, that appellate courts give trial judges wide latitude in evidentiary rulings, and very few cases are overturned on appeal as a result of errors in such rulings.

## 7. Object strategically to plaintiff's exhibits

For each exhibit you expect plaintiff will want to put into the record, determine before trial whether you have a valid basis to object. Here are just some examples: Is it irrelevant, FRE 402, and even if relevant, is it excludable under FRE 403? Does it include hearsay, FRE 801, not within one of the exceptions in FRE 803? Is it properly authenticated, as required in FRE 901, assuming the self-authenticating provisions of FRE 902 do not apply? If it is a summary, has plaintiff complied with FRE 1006?

If you conducted proper discovery, including comprehensive document requests, well before trial you will have received and analyzed all the documents plaintiff's counsel may want to put into the record at trial. Pretrial orders typically require both parties to disclose a list of documents they intend to put into the record. You should have at your fingertips a list of all such documents, and copies of all of them, indexed in a separate three-ring binder, on your computer, or both.

One reason for such comprehensive discovery is avoiding surprises at trial, including that all-time favorite: the smoking gun document. What do you do if, at trial, plaintiff's counsel seeks to put into evidence a document that you had not received in discovery? You don't want to be in the position of the lawyer at counsel table (or the client, for that matter) in the cartoon below.

You must determine whether that document is within your pretrial document requests, whether by request for production of documents pursuant to Rule 34 (note the continuing duty to disclose and correct in Rule 26(e)), or a document to be produced at deposition pursuant to Rule 30(b)(5). You should object to any unproduced document offered at trial that you asked for in pretrial discovery. An informal pretrial document request is likely useless here. See chapter 4, section 6, on drafting and responding to document requests, and chapter 5, section 4, on obtaining documents for depositions.

"Oh-oh, we're in trouble!"

© Gahan Wilson/The New Yorker Collection/Conde Nast

To avoid the risk that the judge will consider plaintiff's failure of production a mere oversight of little consequence, when objecting you should emphasize the significance of the document, how it is clearly within the scope of the documents you sought, and, most importantly, the prejudice your client suffers from the failure of disclosure. Be prepared for the judge to suggest a way to minimize the prejudice by allowing you to take a deposition or conduct other discovery in the middle of the trial. After all, the judge may say, a trial is a search for the truth (see FRE 102), so why keep out of the record a key document just because of a technicality, especially where any prejudice can be minimized?

You can respond, if true, that your trial strategy is based on the documents plaintiff's counsel produced, that further discovery in the middle of trial cannot undo that prejudice, that the court should not condone—and certainly not reward—plaintiff's counsel's gaming the system, and that a break in the trial would be disruptive. This last argument is even more effective in a jury trial.

When appropriate, you can conduct voir dire of a witness in establishing the basis for your objecting to a document being made an exhibit. Such voir dire can give you the opportunity to reinforce your counter-theme, while interrupting the flow of plaintiff's presentation.

## 8. Keep out expert testimony

### FRE 702 and 703.

Rule 702 provides that an expert witness may testify "if scientific, technical, or other specialized knowledge will assist the trier of fact to understand the evidence or to determine a fact in issue" based on the reliability factors summarized below. Rule 703 sets forth the permissible bases of opinion testimony by experts, including hearsay.

### Key cases.

**Daubert v. Merrell Dow Pharmaceuticals, Inc., 509 U.S. 579 (1993).** The court rejects the *Frye* rule, which had required that a scientific theory be generally accepted by the scientific community to be admissible. Frye v. United States, 293 F. 1013, 1014 (D.C. Cir. 1923). Trial court judges are gatekeepers to exclude unreliable expert testimony.

A two-step analysis is required, if the witness is already qualified as an expert: whether the reasoning or methodology underlying the expert's testimony is valid and whether that reasoning or methodology properly can be applied to the facts in issue.

**General Electric Co. v. Joiner, 522 U.S. 136 (1997).**
Abuse of discretion is the proper standard by which to review a district court's decision to admit or exclude scientific evidence. A court of appeals in applying the abuse of discretion standard may not categorically distinguish between rulings allowing expert testimony and rulings disallowing it. The court rejects the position that a *particularly stringent* standard of review applies to the trial judge's *exclusion* of expert testimony.

**Kumho Tire Co., Ltd. v. Carmichael, 526 U.S. 137 (1999).**
Trial court judges' gatekeeping function applies to *all* expert testimony, such as testimony based on technical or other specialized knowledge, not just to scientific testimony. The *Daubert* factors are not exhaustive or definitive, and do not apply exclusively to all experts or in all cases.

## Burden of proof.

FRE 104(a) provides that it is for the court to determine whether someone is qualified to testify. The proponent of expert testimony has the burden of demonstrating, by a preponderance of the evidence, that the testimony is competent (i.e., qualified), relevant, and reliable. The discussion below assumes that a witness is qualified as an expert on the subject at issue—an initial fact that the proponent of the testimony has the burden of proving.

## Relevance issue.

Will the expert's scientific, technical, or other specialized knowledge assist the trier of fact to understand the evidence or to determine a fact in issue? If so, can the expert's reasoning or methodology be properly applied to the facts before the court?

Is an untrained layperson qualified to determine intelligently and to the best possible degree the particular issue without enlightenment from those having a specialized understanding of the subject involved in the dispute? Expert testimony is generally admissible so long as it will assist the trier of fact to understand the evidence or to determine any fact in issue.

### When expert testimony excluded even if relevant.

Even if expert testimony is relevant, the trial court should exclude it if it is directed solely to lay matters that a jury is capable of understanding and deciding without the expert's help, where it is unreliable, or where FRE 403 applies.

FRE 403 provides: "The court may exclude relevant evidence if its probative value is substantially outweighed by a danger of one or more of the following: unfair prejudice, confusing the issues, misleading the jury, undue delay, wasting time, or needlessly presenting cumulative evidence."

### Reliability issue.

The reliability requirement applies to all aspects of the expert's testimony: methodology, facts underlying the expert's opinion, and the link between the facts and the conclusions.

FRE 702 sets forth the requirement of reliability. The testimony of a witness who is qualified as an expert by knowledge, skill, experience, training, or education may testify in the form of an opinion or otherwise as to relevant matters only if the following three criteria are met:

1. the testimony is based on sufficient facts or data
2. the testimony is the product of reliable principles and methods
3. the expert has reliably applied the principles and methods to the facts of the case

No single factor is dispositive. The trial court enjoys broad latitude. Factors trial courts can consider include the nature of the issue, the expert's particular expertise, the subject matter of the expert's testimony, Rule 702 factors, and additional factors courts have developed.

The trial court must rigorously examine

1. the data on which the expert relies: Is the testimony grounded on sufficient facts or data?
2. the method by which the expert's opinion is drawn from applicable studies and data: Is the testimony the product of reliable principles and methods?

3. the application of the data and methods to the case at hand: Has the witness applied the principles and methods reliably to the facts of the case?

Additional reliability factors are

1. whether a theory or technique has been or can be tested
2. whether the theory or technique has been subjected to peer review and publication
3. the technique's known or potential rate of error and the existence and maintenance of standards controlling the technique's operation
4. the existence and maintenance of standards controlling the technique's operation
5. whether a particular technique or theory has gained general acceptance in the relevant scientific community
6. whether the theory or method has been put to any non-judicial use
7. whether the expert's proposed testimony is about matters growing naturally and directly out of research the expert conducted independent of the litigation, or whether the expert developed the opinion expressly for the purpose of testifying
8. whether the expert has unjustifiably extrapolated from an accepted premise to an unfounded conclusion
9. whether the expert has adequately accounted for obvious alternative explanations
10. whether the expert is being as careful as he or she would be in the expert's regular professional work outside paid litigation consulting
11. whether the field of expertise claimed by the expert is known to reach reliable results for the type of opinion the expert would give

Expert testimony *must be* excluded if

1. there is so great an analytical gap between the data and the opinion proffered that the opinion is connected to the existing data only by the ipse dixit of the expert
2. it is speculative or conjectural

3. it is based on assumptions so unrealistic and contradictory as to suggest bad faith or to be, in essence, an "apples and oranges" comparison
4. its prejudicial effect outweighs its probative value

### When expert testimony only on general principle.

If an expert is testifying only about a general principle, without applying that general principle to the facts of a case, all that is required is

1. the expert is qualified
2. the testimony addresses a subject matter on which an expert can assist the fact finder
3. the testimony is reliable

### Expert's reliance on hearsay.

Rule 703 provides: "An expert may base an opinion on facts or data in the case that the expert has been made aware of or personally observed. If experts in the particular field would reasonably rely on those kinds of facts or data in forming an opinion on the subject, they need not be admissible for the opinion to be admitted. But if the facts or data would otherwise be inadmissible, the proponent of the opinion may disclose them to the jury only if their probative value in helping the jury evaluate the opinion substantially outweighs their prejudicial effect."

### Appellate review.

The trial court has wide discretion. A decision to admit or exclude expert testimony may be reversed only on a finding of abuse of discretion, requiring a finding that it is manifestly erroneous. The typical way to raise this issue is by a motion in limine. See chapter 9, section 5.

## 9. CONDUCT AN EFFECTIVE CROSS-EXAMINATION

John Henry Wigmore, the eminent jurist and scholar who wrote the preeminent treatise on the law of evidence, described cross-examination as "the greatest legal engine ever invented for the discovery of truth. You can do anything with a bayonet except sit on it. A lawyer can do anything with his cross-examination if he is skillful enough not to impale his own cause upon it."

Cross can serve many purposes, all of which undermine plaintiff's theme and support your counter-theme: building up your favorable witnesses; corroborating favorable testimony; obtaining admissions; minimizing the credibility of opposing witnesses; and minimizing or destroying the opposing witnesses' testimony. Sometimes it is advantageous to start with friendly cross before proceeding to more adversarial cross.

There are no hard-and-fast rules for cross-examination, just guidelines, so every suggestion here is subject to exceptions. Cross is an art, not a science.

In planning your cross, determine what points to make and know the evidentiary basis for each question and each exhibit not already in the record that you plan to use. Your cross should be concise; like a surgeon, accomplish your task with precision and efficiency. Be prepared to be flexible, adapting your cross to the testimony on direct. Avoid giving the witness the opportunity to repeat the testimony given on direct.

Even when you are prepared to cross a witness, decide whether to cross at all. Has your case been damaged by this witness's direct testimony? If so, can that damage be corrected or minimized, and do you have the means to do so?

Start strong. Use short, simple, understandable leading questions, preferably in the form of statements to which you seek agreement. Often, the best transcript on cross is one in which the witness says only "Yes" or "That's correct."

Be fair to the witness. Don't misrepresent what the witness said on direct, or take testimony out of context. Listen to the answer! Use it to your advantage when you can. Watch the witness's body language. Does it indicate lack of confidence, anxiety, or lying when you ask about a particular subject?

Retain control over the witness, but in such a way that the trier of fact will view you as being fair. How? By asking leading questions, limiting the answers to the questions you asked, controlling the pace, and using your voice and body language. By doing so, you will confine the witness's answers to what you want in the record.

What should you have in front of you as you ask questions on cross? As little as possible, but enough so you cover everything you need to.

You want to focus on the witness (including body language), and cannot do so when your nose is buried in detailed notes.

Key words are usually sufficient, except for any questions that must be worded with extreme care, such as when you want a witness to admit facts using language from a statute. (How satisfying and persuasive it is in a post-trial brief to cite witness testimony that tracks a statutory requirement!) If the witness does not answer your question, but a different question (such as one the witness wished you had asked), make sure your question was clear as stated. If so, say: "You didn't answer my question." Ask that the answer be stricken if it is of consequence in the case. Repeat the same question with the same words. Stay with it until you get your answer!

End your cross strong, with testimony of significance that is helpful to your case. Use a checklist of topics, and review it before saying: "No further questions." Then make sure the redirect is limited to the scope of your cross.

What should you *not* do on cross? Don't begin with a hostile demeanor, although if the witness starts playing games with you, you can be more aggressive. Don't try to trick or confuse the witness, or appear to be trying to do so. Don't cut off the witness's answer unless you have a good reason, such as stopping an obviously nonresponsive or hearsay answer. Don't ask why or how. Don't ask a question you don't know the answer to, unless you don't care what the answer is. Don't ask the one question too many—if you get a good answer, don't try to gild the lily, because you may give the witness the opportunity to weaken the effect of helpful testimony.

## 10. Impeach on cross-examination effectively

You can impeach based on a variety of factors, including bias, prejudice, interest, improper motive, insufficient memory, insufficient perception, inconsistent conduct, acts relating to honesty, reputation or opinion as to dishonesty, certain prior convictions, and, most trial lawyers' favorite, a prior inconsistent statement. The beauty of impeaching by a prior inconsistent statement is that you can use a witness's very own words—or omission of key facts in a prior statement—to belie the veracity of what the witness says in court. For authority to impeach using a prior inconsistent statement, see Rule 32(a)(2) and FRE 801(d)(1)(A).

You should impeach only if the witness's testimony hurt your case on a fact of significance for which you have solid impeachment material. This discussion will be limited to impeachment by prior inconsistent statement, but keep in mind all the other impeachment weapons in your arsenal. See, for example, FRE 607, 608, 609, 613, and 806.

Your mindset must be that the prior statement is the truth, and that the courtroom testimony is *inconsistent* with the truth. Your objective is not necessarily to demonstrate that the witness is lying. After all, the witness may merely remember facts incorrectly, be confused, or simply be mistaken in courtroom testimony.

Impeach one fact at a time. Here are the three steps for an effective impeachment: commit, credit, and contrast. Remember these three C's.

First, *commit* the witness to the courtroom statement, using the witness's own words from direct. In doing so, shut all avenues of escape, avoid words such as "true" and "correct," and use your tone and body language to indicate you don't believe a word of it.

Second, *credit* the impeaching document by building it up, whether it is a letter, report, memo, deposition or trial transcript, or some other document. The effectiveness of your impeachment is no greater than the importance of the impeaching document. Get the witness to admit its significance and trustworthiness.

Third, *contrast* the actual words of the impeaching material. (If you prefer, remember a different "c": *confront*.) Read the prior inconsistent statement to the witness, or play the videotape of it if you have taken a video deposition. Don't risk losing control by having the witness read the prior inconsistent statement, unless you have a good reason to do so. Have the witness admit making the prior inconsistent statement, by simply asking: "I read that correctly, didn't I?" Do not give the witness the opportunity to explain away the inconsistency by asking "Are you lying now or were you lying then?" or a similar question. Even though plaintiff's counsel can try to undo the damage you inflict by giving the same witness an opportunity to explain away the impeaching testimony on redirect, by then it is usually too little and too late. For more on impeachment, see chapter 5, section 17.

Remember that a document used for impeachment is not in evidence—nor is it subject to a hearsay objection, because it is not offered for the truth of the matter asserted. FRE 801(c). If you need the impeaching document to be part of the record to establish a prima facie case, or for some other reason, you must have an independent evidentiary basis to get it in the record.

## 11. Use plaintiff's exhibits against plaintiff

For each exhibit you expect plaintiff's counsel to offer into evidence, ask yourself: Does it hurt my case? If so, is it objectionable? If so, do I have the authority to cite to keep it out? In that circumstance, try to keep it out. But if it comes in, then what?

If you conducted proper discovery, you already deposed the witness on this document. You have already prepared a cross-examination as to this document, with references in your notes to the lines and pages in the deposition transcript you will use for ease of reference, and you are prepared to impeach if you get any bad answers.

In many instances, you can use plaintiff's own exhibits against plaintiff's witnesses. The best way to read any document is from the top left corner to the bottom right corner, keeping a watchful eye for any information that may be of interest, including (beyond the obvious, such as who wrote and received it, the date and contents) fax transmission data, page numbers (any missing pages?), redactions, and all handwriting.

As part of your trial preparation, be ready to use plaintiff's exhibits to your advantage. This same strategy applies to demonstrative exhibits. For example, if plaintiff's counsel uses a blowup of a document, highlighting certain words, use it yourself to highlight other words that benefit your client. (Also keep in mind FRE 106, which provides for introducing the remainder of a writing.) If plaintiff's counsel presents a chronology as a demonstrative exhibit, insert events that were conveniently omitted, to emphasize the importance of the omitted facts.

Keep out demonstrative exhibits that plaintiff's counsel offers in evidence. Only such proffered exhibits that are sufficiently accurate and probative are admissible, although illustrative aids (not made exhibits) may be used to assist a witness to explain testimony.

## 12. When plaintiff rests, consider filing a motion for judgment as a matter of law

If plaintiff's counsel has failed to present a prima facie case as to any count, right after plaintiff's counsel rests, make a motion for judgment as a matter of law (also referred to as motion for directed verdict), if the applicable procedural rules allow you to present your defense case even after doing so, even though judges usually reserve decision or deny such motions. See Rule 52 for bench trials and Rule 50 for jury trials.

Be aware of the consequential limits in your appeal rights if you fail to make this motion. In federal court, the motion is a prerequisite to challenge the sufficiency of evidence on appeal, except for plain error on the face of the record resulting in a miscarriage of justice. Even if you do not file this motion, you still preserve all other appellate issues.

## 13. Adjust your strategy when plaintiff rests

Before trial, you prepared your defense. You decided which witnesses to call, what questions to ask, what exhibits to put into the record, and what demonstrative exhibits to use. But wait. Before you proceed as planned, ask yourself: "Should I adjust my strategy based on what plaintiff's counsel actually put into the record?"

The lesson here is that, just as you adjust your cross-examination of a witness based on the courtroom testimony on direct, adjust your entire defense presentation based on what plaintiff was able to get into the record. Don't revise your basic strategy, except in unusual circumstances; but do fine-tune your presentation so you tailor it to what is already in evidence. Determine what witnesses to call, what to ask them, and what documents to put into the record, based on what plaintiff's counsel put into the record. Keep your presentation fresh, without offering cumulative evidence already in the record in plaintiff's case.

Keep in mind your burden of proof, whether as to any affirmative defenses, counterclaims, or cross-claims, and make sure you sustain that burden. Have a checklist handy of *prima facie* elements, and make sure you have sustained your burden before resting.

## 14. Limit plaintiff's rebuttal, and consider sur-rebuttal

Although judges are not consistent in their exercise of discretion as to the scope of rebuttal, the fundamental principle is that rebuttal is limited to plaintiff's counsel responding to what you put into the record not covered in plaintiff's direct case. Limit plaintiff's scope of rebuttal to this standard. Don't allow plaintiff's counsel to rehash plaintiff's case in chief, and keep in mind FRE 403, which excludes, among other things, cumulative evidence. To object effectively, have sufficiently detailed trial notes or trial transcripts to know what is already in the record, in plaintiff's direct case and in your defense case.

Rebuttal is not the opportunity for plaintiff's counsel to present redundant testimony, repeating what is already in the record. Don't allow that to happen. As soon as plaintiff's counsel advises the court of the proposed rebuttal witnesses, argue, to the extent appropriate, that you object to any testimony of those witnesses that is already in the record, and any testimony that is beyond the scope of proper rebuttal. Keep plaintiff's counsel on a short leash, objecting during rebuttal to any testimony that is beyond the proper scope.

Stay attuned to the opportunity for sur-rebuttal, keeping in mind that this funnel process, each stage limited to the scope of the prior stage, must end at some point. This winnowing procedure is analogous to the narrowing limits on a witness's testimony, cross-examination limited to the scope of direct, and redirect and recross similarly restricted. So, limit sur-rebuttal to something compelling. The additional advantage of sur-rebuttal is that you get the last word in. Under the theory of recency, what is heard last has more persuasive staying power than something in the middle of a trial.

## 15. Preserve issues for appeal

Here is a checklist for preserving issues on appeal. Keep in mind that the appellate court is limited to the trial court record. If you did not preserve an issue for appeal at the trial court, that issue cannot be a basis for an appeal, except for plain error affecting substantial rights, limited to exceptional cases, as provided in Rule 51(d)(2).

- File motions in limine, as discussed in chapter 9, section 5, and in this chapter, section 5.
- File motions to preclude expert testimony based on *Daubert* and its progeny, as discussed in section 8 of this chapter.
- When referring to a document, make explicit what you are referring to, by exhibit number or letter, page reference within the exhibit, and in other specific ways. Avoid using such words as "here," "in this section," "on this page," or any other vague ref-

erence that will not be explicit to the appellate court judges. Be especially diligent when referring to maps, diagrams, charts, and the like, avoiding such vague references as "at this location," and "where I am pointing to on the diagram."
- Make objections timely and with specificity. Error cannot be predicated on a ruling admitting or excluding evidence unless a substantial right of a party is affected and, if the ruling admits evidence, your objection or motion to strike is timely, appears of record, and you state the specific grounds of objection, if not apparent from the context. See FRE 103(a)(1) and sections 5, 6, and 7 of this chapter.
- If a judge excludes evidence that affects a substantial right, make a timely offer of proof. See FRE 103(a)(2) and chapter 9, section 12.
- After plaintiff rests, if appropriate, make a motion for judgment, as discussed in section 10 of this chapter.
- Consider moving under Rule 49 for a special verdict, by which the judge requires jurors to make specific findings, not merely a general verdict. Requiring this specificity may provide you with a better record on appeal, and is an inducement for the jurors to analyze each element of plaintiff's claims with greater deliberation.
- If you have a good-faith basis to do so, after the entry of judgment, file a motion for a new trial, open the judgment if one has been entered, take additional testimony, amend findings of fact and conclusions of law or make new ones, or direct the entry of a new judgment, as provided in Rule 59(a)(2). Any motion for new trial must be filed no later than 28 days after the entry of judgment, as provided in Rule 59(b). If your motion for new trial is based on affidavits, see Rule 59(c). Note that the court can, *sua sponte*, order a new trial for any reason that would justify granting one on a party's motion, giving the parties notice and an opportunity to be heard, and an opportunity to file a motion for a new trial for other reasons, as provided in Rule 59(d).
- If you have a good-faith basis to do so, file a motion to alter or amend a judgment, within 28 days after the entry of judgment, as provided in Rule 59(e).
- If a jury trial, preserve your appellate rights as discussed in section 17 of this chapter.

## 16. Miscellaneous tips

Even if you caution your client that plaintiff has the advantage of putting on testimony and evidence first, sitting through plaintiff's case can be demoralizing for a defendant. You are doing what you can to minimize the impact of the testimony of plaintiff's witnesses, but the fact is that plaintiff's counsel has the advantage of going first. Remind your client that a trial can be like a prize fight, some rounds better than others, and that you will have your opportunity to put on your defense, when you can land your own punches.

Be aware of opportunities to settle a case during trial, especially when plaintiff is vulnerable. You want to negotiate from a position of strength. For example, assume that you have just conducted an effective cross-examination of a key plaintiff's witness, or you have successfully kept a crucial document out of the record. This may be an opportune time, during a break, to suggest to plaintiff's counsel that further settlement discussions may be productive. Depending on the judge, you may even suggest that the judge meet with counsel during a break, and in chambers propose that the judge allow counsel time to discuss settlement—possibly with the assistance of another judge, to mediate.

You have at your disposal an arsenal of technological devices to enhance your defense case. Make the most of them. For example, when cross-examining a witness, you could impeach with a deposition transcript. But consider how much more effective that impeachment would be if you had taken a video deposition and you could, in the courtroom, immediately access the deposition Q and A for impeachment. A larger-than-life image of the same witness appears on the screen, contradicting what he said on direct. Powerful!

## 17. Adjust all this advice for a jury trial

Using your common sense, you'll intuit much of what you must adjust for a jury trial. For example, when cross-examining a witness, your demeanor should be appropriate, depending on the witness. You will cross a brash, arrogant, evasive witness differently than a likable, submissive witness, whether in a bench or jury trial. Likewise, you can become increasingly aggressive with a witness who gives a non-responsive answer on cross-examination only after you establish that the witness is being evasive, and not just confused by your question. Acting in a way that may be perceived as rude or obnoxious will likely have a more devastating effect on the outcome of your case in front of a jury. Unless the members of the jury find you likable, they won't want to follow you to point C.

When you are conducting the cross-examination of an uncooperative witness, don't ask for the judge's assistance unless you have no other choice. Once you do so, the jurors understand that you have lost control of the witness; besides, the judge may not see it your way. Seek judicial assistance only when it is clear that the witness is being intentionally obstreperous, and you have confidence that the judge—the power in the black robe—will support you.

The members of the jury perceive everything, and make up their minds based on much more than what would appear in an appellate court record. They observe how you relate to your client, opposing counsel, your colleagues, the judge, witnesses, and court personnel, whether "on the record" or "off the record." They observe you in the hallway, the elevator, and possibly during a lunch break. Be yourself, but also be aware that what matters is not limited to what is in the official record.

Know when to excuse the jury. It is inconvenient for the jurors to shuffle back and forth to the deliberation room during a trial, but you can't "unring the bell" if they hear testimony or see a document that you want to keep out. Just as you must object timely to avoid evidence coming in and then moving to strike (in which case the jurors hear the testimony that shouldn't be considered *three* times—from the witness, you, and the judge—and it's very difficult not to think about pink elephants when the judge instructs: "Don't think about pink elephants!"), you must ask the judge to excuse the jurors timely when seeking to exclude certain things from the record. You can also ask for a side bar discussion with the judge. One way to avoid this issue altogether is to file motions in limine.

When preparing the jury charge, use plain English, short sentences, and short paragraphs. Include a clear instruction on burden of proof. Unless the jurors understand that the plaintiff has the burden of proof as to all elements of each claim, the standard the jurors apply in their deliberations may be improper—and you may lose without knowing why. See chapter 4, section 7, for more on drafting jury charges.

In opening statement and closing argument, make the jurors care. In a commercial case, many jurors may find the trial boring. How can you make the jurors care? Personalize the dispute, and relate your client's defense to something the jurors will relate to in their own experience. See chapter 8, sections 3 and 4, for more on opening statements and closing arguments.

In a jury case, preserve your appellate rights by doing everything in section 15 of this chapter that applies, and the following:

- After plaintiff rests, file a motion for judgment as a matter of law if a reasonable jury would not have a legally sufficient evidentiary basis to find for the plaintiff on an issue, as provided in Rule 50(a). This motion can be made at any time before the case is submitted to the jury. It must specify the judgment sought, and the law and facts entitling you to move for judgment, as provided in Rule 50(a)(2).
- File proposed jury instructions by the close of evidence, or at such earlier time as the court orders, as provided in Rule 51(a)(1). For tips on drafting jury instructions, see chapter 4, section 7.
- After the close of evidence, file additional proposed jury instructions that could not reasonably have been anticipated by an earlier time the court set for filing them, as provided in Rule 51(a)(2).
- Object on the record to any jury instructions the court intends to give that are properly objectionable, before the instructions and arguments are delivered, as provided in Rule 51(b)(2) and 51(c)(2)(A).
- Object on the record to an instruction you were not informed of, and to any action on a request for jury instructions, promptly after learning that the instruction or request will be, or has been, given or refused, as provided in Rule 51(c)(2)(B).
- Make any objection to jury instructions, or the failure to give jury instructions, on the record, stating distinctly the matter objected to and the grounds for your objection, as provided in Rule 51(c)(2).
- If the court does not grant your motion for judgment as a matter of law made pursuant to Rule 50(a), file a renewed motion for judgment as a matter of law or, in the alternative or jointly, request a new trial as provided in Rule 59. The renewed motion must be filed no later than 28 days after the entry of judgment or, if the motion addresses a jury issue not decided by a verdict, no later than 28 days after the jury was discharged, as provided in Rule 50(b). In deciding a Rule 50(b) motion, the court can allow judg-

ment on the verdict (if the jury returned a verdict), order a new trial, or direct the entry of judgment as a matter of law. See Rule 50(c) for more on a renewed motion for judgment as a matter of law, and conditional grant of a motion for a new trial.
- File a motion for a new trial, as provided in Rule 59(a)(1)(A), no later than 28 days after the entry of judgment, as provided in Rule 50(d).
- For more on the effect of the court's denial of your motion for judgment on your appellate rights, see Rule 50(e).

❖❖❖❖
## PRACTICE CHECKLIST

- Choose a compelling counter-theme that does more than merely refute plaintiff's theme.
- Draft your answer, affirmative defenses, counterclaims, and cross-claims so they are consistent with your counter-theme.
- File a pretrial memo that does more than just refute plaintiff's theme.
- Take limited notes as plaintiff's witnesses testify.
- Keep plaintiff's witnesses' testimony and exhibits out of the record:
  - _____ Protect the record before trial.
  - _____ Know the bases to object to the form of questions.
  - _____ Know the bases to object to the substance of testimony.
  - _____ Know the bases to object to exhibits.
- Object strategically to questions on direct:
  - _____ Listen to each question carefully—is it objectionable?
  - _____ Be poised to object to each question timely, avoiding the need to file a motion to strike, when it is too late to "unring the bell."
  - _____ Object only when you have good reason, and can keep evidence out.
  - _____ Adjust your objections to the judge's rulings.
- Object as appropriate to plaintiff's exhibits:
  - _____ Are they objectionable as violative of any rules of evidence?
  - _____ Were they produced in response to your pretrial discovery?
  - _____ Voir dire on exhibits when appropriate.
- Keep out expert testimony, based on the *Daubert* analysis.
- Conduct an effective cross-examination of each witness.
  - _____ Cross serves many purposes: build up favorable witnesses, corroborate favorable testimony, obtain admissions, minimize the witness's credibility, and minimize or destroy the witness's testimony.
  - _____ Before trial, determine what points you want to make on cross and know the evidentiary basis for each question you plan to ask.
  - _____ At trial, decide whether to cross at all: Was your case damaged by the testimony on direct? If so, can you do something about it?
  - _____ Use short, understandable leading questions, preferably in the form of statements.
  - _____ Be fair to the witness by not misrepresenting what the witness said or taking testimony out of context.
  - _____ Observe the witness's body language when answering questions.

(continued)

_____ Use as few notes as practical.
_____ If the witness does not answer your question, repeat it—but if your question may have been confusing, fix it first.
_____ Start and end strong with each witness.
_____ Use a checklist to be sure you have covered all the points before ending your cross.
_____ Don't start with a hostile demeanor, try to trick or confuse the witness, cut off the answer (unless you have good reason, such as stopping a nonresponsive or improper answer), ask why or how, ask a question you don't know the answer to, or ask the one question too many.
_____ Remember that these are merely guidelines, subject to exceptions, depending on the circumstances in each case.
- Impeach on cross-examination effectively:
  _____ Determine before trial whether you have impeachment material, and use it only if the witness's testimony on direct hurt your case.
  _____ Impeach one fact at a time.
  _____ First, commit the witness to the courtroom statement, making clear you don't believe the statement on which you will impeach.
  _____ Second, credit the impeaching document or statement by building it up.
  _____ Third, confront the witness with the words of the impeaching material.
  _____ Don't give the witness the opportunity to explain away the inconsistency.
  _____ Remember that the impeaching document is not evidence.
- Use plaintiff's exhibits and demonstrative exhibits against plaintiff.
- When plaintiff rests, consider filing a motion for judgment as a matter of law.
- Adjust your strategy when plaintiff rests, based on what is in the record.
- Limit plaintiff's rebuttal to what you put into the record not covered in plaintiff's case in chief, and consider sur-rebuttal, keeping in mind its limited scope.
- Preserve issues for appeal.
- Miscellaneous tips:
  _____ Before trial, caution your client that plaintiff goes first, which can be demoralizing, but that you will have your opportunity to undermine plaintiff's case when you cross-examine and when you present your defense case.
  _____ Be aware of opportunities to settle during the course of the trial.
  _____ Take advantage of technology in your defense.

(continued)

- Adjust all this advice for a jury trial.
    - _____ Adjust your demeanor based on the witness's demeanor.
    - _____ Seek judicial intervention with a difficult witness only when you have no other option.
    - _____ Be aware that during a trial you are "on the record" from the moment you leave the office until the moment you return to the office.
    - _____ Excuse the jurors when necessary to avoid their learning about something you seek to keep out of the record.
    - _____ Minimize disruption for the jurors by filing motions in limine where appropriate.
    - _____ In your jury charge, use plain English, short sentences, and short paragraphs; include a clear instruction on burden of proof.
    - _____ In opening statement and closing argument, make the jurors care by personalizing the dispute whenever possible, and relating your defense to something the jurors will identify with their own experience.

# CHAPTER ELEVEN
# DEALING WITH ETHICAL ISSUES

We begin our discussion of ethics with a word about zeal. As trial lawyers, we have an ethical obligation to represent our clients zealously. The current Model Rules of Professional Conduct (the "Model Rules" or "Rules") provide in the preamble: "As advocate, a lawyer zealously asserts the client's position under the rules of the adversary system." This language is toned down from the American Bar Association's first code of ethics, published in 1908, which included the admonition that "a lawyer owes entire devotion to the interest of the client, *warm zeal* in the maintenance and defense of his rights and the exertion of his utmost learning and ability" (emphasis added). The first Model Code of Professional Responsibility, in 1969, tempered "warm zeal" in Canon 7: "A lawyer should represent a client zealously within the bounds of the law." In 1983, the ABA rewrote the ethical rules once again, relegating "zealously" to the preamble.

Despite this degradation from "warm zeal" in an ethical rule to mere use of "zeal" as an adverb in only the preamble, we cannot allow our zeal in representing clients to overcome our obligation to comply with the ethical rules. Compliance with ethical rules is an enormous topic, the subject of numerous treatises. *See, e.g.*, Peter R. Jarvis, W. William Hodes & Geoffrey C. Hazard, Jr., The Law of Lawyering (Aspen Publishers 3d ed. 2000). An excellent source for state-by-state ethics opinions is Cornell Law School's American Legal Ethics Library, at www.law.cornell.edu/ethics. The *Restatement of the Law (Third) Governing Lawyers* (American Law Institute 2012) covers most ethics issues, except those pertaining to solicitation and advertising. To view the most up-to-date version of the Rules, go to http://www.americanbar.org/groups/professional_responsibility.html. If you are a member of the American Bar Association, get answers to ethics questions by going to www.ambar.org/abaethicsearch. See appendix III for other books on ethics.

This chapter discusses some of the most common ethical issues we confront as trial lawyers, but not all of them. Chapter 12, which provides advice about marketing your litigation practice, discusses ethical issues regarding promotion of your practice.

Some ethical rules are easy to apply. You will not, for example, mingle client funds with yours, disclose client confidences to anyone outside the office (even to your spouse), or discuss a case with an opposing party who is represented by counsel, without consent of opposing counsel. But difficult ethical issues arise frequently for trial lawyers. Ethical issues are not all black and white; gray areas abound.

For example, opposing parties can discuss the case between themselves, without counsel, but are there limits on what you can suggest your client says to the opposing party? If the opposing party is a corporation represented by counsel, which employees of that corporation, if any, can you talk to without first seeking opposing counsel's consent? And what about *former* employees of that corporation? Some answers to these and other ethical questions may surprise you.

The first challenge is to recognize ethical issues when they arise. Otherwise, you could act unethically without even being aware of your lapse. Whenever in doubt whether you are confronted with an ethical issue, check the rules, and talk to someone knowledgeable about ethics. This chapter applies the Model Rules and the very informative comments that supplement those rules. If the Model Rules apply in your jurisdiction, they govern your conduct, including your conduct before any tribunal. A tribunal includes a court, arbitrator, legislative body, administrative agency, or other body acting in an adjudicative capacity. See Rule 1.0(m).

If different rules apply in your jurisdiction, comply with them. In addition to reading this chapter, read *all* the ethical rules that apply in your jurisdiction, and attend seminars on ethics. Then test your understanding of ethical rules by attempting to solve the ethics problems in appendix II. Work through them with your colleagues.

### 1. Make sure you have the competence before undertaking a representation (Rule 1.1)

Having graduated from law school and passed the bar, you are finally in a position, as a bona fide trial lawyer, to give advice to clients, and you are understandably eager to do so. Before giving a client advice, though, you must have the competence to do so, based on the relative complexity and specialized nature of the matter, your general experience, your training and experience in the field in question, your preparation and study of the matter, and whether it is feasible for you to refer the matter to, or to associate or consult with, a lawyer of established competence in the field in question.

Sometimes the most difficult statement to make to a client is: "I don't know." If the issue is one within your competence, you can then say just that, and add: "But I will research the issue and get back to you." However, unless you have specialized training and experience in areas of the law such as tax, securities, bankruptcy, or intellectual property, refer such issues to your colleagues or others.

### 2. Get your client's authority, and communicate with your client as required by the ethical rules (Rules 1.2, 1.4, and 1.6)

Your client has ultimate authority to determine the purposes to be served by your legal representation, within the limits imposed by law and your professional obligations. You must promptly inform your client of any decision or circumstance with respect to which your client's informed consent is required. Before a client can give you "informed consent," you must communicate to your client adequate information, and an explanation about the material risks of and reasonably available alternatives to the course of conduct you propose. Rule 1.0(e).

Your obligation to communicate with your client also requires that you reasonably consult with your client about the means by which you will accomplish his or her objectives, keep your client reasonably informed about the status of the matter, promptly comply with your client's requests for information, consult with your client about any limits on your representation, and explain a matter to the extent reasonably necessary for your client to make informed decisions about your representation. You must abide by your client's decision whether to settle a matter, and on what terms. Make sure you get your client's authority before proposing any settlement.

For any significant decision related to your representation, confirm your client's informed consent in writing, by email or letter. This confirmation reminds your client of his or her authorization for you to proceed as you advise, and verifies your client's informed consent if any issue about that consent arises in the future.

What if your client disagrees with you about the means to accomplish your client's objectives, and you can't resolve that disagreement? If the disagreement is fundamental, you can seek to withdraw as counsel, as provided in Rule 1.16(b)(4), or the client may discharge you, as provided in Rule 1.16(a)(3), discussed in section 6 of this chapter. Before the situation deteriorates to that point, do your best to explain why you can't do as your client requests. If necessary, arrange for another lawyer in your firm to work with you and your client in resolving the disagreement.

You cannot counsel or assist your client in committing a crime or fraud, although this prohibition does not preclude you from giving your honest opinion about the actual consequences likely to result from your client's conduct. The distinction is between presenting your analysis of legal aspects of questionable conduct (permissible) and recommending the means by which a crime or fraud might be committed (not permissible). If a client has already undertaken such conduct, you must seek to withdraw as counsel—and withdrawal alone may be insufficient. You may need to give notice of your withdrawal and disaffirm as provided in Rule 4.1.

With certain exceptions, Rule 1.6 prohibits you from revealing information relating to your representation of a client absent informed consent. This rule has broad application, not limited to communications within the attorney-client privilege and work product doctrine. The range of protected information covers information from any source, even public sources, and even information that is not itself protected but may lead to the discovery of protected information by a third party.

As a practical matter, this means that, unless you have client consent, you cannot reveal client-related information encompassed within Rule 1.6 in response to a third-party subpoena, in advertising or marketing, or in casual conversation. The best advice is to obtain the client's written informed consent before disclosing any such information.

## 3. AVOID CONFLICTS OF INTEREST WITH CURRENT CLIENTS (RULES 1.7, 1.8, AND 1.10)

Conflicts of interest present especially difficult ethical issues. For a thorough analysis of the sometimes subtle considerations required in determining whether you have a conflict of interest, consult the comments to the Model Rules, treatises on ethics, and the online Cornell Law School source referenced at the beginning of this chapter—and discuss conflict issues with your colleagues.

You must have an effective conflicts check system that includes information about present and former clients for you to comply with ethical conflicts rules. When you represent an entity, your conflicts check system must include the names of principals. For example, if you represent a partnership, you must include in your conflicts check the names of all partners. For more on conflicts checks, see chapter 1, section 1.

Rule 1.7(a) provides that, except as provided in 1.7(b), you cannot represent a client if the representation involves a concurrent conflict of interest. Such a conflict exists if (1) your representation of one client will be directly adverse to another client or (2) there is a significant risk that your representation of one or more clients will be materially limited by your responsibilities to another client, a former client, or a third person, or by your own personal interest.

Rule 1.7(b) allows you to represent a client, despite a concurrent conflict, if four conditions are met: (1) you reasonably believe that you will be able to provide competent and diligent representation to each affected client, (2) your representation is not prohibited by law, (3) your representation does not involve asserting a claim by one client against another in the same litigation or other proceeding before a tribunal, and (4) each affected client gives you informed consent, confirmed in writing (which may be by electronic transmission).

Resolution of a conflict of interest problem requires you to (1) clearly identify the client or clients; (2) determine whether a conflict exists; (3) decide whether you can undertake the representation despite the conflict if it exists (i.e., whether it is consentable); and (4) if so, consult with the affected clients and obtain their informed consent, confirmed in writing.

If your client is an organization, by virtue of that representation, you do not necessarily represent any constituent or affiliated organization, such as a parent or subsidiary. See Rule 1.13(a). Thus, in that circumstance, you can accept representation adverse to an affiliate in an unrelated matter, unless the circumstances are such that the affiliate should also be considered your client; you have an understanding with the organization that you will not undertake such representation; or such representation is likely to limit materially your representation of the other client.

Even in the absence of any direct adverseness, a conflict of interest still exists if there is a significant risk that your ability to consider, recommend, or carry out an appropriate course of action for one client will be materially limited as a result of your responsibilities to another client, or your own interests. A conflict of interest also exists if there is a significant risk that your action on behalf of one client will materially limit your effectiveness in representing another client in a different case, as when a decision favoring one client will create a precedent likely to seriously weaken the position you have taken on behalf of the other client.

In seeking informed consent, you must discuss with each affected client the relevant circumstances, as well as the material and reasonably foreseeable ways the conflict could have adverse effects on the interests of that client. If you are considering representing more than one client in a single matter, you must discuss with each client the implications of that common representation, including possible effects on loyalty, confidentiality, the attorney-client privilege, and the advantages and risks involved.

Some conflicts are, by their nature, *not* subject to consent. If you are considering representing more than one client where there is a concurrent conflict, you must resolve the issue of consentability as to each client. You must carefully consider whether you can provide competent and diligent representation as to each, even if the clients are willing to consent to your representation. See Rule 1.1 for the meaning of "competence" and Rule 1.3 for the meaning of "diligence."

Rule 1.8 covers more specific conflict-of-interest issues pertaining to current clients: your entering into business transactions with clients; your using information from one client to the disadvantage of another client; your soliciting any substantial gift from a client; your providing financial assistance to a client in connection with litigation; your accepting compensation from someone other than your client; your making an aggregate settlement of claims of or against concurrent clients; your acquiring a proprietary interest in your client's cause of action or subject matter of the litigation; your having sexual relations with a client; and other matters. Rule 1.10 covers the imputation of your conflict of interest to others in your firm, including issues that arise when you move from one firm to another.

## 4. Avoid conflicts of interest with former clients (Rules 1.9 and 1.10)

Even after termination of an attorney-client relationship, you have continuing duties with respect to confidentiality and conflicts of interest, and thus you may not be able to represent another client unless you comply with Rules 1.9 and 1.10. If you have formerly represented a client in a matter, you cannot represent another client in the same or a substantially related matter in which that person's interests are materially adverse to the interests of your former client, unless your former client gives informed consent, confirmed in writing. So, for example, if you represented multiple clients in a matter, you cannot then represent one of them against the others in the same or a substantially related matter if a dispute arises among them in that matter, unless all affected clients give their informed consent.

What is a "substantially related" matter for purposes of this rule? Matters are substantially related if they involve the same transaction or legal dispute, or if there otherwise is a substantial risk that confidential factual information would materially advance the client's position in the subsequent matter. Such information does not generally include information (1) disclosed to the public, (2) disclosed to other parties adverse to the former client, (3) rendered obsolete by the passage of time, or (4) pertaining to an organizational client's policies and practices. However, knowledge of specific facts you learned in a prior representation relevant to the proposed representation ordinarily does preclude that representation.

If you, or anyone in your present or former firm, represented a former client in a matter, you cannot use information relating to that representation to the disadvantage of that former client, except as the Model Rules permit or require with respect to a client, or when the information has become generally known. You also cannot reveal information relating to that representation, except as the Model Rules permit or require with respect to a client.

Rule 1.9(b) covers your duties to former clients when you move from one firm to another. It provides that you cannot knowingly represent a person in the same or a substantially related matter in which your former firm had represented a client whose interests are materially adverse to that person and about whom you acquired information protected by Rules 1.6 and 1.9(c). For conflict imputation rules that apply to a former representation, see Rule 1.10.

## 5. Comply with the ethical rules when you represent an organization (Rule 1.13)

Commercial trial lawyers frequently represent organizations, such as corporations, limited liability companies, partnerships, and limited partnerships. When representing an organization, you must keep in mind that your duty is to the organization, not to the constituents of the organization, even though an organization can act only through its constituents.

Who are the constituents of an organization? They are its members, partners, limited partners, officers, directors, employees, and shareholders, among others, depending on the nature of the organization.

Rule 1.13(b) provides that if you know that a constituent of your organization client is engaged in an action, intends to act, or refuses to act in a matter related to your representation of the organization that violates a legal obligation to the organization, or is a violation of law that reasonably might be imputed to the organization, likely to result in substantial injury to the organization, you are obligated to proceed as is reasonably necessary in the best interests of the organization. This may include referring the matter to higher authority within the organization. What does it mean for you to "know" in this context? As defined in Rule 1.0(f), your knowledge can be inferred from circumstances. You cannot ignore the obvious.

Subject to the exception in Rule 1.13(d), Rule 1.13(c) provides that if the highest authority within the organization insists on, or fails to address in a timely and appropriate manner, an action or refusal to act that is a violation of a legal obligation to the organization, or a violation of law that reasonably might be imparted to the organization, likely to result in substantial injury to the organization, you may reveal that information relating to your representation, even if Rule 1.6 does not permit such disclosure.

The exception in Rule 1.13(d) is that Rule 1.13(c) does not apply to information relating to your representation of an organization to investigate an alleged violation of law, or to defend the organization or a constituent associated with the organization against a claim arising out of an alleged violation of law.

In dealing with an organization's constituent, you must explain that you represent the organization, not the constituent, when you know or reasonably should know that the organization's interests are adverse to those of the constituent with whom you are dealing. Thus, for example, when gathering information from an employee or preparing an employee for a deposition in a case in which you represent the employer, you must explicitly inform that employee, at the beginning of your first conversation with that employee, that you represent his or her employer, not the employee, if you know or reasonably should know that the organization's interests are adverse to that employee. The better practice is to make this explicit statement to the employee even if there are no such adverse interests, to avoid the employee's understandable assumption that you are his or her lawyer.

Subject to Rule 1.7, you can represent a constituent of an organization as well as the organization itself. If the circumstances are such that Rule 1.7 requires the organization's consent, you must seek such consent from an appropriate official of the organization other than the individual who is to be represented, or from the shareholders.

If you reasonably believe that you have been discharged because of your actions pursuant to Rule 1.13(b) or (c), or if you withdraw as counsel for the organization pursuant to those rules, you must proceed as you reasonably believe necessary to assure that the organization's highest authority is informed of your discharge or withdrawal.

### 6. Comply with the ethical rules when you decline or terminate representation of a client (Rule 1.16)

If you decline a representation, be explicit that you will not be representing the prospective client. It is preferable to convey that message in writing. Do not give legal advice when you decline a representation, but do suggest that the prospective client consult with another lawyer. If any statutes of limitations are about to run, you can suggest that the prospective client consult with other counsel promptly, because certain rights may otherwise be extinguished. For more on declining representation, see chapter 1, section 3.

Subject to complying with the law in your jurisdiction requiring notice to your client, and permission of the court if you have filed a court appearance, you *must* withdraw if your client demands that you engage in conduct that is illegal or violates the ethical rules, and you *may* seek to withdraw as counsel if

- withdrawal can be accomplished without material adverse effect on your client's interests,
- your client persists in a course of action involving your services that you reasonably believe is criminal or fraudulent,
- your client has used your services to perpetrate a crime or fraud,
- your client insists on taking action you consider repugnant or with which you have a fundamental disagreement,
- your client fails substantially to fulfill an obligation to you regarding your services (such as failing to pay you as agreed in your retainer agreement) and you have given reasonable warning to your client that you will withdraw unless that obligation is fulfilled, or
- you have other good cause to withdraw.

If you plan to withdraw as counsel, in addition to complying with applicable rules of practice, you must take steps, to the extent reasonably practicable, to protect your client's interests, such as giving reasonable notice to your client, giving your client time to employ other counsel, giving your client papers and property your client is entitled to, and refunding any fee and advances for expenses you have not yet earned or incurred. You can retain papers only to the extent allowed in your jurisdiction, as provided in statutes and rules that provide for retaining liens.

If you have filed an appearance for a client, you must do what is required to protect your client's interests until the tribunal has granted your motion to withdraw as counsel.

## 7. Know your ethical obligations if you discuss a matter with a prospective client (Rule 1.18)

If you meet with a prospective client and do not undertake the representation, what are your ethical obligations to that person? Even in the absence of an attorney-client relationship, you cannot use or reveal any information you learned from the prospective client, except as provided in Rule 1.9.

To avoid being disqualified by your initial conversation with a prospective client (and disqualification of all lawyers in your firm), limit your discussion to only what you need to know to do a conflicts check, explaining that the ethical rules require you to learn information about the parties involved before you can have a substantive conversation, and that you will do a conflicts check. Complete that conflicts check promptly, and call back the prospective client. If you have no conflict, then you can have a substantive conversation.

## 8. Comply with the ethical requirement regarding meritorious claims and contentions (Rule 3.1)

You cannot bring or defend a proceeding, or assert or controvert an issue therein, unless you have a basis in law and fact for doing so that is not frivolous. So the question is: What is the meaning of "frivolous" in this rule? For Federal Rules of Civil Procedure dealing with frivolousness, see Rules 11(b)(2), 16(c)(2)(A), and Federal Rules of Appellate Procedure 38.

Your action is not frivolous merely because you have not yet fully substantiated the facts, or because you expect to develop vital evidence only by discovery. You are required, though, to inform yourself about the facts of your client's case—and the applicable law—and determine whether you can make good-faith arguments in support of the action you intend to take. Your action is not frivolous even if you believe that your client's position ultimately will not prevail. Nor is it frivolous if your action is based on your good-faith argument for an extension, modification, or reversal of existing law.

However, your action *is* frivolous if you are unable either to make a good-faith argument on the merits of the action you plan to take or to support that action by a good-faith argument for the extension, modification, or reversal of existing law.

## 9. Comply with the ethical requirement of candor to the tribunal (Rule 3.3)

You cannot knowingly make a false statement of fact or law to the tribunal or fail to correct a false statement of material fact or law you previously made to the tribunal, fail to disclose to the tribunal legal authority in the controlling jurisdiction known to you to be directly adverse to your position and not disclosed by opposing counsel, or offer evidence that you know to be false. In an ex parte proceeding, you must inform the tribunal of all material facts you know that will enable the judge to make an informed decision, even if some of the facts are adverse to your position. One of the most difficult issues that arises in complying with this rule is dealing with your client's truthfulness, which warrants an extended discussion.

The oath swearing to tell the truth, the whole truth, and nothing but the truth, which dates back to Roman times, has been in its present form since the 13th century, in England. The issue of truth-telling under oath, though, is not new. Cicero stressed the importance of legally binding oaths by warning that perjurers "shall be hurled down from the Tarpeian Rock." Death by being hurled off that steep cliff near Rome was reserved for murderers, traitors, and perjurers—which reveals how seriously Romans took the oath. That punishment is not available to us, so how do we get our clients to tell the truth under oath? And what should we do if we think they are lying under oath?

We know that our adversarial system and the rules of evidence are designed to ascertain the truth. See FRE 102. But what is truth? Certain truths are unassailable: The San Francisco Giants won the World Series in 2012; A squared plus B squared equals C squared (at least in the world of triangles); Lincoln is the capital of Nebraska. But these are not the kinds of facts we deal with as trial lawyers.

Our "facts" are subjective. Truth is elusive, subjective, and ephemeral. In every case, the oath-taker is testifying about something that occurred in the past, so memory is necessarily in play. But what we remember and how we remember "facts" is a function of many factors: ability to perceive, bias, prejudice, motive, truthfulness, point of view, and desire to make our experience coherent, to name a few. As Oscar Wilde put it: "The truth is rarely pure and never simple." And consider Mark Twain's cynical observation: "Truth is mighty and will prevail. There is nothing the matter with this, except that it ain't so."

> Things happen; we witness some aspects of an event from a particular vantage point; we interpret what we have taken in with our senses; we discover or compose an acceptable meaning from that subjectively limited rendering of "fact." . . . There is a vast psychological distance between the "things that happen" and what we are later able to say about them, no matter how sincerely we try to be objective and to get it

right. Lifelong uncertainty about the "truth" is an attribute of human sensibility; it is a product of the interplay of memory and imagination, history and choice. D. Nyberg, The Varnished Truth: Truth Telling and Deceiving in Ordinary Life 9 (Univ. of Chicago Press 1995).

Lacking a Tarpeian Rock to hurl perjurers down, you need strategies to prepare your own clients so they tell the truth, without suborning perjury yourself.

Truthfulness can be an issue when preparing your own witnesses. When preparing a nonparty witness, you are naturally on your guard, because nothing is within the attorney-client privilege. When preparing your own client, you may feel insulated from disclosure of your preparation. Even so, the crime/fraud exception to the attorney-client privilege hangs like the sword of Damocles over your head, not to mention your own sworn oath to comply with the ethical rules.

Here are some things you *can* do when preparing your client to testify at deposition or in court:

- You can advise your client about applicable law, so your client testifies consistently with what the law requires for each cause of action. For example, you can inform your client that sexual harassment does not require touching.
- You can advise your client about the most credible way to present true testimony.
- You can make suggestions about wording of testimony, so long as you do not encourage what you know or reasonably believe to be false or misleading testimony.
- You can advise your client to avoid technical jargon, colloquialisms, formal speech, pejorative terms, and such phrases as "to tell you the truth. . . ."
- You can reveal to your client testimony of others and evidence for review in preparation for testimony.

But you *cannot* suborn perjury, which means, specifically, that you cross the ethical line if you violate any of these prohibitions:

- You cannot ask a question or make a statement overtly or covertly telling your client that you want your client to testify to something you know or reasonably believe to be false.

- You cannot recommend that your client modify the intended meaning in such a way as to mislead.
- You cannot impart or supply recollection of purported facts.
- You cannot instruct your client to testify as to something without regard to whether or not it is true.
- You cannot tell your client to feign emotion.

If you follow these guidelines during client preparation, but you believe your client is not telling you the truth, put your client through cross-examination to demonstrate the weaknesses in the "story." "It's my story and I'm sticking to it" does not work in the crucible of the courtroom.

What do you do if your own client tells you, in effect, "I will testify to whatever I need to say to win this case, even if I commit perjury!" And what if your client commits perjury at trial, like the fellow in this cartoon, for whom the desire to win overwhelms his obligation to tell the truth under oath? These two situations present similar but distinct issues.

*"I know I'm perjuring myself, but I'm trying to make a point!"*

As to the first situation, you are obligated, under Rule 3.3(a)(3), to seek to persuade your client not to testify falsely, explaining the consequences of committing perjury (a criminal offense), as well as the many potential strategic problems—potential for effective impeachment and loss of credibility as to all your client's testimony. If your persuasion is not effective, and you continue to represent that client, you cannot offer the false testimony, although your client can testify as to matters that are true.

As to the second, in which your client testifies about a material fact contrary to what your client told you privately, you first must determine which statement is true. Even if you have a reasonable belief that the testimony is false—but you do not *know* it to be false—that belief does not preclude your client's testimony. However, your *knowledge* of such falsity can be inferred from the circumstances. Thus, although you should resolve all doubts about the veracity of your client's testimony in favor of your client, you cannot ignore an obvious falsehood.

If, in a civil action, to your surprise your client testifies falsely, or if you have offered material evidence that you believed to be true, but come to know is false, you must remonstrate with your client confidentially, advise your client of your duty of candor to the court, and seek your client's cooperation to correct the false statement. If that fails, you must take further remedial action. You should seek court permission to withdraw as counsel. However, if withdrawal is not permitted, or if it will not undo the effect of the false testimony or evidence, you must make such disclosure as is reasonably necessary to remedy the situation, even if otherwise protected by the attorney-client privilege, set forth in Rule 1.6.

The rationale for such disclosure of what is otherwise privileged is well articulated in the comment to Rule 3.3(a)(3): "The disclosure of a client's false testimony can result in grave consequences to the client, including not only a sense of betrayal but also loss of the case and perhaps a prosecution for perjury. But the alternative is that the lawyer cooperates in deceiving the court, thereby subverting the truth-finding process which the adversary system is designed to implement. See Rule 1.2(d). Furthermore, unless it is clearly understood that the lawyer will act upon the duty to disclose the existence of false evidence, the client can simply reject the lawyer's advice to reveal the false evidence and insist that the lawyer keep silent. Thus the client could in effect coerce the lawyer into being a party to fraud on the court."

## 10. Comply with the ethical requirement of fairness to the opposing party and counsel (Rule 3.4)

As with other ethical rules, this one is easier to state than to apply in its far-reaching ramifications. You cannot do any of the following:

- unlawfully obstruct another party's access to evidence
- unlawfully alter, destroy, or conceal a document or other material having potential evidentiary value
- counsel or assist another person to do either of those things
- falsify evidence
- counsel or assist a witness to testify falsely
- offer an inducement to a witness that is prohibited by law (e.g., you can't pay a fact witness for testifying or pay an expert witness a contingent fee, but you can pay a fact witness's expenses and an expert witness an hourly fee)
- knowingly disobey an obligation under the rules of a tribunal, except an open refusal based on an assertion that no valid obligation exists
- in pretrial procedures, make a frivolous discovery request
- in pretrial procedures, fail to make a reasonably diligent effort to comply with a legally proper discovery request by an opposing party
- at trial, allude to any matter that you do not reasonably believe is relevant
- at trial, allude to any matter that will not be supported by admissible evidence
- at trial, assert personal knowledge of facts in issue, unless you are testifying as a witness (which presents ethical issues of its own)
- at trial, state a personal opinion as to the justness of a cause, the credibility of a witness, or the culpability of a civil litigant
- request a person other than your client to refrain from voluntarily giving relevant information to another party, unless the person is a relative or an employee or other agent of your client and you reasonably believe that the person's interests will not be adversely affected by refraining from giving such information

## 11. Be truthful in your statements to others (Rule 4.1)

You cannot make a false statement of material fact or law to a third person, or fail to disclose a material fact when disclosure is necessary to avoid assisting a criminal or fraudulent act by a client, unless disclosure is prohibited by Rule 1.6. Whether a particular statement is one of "fact" depends on the circumstances.

Your obligation to be truthful in dealings with others does not impose on you an affirmative duty to inform an opposing party of relevant facts (absent appropriate discovery requests). But you violate this rule if you incorporate or affirm a statement of another person that you know is false—or if you make partially true but misleading statements or omissions that are equivalent of affirmative false statements. See also Rule 8.4(c).

You cannot counsel or assist a client in conduct that you know is criminal or fraudulent. Ordinarily, you can avoid doing so by withdrawing from the representation. It may be necessary for you to give notice of the fact of withdrawal and disaffirm an opinion, document, affirmation, or the like. In extreme cases, the law in your jurisdiction may require you to disclose information relating to the representation to avoid being deemed to have assisted the client's crime or fraud. If the only way you can avoid assisting the client's crime or fraud is by disclosing such information, then you are required to do so, unless prohibited by Rule 1.6.

For example, although the ethics rules permit a lawyer to warn authorities that a client threatened to burn down a building, the lawyer could not be compelled to testify about a conversation with the client about it, because that conversation is covered by the attorney-client privilege, and is not covered by the crime/fraud exception because the client is not seeking advice in furtherance of criminal conduct.

## 12. COMPLY WITH THE ETHICAL RULES WHEN DEALING WITH OPPOSING PARTIES WHO ARE REPRESENTED BY COUNSEL, AND THOSE NOT REPRESENTED BY COUNSEL (RULES 4.2 AND 4.3)

Even if someone represented by counsel initiates or consents to communicating with you about the subject matter of your representation, you must not engage in that conversation, although you can discuss unrelated matters. You cannot evade this obligation by failing to inquire whether someone is represented by counsel.

You cannot communicate with someone represented by counsel through the acts of another. See Rule 8.4(a). What about your own client? Can you convey a message to the opposing party by suggesting that your client make certain statements to the opposing party if he or she is represented by counsel? Why not? After all, you may think, clients can always talk to each other. But you can't do indirectly what you are prohibited from doing directly. "The acts of another" in Rule 8.4(a) include your client.

Here's another example, this one involving a private investigator: Assume that you are considering hiring a private investigator to "friend" adverse parties on Facebook to obtain information you can use against them in litigation. If you did so yourself, you would violate Rule 4.2 (if the party is represented by counsel), Rule 4.3 (if not represented by counsel), Rule 4.1 (you cannot knowingly make a false statement of material fact or law to a third person—even by omission), and Rule 8.4 (you cannot engage in conduct involving dishonesty, fraud, deceit, or misrepresentation).

Just as you cannot seek to "friend" an adverse party yourself in these circumstances, you cannot do so through anyone else. In this scenario, doing so violates not only Rule 8.4(a), but also Rule 5.3(c), which provides that you are responsible for the conduct of a non-lawyer you retain who violates the ethical rules, if you order specific conduct or, with knowledge of that specific conduct, you ratify it. So, what may seem at first like a good idea—"friending" an adverse party through an investigator—violates the ethical rules.

When the opposing party is an organization, whether your communication with a constituent is ethical depends on whether that person supervises, directs, or regularly consults with the organization's lawyer concerning the matter or has authority to obligate the organization with respect to the matter, or whether that constituent's act or omission in connection with the matter may be imputed to the organization for purposes of civil or criminal liability. If that person is represented by counsel in the matter, however, you cannot communicate with that person without his or her counsel's consent.

What about former employees? You must learn the law in your jurisdiction on this issue. Generally, the analysis is this: Since *former* agents and employees cannot bind the organization, their statements cannot bind it. Accordingly, your communicating with former employees does not harm the policy of Rule 4.2, which is to avoid undercutting an ongoing attorney-client relationship, but only if you refrain from discussing any communications that person may have had with the organization's counsel about the matter. Furthermore, restricting your communications with former employees would inhibit your acquiring information about your case.

However, you cannot communicate *at all* with a former agent or employee if he or she is acting as a trial consultant or otherwise is actively and extensively working with the organization's attorney in gathering evidence and preparing for litigation. This ban is based on such an individual's extensive exposure to privileged communications and sustained access to the party's litigation strategy and the attorney's work product. There is a presumption that, if you communicate with a person who has acted in this role, he or she did disclose confidences.

If there is any doubt about whether the ethical rules allow you to communicate with a former agent or employee, seek a court order. If you don't, you risk being disqualified as counsel in the case.

The ethical rules governing your communications with unrepresented parties are more straightforward. If the unrepresented party is adverse to your client, you must confirm that he or she is not represented by counsel. Then, you must clearly state whom you represent, make explicit that your client has interests opposed to those of the person you are communicating with. You can negotiate with that person, prepare documents that require his or her signature, and explain your own view of the meaning of the settlement documents and your view of the underlying obligations in those documents. You cannot give any legal advice to that person, other than to suggest that he or she obtain legal counsel.

## 13. Know and comply with all applicable ethical rules

This chapter covers only the ethical rules trial lawyers encounter most frequently. Of course, you must comply with *all* applicable ethical rules.

Other Model Rules include those dealing with diligence (Rule 1.3); your fees (Rule 1.5); confidentiality of information (Rule 1.6); conflicts of interest applicable to a government officer or employee (Rule 1.11); conflicts as to a former judge, arbitrator, mediator, or other third-party neutral (Rule 1.12); dealing with clients of diminished capacity (Rule 1.14); your obligations for safekeeping property of clients and third persons (Rule 1.15); sale of a law practice (Rule 1.17); your role as advisor (Rule 2.1); your evaluation for use by third persons, such as letter opinions (Rule 2.3); your serving as a third-party neutral (Rule 2.4); expediting litigation (Rule 3.2); impartiality and decorum of the tribunal (Rule 3.5); trial publicity (Rule 3.6); your role as a trial witness (Rule 3.7); your role as an advocate in a non-adjudicative proceeding (Rule 3.9); respect for rights of third persons, including inadvertent disclosure to you (Rule 4.4); rules pertaining to law firms and associations (Rules 5.1–5.7);

rules pertaining to public service (Rules 6.1–6.5); rules pertaining to information about legal services (Rules 7.1–7.6); and rules pertaining to maintaining the integrity of the profession (Rules 8.1–8.5).

One last word, about your obligation to report professional misconduct. Rule 8.3 provides that if you know that another lawyer has committed a violation of the ethical rules that raises a substantial question as to that lawyer's honesty, trustworthiness, or fitness as a lawyer in other respects, you *must* inform the appropriate professional authority. Similarly, you *must* inform the appropriate authority if you know that a judge has committed a violation of applicable rules of judicial conduct that raises a substantial question as to the judge's fitness for office.

Rule 8.3 does not, however, require disclosure of information otherwise protected by Rule 1.6 or information you learn while participating in an approved lawyers' assistance program. Even where Rule 1.6 protects disclosure of confidential information, you should encourage a client to consent to disclosure where making the disclosure would not substantially prejudice your client's interests.

❖❖❖❖
## PRACTICE CHECKLIST

- Read and comply with all ethical rules applicable in your jurisdiction.
- Make sure you have the competence before undertaking a representation.
- Get your client's authority, and communicate with your client as required by the ethical rules.
- Avoid conflicts of interest with current and former clients.
- Comply with the ethical rules when representing an organization.
- Comply with the ethical rules when you decline or terminate a representation.
- Comply with your ethical obligations if you discuss a matter with a prospective client.
- Assert only meritorious claims and contentions.
- Be candid to the tribunal.
- Comply with the ethical rules in preparing your client for deposition and court testimony.
- Be fair to the opposing party and opposing party's counsel.
- Be truthful in your statements to others.
- Comply with the ethical rules in dealing with opposing parties, whether represented or not.

# CHAPTER TWELVE
# MARKETING YOUR LITIGATION PRACTICE

You are already overloaded with work. You have deadlines to meet. Memos to write. Pleadings and briefs to file. Emails to respond to. Client calls to return. Billable hour requirements to meet. Who has time to market your practice? You do. Why? Because, unless you want to be no more than a drone churning out work for your superiors for the rest of your legal career, you must learn how to market your skills and your experience as a trial lawyer, create a marketing plan, and follow through on it. Consider your marketing efforts an investment in your professional future. No one can do this for you. And you will likely be compelled to go outside your comfort zone. It's well worth it.

Marketing is more important now than ever before. Competition is intense, for a variety of reasons. Law schools keep pumping out about 45,000 lawyers a year, and one of the most fertile areas for young lawyers is litigation. Mergers, acquisitions, and consolidations have reduced the number of clients for commercial litigation. Shrinkage of the client base is exacerbated by companies having in-house legal departments. Many companies seek to avoid litigation expenses by resolving disputes without benefit of counsel and, even then, utilizing various alternative dispute resolution techniques, in part to avoid costly litigation fees. And many potential clients—executives of companies and those with individual claims—think of lawyers as fungible, one as good as the next.

You must differentiate yourself from the crowd. How?

In this chapter, you will learn how to become a rainmaker, bringing in business to keep you and others in your firm busy with productive, stimulating, profitable work. You may think that some people just have a natural knack for marketing, a skill that you may think cannot be taught. While it is true that some people come by it more naturally than others, every trial lawyer can become an effective marketer and successful rainmaker. In your marketing efforts, get advice from others in your firm about the areas of your practice you may want to promote, and get advice from your marketing director (if your firm has one) about implementing your marketing plan.

Before getting to marketing strategies and tips, though, a discussion about ethics is necessary. You don't want to be so zealous in your marketing efforts that you find yourself defending your conduct before the ethics committee.

### 1. How to comply with the ethical rules governing your marketing efforts

Rule 7.1 provides that you cannot make a false or misleading communication about yourself or your services. Your communication is false or misleading if it contains a material misrepresentation of fact or law—that much is self-evident. But this rule also prohibits even *truthful* statements, if they are misleading. This occurs if you omit a fact necessary to make your communication, considered as a whole, not materially misleading, or if there is a substantial likelihood that it will lead a reasonable person to formulate a specific conclusion about you or your services for which there is no reasonable factual foundation.

So, for example, if you place an ad that truthfully reports your achievements on behalf of clients, it may be misleading if presented so as to lead a reasonable person to form an unjustified expectation that you could obtain the same results in similar matters without reference to the specific factual and legal circumstances of each client's case.

Similarly, an unsubstantiated comparison of your services or fees with those of other lawyers may be misleading if presented with such specificity as would lead a reasonable person to conclude that the comparison can be substantiated. An appropriate disclaimer, or qualifying language, may preclude a finding of such unjustified expectations or otherwise mislead a prospective client.

Rule 7.3(a) imposes restrictions on direct contact with prospective clients. You cannot solicit work from a prospective client for your pecuniary gain by in-person, live telephone, or real-time electronic contact, unless the person you contact is a lawyer, a family member, you have a prior professional relationship with that person, or you have a close personal relationship with that person.

Rule 7.3(b) provides that you cannot seek work from a prospective client by any of the means listed above or by written, recorded, or electronic communication if the prospective client has made known to you a desire that you not solicit him or her, or if your solicitation involves coercion, duress, or harassment. Any solicitation you make to someone you know needs legal services in a particular matter must include the words "Advertising Material" as provided in this rule, unless the recipient is within Rule 7.3(a).

Despite the restrictions in Rule 7.3(a), you can participate with a prepaid group legal service plan operated by an organization you do not own or direct that uses in-person or telephone contact to solicit memberships or subscriptions for the plan from people not known to need legal services in a particular matter covered by the plan.

Rule 7.4 restricts what you can communicate about your expertise. You can communicate that you practice in particular fields of law, but you cannot state or imply that you are certified as a specialist in a particular field of law unless you have been so certified by an organization that has been approved by an appropriate state authority or has been accredited by the American Bar Association, and you clearly identify the name of the certifying organization in your communication.

Generally, this rule allows you to state that you are a "specialist," that you practice a "specialty," or you "specialize in" a particular field of law, subject to the "false and misleading" standard in Rule 7.1. Before promoting your legal services, check the specific rules in your state that govern promotion of your legal services. If in doubt, seek advance approval of the contents of any promotional material from the regulatory agency in your state.

The other Model Rules relevant to this chapter are Rule 7.2, which allows advertising subject to Rules 7.1 and 7.3 and imposes restrictions on giving anything of value to someone who recommends you, and Rule 7.5, which pertains to firm names and letterheads. See also Rule 1.6, which limits your disclosure of information related to your representation of clients, as discussed in chapter 11, section 2.

## 2. How to create a niche you can market

A lawyer with a specialized practice is more likely to develop a successful practice than run-of-the-mill general litigators, who are a dime a dozen. Do you have a unique skill to market? The typical prospective client will pass over the general trial lawyer, selecting a specialist. If you had a blood disorder, would you see a hematologist, or a general physician? A hematologist, of course. So it is with prospective clients who need legal advice. They want advice from a specialist. You must distinguish yourself from all the other trial lawyers out there. Answer this question: Why should a client do business with *you* rather than with another lawyer?

As you gain more experience practicing law, ask yourself: What subjects of litigation do you find most interesting and stimulating, for which you have a natural proficiency. Attend seminars on those subjects. Develop expertise. Make it known to others in your firm and to clients, prospective clients, and referral sources that you have experience in that niche. Feature that niche in all your marketing materials, starting with your website biography. Keep your biography up-to-date. More than half the time people spend visiting law firm websites, they are reading bios. Entice prospective clients and referral sources with your well-crafted, current, and 100 percent accurate bio.

Niches can be by type of law (e.g., tax appeals, intellectual property disputes, insurance coverage disputes, environmental law) or by type of client (e.g., title insurance companies, telecommunications companies, high-tech companies). You are not limited to a single niche. Promote your niche practices to prospective clients who need your specialized services through target marketing.

## 3. How to create a plan to market your practice

If you were to go on a long trip, you would not just head out, not knowing where you're off to. You would carefully consider your objectives in going on that trip, where you would like to go, how you would get there, whom you would like to visit along the way—your entire itinerary. Likewise with your journey in your career as a trial lawyer. You cannot expect that work will just come your way; nor can you expect to advance in your firm unless you become a rainmaker. You will become a rainmaker only by having a plan to market your practice.

Creating a plan to market your practice requires four steps:

1. *Set a goal.* Think about where you want to be professionally five and 10 years out, and beyond. Think of it as a vision statement. Write it down. Make it concrete. Focus on high-end work you enjoy. Review it periodically, and revise it as appropriate.
2. *Select marketing targets.* Where has business come from in the area you want to promote? Identify former and current sources of that work. Cultivate those sources.
3. *Select marketing activities.* Decide what to do to market those sources. See the discussion in the next section for details.
4. *Write your marketing plan.* Make it specific. Your plan should include *annual* objectives, and specific means to achieve them, a *monthly* plan, and a *weekly* plan. Periodically, review your progress, and keep on track. Revise your plan as necessary to achieve your marketing goals.

This may seem like a daunting task. Start with something small and specific, such as making one call a day to a referral source, or having lunch once a week with a client, prospective client, or referral source. Create effective marketing habits. Track your results.

## 4. How to cultivate relationships with clients and referral sources

Even though you cannot bill your time for marketing, and your marketing efforts typically do not yield immediate results, you must take a long view. Developing business is based on establishing lasting relationships, a process that necessarily takes time and effort. And you must be willing to put yourself outside your comfort zone. Many aspiring lawyers are skilled in the practice of law, but what sets good marketers apart is their willingness to make that extra effort, even if somewhat disquieting—whether having lunch with a prospective client, speaking before a group, or walking up to someone you don't know at a cocktail party and introducing yourself. You'll find that the more you extend yourself this way, the easier it will be to market your services in the future. Even if you don't heed Eleanor Roosevelt's admonition to "do one thing every day that scares you," venturing beyond your comfort zone in your marketing efforts (and, more generally, in your career as a lawyer) is well worth your perceived risk.

Former and current clients are the best source for new work. When representing a business client, develop relationships with the people who are in a position to send you work, or who can serve as referral sources. Establish long-standing relationships so that, as those people are promoted, they will be in a better position to send you more substantial work.

Even after you complete your representation in a particular matter, keep in contact with clients. Send them articles of interest to them, acknowledge clients' successes, keep clients informed of your successes, take clients to lunch, and visit your clients' places of business, at no cost to the clients, without making a pitch. Show an interest in clients' families and businesses. Ask about clients' needs, what issues they confront that involve legal matters; then follow up by informing clients how you can fill those needs.

A second source of work, other than satisfied former and current clients, is referral sources, including, for example, college classmates, law school classmates, bar association members, opposing counsel in cases you handle, expert witnesses, members of organizations in which you are active, neighbors, friends, accountants, and bankers. How do you make the most of referral sources to bring in new work? All the ways described above, as well as acknowledging referral sources when they send you work, which may involve more than just making a call or writing a handwritten note to express your gratitude, such as arranging for an evening out together.

Here are some specific ways you can cultivate relationships with clients and referral sources:

- Build on your strengths: Are you better at speaking in front of a crowd? One-on-one meetings? Writing articles?
- Join your local chamber of commerce.
- Give out your business card.
- In your emails, add a signature block with your contact information.
- Apply to teach at a local college, community center, or other venue.
- Offer to speak to community groups.

- Register with your local bar's speaker's bureau.
- Send holiday, birthday, and anniversary cards, in paper form or electronically.
- Ask clients to refer others to you.
- Advertise in your local newspaper.
- Mail or email newsletters on a periodic basis.
- Send out copies of articles of interest.
- Send congratulatory notes.
- Get involved in community activities—but only those in which you have a genuine interest.
- Have lunch with lawyers in other firms in a position to refer you work.
- Get to know your clients' businesses.
- Inform clients about all the services you and others in your firm provide, with updates.
- Send out press releases.
- Join your local trial lawyers' association, and network.
- Become involved in bar association activities.

## 5. HOW TO DEVELOP IN-PERSON NETWORKING SKILLS

You will have plenty of opportunities to attend social gatherings of prospective clients and referral sources—celebrations, fund-raisers, bar association events, parties involving organizations of which you are a member, alumni gatherings, conventions, and the like. You don't want to come across as an overly aggressive marketer at these events, but you don't want to pass up marketing opportunities.

Before attending, ask yourself how you can use an event as a marketing opportunity. Who will attend? If possible, get a list of people attending. Which people do you want to meet? Learn about people you want to focus on, using Google, LinkedIn, and other means. Think about topics you may want to discuss and what your goals are for this gathering. Bring business cards. Failure to do so is marketing malpractice.

Think about what you will say when asked: "What do you do?" Prepare a brief, effective introduction for yourself. Come up with an "elevator pitch"—something effective you can say that is simple, direct, and credible in 30 seconds or less. Like the guy in the cartoon on the next page, this may take some practice.

"What do you do?"     "I'm a lawyer."
"The law."
"I do law."
"I practice law."
"I'm an attorney."
"Something legal."

At the event, if you have the opportunity, briefly explain what your firm does, what you do, and how you help your clients. Be cautious, though, about what you disclose. Even independent of ethics issues (see Model Rule 1.6, discussed in chapter 11, section 2), you don't want a prospective client thinking that you will breach his or her own confidences for the sake of your self-aggrandizing marketing efforts. And listen—actively—far more than you talk.

After you arrive

- Focus on meeting a number of people, including those you had targeted.
- Focus on introductions and relationships, not selling.
- If you see someone who is alone, introduce yourself.
- Most of your conversation should be finding out about the other person, not talking about yourself.
- Show interest in what the other person is saying, by asking follow-up questions.

- Discuss subjects other than business—what you have in common is bonding; but avoid politics, unless you obviously share political views.
- Remember names by repeating them, and ask for business cards.
- Be proactive, positive, and confident, and make eye contact.
- After the event, follow up promptly, by letters, emails, phone calls; make a reference to what you discussed.

### 6. How to make the most of social media to market your practice

Increasingly, people find lawyers on the Internet. Unless you take advantage of social media, a gaping hole will limit your marketing efforts. However, unless you are prudent in your use of social media, your efforts could backfire, or worse. There are pitfalls to avoid.

For starters, to find out what others searching the Internet will find about you, go to a search engine such as google.com, bing.com, pipl.com, metacrawler.com, and dogpile.com. For websites specifically designed for people searching for lawyers, go to www.legalmatch.com, www.findlaw.com, www.lawyers.com, www.martindale.com, www.attorneyfind.com, www.viewmylawyer.com, and www.lawfirmdirectory.org. While you're at it, do the same for some of your competitors to see how they are taking advantage of social media in their marketing efforts.

In a recent poll, nearly 50 percent of law firms reported that social networking and blog initiatives generated new leads and led to new business. LinkedIn can be an effective marketing tool. Among the more than 100 million LinkedIn users are more than 770,000 in the legal field. Create a strong profile, featuring a professional profile at the top. First impressions matter. Craft your summary statement to convey what singles you out as a trial lawyer. Show it to someone whose judgment you trust and ask what impression it conveys. Your summary statement should highlight your unique skills. For inspiration, review summary statements of your competitors.

Collect recommendations for your LinkedIn profile. Third-party endorsements build your credibility. Include a link to your firm's website. Set your LinkedIn profile to "public" and claim a unique URL for your profile, such as "www.linkedin.com/in/yourname."

Join LinkedIn groups. Display group badges in your profile, such as college, law school, and bar association LinkedIn groups, demonstrating your professionalism and desire to connect with others. Display URLs and add LinkedIn applications to direct people to your website, your Martindale Hubbell rating, and your blog, if you have one. Fill in the "specialties" section with key words and phrases a prospective client or referral source may type into a search engine.

What about LinkedIn connections? Request to connect with others for your mutual benefit, specifying how you know the person you want to connect with. If you want to connect with someone you don't know, explain why you want to connect.

What about responding to people who seek to connect with you on LinkedIn? People are known by the company they keep, and after you allow someone to connect with you, you will be linked with them. So, give thought to whether you want to accept such a request.

Update LinkedIn on a regular basis, enhancing your networking efforts, by including information about cases you win (with the client's informed consent), events at which you speak, and links to articles you publish.

What about Facebook? Some lawyers take the approach that you should use Facebook for your private life, and LinkedIn for your professional life. But, increasingly, Facebook is used as a valuable marketing tool. Here are some guidelines:

- Choose your profile and profile photo with care. Even if you set your privacy settings to be the most restrictive possible, anyone searching for you on Facebook will see your profile and profile photo.
- Consider what your Facebook profile and posts reveal about you to referral sources and prospective clients. Keep your profile and posts up-to-date.
- Spelling, grammar, and punctuation matter, even on Facebook.
- Set restrictive settings for "things others share." Even if you are cautious about what you post on Facebook, your Facebook "friends" may not be as careful. Control your online presence.
- Choose your Facebook "friends" wisely.

- Set Facebook email alerts so you are notified of wall postings and tagged photos of you, so you can quickly remove anything you don't want accessible.
- Actively manage your Facebook account. Review it frequently so it is a positive marketing tool.
- For more details, click on "about," then "resources," and "need help?" to manage your Facebook account.

Should you create a blog—what has become fashionable to refer to as a "blawg"? Some trial lawyers have had great success doing so. But before you commit to that endeavor, keep in mind that you will be successful only if you create a blog of sufficiently interesting content, and only if you keep it updated on a regular basis. Do you have the time to devote to a blog each and every week? Do you have content of value to add each and every week?

As with all your other marketing efforts, when taking advantage of social media, comply with the ethical rules. Social media present unique ethical problems. For example, Model Rule 7.1 limits what you can say about your professional credentials. You cannot overstate your experience and abilities, promise results, or compare those results with those of other attorneys. Yet you do not retain full control over content once you use social media.

Model Rule 7.2(c) mandates that any advertising must include the name and office address of at least one lawyer or law firm responsible for its content. Model Rule 7.3 mandates that every communication (including electronic communications) you transmit soliciting work from a prospective client known to be in need of legal services in a particular matter must include the words "Advertising Material" at the beginning and end of your communication, with certain limited exceptions.

As clever website innovators create new sites that are enticing for you to bring in new work, check the ethical rules. As just one example, go to Shpoonkle.com, a website allowing you to bid on a potential client's case. Any ethical problems?

Check your state's ethical rules to determine if they have been amended to keep up-to-date with technological developments, and be sure to comply with them. And avoid inadvertently creating an attorney-client relationship.

## 7. How to draft and publish articles to market your practice

While practicing law, you are presented with many article ideas, if you have the right mindset, in cases you worked on successfully that involved unique or cutting-edge issues, news events that raise legal issues, new statutes that affect your existing and potential clients, amendments to the rules of practice, recent decisions of interest to your existing and potential clients, and issues that need to be addressed by legislation or otherwise related to your practice. Pick a subject that interests you.

Pitch the subject of your proposed article to editors. Where? Local business journals; newspapers; and local, state, and national journals for the general public, lawyers, or other professionals, and appropriate Internet sites.

Send an email to the editor, pitching your article idea, explaining why your article would be timely and of interest, after finding out the applicable editorial guidelines, typically available online.

If the editor expresses interest, know the deadline you must meet. Outline the entire article. Complete your research. Draft it well in advance, writing for your audience. Put it away. Then redraft it. Polish your prose. Show the revised draft to a colleague for a critique. Revise it once again. Give it a title that will provoke interest. The first paragraph should entice the reader to read the rest of your article. Submit your article on time. When you receive proposed revisions from the editor, be open-minded. Your precious prose can be improved.

Getting your article published is just the first step. Here are some ways you can capitalize on it:

- Send your article to clients, potential clients, and referral sources by email or snail mail. If by email, use an effective subject line so the recipient is more likely to open it. If you send it by snail mail, consider including a typed or handwritten personal note.
- Display reprints in the reception area of your firm's offices.
- Transmit copies to colleagues at the firm for them to send to clients, potential clients, and referral sources.
- Include your article in your firm's website, after getting the publisher's permission as to timing and acknowledging where it was published.
- Add a reference to your article in your résumé.

- Send notice of your article to organizations of which you are a member.
- Send a note to the editor expressing gratitude for publishing your article.

## 8. How to cross-sell to benefit yourself and other lawyers in your firm

Unless you are a solo practitioner, you need to know how to cross-sell the services of other lawyers in your firm. You benefit by being a rainmaker not only for your own work, but for the work you generate for your colleagues. Cross-selling requires a good understanding of your clients' needs, as well as knowledge of the services your colleagues offer. Since existing clients are a fruitful source of new work for your firm, cross-selling is a natural and productive way to generate more work.

Know the range of services your firm provides. Spend time with lawyers in your firm who work in other practice groups. Get to know them and what services they provide. Discuss ways they can work for your clients, and vice versa. Keep up-to-date on the accomplishments of other lawyers in your firm, and make sure they know about yours. If appropriate, suggest a firm newsletter or intranet to keep all the lawyers in the firm up-to-date about everyone's accomplishments. If your litigation group meets regularly (an excellent opportunity for workshopping and discussing recent reported decisions, new cases, new procedures, and cases coming up for trial), invite the head of another practice group to make a presentation about the work of lawyers in that group. Inform your clients about those accomplishments, as appropriate.

When you talk with clients, ask questions that could lead to new business for the firm. How is their business doing? Do they have any employee issues? Do they have an employee handbook? Are they considering merging with another company? Any lease problems? Are their wills up-to-date? What about estate planning? Do they need tax advice? You get the idea. You are limited only by the scope of the services other lawyers in your firm provide, and ethics rules. Be informative without being too aggressive. Avoid the hard sell.

If a client expresses an interest in services other lawyers in your firm provide, arrange a lunch or a meeting with the client, you, and the other lawyer for a smooth transition.

Even though your firm most likely has a website, supplement it with something tangible—group brochures and a firm brochure you can mail to a client, with a letter or handwritten note explaining why you are sending it, to let the client know the full range of services your firm provides. Clients may be more likely to read something tangible than going on the Internet to find out what your firm can do for them. Give those brochures to clients early in your representation.

❖❖❖❖
## PRACTICE CHECKLIST

- Comply with the ethical rules governing your marketing efforts.
- Create a niche you can market.
- Create a plan to market your practice:
  - _____ Set a goal.
  - _____ Select marketing targets.
  - _____ Select marketing activities.
  - _____ Write your marketing plan.
- Cultivate relationships with clients and referral sources.
- Develop in-person networking skills.
- Make the most of social media to market your practice.
- Draft and publish articles to market your practice.
- Cross-sell to benefit yourself and other lawyers in your firm.

CHAPTER THIRTEEN

# COPING WITH STRESS AND CREATING A LIFE BEYOND THE PRACTICE OF LAW

While all the other chapters in this book provide practical advice crucial to your success as a trial lawyer, this is one chapter you may want to re-read periodically. Put that on your "to do" list. Why? Because unless you know how to cope with the stress of your chosen profession, you will not succeed. Applying the practical advice in this chapter is the sine qua non for achieving everything else in this book.

The law, Harvard Law School professor Joseph Story once said, "is a jealous mistress, and requires a long and constant courtship. It is not to be won by trifling favors, but by lavish homage." If we substitute "lover" for "mistress"—after all, about half of law firm associates are women—these words ring as true today as when Professor Story uttered them in 1829. Like a jealous lover, the practice of law can monopolize our time and attention, drive us to drink or divorce, and create dissatisfaction in all areas of our lives, unless we find ways to cope with the stress inherent in what we do as trial lawyers.

A 1990 American Bar Association national survey of career satisfaction and dissatisfaction produced these troubling findings: 71 percent of all lawyers surveyed felt fatigued or worn out by the end of the workday; 17 percent reported that their marriages were unhappy; and 13 percent reported drinking six or more alcoholic beverages a day. The study notes that "these figures are even more disquieting when one considers that self-reported drinking and other types of abuse are typically underreported in survey responses." American Bar Association, THE STATE OF THE LEGAL PROFESSION, REPORT No. 1, 17 (1990).

Among attorneys in private practice (not corporate counsel), 28 percent of the men and 41 percent of the women in the 1990 study were dissatisfied with their jobs.

In 2007, the ABA completed a 10-year study of impairments of lawyers who had been sanctioned between 1998 and 2007. Their impairments included depression and other psychiatric problems, abuse of drugs and alcohol, and gambling problems. Throughout that 10-year period, about 35 percent of impaired lawyers who were sanctioned suffered from depression. The next highest percent was an average of 18 percent for alcoholism.

Consider this: Unrelenting low-level stress, unchecked, can cause physical symptoms, including decreased immune system function, increased cholesterol and triglycerides, high blood pressure, faster heartbeat, increased blood glucose levels, digestive problems, loss of mental sharpness, sleeping problems, chest pains, fatigue, headaches, and back and neck pain. And the psychological symptoms? Anxiety, frustration, irritability, and depression. A litany of woes. You don't want to be like the guy in this cartoon, anxious about whatever may come his way.

You don't want to be on the wrong side of these statistics, and you need not be. This chapter discusses strategies that should enable you to enjoy the practice of law without becoming its slave. Adopting even a few of these strategies should help you handle the stresses inherent in what we do. The more of these you adopt, the better you'll be able to cope.

## 1. Take good care of your body

### *Eat right.*

Litigators are the athletes of the bar. We must be agile, quick on our feet (literally and figuratively), and must maintain the stamina to prepare for and try protracted cases with unflagging energy. All this is possible only if we eat as carefully as disciplined athletes. You should think of food as fuel, not just filler. Keep in mind the Russian proverb: "It is not the horse that draws the cart, but the oats."

What does it mean to eat right? Volumes have been written on this subject. Healthy eating doesn't just happen by chance; it requires pre-planning and being prepared for what the day or week might bring. Your initial investment in devising a nutritious lifestyle that works for you may seem daunting at first but, like many changes, soon becomes part of your routine. Make time to map out an eating game plan on a regular basis. It helps to write down or record your plan as you would any other important commitment.

Be sure to start the day with a nutritious and energizing breakfast. Do not skip breakfast! Eating breakfast will fuel your brain, possibly boost your metabolism, improve your mood, and increase the likelihood that you will eat reasonably the rest of the day, without overeating. You would not start off on a road trip on an empty gas tank, so why do that to yourself? Whenever possible, stop working while you eat lunch. Take a break, and enjoy your food. Whether a marketing lunch or a lunch with colleagues, enjoy the respite, and socialize. Have a plan in mind for dinner. Arriving home at the end of the day tired and hungry without a plan is a recipe for nutritional disaster.

Don't have a huge meal for dinner. If putting on weight is an issue for you, use smaller plates for portion control and visit the National Institute of Health website www.hp2010.nhlbihin.net/portion/keep.htm, which includes useful links for menu planning. When you eat a late dinner, brush and floss your teeth right after your meal and close down the kitchen to avoid those after-dinner snacks that put the pounds on and rev up your body at just the wrong time.

When you are on trial, keep to the same regimen, but make an adjustment for lunch, as needed, since typically you won't have enough time for a proper meal. This is where preplanning and being prepared are particularly important. Whenever possible, pack a lunch or at least bring part of the meal. Consider stocking up on nutrition bars, bananas, apples, baby carrots, cans of low-sodium V8 juice, yogurt, and other healthy snacks so you can reenergize for the afternoon session. Combine nuts, whole-grain cereals, dried fruit, and dark-chocolate chips to create "snack packs" you can stow in your desk drawer, briefcase, or car. Keep in mind that security guards in some courthouses will not let you bring food into the courthouse.

If you do have time for a proper lunch, avoid greasy or spicy food, or too much food. Opt for a vegetable-heavy dish like a broth-based soup or a salad, with dressing on the side. Request sandwiches on whole-grain bread or wrap and add tomatoes, cucumbers, peppers, and greens. When dining out for lunch during trial, practice the Okinawan cultural habit called *hara hachi bu*, which means eat only until you are 80 percent full. The last thing you want to be thinking about during your cross-examination of a key witness is your stomach.

Like any competitive athlete, it is important that you stay well hydrated and limit junk food. Drink water. Carry a water bottle with you. Limit caffeine; while small amounts may increase mental acuity, larger amounts can interfere with sleep. You don't need to eliminate junk food altogether, but do minimize your consumption of it—broadly defined. On occasion, indulge yourself with fine chocolate, ice cream, a pastry bursting with calories, or whatever else suits your fancy—but eat only half the amount you would normally. Avoid bringing high-sugar, high-fat foods into your house; if they are not there, you will not eat them. Do you know any successful trial lawyers who are obese?

### *Exercise right.*

Fueling your body properly is just the first step—you must keep your body healthy and in good shape. In the grueling and physically demanding work we do, litigators who exercise right have the advantage over those who don't. Regular, moderate- to high-intensity exercise is sufficient. Before you start on an exercise program, make sure you have a thorough medical exam, or clearance from your doctor. Here's the recommended minimum formula: 30 minutes of moderate aerobic exercise or 10 to 20 minutes of higher-intensity exercise three to five times a week, exerting yourself enough to sustain a pulse rate of between 60 percent and 80 percent of your maximum heart rate. If you exercise for at least 30 minutes three times a week, even if only at moderate intensity, you will achieve positive effects of reduced stress and increased energy levels. Even a brisk walk has some beneficial effect. Why not take a short walk at lunchtime during a workday? Think of your body as a machine that requires regular tune-ups to avoid breaking down. As the Earl of Derby once observed, "Those who do not find time for exercise will have to find time for illness."

Consider such activities as aerobics, cross-country skiing, cycling, jogging, speed walking, and swimming, to mention a few. Find an activity you enjoy and then establish a regimen that suits your lifestyle, so you look forward to exercising rather than viewing it as drudgery. Make a commitment to yourself to get regular exercise. Think of it as investment in your health, and in your physical and mental well-being.

For an extra inducement, and socialization, join a fitness club for a group aerobics class and strength training with a qualified personal trainer, or some other club for golf, tennis, squash, skiing, or whatever other sport you enjoy. If there is a baseball league (law firms have set up such leagues), join in the fun. No matter what form of exercise you decide to pursue, learn proper warm-up and stretching routines. Don't worry about your skill level. You will find others at the same level, and enjoy yourself while getting a good workout. Focus on lifetime sports you can enjoy for decades. Find a buddy whose exercise regimen is similar to yours. Examples include jogging and biking together, on a set schedule. You would not want to disappoint your buddy by not showing up. One more idea: If you have enough space in your apartment or home, put in some exercise equipment and weights—and use them regularly! For more information, go to the website of the American College of Sports Medicine, www.acsm.org.

Physiologically, exercise increases oxygen flow throughout the body, stimulates the nervous system, and affects levels of brain chemicals like serotonin, which relieve tension, induce calm, and make it easier to handle anxiety and stress. In addition, during exercise the pituitary gland releases endorphins, creating a sense of well-being.

The ancillary psychological benefits are tremendous. Studies show that even moderate regular physical activity improves one's sense of well-being, reduces stress, improves the ability to cope with stress, improves self-esteem, increases feelings of energy, and decreases symptoms associated with depression. These benefits are self-reinforcing (think of B.F. Skinner's concept of "positive reinforcement"), and so you will be motivated to continue your exercise program. One more benefit: Each day you exercise, even with moderate intensity, you'll sleep better that night, and wake up the next morning refreshed.

### Sleep right.

Lawyers rank second on a list of most sleep-deprived occupations, just behind home health aides, and just ahead of police officers, physicians, and paramedics, according to a recent U.S. government National Health Interview Survey.

Would you take a magic pill if it enabled you to focus sharply, learn faster, remember better, enhance your mood, reduce fatigue, and boost your energy level? Of course you would, depending on side effects and cost. (See the 2011 thriller, *Limitless*, about just such a pill.) Proper sleep produces all those salutary effects, with no side effects, and it's free. Shakespeare put it well in *Macbeth*, act II, sc. 2: "Sleep that knits up the ravell'd sleave of care, the death of each day's life, sore labour's bath, balm of hurt minds, great nature's second course, chief nourisher in life's feast." Your body requires at least a minimum amount of sleep, and the mind requires enough dream time. In sleep deprivation experiments, dream-deprived subjects developed psychotic tendencies. Even moderate sleep deprivation diminishes mental functioning, decreases motivation, and can increase impatience and irritability. How do you get enough sleep, with all the stresses of work—and all the other stresses in your life—keeping you awake at night? And what about during a trial, when your stress level is 12 on a scale of 1 to 10?

So many thoughts can keep a trial lawyer awake at night, even when not on trial! Deadlines loom. Opposing counsel just filed a memorandum you have difficulty rebutting. Some of your clients are overbearing, never satisfied, overly emotional, or worse. How will the judge rule on a key motion? What will the jury verdict be? What if you lose the case? Because successful trial lawyers are creative, their minds can run amok in the middle of the night. What if your expert misses her flight and doesn't make it to the *Daubert* hearing? What if her plane is diverted because of bad weather? What if the plane crashes? What if, at the hearing opposing counsel . . .? What if the judge . . .? Aaarrggghhhh!!!

Here are some practical techniques to get you back to sleep when you lie in bed staring at the ceiling, becoming all the more anxious because you know you need your sleep. These tips assume that you have already dealt with your physical surroundings by minimizing light and sound, and setting the right temperature, and that you have done something relaxing for at least a half hour before getting into bed. You need to wind down before heading off to slumber. Just as your car engine does not cool down immediately after you've driven a distance, your brain does not switch into repose immediately.

First, figure out just what is on your mind that is keeping you awake. If you are concerned that you will forget an inspirational thought, or something on your "to do" list that you don't want to forget, write it down then and there, in the middle of the night. Put a pad by your bedside, if that helps. Write well enough so your brilliant idea in the middle of the night isn't just illegible gibberish in the morning. By this process, purge your mind of what kept you awake, and get back to sleep.

You may be anxious about something over which you have no control that already happened (such as why you blundered by asking a key witness that one question too many), or something that may or may not ever happen in the future (such as the dire consequences of a possible adverse ruling in a case). Remind yourself that it is futile to agonize over something you cannot control, even though you can learn from your mistakes, or to agonize over something that may never happen.

It is natural to be anxious about what may happen. As Pliny the Younger put it: "Grief has limits, whereas apprehension has none. For we grieve only for what we know has happened, but we fear all that possibly may happen." Here is Mark Twain's wry observation on this subject: "I am an old man and have known a great many troubles, but most of them never happened." Gradually, let go of this natural impulse to worry about what might happen, and get back to sleep.

If you have purged yourself of those anxieties, but still can't get back to sleep, try visualization. In your mind, go somewhere that diverts your attention to something pleasant. You may want to take a virtual soothing walk in the woods or a relaxing stroll along the beach, the waves hypnotically lulling you back to sleep; re-experience your last vacation or fantasize about your next one; or go somewhere in your mind you invent. You are limited only by your imagination. As Shakespeare observed in his Sonnet 44, "Nimble thought can jump both sea and land / as soon as think the place where he would be." When you visualize, though, put yourself entirely where you want to be, unlike this hapless guy in the cartoon on the next page.

"Relax, and just try to imagine you're on a sunny beach."

If none of this works after about a half hour, get out of bed, and do something mindless. Watch TV (something not mentally stimulating). Read something boring. Your eyes will soon glaze over, and you'll return to slumber soon enough. If sleep deprivation becomes an ongoing problem, seek professional help.

If getting to sleep is not a problem for you, consider taking advantage of your subconscious brain activity in working on solving a problem. Before going to bed, focus on a problem to solve, such as which causes of action to assert in a complaint. Read whatever documents you need to focus your attention on that problem. Then do something relaxing before heading off to sleep. While you are sleeping, your brain will process that problem. There is no guarantee that you will wake up with a brilliant solution, but you may find that you have a greater insight in solving that problem than you did the night before.

## 2. CREATE AND NURTURE YOUR SUPPORT SYSTEM

### Make time for family and friends.

You spend most of your waking hours working. In your remaining waking hours, make time for family and friends, undistracted by professional concerns. Keep the courtroom out of the bedroom and living room. What's the sense of marrying and having kids if you never see your spouse or kids? Is it fair to them if you're never around? On your deathbed, is it more likely you'll be thinking "I wish I had billed more hours" or "I wish I had spent more time with my family"?

Make a commitment to yourself and your family to get home for dinner at a set time each day. To the extent possible, keep that commitment. If you can't on a particular day, call in advance to let them know you'll be late.

Know your firm's maternity and paternity leave policy. Take advantage of it. As your kids grow up, whenever possible, attend events, such as parent-teacher conferences, school plays, and sports competitions in which your kids participate—even if during working hours. Be there for your kids on weekends, not just for soccer matches and Little League ball games; be with your kids to have meaningful time together, to create memories that will last a lifetime. You will get your work done, just at different times of the day or week. Hours are fungible. Your kids will grow up only once.

And don't give up your social life. As Samuel Johnson said, "If a man does not make new acquaintances as he advances through life, he will soon find himself left alone. A man, sir, should keep his friendships in constant repair."

### Advise family of trial demands.

Inform family members in advance that you will be very much preoccupied, if not incommunicado, just before and during a trial. Trial work is stressful enough without burdening yourself with avoidable marital or family stress. Discuss your needs before trial so that people in your support system will be there for you when it counts. Don't be surprised if your sexual and parental interests diminish during this period.

### Make time for yourself.

Socrates said it best: "The life which is unexamined is not worth living." Make time for yourself—for introspection, meditation, yoga, daydreaming, and even self-indulgences. Doing so should relax you, clarify what's important to you, and enhance your enjoyment of life. It will also reduce the likelihood that you will begrudge the time you devote to your work.

### Take fulfilling vacations.

The prerequisite is to *take* vacations. Don't skip them unless you've been assigned a conflicting date for trial that you cannot reschedule. Plan a vacation that will be fun for you and your family.

Leave a number where you can be reached, but only in an emergency. Don't take a pseudo-vacation by calling in every day. Likewise, unless you have a very good reason to do so, when on vacation do not check your emails each day. (See the discussion about emails in chapter 3.) Your mind must be on vacation as well as your body, or it's a useless exercise. Don't be like this guy on the beach in business attire.

"Will you relax, Harold, we're supposed to be on vacation!"

You should return to work refreshed and invigorated.

Take some time off after a major trial—you'll return to your other cases with renewed vigor. Try planning your next vacation right after you return from your last one.

### Vary your routine.

Work routine has advantages—predictability, reliability, and regularity. But routine can also be mind-numbing. It is revivifying to alter your routine occasionally. Change your time of arrival, departure, or lunch; your route to work; your lunch companion; your office furniture or decor. Bring a plant to your office. Breathe fresh life into your daily habits.

Go where your peripheral vision takes you, in a responsible way. What does that mean? Just as your eyes take in sights on the edge of your vision, life presents many opportunities just beyond your daily routine. Explore.

### *Expand your horizons.*

Remember life before law school? You probably had interests, hobbies, and intellectual pursuits that have lain dormant many years. Get out that old musical instrument; read a novel; go to the theater, movies, concerts, art galleries, sporting events—whatever you enjoy, so long as it's unrelated to the practice of law. Develop friendships with non-lawyers. Doing so is healthy not only for you personally but for you as a litigator. As Oliver Wendell Holmes Jr. observed, "The life of the law has not been logic: it has been experience."

### *Create oases.*

An oasis is a place for respite and sustenance. Create oases for yourself that present opportunities for meaningful respite, such as a picnic; a walk in the woods, a park, or botanical garden; or just lie in a hammock.

## 3. WORK SMARTER

### *Keep a current "to do" list.*

Like a juggler with many balls in the air, you have many tasks to perform, and you don't want to let any of the balls drop. Whether on your computer or on paper, keep a current, updated "to do" list of discrete tasks you need to perform. Determine which have priority, and complete your tasks in a logical sequence. Don't try to keep all this in your head; it only creates anxiety about what you may have forgotten. At least once a week, review your list to keep it current. Cross off each task as you complete it, for the satisfaction of positive reinforcement.

### *Plan a realistic work schedule.*

Don't schedule client conferences too close together, and avoid conflicting court appearances whenever possible. Do priority and difficult work early in the day. Give yourself enough time—extra time if possible—to complete tasks. Reasonable deadlines allow you to polish and refine. Pace yourself. And when you leave for court, give yourself extra time. You never know when you will be delayed by traffic congestion, foul weather, or security backups at the courthouse. Better yet, plan to arrive even earlier than you need to, and work at the courthouse before the court session starts.

### *Establish realistic expectations.*

Even though you should be a zealous advocate, avoid harboring unrealistic expectations about the likely outcome of a case or communicating such expectations to your client. If you don't avoid this trap, you are setting up both yourself and your client for disappointment. Your goal should be to do your best, not to achieve perfection. See chapter 1, section 6, on how to deal with client expectations.

And know that losing a motion, or even a case, is not the end of the world. Analyze what you might have done differently, with the benefit of input from colleagues, and move on. The only trial lawyer who has not lost a case is one who does not try cases. If you played in Little League or on high school or college sports teams, you learned how to lose—a lesson at least as valuable as knowing how to win. You can learn something new and useful from each case. Your cumulative experience will make you a better lawyer, whether you learn from your wins or your losses. Sometimes, you learn even more from your losses than your wins.

### *Don't beat yourself up when you make mistakes, but do learn from them.*

You certainly don't want to give credence to Ambrose Bierce's sardonic definition of "attorney" as "a person legally appointed to mismanage one's affairs which one has not himself the skill to rightly mismanage." But you will make mistakes.

Assume that you complete only 50 discrete tasks a week (a very low assumption), and that you work 50 weeks a year. On that basis, you perform 2500 discrete tasks a year. Over a career of 40 years, that adds up to 100,000 discrete tasks.

Now assume that you are error free 98 percent of the time (an optimistic assumption for mere mortals). That means you will make mistakes only 2 percent of the time. Over your career, that's 2000 mistakes. Unless you are perfect (and nobody is), you will make mistakes.

What should you do when you realize you've made a mistake? Don't blame anyone else if it is your mistake—not your secretary, your paralegal, your colleagues, or your dog—who did not, after all, "eat your homework." First, ask yourself if you actually *did* something incorrectly. If you are not sure, check with a colleague. Then promptly rectify your mistake, if you can. As Confucius said: "A person who has committed a mistake and doesn't correct it is committing another mistake." Don't put it off, because your mistake will only loom larger over time. On the other hand, don't act impulsively. Make sure your head is clear and you're not stressed out about what you did wrong before you attempt to fix it.

Most mistakes are readily fixable. But what if you think you've made a major blunder, such as blowing the statute of limitations? Analyze carefully. In the case of the blown statute of limitations, ask: Have I actually missed the statute of limitations? What statute of limitations applies? Was the defendant subject to service at all times that the statute of limitations was running? Can I take advantage of any statutes or procedural rules, such as an accidental failure of suit act? Can I amend to fix the problem? Do I have a basis to assert continuing course of conduct or fraudulent concealment of a cause of action? Brainstorm all these issues, and others, with your colleagues.

Now let's take the worst possibility in this hypothetical fact pattern. You've blown the statute of limitations and you have no remedy. That's why you have malpractice insurance. Talk to the person in your firm responsible for reporting incidents to your carrier, and do what needs to be done. Be straightforward with your client about what happened, and suggest that your client get advice from independent counsel.

### *Don't internalize your case.*

To be an effective advocate, you must identify with your client. But if you do this to the extent that your client's case becomes your own, you can lose the very professional objectivity your client relies on—and your own perspective as well.

### *Don't put off the worst until last.*

Inherent in the work of trial lawyers are annoying and anxiety-producing tasks—returning the call of a difficult client, taking a confrontational deposition, working on a burdensome file, or giving a client bad news.

Delay in dealing with these events only exacerbates the situation; your anxiety increases while the problem festers.

What's more, anxiety interferes with clear thinking. There is a Hasidic saying: "To worry is a sin. Only one sort of worry is permissible: to worry because one worries." Figure out what it is that's making you anxious. Then do what's got to be done. Get it over with. Do first what you resist most. What causes you anxiety may in fact be an opportunity. As Joseph Campbell put it: "The cave you fear to enter holds the treasure you seek."

## *Be organized and focused.*

Your sub-files, files, file cabinet, desk, and office should be tidy and well organized, enabling you to be efficient and in control of your physical space. Such tidiness may seem like a daunting task. Start small, with your top desk drawer. Clean it out. Then progress to the piles of paper on your desk. And, while you're at it, ask yourself: In this electronic world, do I really need all this paper?

Likewise with everything on your computer. How much clutter have you accumulated by keeping (rather than deleting or archiving) documents and emails that have no further utility? Delete whatever you have no further use for so you will have on your computer only what you will need.

Being focused mentally is the analogue to being organized physically. Devote all your mental energies to one task at a time, rather than scattering them. A laser beam is far more penetrating than a flashlight. When you must do heavy thinking, go where you will not be disturbed—a conference room, a law library, or even your own office, if you can arrange to be left alone there.

## *Complete tasks on time.*

"The leading rule for the lawyer," Abraham Lincoln wrote, "is diligence. Leave nothing for tomorrow which can be done today. Never let your correspondence fall behind. Whatever piece of business you have in hand, before stopping, do all the labor pertaining to it which can then be done."

But even if you are organized and focused, you may have difficulty completing tasks on time. No good can come of procrastination. As Benjamin Franklin put it: "You may delay, but time will not." Figure out what interferes with your getting things done on time.

Possible roadblocks are being overwhelmed with work, being distracted by emails (business and social), concern about what others may think of your final work product, being a perfectionist, fear of failure, even possibly fear of success (if you do well on this, what additional work will be added to your already heavy workload?), and concern that the task at hand is too monumental to achieve in the time allowed. Make an honest assessment of what holds you back, and deal with it.

If you are being offered an assignment when you already have a full plate, do not hesitate to speak up. Better to be up front about your workload than to do a mediocre job by the deadline. If you need extra time to do a proper job, ask for it, unless you know the deadline is not flexible. If the task can be broken down into stages, accomplish one stage at a time, with the satisfaction that, each step of the way, you are making progress. If the impediment is psychological, then discuss your emotional impediment with someone in a position to give you good advice.

## *Be prepared.*

Use a tickler system, on your computer or otherwise, that will keep track of deadlines and give you adequate notice well ahead of the due date. Anticipate and comply with court-imposed scheduling orders, and set your own timetable in their absence. When you begin a new case, think it through carefully. Start trial preparation the day of your first client conference. Conduct your factual and legal investigation early, and modify it as appropriate. Unless you handle only one case at a time (highly unlikely), you are like a juggler who must keep all the balls in the air, without dropping any. You do not want to drop the ball on any of your cases.

Here's another analogy: For each case, you are on a conveyor belt, heading inexorably toward a deadline, like this guy carried along toward the maw of deadline oblivion on the next page.

Unlike this guy, though, you are on multiple conveyor belts simultaneously in a multidimensional world, as each day ticks by toward multiple deadlines. Cosmologists call this a multiverse. As a trial lawyer, you live in a multiverse, in which you must know where you are, at all times, in all dimensions, on each conveyor belt you're on. As you are carried along simultaneously on all conveyor belts, you don't want to get anywhere near the maw of deadline oblivion looming at the end of any of them.

## Plan ahead.

You don't want to wake up the morning you are to pick a jury only to discover that the clothes you planned to wear are at the cleaners, your car won't start, part of the file is missing, and a key witness is nowhere to be found. In advance, think about what you will need and when you will need it. Then prepare.

## Review all files regularly.

At least once a month, go through all your files to make sure each case is progressing appropriately, and none has languished—especially not the one that hangs around your neck like an albatross. You don't want to discover too late that the time for completing discovery has already passed, the statute of limitations has expired, or you missed some other deadline. Pull out all the files that you have avoided working on, for whatever reason, and get busy.

## 4. TAKE ADVANTAGE OF TEAMWORK

### Get help with work when needed.

Getting help can take many forms: workshopping a case with other lawyers, assigning responsibility for different tasks in a case among colleagues and paralegals, arranging for other lawyers to cover for you when you are on vacation or on trial, and making use of staff support services. Whenever you share responsibility, it is absolutely crucial that the allocation of tasks be clearly understood so that nothing falls through the cracks.

### Keep your client informed.

Send your client copies of significant pleadings and correspondence and return phone calls promptly. Keep your client up-to-date on the progress of the case, including positive and negative developments, and on settlement proposals. Ask yourself: "If I were the client, would I want to know this?" Don't wait for the client to call inquiring about the case. Take the initiative. A well-informed client is more likely to be a satisfied client. For more, see chapter 1, section 5, and chapter 11, section 2.

### Cultivate staff relationships.

You are only as effective as the people working with you—other lawyers, paralegals, secretaries, messengers, and clerks. Praise good performance promptly and appropriately and critique inadequate performance constructively. Relate to members of your staff as people whenever you see them, and not just once a year when you wish them a happy birthday. For more, see chapter 2, sections 1 and 2.

### Seek feedback.

As an associate, you should seek feedback from partners about your performance—not just at your annual or semiannual review, but whenever you have completed a significant assignment. When you become a partner of the firm, initiate that feedback for associates, and solicit their views of the firm and their relationships with the partners. Both associates and partners should seek input about the firm from clients. This fosters a good attorney-client relationship and enhances client satisfaction.

## 5. BENEFIT FROM SAFETY VALVES

### Expect the unexpected.

Whether in the course of a deposition or at a crucial moment during a trial, you will be surprised (maybe flabbergasted) by detrimental testimony contrary to your expectations, or an adverse evidentiary ruling, to name just two hazards of litigation. Even though you have acted diligently in discovery and trial preparation, these unexpected events do occur, and they provide some of the less-welcome thrills of being a trial lawyer. Expect them. When upsets occur, buy time, think, plan your course of action, and execute on it.

There will come a time when you will lose a case you expected to win. Analyze that experience to learn what you should have done differently, do postmortem workshopping with others, and get on with the next case. There is truth in the Welsh proverb that failures are the pillars of success.

### *Discuss your feelings.*

Litigators know the importance of keeping emotions in check. Just as an upset or angry witness is more vulnerable to effective cross-examination, an overly emotional litigator lacks the professional objectivity and control to be an effective advocate. Of course, litigators should display emotion in adversarial proceedings, but only in a controlled, honest way that promotes the client's goals.

But litigators do have emotions and must give vent to them or risk being stymied by their own emotional baggage. Make sure you have someone—a spouse, colleague, or friend—you can talk to about how you *feel* about your work and its stresses.

### *Listen to your body.*

Be conscious of the warning signals your body sends when you are stressed—headaches, malaise, neck pain, queasy stomach, twitching eyelids. Ask yourself, "Why am I stressed now?" Change what you can to reduce your level of stress; your body will tell you if the change is working. Ideally, you will know you are overstressed well before your body sends you these alarm signals.

### *Have fun.*

When did you last have a belly laugh? Experience an adventure? Break loose? Do something spontaneously? The possibilities are all around you—it's just a matter of deciding what would delight you and doing it. Figure out what nourishes your soul and, in a responsible way, enjoy!

### *Evaluate professional satisfaction.*

Periodically, at least once a year, assess what makes your work fulfilling and list impediments to that fulfillment. Consider such factors as the type of litigation you do and would like to do, the people you work with, the quality and depth of your support staff, and the level of your professional development compared with what you had originally expected to have achieved at this stage of your career. If you think making changes could promote your professional satisfaction, make them, if possible. Likewise, evaluate your stressors. Look for ways to reduce tension and strain.

If, despite all these measures, you continue to feel stressed out, consider your options. You can call your state bar association's hotline, especially if you have an urgent need to talk to someone for emergency advice and guidance. Maybe you just aren't temperamentally suited to be a trial lawyer. Not everyone who starts down this path is. You can consider other areas of the law, or venture into other professions, with the benefit of your training and experience as a trial lawyer. Consider reading books on career alternatives, or consulting with a career counselor. See appendix III for books on this subject.

Mark your calendar for three months from now and read this chapter again. Ask yourself how effectively you are reducing stress. What could you do better? What should you stop doing? Return to this exercise as often as suits you.

Adopting these stress reducers on an ongoing basis should enable you to concentrate your energies on the substantive tasks that you have at hand. The law, for you, need not be a jealous lover. With the proper perspective, you can make the law a pathway to a long and very satisfying career as a trial lawyer.

## 6. Navigate up the Flow Channel to Advance Your Career

In a groundbreaking book, University of Chicago psychology professor Mihaly Csikszentmihalyi presented his theory of "flow," which describes the state of optimal experience, times when people report feelings of enjoyment, concentration, and deep involvement (see appendix III). People in flow typically feel strong, alert, in effortless control, and unselfconscious, performing at the peak of their abilities. In flow, people experience an exhilarating feeling of transcendence; they are in the zone, centered. If you can learn to maximize flow, you can succeed in turning your life as a whole into a unified flow experience, achieving intense feelings of enjoyment, improvement of your work performance, and a sense of harmony in your life.

It all sounds too good to be true, perhaps. But Professor Csikszentmihalyi bases his theory on scientific experiments verifying the conditions for flow and the benefits of being in flow. An analogy is useful here.

Assume you want to learn how to play tennis. If in your first lesson the tennis pro (we'll call her Liz) tries teaching you an advanced skill, such as the heavy topspin kick serve, rather than basic strokes, you will become frustrated and anxious about ever learning how to play. You may feel like just giving up altogether. But if Liz starts off teaching you rudimentary skills, you will soon have a sense of achievement, because you perceive that the challenge is commensurate with your skill level.

If Liz has you continue doing rudimentary drills without teaching you more advanced skills you're ready for, you'll get bored and may think about giving up the game for the opposite reason—it's not challenging enough. But if Liz continues to increase the level of difficulty of drills as your skill level increases, you will enjoy tennis as you continue to improve as a player.

When you perceive that the challenge you face is commensurate with your skill level, you are in flow. The same "flow" theory applies to any skill—how to play a musical instrument, how to juggle, how to use a new computer operating system, how to do carpentry, how to cook—any skill at all. Here is a self-explanatory chart showing where the flow channel is—45 degrees between perceived challenge and perceived skill level—where the two equate.

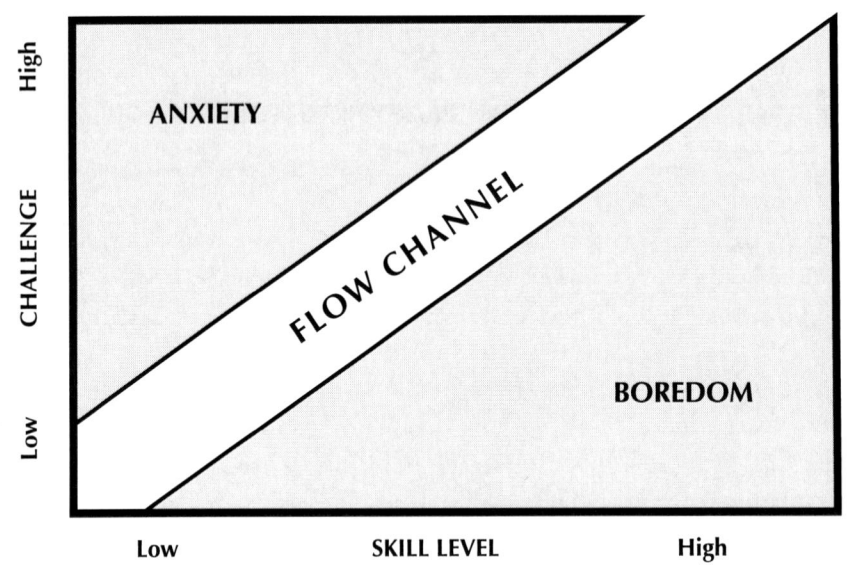

Flow is enhanced when three conditions are met: perceived challenge and perceived skill levels match; you are involved in an activity with a clear set of goals, adding direction and structure to the task at hand; and you get clear and immediate feedback so you can adjust your performance to remain in the flow state.

And so it is with your career as a trial lawyer. If the assignments you get match your skill level as you see it, you will move along in the flow channel, advancing your career by taking on increasingly sophisticated work, with more and more at stake. If you are stuck over time doing low-level work, speak up. Talk to lawyers in your firm in a position to assign you work; let them know you are ready for more-challenging assignments. And seek feedback about each assignment you complete so you know how to improve.

If you are given an assignment that you think is over your head, carefully assess whether that is so. Speak up if it is. But be aware that sometimes you need to make an intellectual and emotional breakthrough to realize that you *can* take on more challenging assignments, such as your first argument of a motion, deposition, evidentiary hearing, or trial. The lawyer assigning you the work has confidence in you or would not assign it to you. So, have confidence in yourself.

Likewise, if you have too much work with too many deadlines looming, you will be anxious; if you have too little work, you will be bored. If you find yourself in either situation, do something about it: If too much work, talk to those assigning you work about extending deadlines or getting other relief. If too little work, ask for more assignments, and step up your marketing activities.

Be the protagonist in the story of your professional career, as you keep a steady course, moving up in the flow channel, for a productive and satisfying life as a trial lawyer. Take to heart Joseph Campbell's insight, noted above, about the cave you fear, because it *does* hold the treasures you seek. And heed Ralph Waldo Emerson's advice: "[D]on't be too timid or squeamish about your actions. All life is an experiment. The more experiments you make the better."

## 7. Aspire to achieve holistic success

What is "holistic success"? For a trial lawyer, it is achieving your professional goals while having balance in your life. It is understanding that whether you are a successful trial lawyer is not merely a function of how many cases you win or how many you settle favorably for your client. Holistic success is achieved by realizing your full potential not only as a trial lawyer, but also as a person of value, in all the roles of your life. "The purpose of life," wrote Emerson, "is to be useful, to be honorable, to be compassionate, to have it make some difference that you have lived and lived well." And by "living well," Emerson certainly did not have in mind driving a fancy car and living in a luxurious home. "Living well," in Emerson's sense, is to be a person of upstanding character.

How do you achieve holistic success? By a constant awareness that success as a trial lawyer requires discipline, focus, commitment, and time-consuming hard work in your professional life, balanced with fulfilling your obligations to your family, friends, and yourself, for a dynamic equilibrium in all the aspects of your life. If you heed all the advice in this chapter, you will be well on your way to achieve the kind of holistic success that, looking back on your career years hence, you will be able to say that the world is a better place because, for a brief time, you lived in it.

❖❖❖❖
## PRACTICE CHECKLIST

- Take good care of your body by eating right, exercising right, and sleeping right.
- Create and nurture your support system by making time for family and friends, advising family members of trial demands, making time for yourself, taking fulfilling vacations, varying your routine, expanding your horizons, and creating oases.
- Work smarter by keeping a current "to do" list, planning a realistic work schedule, establishing realistic expectations, accepting that you will make mistakes and learning from them, not internalizing your cases, not putting off what you want to avoid, being organized and focused, completing tasks on time, being prepared, planning ahead, and reviewing all your files regularly.
- Take advantage of teamwork by getting help with work when you need it, keeping your client informed, cultivating staff relationships, and seeking feedback.
- Benefit from safety valves by expecting the unexpected, discussing your feelings, listening to your body, having fun, and evaluating your professional satisfaction.
- Read books by Mitch Albom, Richard Carlson, Thich Nhat Hanh, Jon Kabat-Zinn, Steven Keeva, Deng Ming-Dao, and Matthieu Ricard, listed in appendix III.
- Aspire to achieve holistic success.
- As you advance in your career, navigate up the flow channel to avoid boredom and anxiety.

# CHAPTER FOURTEEN
# SUCCEEDING AS A TRIAL LAWYER: A PERSONAL ACCOUNT

The insights in this book are from my own professional and personal experience, although, as I make clear in my "But For" acknowledgments, many other people made this book possible. Even so, I intentionally omitted from other chapters of this book any account of my own journey as a trial lawyer.

In this chapter, I tell you my own story, not out of shameless self-indulgence, but rather in the hope that you will learn something valuable, enabling you to assimilate everything else in this book in the context of one trial lawyer's experience. I certainly don't hold myself up as a model of the quintessential trial lawyer, but I have learned a few things worth sharing over nearly 40 years in practice. We'll start with my disastrous first court appearance. . . .

I join Cohen and Wolf PC in Bridgeport, Connecticut, as an associate, right out of law school, doing legal research and writing. The firm has a tradition—a rite of passage, really—that as soon as a new associate passes the bar, off to court to argue a motion. Diligently, I prepare for my first oral argument of a pretrial motion as I did when I was on Cornell Law School's moot court team. I learn the issues, the facts, the law, and the procedural rules; prepare what I will say; and am eager to argue. I enter the large courtroom, for the weekly call of pretrial motions. It seems that the entire Bridgeport litigation bar is present.

My case is one of the first called. I stride confidently to the front of the courtroom, secure in the knowledge that my thorough preparation, and the rightness of my position, will trump opposing counsel's far greater experience as a trial lawyer. As I am about to launch into my argument, Judge Irving Levine, who looks like a wizened, curmudgeonly judge straight out of typecasting, peers down at me, and this colloquy ensues:

"New to the bar, are you?"

"Yes, your honor."

"Welcome to the bar, son. Have you read the most recent revisions to the rules of practice, which went into effect last month?"

"I believe so, your honor, but you may be referring to a rule change I am not aware of."

"You're right about that. I'm denying your motion. Go back to your office and read the updated rules."

"Thank you, your honor."

"What are you thanking me for? I just denied your motion!"

Laughter fills the courtroom. With my tail between my legs, embarrassed that my first court appearance is such a disaster, I return to the office, immediately explain what happened to the partner who assigned this simple but ill-fated task to me. He responds with great understanding and support, without castigation. Whenever associates at my firm wonder why I stress so much keeping abreast of the latest rules changes, I tell them that story.

And now for some context, let's venture back to my college days.

It's my senior year at Oberlin College, where I am an English major. For many reasons, Oberlin is the ideal college for me. I develop a facility for critical thinking across a range of disciplines in the liberal arts curriculum, and the ability to write cogent, analytical prose. As a bonus, I take advantage of Oberlin's Conservatory of Music, where I take French horn lessons and play in ensembles with very talented musicians. I began playing the French horn when I was nine and had graduated from the Preparatory Department of the Eastman School of Music in Rochester, New York, at the same time I graduated from public high school.

In the Oberlin placement office, browsing through graduate school catalogs, I consider getting a PhD in English Literature, to become an English professor, graduate studies in clinical psychology, and law school. The law school curriculum entices me. I'm hooked.

I'm now in my third year of law school, recruitment season. I get callbacks from several firms, including one in Washington, DC, that wines and dines me at a posh four-star restaurant. A couple weeks later, I drive to Bridgeport, Connecticut—not exactly the mecca of political power, the arts, and culture that is Washington, DC—for an interview with a 12-lawyer firm, Cohen and Wolf, PC. Around noon, I join several lawyers in the firm for lunch. Where? At a greasy-spoon diner featuring food that, while edible, would not get any stars. During the course of interviews that day, I become aware that I'm meeting with the lawyers I want to join up with for my entire career. I come to realize that it's not the glitz that counts, but the personalities and character of the people I'm planning to share my professional career with.

As I'm ushered into the office of the senior partner, Herb Cohen, I'm prepared to answer all the stock questions about why I went to law school, what area of practice I'm interested in, my strengths and weaknesses as a lawyer, and other subjects of so many cookie-cutter interviews. To my surprise, Herb begins by asking about my experience as a French horn player, at the Eastman School of Music and at Oberlin. We talk about music, and little else, for about 20 minutes.

I later learn that Herb played an instrument himself—each Wednesday evening, he played string quartets with his cronies. And, by the way, he had his own Stradivarius. He was also very active in the arts and in community affairs. I join the 12-lawyer firm, as one of two spanking-new associates.

Then my first, disastrous appearance in court, when Judge Levine put me in my place, which you read about at the beginning of this chapter. I learn to appreciate that difficult lesson and, over time, manage to earn Judge Levine's respect.

Even after feeling like the laughingstock of the local bar, I remain undaunted. Despite having started off my courtroom career on the wrong foot, I remain confident that I can get my footing in my next court appearance. This time, I join an experienced partner in criminal court. This particular partner, like Judge Levine, is also out of typecasting, as the former New York City Assistant District Attorney turned defense lawyer—tall, movie-star looks, dressed the part, and flamboyant. He knows all the lawyers and prosecutors, glad-hands the prosecutor in our case, tells stories and jokes, and, by sheer force of personality (as well as solid lawyering), achieves his client's purpose.

I, on the other hand, am a rather academic, nose-to-the-grindstone young lawyer, just learning the ropes. I question, for the first time, whether I have the personality to succeed in the world of big-personality trial lawyers. The same day as I see this dazzling lawyer in action, I seek guidance from one of the other partners. I tell him that it's suddenly obvious to me that I'm not cut out to be a trial lawyer, because I don't have the personality for it. He assures me that trial lawyers come in all personality types, and that I have a very promising career as a trial lawyer. "Just be yourself," he assures me, "and you'll do fine." His advice rings true to this day.

A couple years later, I take a five-day National Institute for Trial Advocacy (NITA) course in trial advocacy. This is a learning-by-doing course, in which participants are videotaped. I vividly recall seeing the video of my direct examination of my client, a little old lady who was the victim of stock churning. I intended to look at her sympathetically, as I paid close attention to her well-rehearsed answers. Well, the videotape reveals that I was scowling at her—because I was concentrating so hard. That was an eye-opener.

After a few years of practicing law, I realize that I am missing something important in my life—making music. I had put away my French horn when starting law school, figuring I had no time for it, and so had not taken it out of its case since. I dust off the case, take out my French horn, and play. Awful. Really awful. Such sour notes!

I determine to get back into playing mode, to be at least as proficient as at Oberlin. I take lessons for a year. Then I put together a woodwind quintet, with other like-minded and similarly adept professionals who are likewise amateur musicians. We rehearse together until we are ready for our first concert. We've been together for more than 30 years now, and have performed for weddings and charitable events, at nursing homes, and in concert halls. Each year, we perform a children's concert at the local library. For an encore, we play a Sousa march, while the kids march around playing kazoos we give them. Delightfully raucous.

Because physical exercise has always been important to me, I join the local squash club and tennis club, and keep up my cross-country skiing, snowshoeing, hiking, and long-distance cycling. I come to realize how vital regular physical exercise is to maintain a career as a trial lawyer over decades. I set an exercise routine and stick to it.

As just one example, early in my career I develop the habit of cycling before work, for about an hour. One morning, while climbing a long hill, another cyclist whizzes by me. He slows up. We talk. It turns out he lives near me, cycles about the same distance at about the same time in the morning. We arrange to meet a couple days later. We cycle together several times a week, for decades, and become best of friends.

My son and daughter, when in high school, are on varsity soccer, lacrosse, field hockey, and ski teams. As a parent very active in their lives, I decide that it's important to me to go to some of their games during the workweek. I figure that billable hours are fungible, so that if, on a given day, I devote a couple hours to attending one of their sporting events, I can work a couple hours that night (or another night) to make up for it. My only regret about that is that I didn't attend more of their games.

Over time, I become more active in my community, serving on the boards of the local symphony, historical society, a child advocacy coalition, and a public education organization. I find that work comes my way from being active in the community.

As I handle more cases and became more experienced, I realize that I am in a position to share what I know with other lawyers. I write articles that are published in local and national litigation magazines, and begin presenting seminars for lawyers. Over time, I become chair of the Litigation Group at my firm of over 50 lawyers, and a special master in federal court, serving as a mediator to help settle cases. I become certified as an American Arbitration Association arbitrator for commercial disputes. I serve as a faculty member for NITA programs. I serve as counsel to the federal grievance committee in Connecticut.

One memorable day, I attend a seminar at which one of the presenters, a practicing trial lawyer, is introduced as someone who also teaches trial practice at Yale Law School. During the lunch break, I ask how he managed to teach at Yale. He explains that Yale has a clinical course, eight students in each section, in which law students learn how to try cases by being critiqued doing the direct and cross-examination of witnesses, selecting jurors, and giving opening statements and closing arguments.

Having mentored associates at my firm, and been a faculty member at NITA seminars, I know that this is for me. I inquire further, and the next thing I know, I'm teaching one of the sections of Trial Practice at Yale. I teach Trial Practice each year for about 15 years.

Then Steve Wizner, who is in charge of all clinical programs at Yale, taps Fred Gold and me to teach a more comprehensive course, Civil Litigation Practice, that we need to create from scratch. Fred and I had done the NITA teacher training course at Harvard Law School many years earlier, had served as co-faculty members in NITA programs, and had been colleagues in the practice of law. We are totally compatible, sort of like Tweedledum and Tweedledee, but without the girth. We devise the course, and the students enroll. It gives me great satisfaction to see the progress in the students' pretrial and trial skills from the first class to the last, knowing that they will benefit from those skills throughout their careers.

Over the years, I make a point of following my own advice about reducing stress, creating a life beyond the practice of law, and making quality family time. I sleep seven hours a night, usually getting up at 5:00 a.m., thereby getting a jump on the day. My wife, Lynn, and I never skip breakfast, enjoying a hearty meal in the morning (oatmeal and homemade granola are staples for us). Lynn makes delicious dinners (we're both vegetarians), and I often take leftovers for lunch. On weekends I'm the sous-chef.

When my son and daughter were young, we hiked together often and went on wilderness backpacking trips together and Outward Bound white-water rafting trips together. All four of us vacationed together to America's national parks and beyond our country's borders. I arranged my schedule so the four of us had dinner together whenever possible (most of the time), and I still make sure I'm home in time to enjoy my evenings with Lynn. Lynn is at least as fit as I am, so we enjoy playing tennis, kayaking, hiking, snowshoeing, and cross-country skiing together. She has sustained and supported me all these years, through the best of times and the worst of times.

I create a life beyond the practice of law in my music ensemble groups (my quintet, Prevailing Winds, and a dectet, Cumulus Wind Ensemble), and the other activities described above. I pursue other interests as well, one of which is etymology, which has fascinated me since college. After years of research, I publish *Dubious Doublets: A Delightful Compendium of Unlikely Word Pairs of Common Origin, from Aardvark/Porcelain to Zodiac/Whiskey* (John Wiley & Sons 2003). After I turn 60, I take up the flugelhorn, which is like an oversize trumpet, a perfect, mellow instrument for playing the best of the Great American Songbook (think Tony Bennett, Frank Sinatra, Billie Holiday, and Ella Fitzgerald). I'm doing my best to learn how to improvise, which is quite a challenge for a classically trained musician. It's never too late to learn something new.

Having published many articles pertaining to trial practice, written materials for in-house seminars and bar association seminars, and written materials for my Yale course, it dawns on me that I can incorporate all of them into one comprehensive book about succeeding as a trial lawyer. I recast what I have written, and write new chapters. Thus this book.

One of my articles, published in the June 2000 edition of *Trial*, sprang from my experience at my 25th Cornell Law School reunion. As you will see, it is based on my own experience in my career as a trial lawyer. Here it is.

## TWENTY-FIFTH REUNION CATHARSIS: LEARNING TO AVOID BURNOUT

I do some of my best thinking at thirty thousand feet. The steady drone of the jet engine muffles extraneous sounds. I'm sitting comfortably, with no distractions. During this brief interlude in the sky, I have no faxes, letters, or e-mail to read, no client conferences, office meetings, or court appearances to rush off to, and no urgent calls to return. I've just recharged the battery in my laptop, and now I just have to figure out how to recharge my own battery.

I'm on my way to my law school reunion, and I have some anxiety about it. Until I got a call from Dave, I didn't really think seriously about attending.

I'm busy at the office and can hardly find time to do anything other than work, let alone attend a reunion. Besides, there are only a few classmates I'd really like to see, and I don't know if they'll be there. More fundamentally, do I want to go to a reunion to hear about how satisfied and successful all my classmates are, when I'm in a quandary about my law career?

Then again, maybe I'll get some insight from this reunion. After all, it's my first time back in twenty-five years, and just being at the school may evoke something in me. Even better, maybe I'll find some other classmates who are wrestling with the same issues I'm facing—how practicing law has taken over my life and left me with little time or energy for anything else. I am almost ready to move on to something else, but what?

My chat with Dave convinced me that it will be worth my while to go to the reunion, and now I'm on my way. If I've got the guts, I'll let Dave, or possibly another classmate, know what I'm going through. Maybe I'll introduce this subject right off the bat. It's possible that I'm not alone in this turmoil. I'll just see how it goes.

**At the reunion**

The first person I see is Dave.

**Dave**: Ted, it's so good to see you! I'm sure glad you showed up. We've got a lot of catching up to do.

**Ted**: Do you recognize any other people from our class?

**Dave**: I just saw Swift (Albert Wickware Swifton III). As a matter of fact, here he comes.

**Swift**: How the hell are you guys? Ted, Dave, I almost didn't recognize you, but the voices are familiar! Remember those study sessions? Those are the voices that got me through law school. We gotta talk. But first, want any brews? I'm buying.

**Dave**: Sure.

**Ted**: Make that two.

**Swift**: (delivering brews) So, Ted, this is really quite weird. It looks like someone put fifty-year-old faces, and wider bodies, on you guys and all the other people I remember from law school. Anyway, what are you up to?

**Ted**: I'm a commercial litigator and head of our litigation department. How about you?

**Swift**: PI work, with one partner and a few associates. How about you, Dave?

**Dave**: I'm a commercial litigator, like Ted. I'm not surprised that Ted and I took the same path. Ever since we were on the moot court team together, I figured we'd both go that route.

**Ted:** Remember how idealistic we were back then? With our new law degrees we were going to change the world—public interest law, a storefront office to help people get their food stamps. But then reality set in with school loans, the lure of a sophisticated practice, and the promise of a comfortable living.

**Swift**: Well, you can always do some pro bono work on the side.

**Ted**: If I could ever find the time.

**Dave**: At least we chose a secure profession. As long as people make contracts and get into accidents, we'll have plenty to do.

**Ted**: Sometimes too much! I must admit that on occasion it gets to me. I wonder how many would say that the pressures are hardly worth it, especially for litigators. The clients have unrealistic expectations, opposing counsel is on a mission to thwart everything I'm trying to do, judges can be unreasonable.

And it's much more of a business than a profession. Civility is a thing of the past. Beyond all that, I've got to put in a huge number of billable hours and collect enough fees each year, only to start from zero at the beginning of the next year—like Sisyphus, endlessly (and futilely) pushing a boulder up a mountain, only to start over again. Where's the satisfaction?

**Dave**: It can be like that sometimes, but, as you look back, don't you find satisfaction in helping your clients? After all, you are the last resort for them.

**Swift**: Ted, you just take everything too seriously. Lighten up! Sure, I work hard, too. When I'm on trial, I do nothing else. But you've got to be philosophical about it.

**Ted**: What do you mean?

**Swift**: If you take the practice of law too seriously, it will be the eight hundred pound gorilla that takes over your life. Then you'll have nothing left for yourself, your family, your friends, or your clients, for that matter. You'll be consumed and burn out at the ripe old age of fifty.

**Dave**: So how do you deal with all this?

**Swift**: I work hard on each case, do the best I can, and don't get so caught up in practicing law that I lose perspective. I make time for myself and my family so that when I return to the office I'm fresh. At the end of each case, I assess what I've accomplished, learn from my mistakes, and move on to the next case.

**Ted**: So you think it's just in my head?

**Swift**: Well, your mind-set governs how you deal with any situation. Let's try a little experiment. If there were a hidden camera in your office and you were filmed during a typical day, what would you see when you viewed it? And if there were a hidden camera when you arrived home, what would you see?

**Ted**: To be honest, one very stressed-out lawyer and a grumpy husband and father.

**Dave**: It doesn't have to be like that. Think about varying your routine. Small adjustments in your schedule can make a big difference. Experiment and see what works for you. And while you're at it, you can vary your routine in other ways. As I recall, when we were in law school, you played the oboe. What ever happened with that?

**Swift**: And, Dave, you played the trumpet back then, didn't you?

**Dave**: I did, but right after law school I decided I had no time for the trumpet. After about five years, I realized I missed it. So I tried playing some notes, and it sounded terrible. I took lessons and eventually played well enough to put together a brass quintet.

**Ted**: When do you find the time to play?

**Dave**: I practice a few times a week, in the evenings. We rehearse a couple of times a month, and then perform. We do an annual concert for kids at the local public library, concerts at nursing homes, in the local town hall, and some weddings. And what about your oboe?

**Ted**: I still have it. But I'm not sure I'd even remember the fingerings.

**Dave**: Well, just think about the possibilities—you could dust it off and find out. Besides, you may find, as I do, that playing an instrument puts you in a different frame of mind. Picture this: It's 7:30 at night. Everyone in the quintet has put in a full day of work. We start rehearsing. We're all tired, but it's like there's a new energy source—the music part of our brains—that's been untapped. So we play, and before we know it, it's 10 p.m. One time, we hired a coach to help us prepare for a concert, and we played until after midnight without even realizing it.

**Ted**: Different energy source? That sounds like far-out New Age stuff.

**Swift**: It's for real. Here's another example of varying your routine while at the same time taking care of yourself. What are you doing for exercise?

**Ted**: Exercise? Who has time? By the time I get home from the office, I'm too tired.

**Swift**: But exercise—if it's something you like doing—can be invigorating. For me, it's squash. Besides, exercise is good for you, good for your heart and lungs, and you'll sleep better. If you're in good shape, you'll have more stamina for the time you're working.

**Ted**: I do get some exercise, but it's hard to find the time.

**Swift**: If a client needed to meet with you at a certain time, you'd arrange your schedule to accommodate him. So why not arrange your schedule to accommodate your own needs?

**Ted**: I suppose I could do that, but not early in the morning. I'm not a morning person.

**Swift**: OK, then. How about twice a week after work and then on weekends? If you scheduled your exercise like everything else and commit to it, you'll do it. Just ease into it and make sure the exercise you choose is something you like to do. Otherwise, it will just be a chore.

**Ted**: Why do you like squash?

**Swift**: For a few reasons. It's a great workout in a short amount of time. It combines physical fitness with the strategy of chess. And I learn things that help me in my law practice: how to deal with crucial moments, like when it's down to the last point; how to change strategy when I'm losing; how to handle winning and losing; and how to deal with my opponent as my adversary, not my enemy. All these things apply in both courts—the squash court and the trial court.

And I find squash mentally relaxing. On the court, nothing exists but me, my opponent, the ball, and the four walls—it clears the mind. Besides, I've brought in some clients from the guys at the squash club.

**Dave**: And you can reduce your stress by taking vacations. What about that?

**Ted**: Vacations! I've had to postpone or cancel vacations because of work. And even when I take my one-week vacations, I spend the first few days depressurizing and the last few thinking about getting back to the office. To make matters worse, when I return to the office, I have this let-down feeling.

**Dave**: Some of that is a matter of planning and some is in your head. If you plan ahead and are protective of your vacation time, you should usually be able to schedule trials and other work-related activities around your vacations. You can delegate to other lawyers in your firm to avoid the post-vacation crunch. Isn't that one reason you're not a solo practitioner?

And the no-vacation vacation is self-imposed. If you arrange your schedule appropriately—and delegate responsibly—you won't have to call the office or be near a computer while you're on vacation.

**Ted**: What about thinking about work while on vacation?

**Dave**: It's unavoidable to some extent. But if you have planned, tied up as many loose ends as possible before leaving, and delegated pending matters to others you can rely on, you can go off on vacation secure in the knowledge that everything will be handled in your absence.

**Ted**: Sometimes it's tough to get away and it can be expensive, so I just take vacations at home.

**Dave**: That's risky. The best vacation doesn't mean spending a lot of money, but staying around deprives you of the advantages of getting outside your day-to-day environment. Get out of your box and explore new territory. You'll return to the office refreshed and reenergized.

**Ted**: I suppose. But I only get three weeks of vacation a year. That's not a lot.

**Dave**: Ah, but you don't need to take time off to take a vacation. What I mean is this: "Vacation" is as much a state of mind as it is designated time off. If you plan ahead, you can take a "vacation" over the course of a weekend. Think of something everyone in your family likes to do and do it. I know it may be difficult with teenage daughters. I remember when my kids were still at home—before they went to college. But keep in mind that your time together is limited. So make the most of the time you have.

**Ted**: It would be good to have something enjoyable to look forward to on a regular basis.

**Dave**: Sure! And you can apply the same approach to getting tickets for a play, concert, sporting event, or whatever suits your fancy. That's what I do. Also, create special occasions to look forward to. I had an informal party for my fiftieth birthday, and my son surprised me for the occasion by returning all the way from Brazil, where he lives. You're limited only by your imagination and your budget.

**Ted**: But how do you find the time?

**Dave**: Time is a function of organization and focus. What I mean is that if you are careful about organizing your time and what you fill it with, you can be more efficient. For example, is your desk neat and tidy, so you instantly know where everything is, or is it full of clutter? Are your files up to date and in order? For that matter, is your closet at home in order?

I struggle with this all the time, but I make a concerted effort to keep everything organized and use a tickler system that works. That way, I don't waste time looking for things and wondering if I've missed deadlines.

**Ted**: How does your tickler system work?

**Dave**: Well, I calendar ahead all meetings, court appearances, trials, and pleadings deadlines. I put each one on my tickler not just for the day in question but days ahead of time as well, so I don't get stuck preparing at the last minute.

**Ted**: I've tried that too, but I find that I still put off certain things. I guess it's just natural procrastination.

**Dave:** I have to fight that tendency, too. When you have so many files to work on, it's easy to put off the ones you have some anxiety about, whether it's because of an expected unpleasant confrontation, a tough argument, a difficult client, or an obnoxious opponent. The best thing to do is recognize what's bothering you, deal with it head-on if you can, and commit yourself to getting the job done well before the deadline. Determine the date you will tackle the task, clear your desk and mind of everything else, and do it. And remember, the longer it sits, the larger it looms, and the more difficult it will be to finally get it done. For all the energy you use worrying about it, you could finish the task.

**Ted**: OK, and what about focus?

**Swift**: I'll tell you about focus. Focus is simply a matter of directing all your attention to what you're doing as you're doing it. For example, when I'm in the middle of a squash match, if I start thinking about what I have to do in the office that day, I lose my concentration for an instant. That's all the time it takes to lose the point. I know, because it happens. Likewise, if I think about squash when I'm in the office, I've lost my concentration, and there's slippage that consumes time.

**Ted**: I think I get the idea now. But tell me, don't you guys ever get stressed out?

**Dave**: Of course! Sometimes I ask myself why I put up with all the aggravation. I occasionally feel overwhelmed and consumed by the law, much as you were describing before.

**Ted**: Do you do anything else to handle the stress?

**Swift**: I make sure that on a regular basis I have a good laugh, whether it's from a funny movie, a cartoon, a book, or even a sitcom. And not just something that makes me chuckle but something that's laugh-out-loud funny. It feels good, and I've read that laughter improves respiration, circulation, and the immune system and reduces physical as well as psychological stress. Just figure out what makes you really laugh and go for it, so long as it's not at someone's expense.

**Ted**: But what if I take all this good advice, and I'm still really dissatisfied with the practice of law?

**Dave**: Take a close look at the source of your dissatisfaction. Ask yourself some tough questions: What are your life goals and objectives? Are they realistic? Do you have a clear sense of what you want to and are able to accomplish, professionally and otherwise? What sacrifices are you willing to make for your career?

Have you recognized your own strengths and weaknesses? What are your priorities in life? Do your priorities regarding material goods, relationships, and professional status make sense? Are you attending to your own personal needs?

**Ted**: That's an awful lot to deal with. I suppose it's easier to get caught up in the day-to-day routine than to grapple with these bigger issues. The irony is that if I ignore them, I'm like a robot on automatic pilot, unmindful of the life choices I'm making as I go to the office each day. Maybe if I examine these things, I'll decide I love the practice of law but need to make some minor adjustments. On the other hand, I may decide it's time for a change.

**Dave**: Right. You've got choices. Every year, thousands of lawyers leave the practice of law to explore other career paths. You could talk to a career counselor about options.

And if your issues go deeper, you may want to consider seeing a therapist. After all, if you had a toothache, you wouldn't hesitate to go to the dentist. If you have an ache inside your soul you can't resolve, why not seek professional help?

**Ted**: This chat has been helpful. I think I'll make some adjustments in my life and expand my horizons. I might even get out my oboe.

**Dave**: Why not? And while you're at it, I'll suggest some books that you may find worth reading. I recommend *Flow: The Psychology of Optimal Experience*, by Mihaly Csikszentmihalyi. It's a practical book describing steps toward enhancing your quality of life, including ways to make your professional life more fulfilling.

**Ted**: Any other books?

**Dave**: *Tuesdays with Morrie*, by Mitch Albom. It's a chronicle of a man's weekly visits with his dying college professor, recounting their consciousness-raising conversations about family, emotions, fear of aging, money, marriage, and forgiveness. There's a lot of wisdom in this book.

You might take a look at a book about mindfulness. How often do you go through the day on automatic pilot, without really being attuned to the moment? This book, *Wherever You Go, There You Are*, is by Jon Kabat-Zinn, a professor of medicine and director of a stress reduction clinic at the University of Massachusetts Medical Center. It provides a practical, easy approach to meditation. And it offers advice about how to deal with feelings of stress.

One last book, and the shortest. You can read it in an hour or so. *Don't Sweat the Small Stuff. . .and It's All Small Stuff: Simple Ways to Keep the Little Things from Taking Over Your Life*, by Richard Carlson. The title says it all.

**Ted**: Can you suggest anything that's less serious?

**Swift**: Forget all that heavy stuff. You're about to turn fifty, right? For a good hoot, read *Dave Barry Turns 50*. There's nothing quite like a good belly laugh.

**Post-reunion journal entry**

Well, I'm on my way back home, and I sure have a lot to think about.

I guess the first thing is to recognize that I have more control and more choices than I realized. Right now I need to get back in balance. How do I do that? By making some changes. Nothing monumental, like changing careers, but changes to get me closer to my balance point so I don't feel that I'm always inundated with and preoccupied by work.

What am I going to do differently? Part of me wants to make a lot of changes all at once, but I know it's smarter to make these changes gradually. So, here's a list of specifics, which I'll keep and refer back to as time goes by. Some of these things I can do right away; others will require ongoing effort. The real challenge will be to avoid just reverting to the status quo, even though it's unacceptable. My list:

1. Talk to Alice and the kids about our next vacation and, together, make all the arrangements. Then, I must not let anything interfere with that vacation. I'll schedule around it.
2. Create a tickler system that works.

3. Get out my oboe. Start with simple scales and be patient with myself. I expect that it'll sound pretty awful for a while. Maybe I'll take lessons.
4. Arrange my schedule so I can get to some field hockey games before the girls graduate.
5. Delegate more work to others in the office, when possible.
6. Exercise regularly. Start with something I enjoy: biking. Schedule time to go biking, and find a buddy (Chuck?) to bike with so it's more fun.
7. Buy those books Dave and Swift told me about and read them.
8. Laugh. Find books, articles, anything that will make me laugh. Rent movies that make me laugh out loud. Get a subscription to the *New Yorker*, even if I only have time to read the cartoons.
9. Don't take myself too seriously. Lighten up. (But how?)
10. Have some fun.

I have now been practicing law nearly 40 years, and it has been more than a decade since I wrote that article. From this vantage point, I can say that, professionally, I have, in Joseph Campbell's terms, "followed my bliss." To Campbell, a scholar and mythologist, if you follow your bliss, you put yourself on a kind of track that has been there all the while, waiting for you, and the life that you ought to be living is the one you are living. Wherever you are—if you are following your bliss—you are enjoying that refreshment, that life within you, all the time. If your professional "bliss" is to be a successful trial lawyer, take to heart the advice I offer in this book, and enjoy a full, robust professional life as a zealous advocate.

*"What if my bliss happens to be suing people?"*

# APPENDIX I
# COGENCY: MOLLY COGENT DEBATING AND MENTORING

## 1. Bombast v. Cogent

**Moderator**: This debate goes to the heart of how we conduct litigation today. The participants are Molly Cogent, author of *Less Is More: The Simplification Strategy* and head of the litigation department at Cogent and Sage, and Ulysses S. Bombast, senior partner at Bombast, Bunkum, Bluderbuss, Billingsgate and Blarney. He is the author of the two-volume treatise *Rambo Litigation: Maximizing Body Count by Papering the Enemy to Death*. They see things differently.

Ms. Cogent, what is "simplification strategy"?

**Cogent**: The strategy is based on a notion of simplicity best described by Oliver Wendell Holmes when he said that "the only simplicity for which I would give a straw is that which is on the other side of the complex—not that which has never divined it." Thus, this strategy is based on mastery of complexity and then distillation, reduction to essence. It is not a simplistic approach. It is a strategy that applies to everything litigators do, from the first client interview to appellate court argument. Simplicity works in many other pursuits, and it does in litigation as well.

Think of the powerful simplicity of the Great Pyramid at Giza, the Acropolis, or, for a modern example, the Guggenheim Museum in New York City. Examples from music are the four-note theme in Beethoven's Fifth Symphony, Harry Chapin's "Cat's in the Cradle," Bobby McFerrin's "Don't Worry Be Happy," and even John Coltrane's "My Favorite Things," in which he does incredible jazz riffs without losing the essential simplicity of the musical theme.

Some years ago, Irving Younger wrote: "It has long been observed by practitioners of disciplines other than the law that simplicity marks the master. Simplicity walks hand in hand with high seriousness, not as a child better left behind, but as the very herald of large intention and great accomplishment."

**Moderator**: Mr. Bombast?

**Bombast**: If what litigators do were so simple, we wouldn't have to go to law school. The litigator is in a position very different from that of the artist or composer. Perhaps simplicity can be achieved when you select the notes or invent the characters. But the litigator is not, as it were, present from the creation. You typically come to a case after all the facts are in and must work with these facts in putting together a claim or defense. To be a good litigator, you've got to bring out all the complexities of your case. Don't leave any stone unturned, paper the hell out of the opposition, attack on all fronts; the more you say and write, the more likely that something will stick. Use the shotgun approach; an AK-47 is even better.

**Moderator**: Ms. Cogent, how does your simplification strategy affect the way you develop a case?

**Cogent**: No matter how complex a case you have, you can state its essential facts simply, laying out the central theme of your case. You must think about themes from the first client interview and not wait until the eve of trial. The themes of your case may evolve over time, as with your factual and legal investigation, but everything you do in working up a case has to be evaluated in light of how it ties in with your themes.

I disagree with Mr. Bombast when he suggests that the complexity of the cases we handle makes reduction to essence impossible. I see truth in the words of the Indian poet Rabindranath Tagore: "[L]ife is simple, however complex the organism may be. Everything goes to pieces when the living truth of the central simplicity is lost."

Think of Seurat, the great pointillist painter. All he put on his canvas were dots and dashes, each less than an inch long. If you stand close to one of his paintings, you see only these colorful but meaningless dots and dashes. Move back a dozen feet or so, and a coherent picture emerges. For a modern example, look at any of Chuck Close's large-scale portraits, created in a similar way. Each fact in a case is like one of those dots and dashes. The litigator's job is to organize them on the canvas to make a coherent whole so that the trier of fact gets the big picture.

If you prefer, you can think of what we do as gathering pieces of a puzzle (each fact being one piece) and then assembling those puzzle pieces to make a compelling picture.

**Bombast**: Let me say right here that the more pieces the better. Take discovery, for example. You've got to do a thorough factual investigation in order to represent your client properly. Depose everybody in sight. Ask each deponent everything you can think of that you can get away with. Make the enemy's life miserable. Pose interrogatories about everything you can imagine, including conversations, meetings, dates, times, places—the works. If you have a local rule that limits the number of interrogatories, overwhelm your enemy with waves of interrogatories. File requests for production to get every document in sight. Be creative. Make these requests as broad, oppressive, burdensome, and unbearable as your fertile imagination can conjure up.

This approach makes the enemy's life miserable, keeps the enemy off balance, and saps time and energy so that it is harder for the enemy to take the offensive. Litigation is war, and you must keep the enemy scrambling. Get information. Knowledge is power, and the more of the enemy's facts you know, the more powerful your position will be.

**Moderator**: Ms. Cogent, are you opposed to thorough discovery?

**Cogent**: No. It is important to conduct comprehensive discovery. You can get information from your client, from independent sources (such as state and federal Freedom of Information Acts, Internet searches, and public records), and from implementing court rules.

I disagree with Mr. Bombast, however, when he suggests that the more interrogatories and the more requests to produce, the better.

For example, unless interrogatories are limited to solid facts (such as dates of events and sources of additional information), the answers are generally useless, carefully crafted by lawyers. Furthermore, if you serve detailed interrogatories before taking depositions, you are merely giving opposing counsel the opportunity to prepare his or her client to give carefully stated, unhelpful (for you) answers to important questions.

My preference is to serve a narrowly focused document request and set of interrogatories on the opposing party and to then take an early deposition based on the results of that discovery. At the deposition, I ask about the substance of conversations, and I elicit details that are far beyond the scope of the interrogatories.

I find this approach much more effective than drafting many interrogatories, at considerable expense to my client, only to get back canned responses, drafted by a lawyer, that are of no use to me.

**Moderator**: Ms. Cogent, what do you do with all these facts once you gather them?

**Cogent**: I organize them. There are various ways to do this. Of course, you can digest deposition transcripts and prepare chronologies, using a box calendar if appropriate. You can also prepare organization charts for complex organizational structures, flowcharts for complex processes (such as a manufacturing process in a Uniform Commercial Code case or the critical path for erection of a building in a construction case). There are many ways to summarize and diagram facts.

The task for the litigator is to distill all these facts to the essential documents, key events, and key witnesses. As Winston Churchill said, "out of intense complexities, intense simplicities emerge."

**Moderator**: We've talked about the factual investigation. What about the legal investigation? Mr. Bombast?

**Bombast**: Just as a general going to war has to have all weapons ready for deployment, a litigator must have an arsenal stocked with all the weapons available. This means doing thorough legal research on all possible legal theories and then including in your complaint a count for each legal theory. Remember, if you don't allege it, you can't prove it. Your client can accuse you of malpractice if you don't allege all causes of action. The more causes of action, the more likely you are to hit and destroy your target.

**Cogent**: I agree in part. Mr. Bombast talked about the importance of considering all possible legal theories. I agree with that. Think of all the facts in your case as encompassed within a square. Considering all possible legal theories is like dividing that square into four equal parts in as many different ways as possible. You should try this exercise yourself.

You will probably find that it's easy to think of four or five ways to divide the square into four equal parts. Then challenge yourself to be even more imaginative and to divide the square into four equal parts in other ways. This is an exercise from Edward De Bono's book *Lateral Thinking*, which espouses looking for as many *different* approaches as possible, rather than immediately looking for the *best* approach.

And so, for example, when presented with a bundle of facts in a commercial case, don't limit your analysis to just whether there was a breach of contract. To borrow Mr. Bombast's phrase, go to your arsenal and see what weapons are available. In addition to breach of contract, your arsenal includes such theories as negligent and fraudulent misrepresentation, fraudulent inducement to contract, tortious interference with contract, tortious interference with business expectancy, breach of fiduciary duty, breach of implied covenant of good faith and fair dealing, promissory estoppel, unjust enrichment, quantum meruit, and a whole host of statutory causes of action.

This arsenal is not limited to causes of action; it includes a variety of remedies. In addition to compensatory damages, consider seeking attorneys' fees, double and treble damages, punitive damages, where appropriate, and various equitable remedies, such as an accounting, appointment of a receiver, declaratory relief, reformation of contract, mandamus, or declaration of a constructive or resulting trust.

**Moderator**: So how do you disagree with Mr. Bombast?

**Cogent**: I don't assert all these claims and remedies. I evaluate the merits of each, then discard those theories and remedies that are weak or inapplicable or that impose a greater burden than I need to assume. As Abe Lincoln put it, "in law, it is good policy to never plead what you need not, lest you oblige yourself to prove what you cannot."

I also evaluate very carefully which parties to name as defendants. More is not always better. The more defendants, the more lawyers who will be hired to thwart my purposes and, in the event of a jury trial, the more peremptory challenges against me. Of course, you have to name all necessary parties, and, as a general matter, you want to include as defendants all those who have liability and who could contribute to a settlement or judgment. But you have to pick your targets with care.

To borrow the war analogy, you have to pick your shots. If you spray all your ammunition indiscriminately, you will expend a lot of energy and run out of ammunition, to no avail.

One cautionary note about limiting the legal theories you allege: It's important to advise your client before filing the complaint that you are limiting the legal theories to those that are most effective and impose no greater burden of proof than necessary. Advise the client carefully about the legal theories available and the reasons you are limiting those you assert. Follow up with an appropriate letter. That way you educate your client while safeguarding yourself against a potential malpractice suit.

**Moderator**: Mr. Bombast, what is your philosophy about how a lawyer should state the facts in a complaint?

**Bombast**: The complaint may be the only pleading I draft that ever gets into the jury room or is read by the judge. I want to tell my whole story in the complaint. I make it as factually detailed as possible to overwhelm the opposition and induce an early settlement—not to mention impress the client.

**Moderator**: Ms. Cogent, aren't you interested in fleshing your story out for the judge?

**Cogent**: Flesh, yes. But not fat. A judge who reads such a complaint is going to get weary plowing through the myriad of factual minutiae, and so will a jury. Even more important, by alleging all those facts, you are assuming the burden of proving them, a burden you may not be able to meet. My comments about not assuming any needless burdens apply to the facts as well as to the law.

Complaints I draft tell the story in chronological order. I limit each numbered paragraph to one fact or cluster of facts. I use simple, short declaratory sentences in the active voice. And I assert only the most viable causes of action, to avoid diluting them with weak causes of action, after discussion with my client, getting informed consent.

**Moderator**: What about defending a case? What's your approach then?

**Bombast**: If there is any technical defect in service, I move to dismiss; I move for change of venue; I remove the case to federal court if possible, just to screw up the plaintiff; I move to force the plaintiff to revise the complaint just to keep the plaintiff off balance; I move to strike any count that I think I can get rid of; I move for summary judgment in all my cases, because it causes delay and helps me discover the enemy's factual and legal claims.

**Moderator**: Ms. Cogent, surely you challenge your opponent at the outset?

**Cogent**: True, but you don't gain anything by moving to dismiss on a technical ground that can promptly be rectified by reserving the summons and complaint. Unless you really need to buy a couple of weeks to gear up for a defense or you can take advantage of the running of the statute of limitations, you have accomplished nothing other than increasing your legal fees.

Even worse is the idea that you should move to dismiss or strike any count that fails to state a claim. In many instances, filing the motion merely educates opposing counsel, who promptly files an amended complaint that is immune to such attack. For example, a RICO count may fail to allege the requisite predicate acts. Unless there is no good faith basis for amending to allege those acts, plaintiff's counsel will merely amend.

**Moderator**: How does Rambo approach brief writing, Mr. Bombast?

**Bombast**: Argue every point of law. Make the brief long so that the enemy has to spend lots of time reviewing and analyzing it. Cite as many cases as you can. File briefs that will keep the enemy scrambling and drafting responsive briefs till the wee hours.

**Cogent**: I disagree. The fewer words the better. Lay out your preliminary statement, statement of facts, argument, and conclusion, then stop.

The hardest part of brief writing is editing. It's much easier to write a long brief than a short one. As Pascal wrote apologetically to a friend, "I have made this letter longer than usual because I lack the time to make it shorter."

A useful exercise in editing is to underline the words that work for you and see how many other words you can eliminate without losing meaning. Let's take an example from Richard Wydick's book *Plain English for Lawyers*. Your draft may read: "The ruling by the trial judge was prejudicial error for the reason that it cut off cross-examination with respect to issues that were vital." Excise the nonworking words: "The trial judge's ruling was prejudicial error because it cut off cross-examination on vital issues." The edited version is two-thirds as long and more effective.

**Moderator**: Do you agree with Mr. Bombast's suggestions about case citations in briefs?

**Cogent**: For well-recognized legal principles, such as the requirement of consideration for a binding contract, I cite only one or two cases decided by the highest court in the appropriate jurisdiction. For more obscure points of law, I cite more cases, providing a succinct summary of each. Cases directly in point I discuss in detail.

**Moderator**: How about the trial itself?

**Bombast**: The more witnesses, testimony, and exhibits, the better. If you can get more than one witness to corroborate the same story, all the better. On cross-examination, ask all the questions you can think of until you find a weak point and then slam 'em hard. Then use all those facts in your summation to a jury or your closing argument and brief to the court. It's especially important to do that when you're opposing a change in the status quo—for example, representing a defendant in a criminal case. If I raise enough factual issues, the jury will have difficulty finding guilt beyond a reasonable doubt.

**Moderator**: Ms. Cogent?

**Cogent**: Put into the record only testimony and evidence that gets across your theme. From your first client interview, you should be formulating the theme of your case. By the time you are ready to try your case, your theme should be well developed and refined. Your theme provides the basis for crafting the voir dire, the opening statement, the choice of witnesses, the direct and cross-examination, the documents you choose to put into evidence, the closing argument, the proposed charge to the jury, and any post-trial briefs.

Streamline the trial by stipulating to uncontested facts and unobjectionable exhibits and taking advantage of requests to admit, as appropriate. Call only those witnesses who are necessary to present your case or defense and ask them only those questions that are necessary to accomplish your purposes. Select your exhibits carefully and don't clutter the record with inconsequential documents. If there are voluminous exhibits, introduce summaries, as provided in Rule 1006 of the Federal Rules of Evidence and various state court rules. Cross-examination of witnesses should be crisp, forceful, and clean. Make a few surgical strikes and sit down. Otherwise, you're looking for trouble.

**Moderator**: What about objections at trial?

**Bombast**: I want to derail the enemy's case every chance I get. I do that by objecting to every question that is technically objectionable, and I insert my foot, blocking the enemy's case every chance I get—in voir dire, for example, and during a witness's examination when the enemy tries to put a document into evidence.

**Cogent**: I don't object to every objectionable question. Instead, I object strategically. For example, if opposing counsel asks leading questions on preliminary matters, such as the background of a witness, an objection serves no useful purpose.

The case will proceed more efficiently with leading questions on such matters. But if opposing counsel asks a leading question on a matter in dispute, I certainly do object. The court is more likely to give credence to carefully chosen objections than to a barrage of sometimes meritorious and sometimes frivolous objections.

**Moderator**: I'd like to cover appeals before our time runs out. Mr. Bombast, what is your approach?

**Bombast**: I raise all possible issues on appeal to make sure I cover the bases. Besides, that way I can't be accused of legal malpractice. I always limit myself to the number of pages allowed by the rules, but I usually come mighty close. On a few occasions, I've had to tinker with margins and typefaces, but I've always squeezed all my arguments into the number of pages allowed.

**Cogent**: Exactly wrong. You want to limit the number of issues on appeal to those most likely to succeed. Appellate judges don't like shotgun appeals. Chief Justice Ellen Peters of the Connecticut Supreme Court recently criticized an appellant who raised more than a dozen issues on appeal: "Appellate pursuit of so large a number of issues forecloses the opportunity for fully reasoned discussion of pivotal substantive concerns. A shotgun approach does a disservice both to this court and to the party on whose behalf it is presented."

I searched "shotgun approach" on Westlaw and found nearly three hundred cases in which a judge used the term. I haven't read all these cases, but I'm sure few refer to a criminal's modus operandi. Furthermore, a shotgun approach can result in lengthy and convoluted briefs—and even tinkering with margins, as Mr. Bombast suggests. The Texas Supreme Court threw out an appeal of a $550,000 judgment solely because the size of the print on the appellant's brief was too small. The typeface was reduced so that the brief would fit into the number of pages the rules allowed. The court apparently accepted the earthy argument that an appellate advocate should not be allowed to squeeze seventy-five pounds of manure into a fifty-pound bag.

In oral argument on appeal, I limit myself to the essential appellate issues and focus on the policy considerations that promote my client's cause.

**Moderator**: Summations?

**Bombast**: Litigation is war. Fight on every front. Keep your enemy scrambling. Vex, annoy, and harass your enemy. Take no prisoners.

**Cogent**: Less is more.

## 2. Cogency: Beyond "Less Is More"

*Molly Cogent is back! Here she is mentoring associate Tim Smithers on one of her favorite subjects: cogency. He wrote a draft of a brief supporting a motion for summary judgment. Here she explains to Tim how to make his writing, and so much else we do as trial lawyers, more cogent, and thereby more persuasive.*

**Molly**: I arranged this meeting to discuss your brief. Our discussion this morning will help you write better, and will be useful to me in preparing for a seminar I'm presenting to the bar association about cogency. I'm calling it "Beyond 'Less Is More,'" because, even though that pithy statement is true, to understand its meaning, and how to apply it, requires a deeper understanding.

**Tim**: So, you liked my draft, but you think it needs improvement?

**Molly**: Well, it was good for a first draft, but it needs editing. You researched well, but you need to tighten up your writing. Just because the rules allow you a certain number of pages does not mean you should use them all! Picture the judge, or the judge's clerk, wading through piles of briefs. We want our brief to stand out as tightly written, not just another overly-long ironically-called "brief" to wade through in search of what matters. What is our goal here?

**Tim**: To persuade the judge that there is no genuine dispute as to any material fact, and that we are entitled to judgment as a matter of law. That's the summary judgment standard.

**Molly**: Right! And the best way to do that in a brief is by presenting, on a silver platter, the most focused statement of facts and legal argument. Before we talk about specifics of editing your draft, let's talk about some fundamentals of cogency.

**Tim**: OK. You're going to do a dry run for your seminar, right?

**Molly**: Right you are! Here are some guidelines for writing an effective brief. Of course, before you start writing, know your objective, write down each point you may want to make, organize your points, and prepare a sentence outline. Include your strongest arguments and reject weaker ones.

1. Start with a preliminary statement that grabs the judge's attention, to predispose the judge to rule in your favor. Do so in as few words as possible. Mark Twain put it best: "Anybody can have ideas—the difficulty is to express them without squandering a quire of paper on an idea that ought to be reduced to one glittering paragraph." Can you tell I've done some research for my seminar, Tim?
2. In your fact section, include only facts that make a difference, and be succinct. In referring to parties, use shortened forms (not the generic "plaintiff," "defendant," "intervening party," or "counterclaim plaintiff"), thus: Intercontinental Widget Manufacturing Corporation becomes "IWMC." While you're at it, leave out the "hereinafter," because it is implicit. Focus on facts supporting your position but don't shy away from including bad facts—present them in context to inoculate the judge from their impact when your opponent presents them.
3. Use short, persuasive section headings.
4. Write simple, short sentences. Heed William Strunk's advice: "A sentence should contain no unnecessary words, a paragraph no unnecessary sentences, for the same reason that a drawing should have no unnecessary lines and a machine no unnecessary parts."
5. Cite only pertinent cases and authorities. Even if you find good language in a case, if the holding is against your position, don't cite it—with two exceptions: one is if you find a controlling case that the ethical rules require you to cite; the other is if, after thorough research, you can't find any better case. Don't cite cases from other jurisdictions, unless you find a dearth of authority in your jurisdiction—and then cite only cases directly in point that are highly persuasive, especially those that explain in detail the rationale for the court's ruling.
6. When citing a case, let the judge know what the holding is. The most efficient way to do so is by putting the holding in parentheses after the citation. If the case warrants extended discussion, limit that discussion to what matters.
7. When quoting from a case, a treatise, or any other source, limit the quote to only what is persuasive. Avoid long quotes. No judges like to read them.
8. Avoid redundancy. Put differently, whenever possible, do not repeat what you have already written or say the same thing twice

or make your points more than once. See how annoying that is? The only exception is in summarizing your argument.

9. Avoid personal attacks on your opponent. You use risk antagonizing a judge. Besides, attacking your opponent looks desperate. You know the old saying: "When you're weak on the facts, pound the law! When you're weak on the law, pound the facts! And when you're weak on both, pound the table!" And, by the way, never use the word "disingenuous" when attacking an opponent's motives in making an argument. Judges wince every time they see it.

10. Use simple English words whenever possible. For example, replace "subsequent to" with "after" and replace "approximately" with "about." For some reason, even college students who can write in simple English, after graduating from law school, feel the need to justify their existence as lawyers by writing in polysyllabic words. Don't do it. You will justify your existence as a lawyer by writing persuasive English prose.

11. Replace several words with one whenever possible. For example, replace "in the event that" with "if"; "despite the fact that" with "though"; "in close proximity to" with "near"; "during the time that" with "while"; and never write "it is respectfully submitted that. . . ." Just make your submission! I'm sure you get the idea from these examples.

12. Edit. Edit. Edit. Prepare your draft well enough in advance of the filing date so you can edit. How? Remove all words that do not do work. Eliminate weak arguments. Omit redundancies, overly long quotes, and authorities of little value. The great lexicographer Samuel Johnson employs a memorable analogy do drive this point home: "A man who uses a great many words to express his meaning is like a bad marksman who instead of aiming a single stone at an object takes up a handful and throws at it in hopes he may hit." And here is William Zinsser's way of putting it: "Writing improves in direct ratio to the things we can keep out of it that shouldn't be there." Zinsser wrote *On Writing Well*, which I commend to you. When doing your final edit, try this: omit each word you can, without losing meaning.

13. When you are done, stop.

**Tim**: That's quite a list!

**Molly**: It is. And I want to focus a minute more on editing. On a computer, it's so easy to type many words, and to copy and paste from cases. In a first draft, be expansive if you like, but know that you will edit down to the essence of what you need to convey. When you edit, think about this: What if you were writing longhand, and had a limited amount of ink, or paper? You would choose your words very carefully.

**Tim**: But sometimes isn't a longer brief more persuasive than a shorter one? After all, in a longer brief, I can discuss my points more fully.

**Molly**: Usually not. Consider this: The original U.S. Constitution is 4543 words (about eighteen pages); Martin Luther King's "I Have A Dream" speech is 1579 words (fewer than seven pages); the Declaration of Independence is 1330 words (fewer than six pages); and Winston Churchill's "blood, toil, tears, and sweat" speech to the House of Commons is only 684 words (fewer than three pages). Lincoln's Gettysburg Address is just over a page. How long is your draft of the memo supporting our motion for summary judgment?

**Tim**: My draft is 31 pages. I get the point. My second draft will be a lot shorter. Does the same advice apply to other things I write?

**Molly**: Certainly! Everything I just told you applies—adjusted for context—to internal office memos, letters, and emails. How many times have you had to read through lots of words in an email before someone gets to the point? Remember what Blaise Pascal wrote: "The letter I have written today is longer than usual because I lacked the time to make it shorter." Of course he said it in French, in even fewer words. So, before pushing "SEND," ask yourself: What words can I eliminate without losing meaning?

**Tim**: I see what you mean. What about cogency in other contexts?

**Molly**: Cogency applies to everything we write. Consider Mark Twain's reply to his publisher. Twain received this telegram: "NEED 2-PAGE SHORT STORY TWO DAYS." Twain replied: "NO CAN DO 2 PAGES TWO DAYS. CAN DO 30 PAGES 2 DAYS. NEED 30 DAYS TO DO 2 PAGES."

**Tim**: Did you make that up?

**Molly**: Nope. I don't have the wit to make up something like that. But there's more. Cogency applies to everything we do as trial lawyers! We distill to the essence in so much that we do. For example, in drafting a complaint, do you include every possible cause of action?

**Tim**: Well, my client can't criticize me if I include all possible causes of action. Besides, that way I hedge my bets, in case I lose on some but not on all my claims.

**Molly**: But consider how your weak and far-fetched counts dilute your strong ones, and divert the attention of the judge and jury from what really matters. Choose the strongest claims, and zealously advocate for all of them. Certainly, discuss with your client why you advise against asserting the weaker claims, but recommend and get authority for omitting them. Then, if your client consents, include only your best claims. Keep in mind Model Rule 1.4 regarding a client's informed consent. Sure, it takes guts to leave out claims, but consider what Albert Einstein said: "Any fool can make things bigger, more complex . . . it takes a touch of genius—and a lot of courage—to move in the opposite direction."

**Tim**: What about the facts I include in my complaint?

**Molly**: Be succinct. You want to include enough facts to tell your story, and to avoid a challenge under *Ashcroft v. Iqbal*, 556 U.S. 662 (2009) and *Bell Atlantic Corp. v. Twombly*, 550 U.S. 544 (2007). Those cases hold that, to survive a motion to dismiss, you must set forth a cause of action that is *plausible*; that is, it must allow the court to draw the reasonable inference that the defendant is liable for the misconduct alleged—not merely the *possibility* that the defendant has so acted. If your complaint pleads only facts that are merely consistent with a defendant's liability, it stops short of the line between possibility and plausibility of entitlement to relief.

You also want to keep the story moving and make it compelling, so the reader—whether a judge or jury—will want to rule in your favor after reading it. Look at Federal Rule of Civil Procedure 8(a) and you'll see that the complaint must be "a short and plain statement"—and see rule 8(d)(1), mandating that pleadings must be "simple, concise, and direct." I can't put it better than that.

**Tim**: OK, so I get the idea. Does all this apply to other things, like discovery?

**Molly**: You want to conduct thorough discovery so you learn about all the strengths and weaknesses of each party's position well before trial, but then you must distill all the facts and documents down to what makes a difference in the case. By doing so, you can focus on what will be most persuasive at the trial. Depositions present a unique opportunity to learn about cogency.

**Tim**: Why is that?

**Molly**: Before you take any deposition, you must decide whom to depose, why, when, and what you seek to accomplish from the deposition. Only then can you proceed to take it. Your questions should exhaust the witness's memory on each subject that makes a difference. Keep in mind, though, that what is most important, especially for party deponents, is the admissions you get. So you need to determine in advance what admissions you need. You could spend one of your seven hours allowed by the Federal Rules of Civil Procedure exploring the party deponent's educational background and employment experience, but before you use up your precious time that way, ask yourself: will the answers make a difference in my case? You want admissions you can distill down to a powerful cross-examination at trial.

**Tim**: What is the unique opportunity that depositions present?

**Molly**: You get a transcript of every word. When you review it, ask yourself: What did I accomplish? Could I have been more efficient in achieving my objectives? Did I ask overly long or unduly convoluted questions? How can I use my limited time taking depositions more efficiently so I learn more in less time?

**Tim**: I suppose the same distillation process applies to the trial itself.

**Molly**: Right you are! You must distill your case to its essence before you can decide which witnesses you need, what questions to ask, what documents to put into evidence, and what arguments to make. Cicero's words thousands of years ago ring as true today as when he wrote them: "When you wish to instruct, be brief; that men's minds take in quickly what you say, learn its lesson, and retain it faithfully. Every word that is unnecessary only pours over the side of a brimming mind." Likewise, every superfluous witness, question and answer, exhibit, and argument, only dilutes your message, when you should be distilling it.

**Tim**: Like a billboard or bumper sticker?

**Molly**: Exactly! You should be able to summarize your case in a few choice words. As David Belasco, a renowned Broadway producer, put it: "If you can't write your idea on the back of my calling card, you don't have a clear idea." If you created a billboard to convince each person who sees it that you should prevail, what would it say? Another way to think about it is this: You are on an elevator that is about to descend from the 15th floor to the lobby. You are with the person you want to convince. You have until the elevator door opens. What do you say?

**Tim**: I thought you told me that I should never discuss a case in an elevator.

**Molly**: That's still good advice. But in this hypothetical, it's just the two of you.

**Tim**: I think I understand. So, in pretrial and trial work, I must distill to the essence to present my best case.

**Molly**: Right! And everything we just talked about applies to your oral presentation as well, whether in a pretrial argument, your opening statement and closing argument to a jury, or your appellate argument.

**Tim**: So what you're telling me applies across the board in everything we do as lawyers.

**Molly**: Not quite. There are exceptions. When we workshop cases, creative, nonlinear thinking often is more productive than straight-ahead analytical thinking. You know, thinking outside the box. And when you take a potential client out to lunch, the conversation should flow freely, even if it meanders. At some convenient point, you'll have the opportunity to talk about the services our firm provides, but only after you do a lot of listening.

**Tim**: I get it. So, with those exceptions, in my professional work I should stay focused and get right to the point.

**Molly**: Exactly. Here's a perspective for you: It takes 40 to 50 gallons of tree sap to make one gallon of maple syrup. In litigation, all the information and documents you glean through pretrial discovery, all the pretrial testimony, and all the potential trial witnesses, are the tree sap. You must boil all that down to the maple syrup, which is the essence of your case.

**Tim**: I never thought of trial work like making maple syrup, but I see your point.

**Molly**: Now let's focus for a minute on appellate work. Just as trial judges are mired in piles of not-so-brief briefs, appellate judges must plow through pages and pages of appellate briefs to understand the central points on appeal. Make it easier for the appellate judges, just as you do for the trial judges, choosing your arguments carefully, discarding the weaker ones (think of a Darwinian process of survival of the fittest, winnowing out the weak), distilling your appeal to its essence, and writing cogently. In appellate oral argument, you have just minutes to present your case, so choose your words wisely.

**Tim**: And keep my briefs brief, right?

**Molly**: Yes. Keep in mind that the word "brief" derives from Latin *brevis*, meaning "short." So "brief" is related to "brevity," as in the adage: "Brevity is the soul of wit." Keep it short!

**Tim**: Where did that come from?

**Molly**: Shakespeare. It's ironically from a long-winded speech of Polonius, right-hand man to King Claudius, who was Hamlet's stepfather. Claudius asked Polonius to spy on Hamlet, to find out what he was up to. The extended quote is so good, I may use it in the seminar: "Since brevity is the soul of wit, [a]nd tediousness the limbs and outward flourishes, I will be brief. Your noble son is mad. . . ." Observe how Shakespeare contrasts brevity with tediousness, and how Polonius summarizes his point in five words: "Your noble son is mad." Those five words demonstrate cogent prose.

**Tim**: But I don't get it. What does brevity have to do with being witty?

**Molly**: In Shakespeare's day, "wit" referred to intelligence, not being quick witted. Think about a nitwit as the opposite of someone of intelligence. So, to Shakespeare's audience, "brevity is the soul of wit" meant that the essence of intelligence is the ability to convey thoughts as briefly and efficiently as possible.

**Tim**: Looks like you've done a lot of work to prepare for this seminar. It seems like you are a student of words.

**Molly**: Think about it: a painter has a spectrum of paints; a mason has different kinds of bricks; a composer has all the notes of the scale; a carpenter has a variety of woods; a gourmet chef has an assortment of edible ingredients. As lawyers, all we have is words—yet we have an almost limitless lexicon to choose from. We should employ the best words for the task at hand, and the fewest.

**Tim**: How many minutes do you have to make your presentation?

**Molly**: Only one hour. I'd better get busy, distilling my presentation to its essence, just as I'm advising you to do with your brief.

**Tim**: Are you going to use my draft brief?

**Molly**: That will be the first handout for my seminar.

**Tim**: What is the second handout?

**Molly**: Your revised draft, in which you heed all the advice I just gave you. Be sure to redline all your changes. So get busy! Our deadline for filing is just a week away!

# APPENDIX II
# ETHICS PROBLEMS

## 1. Are these conversations forbidden?

You represent Bixby Real Estate Development LLC, a developer of apartment complexes, whose managing member is Bill Bixby. Bixby obtained $20 million financing for his company from Midas National Bank to develop an apartment complex, pursuant to the terms of a construction loan agreement. Because of tough economic times, Bixby met with Len Hinkley, senior vice president of Midas National Bank, requesting a modification of the loan, including an extension of the maturity date of the loan for an additional year. After negotiation, they reached an agreement on all terms, and both parties executed a loan modification agreement, entitling Bixby's company to extend the maturity date on the loan for an additional year, on certain conditions. Those conditions included the requirement of a new appraisal of the subject property satisfactory to the bank, by an appraiser approved by the bank, evidencing a value reasonably acceptable to the bank.

Bixby submitted an appraisal to the bank, prepared by the bank's appraiser. The value of the subject property had decreased by 5 percent from the appraisal the bank relied upon in making the original construction loan. The bank denied the one-year extension of the maturity date, solely based on its determination that the appraisal was unacceptable. As a result, Bixby was forced to sell the subject property at a significant loss.

You have learned that, within a month after the execution of the loan modification agreement, and before Bixby submitted the appraisal, Sid Proctor, an investor, took over the bank. Proctor did not want to carry this loan on the bank's books, and did want to increase the capitalization of the bank. Accordingly, he instructed Hinkley to do whatever he had to do to make sure the Bixby loan was not extended, no matter what he had to do.

Bixby has told you that he complied with all conditions for the loan extension, and that the bank's refusal to extend the loan as agreed based on the 5 percent reduction in the appraised value of the property is pretext to comply with Proctor's mandate. You have brought an action against Midas National Bank for breach of contract, and against Proctor for tortious interference with contract.

Based on responses to your interrogatories and document requests (and before you take any depositions), you have reason to believe that Proctor summoned Hinkley to a meeting, attended by Hinkley's secretary, Harriet Longsworth, at which Proctor instructed Hinkley to concoct any reason necessary to deny the loan extension, no matter what the terms of the loan modification agreement. Midas National Bank and Proctor are represented by counsel. Their primary defense is that the bank reasonably rejected the appraisal, which was a condition precedent for the one-year extension of the maturity date of the loan.

1. Assume that Hinkley is still employed at Midas National Bank, as senior vice president. Can you call him and discuss the facts of the case?
2. Is your answer to 1 different if you know that Hinkley, after you brought suit, was fired from Midas National Bank and now works as senior vice president at Century National Bank?
    a. Can you call Hinkley? If so, do you need to call defense counsel first to get approval?
    b. Does it matter if Hinkley calls you, eager to talk?
    c. If it is proper for you to call Hinkley, is there any limit to the subjects you can discuss?
    d. Does it matter if Hinkley tells you that he has discussed your client's claims with counsel for Midas National Bank?

3. Assume that Longsworth is still employed at Midas National Bank, as secretary to Hinkley's replacement. Can you call her and discuss the facts of the case? If so, do you need to call defense counsel first to get approval?

## 2. How do you deal with what really *did* happen in the car?

You represent Fred "Skip" Skipkowicz, president and CEO of Skippy's Inc., a national chain of fast-food restaurants known as Skippy's, in the defense of a sexual harassment case brought by Mindy LaMort, the former marketing director of his company. Skip is a hard-charging chief executive, who is used to getting his way. He is outraged about this lawsuit, and has told you that he will do whatever it takes to win.

Mindy's complaint alleges that, at the convention of the National Franchisors' Association in New Orleans a year ago, he and Mindy were both staying at the same hotel where the convention took place. According to the complaint, Skip took her out to dinner at Feelings Café, a romance-themed restaurant, where they had drinks with dinner. Driving back to the hotel, Skip pulled over and said to Mindy: "You are very attractive. I like you a lot. If you're nice to me, good things could happen for you." He then tried to kiss her on the mouth, but she rebuffed him.

Three months later, Skip told Mindy that he "wanted to go in a different direction" and that her employment was being terminated. Mindy claims that she was fired because she rebuffed Skip's advances. You are in a conference room preparing Skip for his deposition.

1. Ethically, can you inform Skip of all the elements Mindy must prove to establish a prima facie case, and all the elements for affirmative defenses, before you prepare him, knowing that by doing so he may tailor his testimony accordingly?
2. While you are preparing Skip, you play the role of opposing counsel in a dry run of his deposition:
   Q: *Did you stop the car on the way back to the hotel after having dinner with Mindy that night?*
   A: *I don't remember.*

> Q: *Did you, while returning to the hotel that night, say to Mindy "If you're nice to me, good things could happen for you," or words to that effect?*
> A: *I don't remember.*
> Q: *Did you attempt to kiss Mindy on the way back to the hotel that night?*
> A: *No.*

Can you advise Skip to testify that he may have stopped the car that night, but he just doesn't remember doing so?

3. At this juncture, what ethical issues arise, if any, and how should you deal with them?
4. Can you tell Skip to appear outraged at the suggestion that he made any advances to Mindy when questioned about that?
5. Assume Skip tells you, upon further questioning, that he *did* stop the car on the way back to the hotel, and that he *did* say to Mindy something like "You are very attractive, and I like you a lot. And you have good people skills. If you're nice to me, good things will happen for you," intending to convey only that because she has good people skills she will do well at the company—nothing more. Can you tell Skip that if he testifies that way, he could very well lose the case, but if he testifies that he said to her only: "You have good people skills, and so good things will happen for you," he would be far better off?
6. After you grill Skip for a while, he tells you candidly:

   *"Look, she was coming on to me all during dinner, flirting like crazy. We had a lot to drink at dinner. We're on the way back to the hotel, finally alone, just the two of us. I stop the car, and, yes, I did say something like what's in the complaint, and I did try to kiss her. Hell, we're both single, and so what's the harm? Besides, when she rebuffed me, I stopped. I didn't do anything wrong!"*

What do you do now?

## 3. How do you solve this joint defense dilemma?

Elmer Comstock uses the services provided by Mogul Media Enterprises Inc. (MME) for cable to his home. Believing his monthly cable bill is too high, he seeks advice from an antitrust lawyer, Fred Verret, who investigates. Verret brings an antitrust action in federal court against MME and against your client, Cable News and Entertainment LLC (CNE), claiming price fixing, illegal market division, and other antitrust violations.

You enter your appearance for CNE, and begin preparing your defense. Alice Roberts enters her appearance for MME. As you are preparing your Rule 26(a) statement and Rule 26(f) report, you call Roberts to discuss coordinating your efforts. You proceed to exchange many emails, working together. Those emails include candid exchanges about the facts (including facts that Verret would certainly like to know) and about strategy in the defense of this action.

Verret serves a document request on CNE, seeking disclosure, among other things, of all written communications, including emails, between you and Roberts. In response, you assert that all your emails with Roberts are privileged as attorney-client communications and as within the work-product privilege.

Verret's response is that your email exchange with Roberts is not covered by the attorney-client privilege because MME is not your client, and that it is not covered by the work-product doctrine because that doctrine does not extend to such email exchanges—it applies only to your own internal investigation of the facts and the law.

1. Is your email exchange with Roberts within the attorney-client privilege?
2. Is your email exchange with Roberts protected by the work-product doctrine?
3. Is your email exchange with Roberts protected by any other privilege or doctrine?
4. Should you have refrained from exchanging any emails with Roberts?
5. If you limit your communications with Roberts to telephone calls, and you are served with a deposition subpoena, can you be required to reveal the contents of all those oral communications?
6. What could you have done before your first email exchange with Roberts, and before your first conversation with Roberts, about the subject matter of this case, to enhance the likelihood that these communications would not be discoverable?

## 4. How far does the attorney-client privilege reach?

You represent Savvy Investment Partners LLC (SIP), whose members are Roger Smith and Dennis Jones. In 1992, SIP purchased vacant commercial property, and erected a building on it. SIP now leases that property to Best Buy. Mandible Corporation owns the adjacent property, leased to a Target store. SIP received a letter from Mandible's lawyer, asserting that the Best Buy store is on Mandible's property. Mandible demands that the Best Buy store be demolished, to the extent that it is over the property line. In the alternative, Mandible is willing to settle the claim for $1 million. Smith, in a panic, calls you for advice.

You discuss the elements of adverse possession, and ask Smith if Mandible, or its predecessor in title, ever gave notice to SIP of its claim that the Best Buy building is over the deed line, whether by putting up a "NO TRESPASSING" sign or otherwise. Smith candidly tells you that Mandible had put up a "NO TRESPASSING" sign on the deed line five years ago, and that this sign remains there to this day. But Smith never paid much attention to it, other than arranging for a survey, since SIP never received a formal letter from Mandible about the property line.

After explaining the elements for adverse possession to Smith, you tell him that the "NO TRESPASSING" sign stops the 15-year period required to establish title by adverse possession. You ask Smith if he has an accurate survey. He does. The survey Smith arranged for five years ago confirms that the Best Buy building is over the deed line by 15 feet. You tell Smith that SIP has a serious problem, because (1) the "NO TRESPASSING SIGN" makes a claim of adverse possession untenable and (2) the survey confirms that the Best Buy building is over the property line. You advise Smith to authorize you to enter into settlement negotiations with Mandible's lawyer. Smith tells you he must discuss this with Jones before deciding what to do. Smith then calls Jones, recounting your entire conversation with Smith.

1. The lawyer for Mandible deposes Jones. During this deposition, he asks Jones if he had any conversation with Smith about the "NO TRESPASSING SIGN" and about any surveys of the SIP property. Can you advise Jones during his deposition that

he should not answer that question as invading the attorney-client privilege, even though the subject conversation is between Smith and Jones, and you were not a party to that conversation?
2. Assume Roger Smith's wife, Samantha, is not a member of SIP. When Roger Smith is on the phone with you, Samantha joins the conversation, in which she is an active participant. Mandible's lawyer deposes Samantha. During her deposition, Mandible's lawyer asks Samantha about this conversation. Can you instruct her not to answer as invading the attorney-client privilege or any other privilege?

## 5. Is a settlement discussion between parties always ethical?

You represent Seamus McManus, a plaintiff in an action you brought on his behalf against Fenster Corporation for wrongful dismissal of McManus as executive vice president of that corporation. The lawyer for Fenster Corporation, Duke Bombast, has been very aggressive in defending this action, and has rebuffed your suggestions regarding discussion of settlement. Bombast was very explicit in telling you that any settlement discussions, if they ever do occur, must be between him and you, not between McManus and Fenster. Bombast told you that he is very concerned that McManus, in any private meeting with Fenster, could use his Irish charm to induce Fenster to agree to a settlement that is not in Fenster Corporation's best interests, and that McManus, at such a meeting, would likely induce Fenster to make statements of fact that could be admissible against Fenster Corporation at trial.

At your deposition of the president of Fenster Corporation, Oliver Fenster, you observe that McManus and Fenster are on their guard, except during breaks, during which you sense that there is some residual good will between the parties. You realize that it may be worthwhile for McManus and Fenster to meet, without lawyers present, to discuss a resolution of the case.

A few days after the Fenster deposition, you meet with McManus to prepare him for his deposition. McManus, also aware of his residual good will with Fenster, suggests to you the possibility of his meeting with Fenster, without lawyers, to discuss settlement and, even if he is not successful in settling the case, to get Fenster to admit at that meeting certain facts relevant to the case. McManus thinks he has the advantage in any negotiations one-on-one with Fenster.

1. Can you advise McManus to call Fenster to arrange a meeting to discuss settlement without your first calling Bombast?
2. If you do first call Bombast, are you seeking his permission, or merely advising him that McManus will be calling Fenster to arrange that meeting to discuss settlement?
3. Since Bombast told you that he does not approve of McManus calling Fenster to discuss settlement, are you required to advise McManus not to make that call?
4. Can you suggest to McManus that he tell Fenster not to let his lawyer know that they plan to meet to discuss settlement?
5. If McManus asks that you prepare a proposed settlement agreement to present to Fenster when they meet, can you do so?

## 6. Is this an ethical negotiation tactic?

You represent George Hendricks, former head of strategic planning for Northeast Dental Supply Company ("Northeast Dental"), which sells dental equipment to dentists, periodontists, pedodontists, and oral surgeons in New England. A few months ago, Hendricks left Northeast Dental and started working for National Dental Inc. ("National Dental") as its head of marketing and strategic planning. National Dental is a direct competitor of Northeast Dental in the Northeast.

Hendricks had a non-compete agreement with Northeast Dental, prohibiting him from working in any capacity for a competitor for a period of five years. Northeast Dental gave written notice to Hendricks and National Dental that Hendricks must stop working for National Dental immediately, or else it would bring a legal action to enforce it, and for money damages, without further notice. In response, you sent a letter to Northeast Dental's attorney that the non-compete agreement is invalid because Hendricks received no consideration for signing it (six months after Northeast Dental hired him) and because the non-compete is unreasonably broad. The parties agreed to mediate before any litigation commences. The mediation is scheduled for next month.

In preparing for the mediation, you discuss strategy with Hendricks. He tells you that he knows that Northeast Dental routinely—and intentionally—overcharged its customers by fraudulent billing, and that he has the records to prove it. You research the criminal statutes, and see that "larceny" is defined to include fraudulently obtaining property by "any false token, pretense, or device."

Hendricks suggests that at the mediation you should take the position that, unless Northeast Dental agrees not to pursue any injunctive relief, and accepts a nominal sum to resolve the civil dispute, you will report these fraudulent billing practices to the Economic Crimes Unit of the Chief State's Attorney's Office. He is eager for you to make this threat because he sees it as a very strong negotiating tactic.

1. Ethically, can you make this threat?
2. Would your answer be any different if Hendricks says *he* will make the threat himself, *without involving you*, in a separate meeting with his former boss during the mediation?
3. Would it make any difference if a legal action commenced before the mediation, but all other facts are the same?
4. Would it make any difference if Hendricks did not tell you that Northeast Dental overcharged its customers, but instead told you that Northeast Dental intentionally under-reported income on its tax returns. Does that change the result?
5. Assume the same facts, except instead of asking you to threaten Northeast Dental with reporting its fraudulent billing practices to the Economic Crimes Unit of the Chief State's Attorney's Office, Hendricks asks you to let opposing counsel know that Hendricks is aware of Northeast Dental's systematic and fraudulent overcharging of customers, and that he will need a release and indemnification from Northeast Dental regarding all claims by its customers for overcharging them. Can you make that demand?

## 7. How do you deal with a last-minute conflict?

You represent Samantha and Rodney Martin, plaintiffs in an action that has been pending for three years. You claim that a sales agent for the defendant, Home Sweet Home LLC, the broker representing the

Martins in the sale of their home, acted negligently, causing a loss of more than $250,000. Trial is scheduled to begin in two months.

As you are preparing for trial, you read in a newspaper article that Castle Real Estate Inc. (Castle), a long-standing client of the firm for litigation matters, acquired Home Sweet Home effective immediately.

1. What, if anything, do you tell the Martins?
2. Can you ask Castle for a waiver of the conflict?
3. If Castle moves to disqualify our firm, can you urge the court to allow you to continue representing the Martins?
4. Can you choose whether to continue to represent the Martins or to represent Home Sweet Home?

## 8. How do you deal with this deposition crisis?

You represent the plaintiff, Acme Microcomputer Chip Company (Acme), in an action to collect $875,000 from Zebra Telecommunications Inc. (Zebra) for computer chips Acme sold Zebra (IP-17s) for telephone systems it sells to its customers. Zebra has counterclaimed for $2 million, alleging that Zebra installed Acme's IP-17s into its telephone systems, which failed, causing Zebra lost profits and loss of good will. Zebra's counterclaims are for breach of express and implied warranties under the Uniform Commercial Code, breach of contract, negligence, fraud (alleging that Acme knew the computer chips were defective before the sale to Zebra), and violation of your state's Unfair Trade Practice Act.

In preparing Henry Throckmorton, president of Acme, for his deposition, you ask him what he knew about defects in the IP-17s before delivering them to Zebra, and what representations he made to Barbara Zeller, president of Zebra, about the IP-17s before they made their deal. He candidly tells you that he knew of defects in the IP-17s before meeting with Zeller (as a result of quality control tests conducted just a few days before he met with Zeller), but that he was confident his head of production could rectify those defects before any delivery to Zebra. Besides, he tells you, Acme needed the business. He also tells you that when he met with Zeller to discuss Zebra's purchase of the IP-17s, he told her that he was not aware of any production problems or defects in the IP-17s.

At Throckmorton's deposition, he testifies that he was not aware of any defects in the IP-17s before the sale to Zebra, and he denies that he made any representations to Zeller about the IP-17s.

It is now time for a lunch break. You meet with Throckmorton during this break.

1. What do you say to Throckmorton about this testimony? What is your advice to him?
2. Before the afternoon session of Throckmorton's deposition, can you suggest to Acme's lawyer that, rather than completing this deposition, time and effort would be better spent discussing a settlement, while the principals are together with their lawyers?
3. If Throckmorton refuses to correct his testimony (assuming what he told you in your prep session was correct), can you advise Acme's lawyer that his testimony on these two points was wrong, even if Throckmorton instructs you not to do so? Are you ethically obligated to do so?
4. What if the facts are changed: The only change is that Throckmorton gives testimony at his deposition that you know to be false, but on a subject that you consider immaterial. Does that change the analysis?

## 9. WHEN CAN YOU GET OUT OF A CASE?

You represent Hercules Steel Inc. (Hercules), a steel fabrication and erection subcontractor. The general contractor, Atlas Builders LLC (Atlas), owes Hercules $572,000 for work it performed. You have commenced an action to recover this amount, plus interest. You have served interrogatories and document requests, and plan to take depositions. You have a written retainer agreement, providing for payment by the hour, within 30 days of each invoice.

Hercules has not been paying you, and you are about to spend many hours over the short term in the discovery process. Hector Stentor, president of Hercules, tells you not to do a lot of work because, in this economy, the construction industry is very weak, and he doesn't know when he will be able to pay you the invoices that are now long past due, not to mention future invoices. He promises to pay you when work picks up again, but he cannot predict when that will be.

Should you try to withdraw your representation of Hercules? If so, can you get out? What is the proper procedure?

Same facts, with a twist. Hector has been paying you in full, on time. But he urges you to add a claim against the president of Atlas, Luke Atlas, personally, based on piercing the corporate veil. He tells you that only by suing Luke Atlas personally will you be able to get the leverage for a reasonable settlement—from which he can pay you. Besides, Hector tells you, Luke has been siphoning off profits from Atlas for years—he has significant assets, and Atlas does not. You have investigated the facts and researched the law, concluding that you have no good-faith basis to assert such a claim. When you tell Hector you cannot ethically pursue Luke personally, he becomes outraged and insists that you assert that claim.

Now should you and can you get out? If so, what do you tell the judge?

## 10. WHY CONTACT THE PASSIVE SHAREHOLDER?

Roger Avery calls to ask if you will represent Transmedia Enterprises Inc. (Transmedia), in the defense of a lawsuit. Transmedia publishes magazines and has a website for the entertainment industry. The plaintiff, Ralph Geller, claims that Transmedia libeled him when it published a story, both in its magazine, *Entertainment World: Behind the Scenes*, and on its website, about Geller's embezzlement of funds from several of Rupert Murdoch's media businesses. Roger tells you that there is nothing to this claim, and that every word he wrote in the article and on the website is true. Geller claims that Transmedia's libelous conduct has caused the loss of his job as an executive for Fox News Channel, for which he had been paid $375,000 a year, plus a bonus each year, depending on performance.

Roger also tells you that he is a 50 percent shareholder in Transmedia, and that his brother, Thomas, an orthopedic surgeon, is the other 50 percent shareholder. You do a conflicts check and find no conflict. When you call Roger back, you discuss the terms of the retainer agreement, and set up a meeting. Roger tells you that he will meet with you, that he will be your contact with regard to this representation, that all communications should be with him, and that you should not trouble

Thomas, who has a very busy orthopedic practice. Besides, Roger tells you, Thomas has nothing to do with the business or its operation. Thomas put in half the cash to get the business started, and receives half the profits.

1. What do you say to Roger about whether you will be communicating with Thomas?
2. Do you have any ethical obligation to communicate with Thomas? If so, what communication is required?
3. Would your answers to 1 and 2 be different if Roger were a 51 percent owner and Thomas a 49 percent owner, with the profits split in those percentages?
4. Would your answers to 1 and 2 be different if Roger was one of 20 shareholders in Transmedia, and he owned only 5 percent of its stock?
5. Assume that Roger and Thomas, as two 50 percent shareholders in the corporation, disagree as to the approach they want to take. Assume they both agree to hire you as their lawyer, but Roger wants to litigate to the end, and Thomas wants to immediately mediate to make the case go away. Assume they cannot agree with each other. If you undertake to represent the corporation, how do you handle their disagreement?
6. Would your answers to 1 and 2 be different if the plaintiff claimed (instead of the claim in the original fact pattern) that he had a contract to acquire half of Roger's stock in Transmedia?

## 11. Is your email blast ethical?

To drum up business for your firm, you have compiled a list of email addresses of prospective clients who may need your services as a trial lawyer. You have drafted the email blast you plan to send out. You know that the "subject" line is crucial—it must be eye-catching. Your "subject" line is **"Savvy Legal Advice for Business Disputes at Reasonable Rates!!!"** You are about to push the "send" button. What edits should you make to your draft (below), before violating the ethical rules in your jurisdiction?

**Savvy Legal Advice for Business Disputes at Reasonable Rates!!!**

In today's litigious world, sooner or later you will need to defend yourself or your business in court. Or you may need to bring a lawsuit to recover what is due you or your business. You need the best lawyer you can find. And you want to pay reasonable rates.

At Shyster and Shyster, we have been achieving great results for our clients for years. Here's just one example: We recently represented Specialty Wholesale Shoe Supply Company in an action we brought against Soppaz Shoes Inc. Our client didn't get paid for its shipment of shoes, supposedly because they were defective. We proved that Soppaz improperly rejected our client's shipment and won in court, recovering more than $100,000! That's the kind of result we can achieve for you. Ask anyone who knows their way around the courthouse. They'll tell you that Shyster and Shyster is a well-respected law firm that gets results. We have a great track record, second to none.

**Legal tip**: Did you know that some agreements are unenforceable unless they are in writing? That writing requirement applies to any agreement that is not to be performed within one year, any agreement to pay someone else's debt, and any loan for more than $50,000. How would you like to make a handshake deal like that and find out, too late, that you can't collect? What you don't know about the law *can* hurt you! That's why you need Shyster and Shyster!

For a limited time only, we're offering a discount on our services—10% off our normal reasonable rates. A bargain on a bargain! So, call us now at 1-800-SHYSTER (1-800-749-7837). We're the best in the business!

## 12. Which conversations are ethical?

At a cocktail party, you meet people who inquire about your professional work. You see this as a good marketing opportunity. In response to questions you are asked, which statements can you make, as an ethical matter, assuming all of them are true?

1. "I am a trial lawyer, which means that I deal with business disputes."
2. "I'm an attorney with Shyster and Shyster, specializing in commercial litigation, which means that I deal with business disputes."
3. "I have expertise in commercial litigation."
4. "It's interesting that you ask about that. As a matter of fact, I just represented Specialty Wholesale Shoe Supply Company in an action against Soppaz Shoes Inc. and recovered $100,000 for my client. That case was just like the claim you want to bring! I can certainly help you with that."
5. "Based on what you just told me, your buyer failed to revoke acceptance properly, or properly reject the goods you sold. This is governed by the Uniform Commercial Code, which I know something about. Yes, you can recover the agreed price. That's just like the Specialty case I just told you about. You should win that one."

## 13. How should you handle this blown statute of limitations?

Sam Rafter called you six months ago, for legal advice about suing other members of a startup limited liability company, Tragon Internet Consulting, LLC (Tragon), for improperly removing him as a member, in violation of the written agreement of the members. You did a conflicts check, found no conflict, and met with him promptly after his call.

He told you that, even though the other members removed him from the limited liability company years ago, he did not learn until recently, while surfing the Internet, that Tragon was a financial success. Tragon's website touts its successes in marketing software products, including one that was obviously very lucrative for Tragon's members.

You discussed with him possible causes of action: breach of contract, breach of fiduciary duty, promissory estoppel, breach of the implied covenant of good faith and fair dealing, and violation of the applicable limited liability company statute, which provides for recovery of legal fees (unlike the contract among the members). Rafter signed a retainer agreement, which provided that you would pursue "any and all claims, as provided by law and equity, against the members of Tragon resulting from Rafter's improper removal as a member of Tragon."

You drafted a one-count complaint, for breach of contract. You sent it to Rafter, who confirmed that all facts you alleged are true. Rafter did not say anything to you about the missing counts.

In reviewing the file recently while preparing for the deposition of one of the members of Tragon, you realize to your dismay that you failed to include any claims other than for breach of contract, and that the statute of limitations for all other claims has expired.

1. Do you have any ethical obligation to tell Rafter anything, in light of the fact that you preserved his contract count? If so, what do you tell him?
2. Assume that you file a motion to amend your complaint, to add all the other counts referenced above, but the court denies it.
   a. What, if anything, do you tell Rafter now?
   b. Can you tell Rafter that the claim you *did* assert in the complaint is strong, and so he should not be concerned that you did not include the other claims?
   c. At what point, if at all, should you call your liability carrier?
3. Rafter retains other counsel, who tries the contract claim, and loses. In the memorandum of decision, the judge notes that Rafter may have prevailed on other claims, but since they were not alleged, no remedy was available. Rafter sues you for legal malpractice. Can you assert that Rafter himself was negligent for failing to inform you that you omitted all other counts you had discussed with him?

## 14. Is this surreptitious recording ethical and admissible?

You represent Matthew Keating, as trustee of a trust created for the benefit of Brookfield (Brook) Evans III. The trust assets consist largely of stock. Brook brought an action against Keating for breach of fiduciary duty, fraud, conversion, statutory theft, and unjust enrichment, claiming that Keating mismanaged trust assets, and diverted them for his own use.

Brook's attorney, Alan Crowley, suggests that, before he takes Keating's deposition, you and Keating meet with Crowley at his office, for an informal discovery conference. You see this as an opportunity to narrow the issues and possibly lead to a productive settlement discussion.

After advising Keating about the pros and cons of such a meeting, you agree to proceed with it. The meeting at Crowley's office is rather unrestrained, unlike at a deposition. At one point, Keating acknowledges that he reviewed the trust stock portfolio only once a year, and so he was not aware of stock fluctuations during the course of each year, and that, on occasion, he "borrowed" money from the trust to pay personal expenses, "loans" which he "paid back" when he could. Keating also acknowledges that he has not yet repaid all of those "loans." The trust instrument does not allow for any such "loans."

It is now a week before trial. In accordance with the judge's pre-trial order, Crowley lists all his proposed exhibits, including a recording of Keating's statements referenced above, and a transcript of that recording.

1. Was it unethical for Keating to make that recording?
2. Would your answer be the same if, at the beginning of that meeting, Keating stated that everything said during that meeting would be "on the record," even though he did not reveal that he was recording it?
3. What do you do in response to Crowley's including the recording and transcript of it on his list of proposed exhibits? If you object, what is your response if Crowley takes the position that he did not act unethically? And what is your response if Crowley takes the position that, even if he acted unethically, the statements are admissions of a party during what was not a settlement conference (and therefore not privileged), and so Keating's statements are admissible?
4. How would your analysis of any of these issues change, if at all, if the conversation were by phone rather than in person?
5. How would your analysis of any of these issues change, if at all, if the meeting took place in a state that allowed recording even if only one party to a conversation is aware it is being recorded, but the case is pending in a state that allows recording only if *all*

parties to the conversation are aware it is being recorded? What about the reverse situation?
6. Different hypothetical: Your client, without your instruction or knowledge, records a telephone conversation with the opposing party, in which the opposing party makes admissions very helpful to your case. Can you use that recording and a transcript of it? Would it matter if the opposing party was represented by counsel when your client made that recording?

# APPENDIX III
# SUGGESTIONS FOR FURTHER READING & FOR VIEWING

## 1. SUGGESTED READING

JEFFREY P. AIKEN., PETER D. BAIRD, PAUL A. BANKER, BRUCE J. BERMAN, DENNIS BROWN, JOHN R. BURNS, FREDERICK S. GOLD, J. BRIAN JACKSON & JON G. MARCH, STRATEGIES FOR SUCCESSFUL MEDIATION: LEADING LAWYERS ON UNDERSTANDING CLIENT GOALS, COMMUNICATING EFFECTIVELY, AND FACILITATING AN AGREEMENT (2008).

MITCH ALBOM, TUESDAYS WITH MORRIE: AN OLD MAN, A YOUNG MAN, AND LIFE'S GREATEST LESSON (1997).

ALDISERT, RUGGERO J., WINNING ON APPEAL: BETTER BRIEFS AND ORAL ARGUMENT (Nat'l Inst. for Trial Advocacy 2d ed. 2003).

AM. ARBITRATION ASS'N, DRAFTING DISPUTE RESOLUTION CLAUSES: A PRACTICAL GUIDE (2007), *available at* http://www.adr.org.

AM. ARBITRATION ASS'N, HANDBOOK ON COMMERCIAL ARBITRATION (Juris Publishing 2d ed. 2010).

American Law Institute, Restatement of the Law (3d) of the Law Governing Lawyers (2012).

Stephen V. Armstrong & Timothy P. Terrell, Thinking Like a Writer: A Lawyer's Guide to Effective Writing and Editing (Practising Law Institute 3d ed. 2009).

Am. Bar Ass'n, Annotated Model Rules of Professional Conduct (Ellen J. Bennett, Elizabeth J. Cohen & Martin Whittaker eds., 7th ed. 2011).

Ellen J. Bennett, Elizabeth J. Cohen & Helen W. Gunnarsson, Bloomberg ABA/BNA Lawyers' Manual on Professional Conduct, 2013, www.americanbar.org/groups/professional_responsibility/publications/aba_br.

David Berg, The Trial Lawyer: What It Takes to Win (2006).

Joseph Campbell, Joseph Campbell and the Power of Myth with Bill Moyers (1988).

Benjamin Cardozo, The Nature of the Judicial Process (with notes) (2010).

Richard Carlson, Don't Sweat the Small Stuff at Work: Simple Ways to Minimize Stress and Conflict While Bringing Out the Best in Yourself and Others (1998).

Tamar E. Chansky, Freeing Yourself from Anxiety: 4 Simple Steps to Overcome Worry and Create the Life You Want (2012).

F. Gregory Coffey & Maureen C. Kessler, The Reflective Counselor: Daily Meditations for Lawyers (2008).

John W. Cooley & Steven Lubet, Arbitration Advocacy (1997).

Wendy Gerwick Couture & Allyson W. Haynes, Strategies for Managing Expert Witnesses from Retention Through Trial (2010).

Trey Cox, Winning the Jury's Attention: Presenting Evidence from Voir Dire to Closing (2011).

Mihaly Csikszentamihalyi, Flow: The Psychology of Optimal Experience (2008).

Adrian Dayton & Amy Knapp, LinkedIn & Blogs for Lawyers: Building High Value Relationships in a Digital Age (2012).

Edward De Bono, Lateral Thinking: A Textbook of Creativity (2009).

Roberta Larson Duyff, American Dietetic Association Complete Food and Nutrition Guide (John Wiley & Sons 4th ed. 2012).

Neal Feigenson & Christine Spiesel, Law on Display: The Digital Transformation of Legal Persuasion and Judgment (2009).

Ralph Adam Fine, The How-to-Win Trial Manual: Winning Trial-Advocacy in a Nutshell (Juris Publishing 5th ed. 2011).

Ralph Adam Fine, The How-to-Win Appeal Manual: Winning Appellate Advocacy in a Nutshell (Juris Publishing 3d ed. 2012).

Roger Fischer, William Ury & Bruce Patton, Getting to Yes: Negotiating Agreement Without Giving In (Penguin Books 2d ed. 1991).

Lawrence J. Fox & Susan R. Martyn, Red Flags: A Lawyer's Handbook on Legal Ethics (2010).

Lawrence J. Fox & Susan R. Martyn, The Ethics of Representing Organizations: Legal Fictions for Clients (2009).

X.M. Frascogna Jr. & H. Lee Hetherington, The Lawyer's Guide to Negotiation: A Strategic Approach to Better Contracts and Settlements (2001).

Dwight Golann, Mediating Legal Disputes: Effective Strategies for Neutrals and Advocates (2009).

Hindi Greenberg, The Lawyer's Career Change Handbook: More Than 300 Things You Can Do with a Law Degree (1998).

Paul W. Grimm, Charles S. Fax & Paul Mark Sandler, Discovery Problems and Their Solutions (2005).

Ross Guberman, Point Made: How to Write Like the Nation's Top Advocates (2011).

Sonya Hamlin, Now What Makes Juries Listen (2008).

Thich Nhat Hanh, You Are Here: Discovering the Magic of the Present Moment (2010).

Mark Herrmann, The Curmudgeon's Guide to Practicing Law (2006).

Edward J. Imwinkelried, Evidentiary Foundations (Mathew Bender & Co. 8th ed. 2012).

Jon Kabat-Zinn, Wherever You Go, There You Are: Mindfulness Meditation in Everyday Life (1994).

Steven Keeva, Transforming Practices: Finding Joy and Satisfaction in the Legal Life (2009).

Dennis Kennedy & Allison C. Shields, Facebook in One Hour for Lawyers (2012).

James M. Kramon, The Art of Practicing Law: Talking to Clients, Colleagues and Others (2012).

Douglas S. Lavine, Cardinal Rules of Advocacy: Understanding and Mastering Fundamental Principles of Persuasion (2002).

Douglas S. Lavine, Questions from the Bench (2004).

J. Anderson Little, Making Money Talk: How to Mediate Insured Claims and Other Monetary Disputes (2007).

Anne Marie Lofaso, A Practitioner's Guide to Appellate Advocacy (2010).

Steven Lubet, Modern Trial Advocacy (National Institute for Trial Advocacy 4th ed. 2009).

W.I. Lundquist & A. Pyette, The Litigation Manual: Jury Trials (2008).

D.M. Malone, P.T. Hoffman & A.J. Bocchino, The Effective Deposition: Techniques and Strategies that Work (National Institute for Trial Advocacy rev. 3d ed. 2007).

Steve Martin, The Ten, Make that Nine, Habits of Very Organized People. Make that Ten: The tweets of Steve Martin (2012).

Thomas A. Mauet, Trial Techniques (Wolters Kluwer Law & Business 8th ed. 2010).

James W. McElhaney, McElhaney's Litigation (1995).

James W. McElhaney, McElhaney's Trial Notebook (ABA 4th ed. 2005).

Tom Mighell, iPad in One Hour for Lawyers (2012).

Tom Mighell, iPad Apps in One Hour for Lawyers (2013).

Deng Ming-Dao, 365 Tao: Daily Meditations (1992).

John Mortimer, Forever Rumpole: The Best of the Rumpole Stories (2011).

Gary A. Munneke & William D. Henslee, Nonlegal Carrers for Lawyers (ABA 4th ed. 2003).

The New Yorker Book of Lawyer Cartoons (1993).

David Nyberg, The Varnished Truth: Truth Telling and Deceiving in Ordinary Life (1993).

Bennet G. Parker, Mediation Practice Guide: A Handbook for Resolving Business Disputes (ABA 2d ed. 2004).

Matthieu Ricard, Happiness: A Guide to Developing Life's Most Important Skill (2003).

Jennifer K. Robbennolt & Jean R. Strenlight, Psychology for Lawyers: Understanding the Human Factors in Negotiation, Litigation, and Decision Making (2012).

Mark A. Robertson & James A. Calloway, Winning Alternatives to the Billable Hour: Strategies that Work (ABA Publishing 3d ed. 2008).

Charles M. Sevilla, Disorder in the Court: Great Fractured Moments in Courtroom History (1992).

Danny Shanahan, Innocent, Your Honor: A Book of Lawyer Cartoons (2005).

Jacob A. Stein, Eulogy of Lawyers (2010).

Ellen Sue Stern, Yawn!: Bedtime Reading for Insomniacs (2000).

Thomas J. Stipanowich, Curtis E. Von Kann & Deborah F. Rothman, Protocols for Expeditious, Cost-Effective Commercial Arbitration (2010).

D. Stone, B. Patton & S. Heen, Difficult Conversations: How to Discuss What Matters Most (1999).

Michael E. Tigar, Persuasion: The Litigator's Art (1999).

William Ury, Getting Past No: Negotiating Your Way from Confrontation to Cooperation (1993).

Curtis E. von Kann, James M. Gaitis & June R. Lehrman, The College of Commercial Arbitrators Guide to Best Practices in Commercial Arbitration (2006).

Vincent S. Walkowiak, Stephen M. McNabb & Oscar Rey Rodriguez, The Attorney-Client Privilege in Civil Litigation: Practicing and Defending Confidentiality (ABA 5th ed. 2012).

Frederick Bernays Wiener, Effective Appellate Advocacy (2004).

Robert W. Wood, Leonard L. Silverstein, Gerald H. Sherman & Patrick G. Dooher, Tax Aspects of Settlements and Judgments (2012).

Richard C. Wydick, Plain English for Lawyers (Carolina Academic Press 5th ed. 2005).

William Zinsser, On Writing Well: The Classic Guide to Writing Non-Fiction (Harper Collins Publishers, 30th Anniversary ed. 2006).

## SUGGESTED MOVIES

Hundreds of movies have been made about lawyers. Here is a selection of some worth seeing, with a brief synopsis of each. Keep in mind, though, that, as with all movies about lawyers, the objective is to entertain, not to portray accurately what goes on in or out of the courtroom.

12 Angry Men (1957)

> Henry Fonda overcomes preconceived notions and prejudices of other jurors by the force of analytical thinking.

A Civil Action (1998)

> John Travolta sues corporations that may be responsible for leukemia-related deaths of eight children. Robert Duvall defends.

A Few Good Men (1992)

> Tom Cruise breaks down unapologetic commander Jack Nicholson in a stirring court martial at the Guantanamo Bay naval base.

A Man for All Seasons (1966)

> Paul Scofield is Sir Thomas More, the Tudor judge and chancellor of England, caught in a political struggle involving Henry VIII, who wants to divorce his wife to wed Anne Boleyn.

ADAM'S RIB (1949)

Spencer Tracy and Katharine Hepburn take each other on in court, with a twist. In this memorable comedy, they are husband and wife.

ANATOMY OF A MURDER (1959)

James Stewart confronts difficult ethical issues in representing his client, Ben Gazzara, in a murder case.

AND JUSTICE FOR ALL (1979)

A young and very angry Al Pacino represents a judge accused of rape, in an over-the-top performance in which he breaks evidentiary and ethical rules. See how many violations you can find.

AMISTAD (1997)

The true story of the trial of mutinous African slaves who had been transported on a slave ship.

BREAKER MORANT (1960)

An Australian court-martial movie about lieutenants prosecuted for executing prisoners of war.

CLASS ACTION (1991)

Gene Hackman takes on a products liability case involving defective cars with exploding gas tanks. His estranged daughter represents the car manufacturer.

COMPULSION (1959)

Orson Welles defends two rich kids who sought to commit the perfect crime.

ERIN BROCKOVICH (2000)

Julia Roberts, as a single-mom paralegal working for Albert Finney, exposes illegal dumping of toxic chemicals in a memorable class action.

I AM SAM (2001)

Sean Penn is the mentally impaired father of a seven-year-old daughter. His lawyer, Michelle Pfeiffer, confronts ethical issues in seeking to preserve custody for her client, despite the efforts of the child welfare authorities.

In the Name of the Father (1993)

Pete Postlethwaite and Daniel Day-Lewis are falsely accused of participating in IRA bombings. Their lawyer, Emma Thompson, saves the day.

Inherit the Wind (1960)

Spencer Tracy, as Clarence Darrow, takes on Frederic March, as William Jennings Bryan, in re-creating the 1925 Scopes "monkey" trial.

Judgment at Nuremberg (1961)

Spencer Tracy is a lawyer representing defendants in Nazi war crimes trials, trying to understand how German judges could be accomplices to Nazi atrocities.

Kramer v. Kramer (1979)

Dustin Hoffman and Meryl Streep are an estranged couple, battling over custody of their son.

Lincoln Lawyer (2011)

Matthew McConaughey is a small-time criminal defense lawyer who takes on a case of a lifetime.

Michael Clayton (2007)

George Clooney defends a class action involving toxic agricultural chemicals.

Miracle on 34th Street (1947)

Kris Kringle is on the witness stand. Can his lawyer prove he is Santa Claus?

My Cousin Vinny (1992)

Joe Pesci, as a brash Brooklyn lawyer with no trial experience, demonstrates effective cross-examination to humorous and devastating effect.

Philadelphia (1993)

Tom Hanks is a gay attorney who sues his firm for firing him after discovering he had contracted AIDS. Denzel Washington takes the case.

PUNCTURE (2011)

> A David and Goliath story about a drug-addicted lawyer who takes on a health-supply corporation that sells defective needles.

PRESUMED INNOCENT (1990)

> Harrison Ford is a prosecutor accused of murdering a colleague with whom he's had an affair.

REVERSAL OF FORTUNE (1990)

> Claus von Bulow, played by Jeremy Irons, is represented by Alan Dershowitz, played by Ron Silver, in the defense of an attempted murder case.

SOCIAL NETWORK (2010)

> The Facebook story: no courtroom drama, but memorable deposition testimony.

THE CAINE MUTINY (1954)

> Humphrey Bogart is Captain Queeg in this movie about military authority and moral duty.

THE FORTUNE COOKIE (1966)

> Walter Matthau, a crooked personal injury lawyer, provokes Jack Lemmon, his brother-in-law, to feign a serious injury in this comedy.

THE VERDICT (1982)

> Paul Newman, a washed-up alcoholic lawyer, successfully takes on a medical malpractice case.

TO KILL A MOCKINGBIRD (1962)

> Gregory Peck overcomes racism in the courtroom with logic and steadfast courage.

WITNESS FOR THE PROSECUTION (1957)

> Charles Laughton is the pompous barrister, Tyrone Power his playboy defendant, and the witness in question is Marlene Dietrich, Tyrone Power's wife.

# TABLE I

## Federal Rules of Civil Procedure

| Rule | Page | Rule | Page |
|---|---|---|---|
| 5.1 | 71, 72 | 26(b) | 33, 35 |
| 8 | 71 | 26(b)(1) | 10, 78, 85 |
| 8(a) | 70, 320 | 26(b)(2) | 78, 79 |
| 8(b) | 77 | 26(b)(2)(A) | 79, 128 |
| 8(b)(6) | 77 | 26(b)(2)(C) | 82, 128 |
| 8(c) | 77 | 26(b)(3) | 209 |
| 8(d) | 70 | 26(b)(4)(B) | 34 |
| 8(d)(1) | 320 | 26(b)(4)(C) | 34, 121 |
| 9 | 78 | 26(b)(5)(B) | 57 |
| 9(a)(2) | 77 | 26(c) | 102, 128 |
| 10 | 71 | 26(d) | 78, 100 |
| 11 | 96 | 26(e) | 79, 80, 81, 84, 85, 215 |
| 11(b) | 73, 77 | 26(f) | 17, 51, 100, 101, 153, 160, 329 |
| 11(b)(2) | 245 | 29 | 83, 210 |
| 11(b)(4) | 77 | 29(b) | 81 |
| 12(a) | 73 | 30 | 127 |
| 12(b) | 74, 78 | 30(a)(2) | 101 |
| 12(e) | 74 | 30(a)(2)(A) | 101 |
| 12(f) | 74 | 30(a)(2)(A)(ii) | 101 |
| 12(h) | 74 | 30(b)(1) | 101 |
| 13 | 77, 207 | 30(b)(2) | 101 |
| 14 | 77 | 30(b)(3) | 101, 125 |
| 15 | 73 | 30(b)(5) | 125, 215 |
| 16(c)(2)(A) | 245 | 30(b)(6) | 101, 102, 105, 127, 129, 187 |
| 17 | 72 | 30(c)(2) | 105, 106, 117, 210 |
| 18 | 72 | 30(d)(1) | 101, 108, 112 |
| 19 | 70, 72, 74 | 30(d)(2) | 126 |
| 20 | 70, 72 | 30(d)(3) | 119, 128 |
| 23.1 | 70 | 30(d)(3)(A) | 106, 128 |
| 26(a)(1) | 79 | 30(e) | 106, 107, 117 |
| 26(a)(1)(A)(ii) | 83 | 30(e)(1) | 104, 122 |
| 26(a)(1)(C) | 79 | 31 | 127 |
| 26(a)(2) | 120, 209 | 31(a)(4) | 127 |
| 26(a)(2)(C) | 34 | 32 | 210 |

(continued)

| Rule | Page | Rule | Page |
|---|---|---|---|
| 32(a)(2) | 124, 187, 194, 222 | 38(b)(1) | 72 |
| 32(a)(4) | 123, 194 | 38(d) | 72 |
| 32(a)(6) | 125, 210 | 41(a)(1)(A)(ii) | 89, 93 |
| 33 | 79 | 45(a) | 101 |
| 33(a)(1) | 79 | 45(a)(3)(B) | 102 |
| 33(b)(2) | 81 | 45(b)(2) | 102 |
| 33(b)(3) | 81 | 45(c)(3) | 128 |
| 33(d) | 81 | 45(c)(3)(A)(ii) | 102 |
| 34 | 83, 101, 215 | 45(e) | 126 |
| 34(a) | 83 | 49 | 87, 227 |
| 34(b) | 83, 101, 212 | 50(a) | 230 |
| 34(b)(2) | 84 | 50(a)(2) | 230 |
| 35(b) | 34 | 50(b) | 230 |
| 36 | 84, 85, 86, 187 | 50(d) | 231 |
| 36(a)(1) | 85, 187 | 50(e) | 231 |
| 36(a)(3) | 85 | 51(a) | 87 |
| 36(a)(4) | 85 | 51(a)(1) | 230 |
| 36(a)(5) | 85 | 51(a)(2) | 230 |
| 36(a)(6) | 85 | 51(b) | 87 |
| 36(b) | 84, 187, 194 | 51(b)(2) | 230 |
| 37 | 51, 82, 83, 126 | 51(c) | 87 |
| 37(a) | 127, 128 | 51(c)(2) | 230 |
| 37(a)(1) | 43, 44, 82, 127 | 51(c)(2)(A) | 230 |
| 37(a)(3)(B)(i) | 127 | 51(c)(2)(B) | 230 |
| 37(a)(3)(B)(ii) | 127 | 51(d) | 87 |
| 37(a)(3)(C) | 127 | 51(d)(2) | 226 |
| 37(a)(5) | 127, 128 | 52 | 225 |
| 37(a)(5)(A) | 82 | 57 | 70 |
| 37(a)(5)(B) | 82, 127 | 59 | 230 |
| 37(a)(5)(C) | 128 | 59(a)(1)(A) | 231 |
| 37(b) | 128 | 59(a)(2) | 227 |
| 37(c)(1) | 83 | 59(b) | 227 |
| 37(c)(2) | 86 | 59(c) | 227 |
| 37(d) | 128 | 59(d) | 227 |
| 38 | 70, 72, 198 | 59(e) | 227 |

# TABLE II

## Federal Rules of Evidence

| Rule | Page | Rule | Page |
|---|---|---|---|
| 102 | 216, 246 | 613 | 211, 223 |
| 103(a)(1) | 227 | 704(a) | 196 |
| 103(a)(2) | 227 | 801(c) | 212, 223 |
| 105 | 211, 212 | 801(d)(1)(A) | 124, 222 |
| 106 | 125, 194, 210, 224 | 801(d)(1)(B) | 211, 212 |
| 201 | 188 | 801(d)(2) | 124, 187, 194 |
| 201(d) | 188 | 803(6) | 85, 188, 213 |
| 403 | 86, 190, 195, 211, 214, 218, 226 | 804(a)(3) | 124 |
| 502 | 209, 211 | 804(b)(1) | 123, 124 |
| 607 | 223 | 806 | 223 |
| 608 | 223 | 1006 | 195, 212, 215, 314 |
| 609 | 223 | | |

# TABLE III

## Model Rules of Professional Conduct

| Rule | Page | Rule | Page |
|---|---|---|---|
| 1.0(e) | 237 | 1.18 | 244–245 |
| 1.0(f) | 242 | 2.1 | 253 |
| 1.1 | 237, 240 | 2.3 | 253 |
| 1.2 | 237–239 | 2.4 | 253 |
| 1.3 | 240, 253 | 3.1 | 245 |
| 1.4 | 237–239, 320 | 3.2 | 253 |
| 1.6 | 237–238, 237–239, 242, 249, 250–251, 251, 253, 254, 258, 262 | 3.3 | 245–249 |
| 1.7 | 239–241, 243 | 3.3(a)(3) | 248, 249 |
| 1.7(a) | 239 | 3.4 | 249–250 |
| 1.7(b) | 239 | 3.5 | 253 |
| 1.8 | 239–241 | 3.6 | 253 |
| 1.9 | 241, 244 | 3.7 | 253 |
| 1.9(c) | 242 | 3.9 | 253 |
| 1.10 | 239–241, 242 | 4.1 | 238, 250–251, 252 |
| 1.11 | 253 | 4.2 | 251–253 |
| 1.12 | 253 | 4.3 | 251–253 |
| 1.13 | 242–243 | 4.4 | 253 |
| 1.13(a) | 240 | 5.1–5.7 | 253 |
| 1.13(b) | 242, 243 | 5.3(c) | 252 |
| 1.13(c) | 242, 243 | 6.1–6.5 | 254 |
| 1.13(d) | 242 | 7.1–7.6 | 254, 256, 257, 258, 265 |
| 1.14 | 253 | 8.1–8.5 | 254 |
| 1.15 | 253 | 8.4 | 252 |
| 1.16 | 243–244 | 8.4(a) | 251, 252 |
| 1.17 | 253 | | |

# TABLE IV

**American Arbitration Association Commercial Arbitration Rules**

| Rule | Page | Rule | Page |
|---|---|---|---|
| R-1(a) | 145 | R-30 | 154 |
| R-4(b) | 152, 153 | R-30(b) | 153 |
| R-4(c) | 152 | R-31 | 154 |
| R-7(a) | 150 | R-31(a) | 155 |
| R-11(a) | 151 | R-34 | 153, 156 |
| R-12 | 151, 207 | R-41 | 157 |
| R-18 | 151 | R-43 | 156 |
| R-21 | 153 | R-43(d) | 152, 156 |
| R-26 | 153, 156 | R-46 | 157 |

# PRACTICE CHECKLISTS

❖❖❖❖
## Dealing with Clients

- Complete a conflicts check before undertaking any representation.
- Beware of scams in undertaking any representation.
- Decline a prospective representation if red flags are raised.
- If you decline the representation, put it in writing.
- Before doing substantive work, obtain a written retainer agreement.
- Consider alternative fee arrangements:
  - _____ reduced hourly with performance bonus
  - _____ blended rate
  - _____ fixed fee
  - _____ contingent fee
  - _____ retrospective fee based on result
  - _____ straight retainer
  - _____ volume discount
- If you undertake the representation, meet promptly with the client at your client's place of business or your office.
- At the first client meeting
  - _____ establish rapport
  - _____ explain the attorney-client privilege
  - _____ explain the purpose of the meeting
  - _____ get necessary information
  - _____ discuss the document litigation hold requirement
  - _____ get a commitment that the client will devote the resources you need

*(continued)*

|        | discuss options |
| --- | --- |
|        | don't predict outcome |
|        | discuss your fee |
|        | warn your client about preserving the attorney-client privilege |
|        | ask for more information |

- Meet with all representatives of your client from whom you need information.
- Early in the representation, obtain the documents you need.
- If you take the case, inform the client what must be done; arrange for the help you will need from support staff, experts, and others; develop an overall strategy; and follow through.
- Work collaboratively with your client.
- Manage client expectations as to time, cost, and result.
- Deal with difficult clients by understanding what concerns cause them to be difficult.
- When you need to deliver bad news to a client, do so promptly, be direct in explaining the significance of what happened, and discuss options in your strategy going forward.
- In preparing your client to testify in court, tailor your preparation to the experience, sophistication, and personality of your client, following the tips in the text.
- Be conscientious about capturing and recording your billable and non-billable time each day.
- After you have completed your representation, send a letter to the client to that effect, and, if you have not done so already, inform the client of other services your firm provides.

## Dealing with Everyone Other Than Clients You Will Encounter as a Trial Lawyer

- Work in collaboration with your secretary by following the tips in the text.
- Benefit from paralegal assistance by knowing the capabilities of your paralegals and assigning work as appropriate.
- In all communications with witnesses (other than your client), assume that nothing is privileged.
- Know which types of communications with expert witnesses are protected, and which are not, under the Federal Rules of Civil Procedure and the procedural rules in your jurisdiction.
- Limit communications with expert witnesses that are not protected as much as practicable, preferring conversations to writings.
- Brainstorm ideas with colleagues.
- When getting an assignment, know what you are being asked to do, the form of the work, and the deadline.
- As you work on an assignment, if you think of related issues worth exploring, discuss them with the lawyer who gave you the assignment.
- Ask for critiques of your work.
- If you plan to work with a lawyer in another firm representing another party in litigation, obtain your client's informed consent, and draft a joint defense agreement for execution by all affected parties.
- If you act as local counsel only, establish clear lines of responsibility to avoid failure to protect your client's interests.
- Remember that opposing counsel is not your enemy but your adversary, and that you need not be hostile in your dealings. You get what you give in your dealings with opposing counsel.
- Treat mediators and arbitrators with respect, while keeping in mind that mediators often test your position by challenging you.
- Do not communicate ex parte with arbitrators.
- Preserve and promote your credibility with judges by punctuality, preparation, persuasiveness, and professionalism.
- Do not communicate with jurors, while being aware that they observe everything you do, in and out of the courtroom. You can talk to them after they render their verdict, but then only with the judge's permission, within the constraints of Model Rule 3.5(c).

## ❖❖❖❖
## Managing and Drafting Emails and Letters

- Create scheduling mechanisms so you do not get distracted by incoming emails.
- When responding to emails, determine which are easily dealt with; respond to those first and then to those that require more time.
- Be diligent in responding to emails.
- Do not send emails in certain circumstances.
  - _____ when sending a demand letter or other document you may want to use as an exhibit
  - _____ when a phone call is more likely to achieve your purpose
  - _____ when you need to clear the air
  - _____ when it is unnecessary to do so
  - _____ when you are on vacation (with exceptions)
  - _____ when you suspect spam
- Send emails only to those who need them.
- Be specific in your subject line.
- Be cogent.
- Make sure you attach what you intend.
- Beware of email chains.
- Read your draft email carefully before sending it.
- Use proper email etiquette.
- Avoid inadvertent waiver of the attorney-client and work-product protections:
  - _____ Do not send emails to your client's place of employment.
  - _____ Do not send emails to your client's home if not a sole email account.
  - _____ Be wary when copying parties on emails.
  - _____ Do not blind-copy emails.
- If you inadvertently send an email to opposing counsel containing attorney-client privileged or work-product information, take immediate remedial action.
- If opposing counsel ever sends you an email containing attorney-client privileged or work-product information, call opposing counsel immediately so opposing counsel can take remedial action.
- Organize your emails so you can locate them promptly, and archive them appropriately.
- In drafting letters, be cogent, businesslike, and conscientious about each element, from the "re" line to the "cc" line.
- Apply to letters all the advice above about emails, to the extent applicable.
- Send letters when you decide not to take on a matter, when you do take on a matter, and when you complete or terminate a matter.
- Before sending any opinion letter, a colleague in your firm should review it.
- Do a thorough investigation of all relevant matters before responding to an auditor's letter.

## ❖❖❖❖
## Drafting Documents Other Than Emails and Letters

- Apply the following principles to everything you write:
  - _____ think before you write
  - _____ write for your reader
  - _____ divide the writing process into discrete tasks
  - _____ use simple words
  - _____ edit
  - _____ eliminate typos
  - _____ write cogently
- In drafting internal memos, know your assignment, research thoroughly, and use an effective format by setting forth the facts, issues, summary of your conclusion, and analysis.
- Before drafting a complaint, know your client's objectives, the applicable facts, applicable law, available causes of action, and available remedies.
- In drafting a complaint, do not necessarily include all possible causes of action, after obtaining your client's informed consent.
- In drafting a complaint and other pleadings, comply with all applicable Federal Rules of Civil Procedure and state court analogs.
- Before drafting a pleading responsive to the complaint, ask yourself if the court has personal and subject matter jurisdiction, if service was made properly, and what defenses are available so you can determine whether to file a motion before filing an answer.
- Within the constraints of Rule 11, file motions addressed to the complaint before filing an answer.
- In drafting a memo supporting a motion involving complex issues, include a cover page, table of contents, table of authorities, preliminary statement, facts, argument (divided into subsections), conclusion, and supporting documents.
- In drafting discovery requests, know the practical utility of interrogatories, document requests, and requests for admissions, and use them in a sequence that makes sense in your case.
- In responding to discovery requests, meet deadlines. If you need extra time, comply with rules requiring a conference with opposing counsel before filing a motion for extension of time.
- In responding to discovery requests, conduct a good-faith investigation to respond fully and fairly, while preserving all applicable privileges, and objecting as appropriate, within applicable rules.
- Before producing any documents, Bates stamp them so you have a record of what you produced; opposing counsel should do the same.
- Take advantage of requests for admission to obtain admissions conclusive for purposes of your case.

(continued)

- Draft jury instructions using simple English in short sentences, one concept for each instruction with authority for each, in a logical order with appropriate headings.
- Before drafting an appellate court brief, know the record, standard of review, and applicable law. Discuss facts essential to your argument, frame the issues with care, and make your strongest points first in your argument. Explain why the court should rule in your favor, and distinguish opposing counsel's cases. Be specific in stating what you want the appellate court to do.
- In drafting settlement documents, be explicit and include all provisions discussed in the text, keeping in mind tax considerations.

❖❖❖❖
## Preparing for, Taking, and Defending Depositions

- Take a deposition only after you have completed necessary factual and legal research and developed a working theme for your case.
- Obtain all necessary documents and review them before taking a deposition.
- If an opposing party is an entity, serve a notice to take the deposition of the entity, not just individuals, listing topics to be covered, as provided in Rule 30(b)(6).
- In preparing your client for a deposition, explain the deposition procedure in detail; discuss the themes, claims, and defenses of the case; discuss how to answer questions; and put your client through a practice deposition, playing the role of opposing counsel. Explain how you will protect your client's interests at the deposition, and explain how your client can correct any mistakes in his or her deposition testimony.
- In taking a deposition, use the list of subjects or questions you prepared, listen to the answers and observe the deponent's body language, ask follow-up questions, exhaust the deponent's memory, and use the funnel method to obtain admissions you can use.
- In defending a deposition, caution your client the first time he or she volunteers; limit your objections to the word "objection" unless you have justification to say more; during breaks, provide guidance to your client as needed unless prohibited in your jurisdiction; take notes only as you need at the deposition; and know when it is permissible to instruct your client not to answer.
- Ask questions of your own client at a deposition only to correct mistakes or to create a more complete record if your client may not be available at trial.
- In deposing an expert, prepare by learning everything you can about the expert and the expert's writings, cover all subjects that may be useful in cross-examining the expert at trial and for a *Daubert* challenge; and consider refraining from asking certain questions to blindside the expert at trial.
- Unless, for strategic reasons, you have not preserved your client's right to read and sign the transcript of the deposition, preserve that right during the deposition, and make sure that you submit the errata sheet within 30 days of your client's receipt of the transcript.
- After receiving the transcript, prepare a summary of it and include significant facts from it in your working chronology.
- Use deposition transcripts to support motions for summary judgment, in settlement negotiations, and at trial. You can use deposition transcripts at trial as follows:
    - _____ testimony of an absent witness
    - _____ admission of a party opponent

(continued)

- _____ basis for a proffer
- _____ means to refresh recollection
- _____ testimony of a witness whose testimony cannot be refreshed
- _____ means of impeachment
- _____ means for phantom impeachment
- In an appropriate case, consider taking a video deposition, keeping in mind the advantages and disadvantages of doing so.
- Take advantage of applicable Federal Rules of Civil Procedure to compel attendance at deposition and to compel answers to deposition questions.
- Take advantage of applicable Federal Rules of Civil Procedure to obtain a protective order limiting the conduct of a deposition.

## ❖❖❖❖
## Mediating Commercial Disputes

- Determine whether your client has a contractual obligation to mediate before commencing litigation.
- Weigh the advantages and disadvantages of mediation before advising a client whether to mediate; discuss them with your client.
- Explain to your client that offering to mediate is not a sign of weakness.
- Mediate only after you know the facts and law of your case, but before the parties have spent so much on legal fees and their positions are so entrenched that they conclude it would be a waste of time and money to mediate.
- Unless the parties have a preexisting mediation contract, draft one.
- In deciding on a mediator, determine whether you want a facilitative or evaluative mediator, or a mediator who combines both approaches.
- Select a mediator in whom all parties have confidence.
- Prepare for mediation:
  - _____ Know your BATNA and your WATNA.
  - _____ Decide on your opening demand or offer.
  - _____ Get authority from your client regarding your settlement position.
  - _____ Discuss with your client nonmonetary as well as monetary resolution components.
  - _____ Consider principles all parties can agree upon.
  - _____ Determine whether the dispute results from a breakdown in a relationship; if so, determine the best way to deal with it.
  - _____ Prepare demonstrative exhibits for the mediation, as appropriate.
  - _____ Bring to the mediation all documents you may need.
  - _____ Bring to the mediation someone with authority to settle, but no one you do not need.
  - _____ Prepare your opening statement.
- Use effective strategies during the mediation.
  - _____ Deliver an effective opening statement.
  - _____ Be prepared for the mediator's shuttle diplomacy, including the mediator's taking a devil's advocate position with you.
  - _____ As you make each demand or offer during the mediation process, get your client's prior authority, be aware of how the opposing party will interpret it, and be very careful in the words you use in transmitting each demand or offer.
  - _____ As you approach the limit of your authority, decrease each increment in the amount of your offer.
  - _____ Keep in mind creative resolutions.
  - _____ Be very clear with the mediator what information you authorize the mediator to share with your opponent.

*(continued)*

- Use strategies to break through impasse.
  - _____ Challenge perceived BATNA.
  - _____ Challenge perceived WATNA.
  - _____ Focus on nonmonetary factors.
  - _____ Change the players.
  - _____ Change the venue.
  - _____ Ask: What if?
  - _____ Cut to the chase.
  - _____ Accept the "double-blind" proposal.
  - _____ Take a break.
  - _____ Resume another day.
- If your mediation is successful, before leaving the mediation session, get a signed agreement.
- If the mediation is not successful, consider other dispute resolution mechanisms.
- Learn from each mediation so you will be more adept in your next mediation.

## ❖❖❖❖
## Arbitrating Commercial Disputes

- At the inception of a new matter involving a written agreement, determine whether your client has agreed to arbitrate disputes.
- Be aware that, even after a dispute arises and the parties have no pre-dispute arbitration agreement, they can agree to arbitrate their dispute.
- Know the advantages and disadvantages of arbitration, and advise your client accordingly.
- Review the arbitration clause, focusing on what arbitration rules apply, conditions precedent to arbitration, scope of the arbitrator's authority, and unique provisions regarding what is arbitrable and agreed arbitration procedures.
- Know the law in your jurisdiction on the issue of arbitrability.
- Unless your client authorizes you to waive the right to arbitrate, do not inadvertently waive that right by proceeding in a way inconsistent with arbitration, as by prosecuting or defending claims in litigation.
- Know the procedure under the applicable arbitration rules for selecting arbitrators.
- Learn as much as you can about potential arbitrators before making your selection.
- When you commence an arbitration proceeding, include a detailed statement of facts in your statement of claim.
- If the statute of limitations may run soon after you take on a new matter where the parties have a pre-dispute arbitration agreement, bring a legal action, and then move to stay that action to arbitrate the same claim if required in your jurisdiction to avoid the running of the statute of limitations.
- Prepare for the preliminary hearing by discussing with opposing counsel all the issues you should expect will be raised at that hearing, which is analogous to a Rule 26(f) conference in federal court.
- Prepare for the arbitration hearing by completing your factual and legal investigation, stipulating to facts and exhibits, preparing a chronology, and discussing with opposing counsel creative ways to expedite the arbitration hearing.
- Even though the evidentiary rules do not apply in arbitration, be prepared to argue the evidentiary basis for getting testimony and documents in the record.
- Prepare for the arbitration hearing as you would for trial, but keep in mind your greater flexibility in arbitration, enabling you to provide the arbitrator (copying opposing counsel) with such persuasive aids as bullet-point sheets regarding the testimony of each witness, a chronology, and demonstrative exhibits.

(continued)

- In your post-hearing brief, consider including, in an appendix, copies of the authorities on which you rely, transcript excerpts, an index of exhibits, and anything else that may make the arbitrator more likely to rule in your client's favor.
- Be aware of the nonmonetary as well as monetary relief available in arbitration, and seek all relief appropriate in your matter.
- Protect the confidentiality of arbitration by entering into a confidentiality agreement.
- When appropriate, file a motion in court to modify or correct an award within the time allowed by statute.
- If the arbitrator rules in your favor, file a motion in court to confirm the award within the time allowed by statute so that the award becomes a court order.
- If the arbitrator rules against you, determine whether you have a good-faith basis to file a motion in court to vacate the award; if so, file it within the time allowed by statute.
- Be aware that the FAA applies in certain matters, and comply with its provisions when it does apply.

## ❖❖❖❖
# Making Oral Presentations in Court

- In preparing for oral argument of pretrial motions, learn what you need to know about the judge before whom you will argue, find out how much time you will have for the argument, read all briefs and other documents related to the issues presented, and decide what points are most persuasive.
- In preparing for oral argument of pretrial motions, take a devil's advocate position, and determine how you can undercut that position in your presentation, while focusing primarily on arguing your position.
- Bring to court all briefs and other documents related to the issues presented and an outline of the key points you plan to make.
- Expect to be interrupted during your argument.
- As you argue, appear prepared and confident, don't fidget, and don't talk too fast.
- Listen carefully to the judge's questions during oral argument. Think before you answer. If you do not understand a question, seek clarification.
- Answer each question directly, weaving your themes into your answers.
- In answering questions, do not evade, put off until later, misstate anything in the record or any point of law, or answer a question other than the one asked.
- Do not argue with the judge or suggest that the judge's question is off the mark or of no consequence.
- Never interrupt a judge.
- Be respectful, but not obsequious.
- Make concessions, but only as necessary.
- Be wary of hypothetical questions, because they may contain hidden concessions.
- In your opening statement to the jury, introduce yourself, start with a persuasive statement of your theme, provide the jurors with a basis to identify with your client, describe what you will prove in a way that captivates the jurors, use simple language, focus only on facts that matter, inject a sense of morality, make a preemptive strike on your opponent's theme, and end with something powerful related to your themes.
- In your opening statement to the jury, do not make an argument, do not refer to anything unlikely to get into the trial record, do not overstate or exaggerate anything, do not be theatrical, do not refer to the "golden rule," and do not state your personal opinion.
- In your closing argument to the jury, address what you think the jurors will find most persuasive, weave in your theme throughout your argument, and start and end strong. Use simple, powerful words, analogies, metaphors, allusions, aphorisms, apt quotations, images, and words the jurors will hear in the charge to the jurors.

(continued)

- In your opening statement and closing argument to the jury, use as few notes as possible.
- In preparing for an appellate court argument, know the record cold, the issues on appeal, the standard of review, and the key cases. Prepare an argument based on the amount of time the court allows, planning to make your strongest point first. Find out which judges are on your panel and learn what you need to know about them.
- During your appellate court argument, expect to be interrupted constantly and follow the advice as for argument of pretrial motions.
- If you represent an appellant, reserve time for rebuttal.

## ❖❖❖❖
## Presenting an Effective Plaintiff's Case in the Courtroom

- Choose a compelling, succinct, common-sense theme.
- Draft your complaint so it is consistent with your theme.
- Conduct discovery to get admissions and streamline the trial:
  - _____ Get deposition admissions and judicial admissions in response to requests for admissions to promote your theme.
  - _____ Obtain certified copies of public records.
  - _____ Get judicial notice of adjudicative facts.
- Stipulate to admission of documents as full exhibits.
- File motions in limine on key evidentiary issues.
- Prepare a trial notebook.
- File a pretrial memo.
- Select as few witnesses as you need and present them in a logical order.
- Prepare your witnesses to avoid surprises in the courtroom.
- Ask direct examination questions efficiently and effectively:
  - _____ Ask short questions in plain English at a comfortable pace.
  - _____ Ask only questions that promote your theme.
  - _____ Vary the types of your questions.
  - _____ Use headnotes and loop-backs.
  - _____ Don't ask the one question too many.
  - _____ Avoid objectionable questions.
  - _____ Counter defense counsel's objections in a way to reinforce your themes.
  - _____ Cut off voir dire that derails your case.
  - _____ Use your voice like an instrument.
  - _____ Build up significant testimony.
  - _____ Make a preemptive strike on weaknesses in your witnesses' testimony.
  - _____ Review your checklist before ending your questions of each witness, and before resting your case.
- Use exhibits efficiently and effectively:
  - _____ Put into evidence only exhibits promoting your theme, and know the evidentiary basis for each.
  - _____ Build up significant documents.
  - _____ Put into evidence deposition testimony and responses to requests for admissions.
  - _____ Put into evidence summaries of voluminous documents.
  - _____ Use demonstrative exhibits.
  - _____ Make sufficient copies of documents.
  - _____ Keep track of which documents are in evidence and which are for identification only.

*(continued)*

- Select an expert who will support your theme efficiently and effectively:
  - _____ Select an expert with the requisite background and experience who speaks in plain English and who is not subject to a *Daubert* challenge.
  - _____ Have your expert testify on the ultimate issue.
  - _____ Introduce your expert's report into evidence.
- Miscellaneous tips:
  - _____ Do not misrepresent or distort anything.
  - _____ Be prepared for a bad answer from your own witness.
  - _____ Prepare your witnesses for questioning by the judge.
  - _____ Stay organized during trial.
  - _____ Use note cards to communicate with co-counsel during trial.
  - _____ Be flexible during trial.
  - _____ Avoid burnout during trial.
- Adjust all this advice for a jury trial:
  - _____ Workshop your case with a non-lawyer, focus group, or mock jury.
  - _____ Don't promise more than you can deliver in your opening statement and don't mischaracterize the record in your closing argument.
  - _____ Don't bludgeon the jurors with your theme.
  - _____ Try your case at the level of the jurors.
  - _____ Use more demonstrative exhibits than at a bench trial.
  - _____ Publish each exhibit to the jurors in a meaningful way.
  - _____ Promote your theme in opening statement, in closing argument, and in the charge to the jury.
- Listen to Beethoven's Fifth Symphony, focusing on his use of the theme.
- When you settle a case shortly before or during a trial, keep in mind that your case settled so favorably only because you were prepared to try it.

# Presenting an Effective Defense in the Courtroom

- Choose a compelling counter-theme that does more than merely refute plaintiff's theme.
- Draft your answer, affirmative defenses, counterclaims, and cross-claims so they are consistent with your counter-theme.
- File a pretrial memo that does more than just refute plaintiff's theme.
- Take limited notes as plaintiff's witnesses testify.
- Keep plaintiff's witnesses' testimony and exhibits out of the record:
  - _____ Protect the record before trial.
  - _____ Know the bases to object to the form of questions.
  - _____ Know the bases to object to the substance of testimony.
  - _____ Know the bases to object to exhibits.
- Object strategically to questions on direct:
  - _____ Listen to each question carefully—is it objectionable?
  - _____ Be poised to object to each question timely, avoiding the need to file a motion to strike, when it is too late to "unring the bell."
  - _____ Object only when you have good reason, and can keep evidence out.
  - _____ Adjust your objections to the judge's rulings.
- Object as appropriate to plaintiff's exhibits:
  - _____ Are they objectionable as violative of any rules of evidence?
  - _____ Were they produced in response to your pretrial discovery?
  - _____ Voir dire on exhibits when appropriate.
- Keep out expert testimony, based on the *Daubert* analysis.
- Conduct an effective cross-examination of each witness.
  - _____ Cross serves many purposes: build up favorable witnesses, corroborate favorable testimony, obtain admissions, minimize the witness's credibility, and minimize or destroy the witness's testimony.
  - _____ Before trial, determine what points you want to make on cross and know the evidentiary basis for each question you plan to ask.
  - _____ At trial, decide whether to cross at all: Was your case damaged by the testimony on direct? If so, can you do something about it?
  - _____ Use short, understandable leading questions, preferably in the form of statements.
  - _____ Be fair to the witness by not misrepresenting what the witness said or taking testimony out of context.
  - _____ Observe the witness's body language when answering questions.

*(continued)*

- Use as few notes as practical.
- If the witness does not answer your question, repeat it—but if your question may have been confusing, fix it first.
- Start and end strong with each witness.
- Use a checklist to be sure you have covered all the points before ending your cross.
- Don't start with a hostile demeanor, try to trick or confuse the witness, cut off the answer (unless you have good reason, such as stopping a nonresponsive or improper answer), ask why or how, ask a question you don't know the answer to, or ask the one question too many.
- Remember that these are merely guidelines, subject to exceptions, depending on the circumstances in each case.

• Impeach on cross-examination effectively:
- Determine before trial whether you have impeachment material, and use it only if the witness's testimony on direct hurt your case.
- Impeach one fact at a time.
- First, commit the witness to the courtroom statement, making clear you don't believe the statement on which you will impeach.
- Second, credit the impeaching document or statement by building it up.
- Third, confront the witness with the words of the impeaching material.
- Don't give the witness the opportunity to explain away the inconsistency.
- Remember that the impeaching document is not evidence.

• Use plaintiff's exhibits and demonstrative exhibits against plaintiff.
• When plaintiff rests, consider filing a motion for judgment as a matter of law.
• Adjust your strategy when plaintiff rests, based on what is in the record.
• Limit plaintiff's rebuttal to what you put into the record not covered in plaintiff's case in chief, and consider sur-rebuttal, keeping in mind its limited scope.
• Preserve issues for appeal.
• Miscellaneous tips:
- Before trial, caution your client that plaintiff goes first, which can be demoralizing, but that you will have your opportunity to undermine plaintiff's case when you cross-examine and when you present your defense case.
- Be aware of opportunities to settle during the course of the trial.
- Take advantage of technology in your defense.

(continued)

- Adjust all this advice for a jury trial.
    - _____ Adjust your demeanor based on the witness's demeanor.
    - _____ Seek judicial intervention with a difficult witness only when you have no other option.
    - _____ Be aware that during a trial you are "on the record" from the moment you leave the office until the moment you return to the office.
    - _____ Excuse the jurors when necessary to avoid their learning about something you seek to keep out of the record.
    - _____ Minimize disruption for the jurors by filing motions in limine where appropriate.
    - _____ In your jury charge, use plain English, short sentences, and short paragraphs; include a clear instruction on burden of proof.
    - _____ In opening statement and closing argument, make the jurors care by personalizing the dispute whenever possible, and relating your defense to something the jurors will identify with their own experience.

## Dealing with Ethical Issues

- Read and comply with all ethical rules applicable in your jurisdiction.
- Make sure you have the competence before undertaking a representation.
- Get your client's authority, and communicate with your client as required by the ethical rules.
- Avoid conflicts of interest with current and former clients.
- Comply with the ethical rules when representing an organization.
- Comply with the ethical rules when you decline or terminate a representation.
- Comply with your ethical obligations if you discuss a matter with a prospective client.
- Assert only meritorious claims and contentions.
- Be candid to the tribunal.
- Comply with the ethical rules in preparing your client for deposition and court testimony.
- Be fair to the opposing party and opposing party's counsel.
- Be truthful in your statements to others.
- Comply with the ethical rules in dealing with opposing parties, whether represented or not.

## Marketing Your Litigation Practice

- Comply with the ethical rules governing your marketing efforts.
- Create a niche you can market.
- Create a plan to market your practice:
  - _____ Set a goal.
  - _____ Select marketing targets.
  - _____ Select marketing activities.
  - _____ Write your marketing plan.
- Cultivate relationships with clients and referral sources.
- Develop in-person networking skills.
- Make the most of social media to market your practice.
- Draft and publish articles to market your practice.
- Cross-sell to benefit yourself and other lawyers in your firm.

❖❖❖❖
## Coping with Stress and Creating a Life beyond the Practice of Law

- Take good care of your body by eating right, exercising right, and sleeping right.
- Create and nurture your support system by making time for family and friends, advising family members of trial demands, making time for yourself, taking fulfilling vacations, varying your routine, expanding your horizons, and creating oases.
- Work smarter by keeping a current "to do" list, planning a realistic work schedule, establishing realistic expectations, accepting that you will make mistakes and learning from them, not internalizing your cases, not putting off what you want to avoid, being organized and focused, completing tasks on time, being prepared, planning ahead, and reviewing all your files regularly.
- Take advantage of teamwork by getting help with work when you need it, keeping your client informed, cultivating staff relationships, and seeking feedback.
- Benefit from safety valves by expecting the unexpected, discussing your feelings, listening to your body, having fun, and evaluating your professional satisfaction.
- Read books by Mitch Albom, Richard Carlson, Thich Nhat Hanh, Jon Kabat-Zinn, Steven Keeva, Deng Ming-Dao, and Matthieu Ricard, listed in appendix III.
- Aspire to achieve holistic success.
- As you advance in your career, navigate up the flow channel to avoid boredom and anxiety.

# INDEX

## A

admissions. *See* requests for admissions
"adversary," etymology of, 42
advertising, ethical issues of, 256, 265. *See also* marketing
affidavits, 76
affirmative defenses, drafting, 76–78, 206–207
Albom, Mitch, 304–305
American Arbitration Association (AAA)
   arbitration costs, 151, 152
   arbitrator selection, 151
   Commercial Arbitration Rules, 145–147, 148–149
   confidentiality, 157
   *Drafting Dispute Resolution Clauses: A Practical Guide*, 147
   mediators, 134
American Bar Association
   on career satisfaction, 270
   contact information, 236
   Model Rules of Professional Conduct (*see* ethical issues)
American Law Institute, 236
American Legal Ethics Library, Cornell Law School, 236
answers, drafting, 76–78, 206–207
appeal
   arbitration and, 148
   preserving issues for, 226–227
appellate court arguments, 178–182
appellate court briefs, drafting, 88–89
appellate review, excluding expert testimony and, 220
appellate rights, 230–231
arbitration, 145–160
   advantages and disadvantages, 147–148
   arbitrability issues, 149–150
   arbitration clause review, 148–149
   arbitrator selection, 151
   awards rendered, 157–158
   checklist, 159–160
   commencement of proceeding, 152
   Commercial Arbitration Rules (American Arbitration Association), 145–147

arbitration (*continued*)
  confidentiality, 157
  Federal Arbitration Act
    (FAA) applicability, 159
  hearings, 154–157
  inadvertent waiver, 150–151
  mediation as unsuccessful, 142
  preliminary hearing
    preparation, 147, 153–154
  statute of limitations,
    152–153
arbitrators. *See also* arbitration
  authority of, 148–149
  selecting, 151
  working relationship
    with, 45, 48
argument, preparing for. *See* oral
    presentations in court
Armstrong, Lance, 71
articles, publishing, 266–267
*Ashcroft v. Iqbal*, 320
attorney, etymology of, 1–2.
    *See also* lawyers
attorney-client privilege
  email and, 54, 55–57
  ethics and, 238–239 (*see
    also* ethical issues)
  ethics and (example), 330–331
  explaining, to client, 6, 10–11
auditor letters, 61–62

**B**
baseball arbitration, 142
Bates, Edwin G., 84
Bates stamping, 84
BATNA, 135, 139
Beethoven, Ludwig von, 199–201
Belasco, David, 321
*Bell Atlantic Corp. v. Twombly*, 320
*Best Lawyers in America, The*, 134
Bierce, Ambrose, 280
billable hours. *See* fees
Blackstone, William, 99
blended rate fees, 13–14

blogs, 263, 265
body language, in court,
    164–165, 177
"bounded" arbitration, 142
brainstorming, about case,
    11–12
brief banks, 69
burden of proof, 217
"but for," xxix–xxx

**C**
Campbell, Joseph, 306
candor to the tribunal, 245–249
career satisfaction, evaluating,
    270, 286–287
Carlson, Richard, 305
certification, marketing
    and, 257–258
Churchill, Winston, 310, 319
Cicero, 246
clerks, of judges, 47
clients, 1–28. *See also* email;
    ethical issues; marketing
  checklist, 27–28
  client's authority and lawyer-
    client communication,
    237–239
  of co-counsel in other firms, 37
  collaboration with, 16–17
  completion of work
    for, 26, 60–61
  delivering bad news to,
    21–22
  difficult clients, 19–21
  etymology of "clients," 1–2
  expectations of, 17–19
  first client meeting, 6–11
  first client meeting
    follow-up, 11–12
  first contact from prospective
    clients, 2–5
  keeping clients informed, 285
  location of deposition, 102
    (*see also* depositions)

non-engagement letters,
   4, 11, 59–60
organizations as, 240,
   241, 242–243
preparing, for deposition,
   103–107 (*see also* depositions)
preparing, to testify
   in court, 22–23
as referral source, 259–261
retainer agreements, 12–16
time records and billing, 23–26
   (*see also* timekeeping)
closing arguments, oral
   presentation for, 175–178
co-counsel (in other firms). *See
   also* colleagues; law firms
   communication with,
      during trial, 197
   working relationship
      with, 37–41, 48
cogency, 67, 95, 307–323
Cohen, Herb, 293
Cohen and Wolf PC, 291–293
colleagues. *See also* co-counsel
   (in other firms); law firms
   drafting internal memos
      to, 67–69
   professional conduct by, 254
   working relationship
      with, 36–37, 48
Commercial Arbitration
   Rules (American
   Arbitration Association),
   145–147, 148–149
commercial cases, generally, 185
commercial disputes.
   *See* mediation
competence, ethics and, 237
complaints
   drafting, 69–73
   theme and, 186
completed-engagement
   letters, 26, 60–61
confirmation bias, 205

conflict of interest. *See
   also* ethical issues
   client interaction and
      conflicts check, 2, 3
   clients, current, 239–241
   clients, former, 241–242
   example, 333–334
contingent fees, 15
Cornell Law School, 236
correspondence. *See* email; letters
counterclaims, drafting, 206–207
CPR Corporate Policy
   Statement on Alternatives
   to Litigation, 131
CPR Institute for Dispute
   Resolution, 134
cross-claims, drafting, 206–207
cross examination
   effectiveness of, 220–222
   impeachment upon, 222–224
cross-selling, 267–268
Csikszentmihalyi, Mihaly,
   287–289, 304

**D**

*Daubert* analysis
   *Daubert v. Merrell Down
      Pharmaceuticals,
      Inc.*, 216–217
   expert witnesses and, 34, 196
deadlines. *See also* statute of
      limitations; timekeeping
   of clients, 17–18
   organization and, 12,
      67, 73, 158
   preliminary hearing and, 153
   stress management and, 280, 283
De Bono, Edward, 311
defense, 205–234
   checklist, 232–234
   compelling counter-
      theme for, 205–206
   defending depositions of
      clients, 117–119

defense (*continued*)
  drafting answer, affirmative defenses, counterclaims, cross-claims, 206–207
  effective cross-examination, 220–222
  ethical issues and, 2, 3–4, 12–13, 20–21, 25, 237–239 (*see also* clients; conflict of interest; ethical issues)
  excluding expert testimony, 216–220
  excluding plaintiff's witnesses' testimony and exhibits, 209–213
  filing pretrial memo for, 207–208
  impeach on cross-examination, 222–224
  for jury trials, 228–231
  motion for judgment as matter of law as option, 224–225
  motions in limine, 210
  objecting, strategically, 210–216
  plaintiff's rebuttal, 225–226
  preserving issues for appeal, 226–227
  strategy adjustment upon plaintiff resting, 225
  taking notes during plaintiff's witnesses' testimony, 208
  tips for, 228
  using plaintiff's exhibits against plaintiff, 224
depositions
  admissions during, 187
  advantages and disadvantages of taking deposition, 100
  checklist, 129–130
  compelling attendance and answers of deponents, 126–128
  defending, 99–130, 117–119
  ethics and (example), 334–335
  of experts, 120–121
  funnel method for, 109, 111–116
  generally, 99
  length of deposition, 101
  location for taking deposition, 102
  noticing a deposition, 101–102
  number of depositions, 101
  preparing clients for, 7, 103–107
  preparing expert witnesses for, 35
  preparing to take deposition, 103
  procedure, 107–111
  protective orders to limit conduct of deposition, 128
  questioning clients at, 119–120
  terminating, 119
  transcript for impeachment, 228
  transcripts, utilizing at trial, 123–125
  transcripts, utilizing before trial, 122–123
  transcripts of, 121–125
  video depositions, 125–126
  when to take deposition, 100–101
Derby, Earl of, 273
diet, 271–272
direct examination questions, 191–193, 213–214
discovery
  arbitration limitations, 148
  "closed" records and, 17
  drafting documents in response to, 78–87
  Internet searches, 78, 188, 252
  for plaintiff's case, 187–188
  preliminary research, 5, 11–12
  working relationship with opposing counsel and, 43–44
  writing documents and, 68–69

documents, 65–97. *See also*
    email; letters
  affidavits, 76
  answers and affirmative
    defenses, 76–78
  appellate court briefs, 88–89
  Bates stamping, 84
  checklist for, 96–97
  cogent writing, 67, 95, 307–323
  complaints, 69–73
  for deposition, 100–101, 103
    (*see also* depositions)
  disclosure of expert reports, 34
  drafting answer, affirmative
    defenses, counterclaims,
    cross-claims, 206–207
  for first client meeting,
    5, 8, 16–17
  as full exhibits, in
    plaintiff's case, 188
  generally, 65
  internal memos, 67–69
  joint defense agreements, 37–38
  jury instructions, 87
  motions and memos,
    supporting and opposing
    motions, 73–76
  objecting to plaintiff's
    exhibits, 215
  for oral argument in court, 163
  principles applicable to all
    legal writing, 66–67
  requests for, 83
  in response to discovery, 78–87
  settlement agreements, 89–93
  settlement agreements, tax
    consequences, 94–95
  from third parties and
    public record, 188
*Don't Sweat the Small Stuff . . .
    and It's All Small Stuff*
    (Carlson), 305
"double-blind" proposal, 141
drafting. *See* documents

*Drafting Dispute Resolution Clauses:
    A Practical Guide* (American
    Arbitration Association), 147
*Dubious Doublets: A Delightful
    Compendium of Unlikely
    Word Pairs of Common
    Origin* (Edelstein), 297

**E**
Edelstein, Lynn, 296
Edelstein, Stewart I., 291–306
  *Dubious Doublets: A
    Delightful Compendium
    of Unlikely Word Pairs of
    Common Origin*, 297
  early law career of, 291–295
  work/life balance, 295–306
Einstein, Albert, 320
email, 49–63
  appropriateness of, 50–53
  attorney-client privilege
    and, 54, 55–57
  checklist for, 63
  drafting, 53–55
  ethics and (example), 337–338
  etiquette for, 55
  letters and, 50–53, 58–62
  managing, 49–50
  organizing and saving, 57
  from prospective clients, 2–3
Emerson, Ralph Waldo, 289–290
employees, former, 252–253
"enemy," etymology of, 41–42
ethical issues, 235–254
  arbitration and
    confidentiality, 157
  candor to the tribunal
    and, 245–249
  checklist, 254
  client interaction and, 2,
    3–4, 12–13, 20–21, 25
  client's authority and lawyer-
    client communication,
    237–239

ethical issues (*continued*)
  competence and, 237
  conflict of interest and current clients, 239–241
  conflict of interest and former clients, 241–242
  declining or terminating representation of clients, 243–244
  depositions and, 106
  examples, 325–342
  fairness to opposing party and counsel, 249–250
  knowledge and compliance of, 253–254
  of marketing, 256–258
  meritorious claims and contentions, 245
  opposing parties represented by counsel and parties not represented, 251–253
  prospective clients and, 244–245, 256–258 (*see also* marketing)
  recognizing, 236–237
  representing organizations and, 242–243
  truthfulness and, 250–251
  "zeal" and, 235
evidence, exclusion of, 195–196
exercise, 272–274
exhibits
  demonstrative, 136, 191, 195, 224
  excluding plaintiff's witnesses' exhibits, 209–213
  illustrative aids, 224
  objecting to, 214–216
  for plaintiff's case, 194–195
  using plaintiff's exhibits against plaintiff, 224
expert witnesses
  deposing, 120–121
  excluding plaintiff's witnesses' testimony and exhibits, 209–213
  excluding testimony of, 216–220
  selecting, for plaintiff's case, 196
  types of, 33–34
  working relationship with, 32–35, 48

# F

Facebook
  as investigative tool, 252
  for marketing, 264–265
family. *See also* stress management
  as support system, 277–279
  work/life balance, 279–284, 295–306
Federal Arbitration Act (FAA), 159
feedback, benefits of, 285
feelings, venting, 286
fees
  for arbitration, 151, 152
  client expectations, 18
  discussing, with clients, 10
  for expert witnesses, 34
  nonpaying clients, 19
  recording, and good client relations, 23–26
  retainer agreements, 5, 12–16
  types of, 13–16
*Fifth Symphony* (Beethoven), 199–201
files, reviewing, 284
fixed fees, 14
*Flow: The Psychology of Optimal Experience* (Csikszentmihalyi), 304
flow channel, 287–289, 304
funnel method, for deposition, 109, 111–116

## G
*General Electric Co. v. Joiner*, 217
Gold, Fred, 296
Gryphon, xxx–xxxiii

## H
Hammerstein, Oscar, II, xxix
*hara hachi bu*, 272
headnotes, 192
hearing (arbitration)
  determining admissibility, 154–155
  follow-up, 155–156
  persuasiveness for, 155
  preparation for, 154
  remedies, 156–157
hearsay
  hearsay objection, 212–213
  reliance on, 220
"high-low" arbitration, 142
hold order, 8
holistic success, 289–290

## I
illustrative aids, 224
impeachment
  on cross-examination, 222–224
  depositions and, 106, 123, 124–126
inadvertent disclosure, 209, 253
inadvertent waiver, arbitration, 150–151
"in limine," etymology of, 188–189
in-person networking, 261–263
insurance, client coverage, 7
internal memos, drafting, 67–69
interrogatories, drafting, 79–83

## J
Jackson, Robert H., 182
JAMS, 134
Johnson, Samuel, 318
joint defense agreements, 37–38

judges
  activist, 197
  answering judges' questions, during pretrial motions, 165–168
  drafting jury instructions and, 87
  drafting letters to, 58–59
  working relationship with, 45–47, 48
jury trials
  closing arguments to jurors, 175–178
  instructions to jurors, 87
  jury demand, 198
  opening statement to jurors, 168–174
  plaintiff's case presentation, 198–199
  voir dire, 192, 201
  when representing defendant, 228–231
  working relationship with jurors, 47, 48

## K
Kabat-Zinn, Jon, 305
Katz, Joette, 89
King, Martin Luther, Jr., 319
*Kumho Tire Co., Ltd. v. Carmichael*, 217

## L
*Lateral Thinking* (De Bono), 311
law firms. *See also* co-counsel (in other firms); colleagues; opposing counsel
  cross-selling of firm services, 267–268
  specialty certification and marketing, 257–258
lawyers
  career satisfaction of, 270, 286–287

lawyers (*continued*)
  etymology of "attorney," 1–2
  etymology of "lawyer," 1
  working relationships of
    (*see* arbitrators; clients;
    colleagues; expert witnesses;
    judges; lay witnesses;
    mediators; opposing
    counsel; paralegals)
lay witnesses
  preparing, for plaintiff's
    case, 190–191
  selecting, for plaintiff's
    case, 190
  working relationship
    with, 32, 48
letters. *See also* email
  appropriateness of, instead
    of email, 50–53
  auditor letters, 61–62
  checklist for, 63
  completed-engagement
    letters, 26, 60–61
  non-engagement letters,
    4, 11, 59–60
Levine, Irving, 292
lifestyle, healthy, 271–276, 286
Lincoln, Abraham, 143, 282, 319
LinkedIn, 263–265
litigation
  arbitration contrasted
    to, 147–148
  avoiding (*see* mediation)
  litigation hold, 8
local counsel, serving as, 38–41

**M**
mandatory disclosure, 79, 83
*Maples v. Thomas*, 38–41
marketing, 255–268
  checklist, 268
  cross-selling firm services
    and, 267–268
  ethical issues of, 256–258

  ethical issues of
    (example), 338–339
  importance of, 255–256
  in-person networking,
    261–263
  niche marketing, 258
  planning for, 258–259
  publishing articles
    and, 266–267
  referral sources, 259–261
  social media for, 263–265
mediation, 131–144
  checklist, 143–144
  decision to mediate, 131–133
  etymology of "mediation," 134
  impasse-breaking strategies
    for, 138–141
  mediator selection, 133–134
  position statements, 136
  preparing for, 135–137
  settlement terms, 141–142
  strategies for, 137–138
  success of, 143
  unsuccessful, 142
mediators. *See also* mediation
  types of, 133–134
  working relationship
    with, 45, 48
mindfulness, 305
mistakes, handling, 55–57,
    280–281
misunderstandings, resolving, 51
mock depositions, 106
Model Rules of Professional
  Conduct (American
  Bar Association). *See*
  ethical issues
Montaigne, Michel de, 109
motions
  drafting, 73–76
  for judgment as matter
    of law, 224–225
  in limine, 188–189, 210, 220
movies, suggestions for, 348–351

## N

National Institute for Trial
    Advocacy (NITA), 294
networking, 261–263
niche marketing, 258
non-engagement letters, 4, 11,
    59–60. *See also* clients
notes
    paralegals in courtroom
        for, 208
    during trial, when representing
        defendant, 208
    during trial, when representing
        plaintiff, 189
nutrition, 271–272

## O

objections
    at depositions, 105, 110,
        117, 123, 126, 127, 128
    to document requests,
        78, 81–82
    to jury instructions, 230
    at trial, 210–216
offer of proof, 195–196
opening statements, oral
    presentation for, 168–174
opinion letters, 61
opposing counsel. *See also*
    arbitration; depositions;
    email; mediation
    Bates stamping
        documents and, 84
    ethics and, 251–253, 252–253
        (*see also* ethical issues)
    mediator selection and, 134
        (*see also* mediation)
    working relationship with,
        32, 34, 41–45, 48
oral presentations in
    court, 161–184
    appellate court arguments,
        178–182
    checklist, 183–184

closing arguments to
    jury, 175–178
generally, 161
opening statement to
    jury, 168–174
pretrial motions, 162–165
pretrial motions, answering
    judges' questions, 165–168
organization skills. *See*
    *also* deadlines; stress
    management; timekeeping
deadlines, 12, 67, 73, 158
email and, 57
files, 284
for stress management, 282

## P

paralegals
    etymology of "paralegal," 31
    note-taking by, in
        courtroom, 208
    working relationship
        with, 31–32, 48
Pascal, Blaise, 313
performance bonuses, 13
perjury
    depositions and, 110–111
    ethics and, 247–249
persistence of belief, 205–206
Peters, Ellen, 315
phone calls, efficiency of, 51
physical activity, 272–274
physical presentation, in
    court, 164–165, 177
*Plain English for Lawyers*
    (Wydick), 313
plaintiff's case presentation, 185–204
    checklist, 203–204
    commercial cases,
        generally, 185
    compelling theme for,
        186, 199–201
    direct examination
        questions, 191–193

plaintiff's case presentation
(*continued*)
   discovery for, 187–188
   documents as full exhibits, 188
   drafting complaint, 186
   effective use of exhibits, 194–195
   experts, selection of, 196
   filing motions in limine, 188–189
   filing pretrial memo for, 189–190
   for jury trials, 198–199
   location of deposition and, 102 (*see also* depositions)
   motions in limine, 220
   offer of proof as option, 195–196
   plaintiffs as clients, generally, 16
   settlement before or during trial, 201–202
   tips for, 197–198
   trial notebook preparation, 189
   witness preparation, 190–191
   witness selection, 190
Pliny the Younger, 275
preservation order, 8
pretrial memos
   for defense, 207–208
   drafting, 73–76
   for plaintiff's case, 189–190
   when representing defendant, 207–208
pretrial motions
   answering judges' questions during, 165–168 (*see also* oral presentations in court)
   oral presentations in court, 162–165
   oral presentations in court, answering judges' questions, 165–168
primacy effect, 162–163

procrastination, 281–282
professional satisfaction, evaluating, 270, 286–287

## R

reading, suggestions for, 343–348
rebuttal, by plaintiff's lawyer, 225–226
recency effect, 175
reduced hourly fees, 13
referral sources, 259–261
relevance issue, 217–218
reliability issue, 218–220
requests for admissions
   arbitration hearings, 154–155
   conducting discovery for, 187–188
   funnel method and, 113–114
   requests for, 84–87
*Restatement of the Law (Third) Governing Lawyers* (American Law Institute), 236
results, predicting for clients, 9, 18–19
retainer agreements
   client review of, 5
   co-counsel arrangements, 40
   drafting, 12–16
retrospective fees, 15
Rogers, Will, 66
Roosevelt, Eleanor, 260

## S

scams, email, 2–3
secretaries, working relationship with, 30–31, 48
Seinfeld, Jerry, 161
serial position effect, 190
settlement agreements
   drafting, 89–93
   ethics of (example), 331–332
   before or during trial, plaintiff's case, 201–202

successful mediation and, 141–142
tax consequences of, 94–95
during trial, defendant's case, 228
Shakespeare, William, 42, 323
sleep, 274–276
social media
    ethical use of, for investigation, 252
    for marketing, 263–265
Socrates, 46
spell-checking, for emails, 54–55
statute of limitations
    arbitration, 152–153
    ethics and (example), 339–340
stenographers, depositions and, 107–108, 121
Story, Joseph, 269
straight retainer fees, 15
stress management, 269–270
    checklist for, 290
    consequences of stress, 269–270
    flow channel, 287–289, 304
    healthy lifestyle, 271–276, 286
    holistic success, 289–290
    safety valves, 285–287
    support system, 277–279
    teamwork advantage, 284–285
    work/life balance, 279–284, 295–306
support system, need for, 277–279
sur-rebuttal, 225–226
sur-reply memos, 76

## T

Tagore, Rabindranath, 308–309
"Tarpeian Rock," 246–247
taxes, settlement agreements and, 94–95
teamwork, benefits of, 284–285
timekeeping
    client expectations, 17–18
    deposition transcripts, 121, 122
    email and time management, 49–50, 52–53
    meeting deadlines, 37
    recording billable time, and good client relations, 23–26
time management, stress and, 279–280, 282–284
"to do" lists, 279
transcripts, of depositions
    form of, 121
    at trial, 123–125
    before trial, 122–123
*Trial*, 297
trial, preparing clients to testify, 22–23. *See also* clients
trial notebook, preparing, 189
trials. *See* documents; exhibits; expert witnesses; judges; jury trials; lay witnesses; motions
trial "themes"
    brainstorming, 11–12
    counter-themes for representing defendant, 205–206
    refuting, 207–208
    representing defendant and, 225
    representing plaintiff and, 186, 199–201
truthfulness. *See also* ethical issues
    candor to the tribunal, 245–249
    of statements to others, 250–251
*Tuesdays with Morrie* (Albom), 304–305
Twain, Mark, 161, 246, 319

## V

vacations
    emailing during, 52–53
    for stress management, 278
video depositions, 125–126
viewing, suggestions for, 348–351
voir dire, 192, 201
volume discount, 16

**W**
WATNA, 135, 139
*Wherever You Go, There You Are* (Kabat-Zinn), 305
Wigmore, John Henry, 220
Wilde, Oscar, 246
witnesses. *See* expert witnesses; lay witnesses
Wizner, Steve, 296
work/life balance, 279–284, 295–306. *See also* stress management
work-product doctrine
 depositions and, 121
 email and, 56–57
 ethics and, 238, 329 (*see also* ethical issues)
 explaining, to clients, 17
 presenting effective defense and, 209
 witnesses and, 32
Wydick, Richard, 313

**Y**
Yale Law School, 296
Younger, Irving, 207, 308

**Z**
Zinsser, William, 318

# PERMISSIONS

The gryphon illustration on the cover was created by Nina Bolen (www.featherheart.com), who licensed the use of this image.

The flowchart on page 375 is printed with the permission of Mihaly Csikszentmihalyi, Distinguished Professor of Psychology and Management, Claremont Graduate University, and author of *Flow: The Psychology of Optimal Experience*. HarperCollins, New York 2008.

The funnel method chart on page 147 and the flowchart on page 375 were designed by and printed with the permission of Miggs Burroughs of Miggs B. Design (www.miggsb.com).

My article, "Twenty-Fifth Reunion Catharsis: Learning to Avoid Burnout," first published in the June 2000 edition of *Trial*, is reprinted at pages 388 to 402 with the permission of the American Association for Justice.

My article "*Bombast v. Cogent*," first published in the spring 1992 edition of *Litigation* magazine, is reprinted at pages 403 to 415 with the permission of the American Bar Association.

My article "14 Tips for Presenting a Compelling Commercial Plaintiff's Case," first published in the March 2008 edition of *The Practical Litigator*, is reprinted with revisions in chapter 9. For the original article, go to www.ali-aba.org.

My article "14 Tips for a Vigorous Defense of a Commercial Case," first published in the November 2008 edition of *The Practical Litigator*, is reprinted with revisions in chapter 10. For the original article, go to www.ali-aba.org.

# ABOUT THE AUTHOR

At Yale Law School, Stewart Edelstein has taught civil litigation skills for the past twenty years, while chairing the Litigation Group at his firm, Cohen and Wolf PC where he has been a commercial trial lawyer for forty years, mediating, arbitrating, and litigating cases. He has been a faculty member in various programs presented by the National Institute for Trial Advocacy and ALI-ABA (now ALI-CLE), and frequently presents seminars to bar association groups. He is on the Neutral Panel of the American Arbitration Association, on the Executive Committee of the Alternative Dispute Resolution Section of the Connecticut Bar Association, and has served as a Settlement Special Master in federal court and Counsel to the Federal Grievance Committee in Connecticut.

He has published numerous articles for trial lawyers in various publications, including *Litigation*, *Trial*, and *The Practical Litigator*, and is the author of a book about etymology, *Dubious Doublets*, published by John Wiley & Sons Inc., and two bike-tour brochures. He is also a founding member of Prevailing Winds, a woodwind quintet, and a member of Cumulus, a woodwind dectet, in both of which he plays the French horn. Mr. Edelstein has served on the boards of directors of several charitable organizations, and is certified by U.S. Squash as a squash coach.

He is a graduate of the Eastman School of Music (Preparatory Department), Oberlin College, and Cornell Law School, where he was on the moot court team. At Stanford Law School, he completed the Advanced Course in Trial Advocacy, and at Harvard Law School, he completed the Teacher Training Program, both under the auspices of the National Institute for Trial Advocacy.